EVALUATING POLICE USES OF FORCE

Evaluating Police Uses of Force

Seth W. Stoughton,
Jeffrey J. Noble, and
Geoffrey P. Alpert

NEW YORK UNIVERSITY PRESS
New York

NEW YORK UNIVERSITY PRESS
New York
www.nyupress.org

References to Internet websites (URLs) were accurate at the time of writing. Neither the author nor New York University Press is responsible for URLs that may have expired or changed since the manuscript was prepared.

Library of Congress Cataloging-in-Publication Data
Names: Stoughton, Seth W., author. | Noble, Jeffrey J., author. | Alpert, Geoffrey P., author.
Title: Evaluating police uses of force / Seth W. Stoughton, Jeffrey J. Noble, Geoffrey P. Alpert.
Description: New York : New York University Press, 2020. | Includes bibliographical references and index. | Summary: ""Evaluating Police Uses of Force" is an exploration of how police violence is regulated"—Provided by publisher.
Identifiers: LCCN 2019030941 | ISBN 9781479814657 (cloth) |
ISBN 9781479810161 (paperback) | ISBN 9781479830480 (ebook) |
ISBN 9781479803798 (ebook)
Subjects: LCSH: Police brutality—United States. | Police misconduct—Law and legislation—United States. | Police patrol—United States.
Classification: LCC KF5399 .S76 2020 | DDC 344.7305/232—dc23
LC record available at https://lccn.loc.gov/2019030941

New York University Press books are printed on acid-free paper, and their binding materials are chosen for strength and durability. We strive to use environmentally responsible suppliers and materials to the greatest extent possible in publishing our books.

Manufactured in the United States of America

10 9 8 7 6 5 4 3 2

Also available as an ebook

CONTENTS

LIST OF FIGURES AND TABLES

FOREWORD

ARIF ALIKHAN

With controversial police shootings capturing the attention of the nation, it has never been more important to understand when and how a police officer may use force. As a senior police executive, however, I experienced firsthand the difficulty of explaining the law and different policies regarding when an officer may use physical force against a suspect.

There are 18,000 different police agencies in the United States, each following different administrative policies, operating within different judicial districts, and serving different communities with varying expectations. This has resulted in a patchwork of legal interpretations, policies, and community standards that often conflict and can cause significant confusion among police professionals and the public.

Law enforcement experts Seth Stoughton, Geoffrey Alpert, and Jeff Noble provide a comprehensive explanation of the many factors that surround a police officer's decision to use physical force and provide useful guidance on how to navigate the complexities of the law and policy in police uses of force. In these pages, they use their diverse experiences as leading police researchers, accomplished authors, and former police officers to simplify the complex concepts into understandable and useful explanations of when and how an officer may use force to apprehend a suspect, to defend themselves, or to defend others.

I have had many spirited debates with these learned gentlemen and greatly value their important insights about the gaps and contradictions

---

Arif Alikhan is a Senior Fellow at the University of Chicago Crime Lab and the former Director of Constitutional Policing and Policy at the Los Angeles Police Department (LAPD). He previously served as the Deputy Executive Director for Homeland Security, Law Enforcement, and Fire/EMS at Los Angeles World Airports, as a Distinguished Professor of Homeland Security and Counterterrorism at the National Defense University, as the Assistant Secretary for Policy Development at the Department of Homeland Security during the Obama administration, as a senior advisor to Attorneys General John Ashcroft and Alberto Gonzalez, and as an Assistant United States Attorney. The opinions expressed above are his personal opinions and do not necessarily reflect the opinions of the University of Chicago and its affiliates.

in the law. Unlike most books on uses of force, they go beyond the typical constitutional analysis and discuss the impact of dozens of state laws and thousands of administrative policies that influence the subject. Most importantly, they address how community expectations often differ, and even conflict, with what the law allows and policies define as permissible.

Deciding whether to use physical force is among the most serious and consequential decisions a police officer can make. The decisions are often made during intense and uncertain circumstances. They are also captured on video for the world to see and pass judgment on, often with little or no understanding of the law governing these interactions or the policies that guide officers' decisions. This important book, long overdue, will help police executives, legal professionals, researchers, and the public understand, assess, and have the ability to explain when and how a police officer may use force to protect the communities they serve.

PREFACE TO THE PAPERBACK EDITION

This book arose from a shared interest in and appreciation for the importance of police uses of force as a social issue. After many conversations about the frequency and severity of confusion among lawyers and judges, police investigators and supervisors, and community members and elected officials over how to properly assess police actions, we formally began the process of combining our efforts in 2016.

Each of us is a nationally recognized expert in police use of force. Each of us regularly reviews cases, prepares reports, and testifies about police uses of force in state and federal courts across the country. We each have our own, sometimes differing, perspectives. Our original goal was to combine and build on our distinct perspectives—as a veteran police executive, a criminologist, and a law professor—to provide critical, if technical, information about police uses of force in a way that was, we hoped, greater than the sum of our individual parts. But what started as an effort to explain police uses of force became a comprehensive guide that situates the reader in four different evaluative frameworks—constitutional law, state law, agency policy, and community expectations—while also explaining the training, tactics, and tools available to officers as they make what can be difficult, time-compressed decisions.

We believed in 2016, as we do now, that a thorough understanding of police violence will assist law enforcement officers to make better decisions in the field; administrators to reevaluate their training, policies, and oversight efforts; lawyers and judges to have a better understanding of the training and standards that apply to officers; and, perhaps most importantly, everyone in communities affected by policing and the use of force to understand how the existing legal and administrative systems currently distinguish legitimate government action from abuses of power.

When we first began this project, our goal was to go beyond any inherently limited discussion of a single case, although we kept in mind the many high-profile incidents, as well as many lesser-known cases, of police violence. In the few years immediately preceding the publication of this text, Walter Scott, Tamir Rice, Philando Castile, Eric Garner, and many—too many—others brought a national focus to a broad issue that has often been considered in isolation. In the decades-long national discussion about policing, most of the conversation has been dominated by specific cases, with analysis and attention directed at individual agencies, often in large cities. In this book, we sought to provide a broader perspective, one that allows readers to see the forest for the individual trees, as well as the various paths that run through it. As it developed, this book was not intended as an overall criticism of current law or policy, although it does include a number of specific criticisms. Instead, it is intended as a reference for anyone who wants to know what the extant laws and policies *are*, regardless of whether any given reader has a purely academic interest, is in the position of applying those laws and policies, or is an advocate for challenging and changing them.

This book was originally published on May 26, 2020, per the preexisting publication schedule. But the world had changed from the day we submitted the final draft of the manuscript. The day before the book was released, George Floyd died, handcuffed and face down on the ground with Minneapolis Police Department Officer Derek Chauvin kneeling across the back of his neck. Public attention and criticism again turned to policing, especially the use of force. In the time since the original printing of this book, a flood of federal, state, and local legislation has been proposed, and some of those proposals have passed and been signed into law. California, for example, now prohibits police agencies from authorizing chokeholds and neck restraints (discussed in chapter 6) and requires the state attorney general to investigate and, if appropriate, prosecute officer-involved shootings of unarmed civilians.

We believe that the standards and recommendations contained in this book have the opportunity to advance policing by empowering police leaders, at all ranks, and community members to understand the standards, the training, and the law and to allow the justice system and the community to evaluate more completely police violence. This understanding is necessary, but as academics and practitioners who have spent our professional lives in, around, or studying policing, we also want to step outside the relatively narrow focus of this book— which is, after all, dedicated to exploring how police uses of force are evaluated—by offering specific suggestions for the much-needed improvement of policing.

The following commentary was first published, in slightly modified form, in *The Atlantic* on June 3, 2020. That essay can be found in its original form at https://bit.ly/PoliceReformEssay.

How to Actually Improve Policing in the United States

George Floyd's death is the latest in a long series of brutal encounters between the police and the people they are supposed to serve. Police abuse has targeted people of every race and class, but members of vulnerable populations and minority groups, particularly young black men, are especially at risk.

This is well known. The solutions are also well known. Prior tragedies have resulted in a string of independent, blue-ribbon commissions—Wickersham (1929), Kerner (1967), Knapp (1970), Overtown (Miami, 1980), Christopher (1991), Kolts (1991), Mollen (1992), and the President's Task Force on 21st Century Policing (2014)—to make recommendations for meaningful change that could address police misconduct. These groups have developed well-reasoned conclusions and pointed suggestions that are widely discussed and enthusiastically implemented—but only for a time. As public attention shifts, politics moves on, and police-reform efforts wane. The cycle continues unbroken.

The problem that the United States faces is not figuring out what to do. As an industry, American policing knows how to create systems that prevent, identify, and address abuses of power. It knows how to increase transparency. It knows how to provide police services in a constitutionally lawful and morally upright way. And across the country, most officers are well intentioned, receive good training, and work at agencies that have good policies on the books. Knowledge and good intentions are necessary but not nearly sufficient.

The hyperlocalized nature of policing in the United States is one factor here; the country has more than 18,000 police agencies, the majority of which (more than 15,000) are organized at the city or county level. Reforms tend to target single agencies. But it is not just the Minneapolis Police Department that needs reform; it is American policing as a whole.

What we desperately need, but have so far lacked, is political will. The United States needs to do more than throw good reform dollars at bad agencies. Elected officials at *all* levels—federal, state, and local—need to commit attention and public resources to changing the legal, administrative, and social frameworks that contribute to officer misconduct. As University of Colorado law professor Ben Levin succinctly stated on Twitter on May 30, 2020, "Feigned powerlessness by lawmakers is common & frustrating. It reflects political cowardice or actual acquiescence in the violence of policing." It is time for that to change. Here is a blueprint for what they should do.

Federal Intervention

At the federal level, Congress should focus on three objectives.

The first is getting rid of qualified immunity as we know it. Qualified immunity is a judicial doctrine that protects officers who violate someone's constitutional rights from civil-rights lawsuits unless the officers' actions were clearly established as unconstitutional at the time. The Fourth Amendment—

which governs stops, frisks, searches, and arrests—allows officers leeway to act so long as they reasonably, even if they make reasonable mistakes; an officer who has probable cause to arrest someone can lawfully make that arrest even if the officer is wrong and the individual did not commit a crime. Qualified immunity only comes into the picture when officers violate the Fourth Amendment by acting unreasonably. As the University of Chicago legal scholar William Baude persuasively argued in a 2018 California Law Review article, the Supreme Court has provided multiple justifications for qualified immunity—including that it is the modern evolution of a common-law "good faith" defense and that it ensures that government officials are not exposed to liability without "fair warning" that their actions are wrong—but neither the Court's historical nor doctrinal justifications can bear the burden of scrutiny. Nevertheless, as the Court described the doctrine in Malley v. Briggs, qualified immunity "provides ample protection to all but the plainly incompetent or those who knowingly violate the law."

The problem is that the Court has taken an inappropriately narrow view of what it means for a constitutional violation to be "clearly established." Essentially, a constitutional violation is clear only if a court in the relevant jurisdiction has previously concluded that very similar police conduct occurring under very similar circumstances was unconstitutional. The Supreme Court has, for example, applied qualified immunity in a case where an officer standing on an interstate overpass shot at a fleeing vehicle, something not only that contravenes best practices but that the officer was not trained to do, a supervisor had explicitly instructed him *not* to do, and was unnecessary because officers *under* the overpass had set up stop strips and then taken appropriate cover. Nevertheless, because no court had previously reviewed such conduct and found it to be unconstitutional, the Court held that any violation was not clearly established and, thus, that the officer could not be sued for his actions. In San Francisco v. Sheehan, the Court held that qualified immunity protected officers who, contrary to their training, their agency's policies, and longstanding police procedure, rushed into the room of a mentally ill woman who they knew had a knife and had threatened officers—but was no threat to herself—without bothering to wait for the backup officers whom they had already called. When the woman predictably threatened officers with the knife, something she would not have been able to do had they done what they were trained and expected to do, they shot her. Again, the Court found that because no court had yet explicitly held such conduct unlawful, a "reasonable officer could have believed that [such] conduct was justified." This ridiculous standard means that qualified immunity does not protect all but the "plainly incompetent"; it protects *even* the plainly incompetent. And these are just two of many egregious examples.

As a judicially created doctrine, qualified immunity could be modified or eliminated by federal legislation. There is broad bipartisan support for doing so. The right-leaning commentator David French and the left-leaning UCLA law professor Joanna Schwartz have both made the case against qualified immunity. The American Civil Liberties Union, the NAACP Legal Defense Fund, the Cato Institute, and the Alliance Defending Freedom are among the groups that have filed amicus briefs or called publicly for the end of qualified immunity. The onetime Democratic presidential hopeful Julián Castro pledged in a 2019 debate to "end qualified immunity for police officers so we can hold them accountable," and Representative Justin Amash, a former Tea Party Republican who is now a member of the Libertarian Party, recently introduced the Ending Qualified Immunity Act. With this scope of support, legislating the elimination of qualified immunity should be an easy first step. Eliminating qualified immunity will not eliminate police misconduct, but it will help restore trust in the rule of law and provide compensation to individuals whose rights have been violated.

A second thing Congress could do is pass legislation to collect better data, and to encourage states and other actors to collect better data, about what police do and how they do it. For example, no one really knows how often American police use force, why force was used, whether it was justified, or under what circumstances it is effective. No one knows how many high-speed pursuits have been conducted or why they were initiated, how many fleeing drivers have been caught, or the accurate number of collisions, injuries, or deaths that resulted. Only one state—Utah—requires agencies to report forcible entries and tactical-team deployments (Utah Code § 77-7-8.5). Neither the police nor anyone else can tell us how many people have been injured when taken into custody, how many people have been arrested only to be later released without charges, or how many cases local prosecutors have refused to file for lack of evidence, constitutional violations, or police misconduct.

Moreover, no state or federal officials know how many publicly owned surveillance cameras police have deployed or privately owned cameras they can access or where those resources are allocated. No state or federal officials know how many internal or citizen complaints of officer misconduct exist, whether people were dissuaded from making a complaint or their complaint was ignored or minimized, or the ultimate disposition of the complaint and whether the offending officer was disciplined. These data are not the administrative minutiae of policing; this is basic information about the everyday actions of government officials that is crucial to ensuring that such actions are properly regulated. Voluntary data sharing, such as the FBI's current National Use-of-Force Data Collection efforts, is clearly insufficient. The federal government can incentivize agency- and state-level data collection, coupled with a robust auditing system to ensure that accurate data are provided. This, too, is not a matter of partisan politics. Democrats tend to believe that policing suffers from systemic problems, the type that better data collection can help address, but that perspective is gaining support among Republicans, too. Tim Scott, a Republican senator from South Carolina, and Chuck Grassley, a Republican senator from Iowa, introduced the Walter Scott Notification Act, named after the man who was infamously shot in the back and killed by a North Charleston Police Department officer in 2017. Efforts like these are simply common sense.

The final thing the federal government should do is dedicate significantly more resources to support police training, local policy initiatives, and administrative reviews. Police agencies around the country regularly fail to meet what are generally recognized as minimum standards for use-of-force and arrest training, front-line supervision, and internal investigations. Some have a demonstrated pattern of violating the constitutional rights of their community members. Acting with legislated authority, the Department of Justice has intervened in a few of these agencies, mostly through consent decrees, assisted by an appointed monitor and enforced by a federal judge. While the Department of Justice cannot intervene in the actions of the more than 18,000 police agencies in the United States, Congress can instruct and empower it to offer technical assistance, identify conduct standards that can serve as references for courts in civil litigation, and provide a framework for responsive and democratically accountable community collaboration, opening additional avenues of reform. It cannot do any of that, however, if the presidential administration continues to seek to cut funding for such efforts. Congress could also better regulate the industry by requiring or encouraging clear, evidence-based conditions of accreditation, making them a prerequisite for federal funding and putting teeth into police-reform efforts by reducing or cutting off funding when agencies fail to meet those conditions.

State Intervention

State legislatures, which can often move much faster than the pace of national politics, have their own five objectives to focus on.

To begin with, thirty-six states have statutes that govern the use of both deadly and nondeadly force, while six states have statutes only for deadly force. More than three-quarters of the fifty-eight total state statutes (some states have more than one) were adopted prior to or during the 1970s, and most have not been recently amended. In the absence of statutes, states regu-

late police use of force through judicial decisions. But even where state statutes do exist, the courts that interpret them unfortunately tend to rely on the
Fourth Amendment law. This is a problem for two reasons. First, the Fourth
Amendment regulates police *seizures*, but state law is supposed to regulate
use of force; and not all uses of force count as seizures. (Several courts have
held, for example, that an officer shooting at someone but instead striking a
bystander does not constitute a seizure.) State law is supposed to be broader
than the Fourth Amendment, which means that referring to Fourth Amendment doctrines in the interpretation of state law can provide less protection
than state lawmakers intended. Second, and perhaps more important, those
Fourth Amendment doctrines are a mess; they provide little meaningful
guidance that officers in the field can use to determine when and how much
force to use, and the guidance they provide to courts reviewing use of force
is often flawed.

Worse, many of the state statutes and common-law doctrines are contrary
to good practices. Some states allow officers to use force to make an arrest if
they *believe* the arrest is lawful, even if it is not and their belief is unreasonable. Other statutes are woefully outdated and still provide a defense to officers
who use deadly force to prevent the escape of a fleeing felon. And most states
authorize officers to use "reasonably necessary" force but do not bother to define what reasonable force is or explain how officers should determine that it
is necessary. Very few states admonish officers to use appropriate tactics or
punish officers for egregious mistakes that contribute to avoidable use of force.

States can do better. In the past several years, for example, both Washington State and California have amended their statutory regimes, giving officers
the authority to use force in the situations that require it while also providing
meaningful guidance to officers and courts about what those situations are.
California Penal Code § 835a allows officers to use deadly force against "imminent threats of death or serious bodily injury" and says that an "imminent
threat" exists when "a person has the present ability, opportunity, and apparent
intent" to cause such harm. Definitions like this, which draw from best practices in policing, give officers the leeway to protect themselves and others while
also prohibiting them from acting on unfounded or purely speculative fears.

State legislatures can also amend law-enforcement officers' bills of rights
and the laws that govern the collective-bargaining rights of police unions.
Most states permit or encourage collective bargaining for police unions—
even states that, like Wisconsin, otherwise take a dim view of public-sector
unions. Police unions do some good work; research suggests that officers at
unionized agencies are, on average, higher paid and more professional than
are officers at nonunionized agencies. However, unions have leveraged the

collective-bargaining process to create labyrinthine procedural protections that can make it exceptionally difficult to investigate, discipline, or terminate officers. Some of the limits on investigation—such as delaying interviewing an officer after a critical incident for several "sleep cycles"—are based on faulty reasoning and have been thoroughly debunked by credible scientific research. Too often, discipline is precluded by unnecessary or inappropriate procedural violations; in some cities, for example, civilians can file a complaint only during a limited period after an incident, sometimes as short as thirty days. When officers *are* disciplined, that discipline is subject to grievance and arbitration procedures; at one agency, a study published in the Journal of Criminal Law and Criminology found that arbitrators "routinely cut in half" the severity of disciplinary sanctions imposed by agency management. Officers should have a right to appeal disciplinary findings, but only when they are arguing that the agency's decision was arbitrary and capricious or that the agency did not act in good faith. By protecting bad officers, collective-bargaining agreements and state laws contribute to misconduct.

Further, state legislatures can do a better job of certifying and, when necessary, decertifying officers. Currently, most states require most officers to be certified by a standards-and-training commission. Such commissions set minimum training requirements, but state law can impose specific training that the state commission has, thus far, omitted from the academy curriculum. Washington State, for example, now requires both violence-deescalation training and mental health training, and the commission must "consult with law enforcement agencies and community stakeholders" in developing that training (Revised Code of Washington, 43.101.450, 452, 455). And while most states allow for decertification—which prevents someone who has engaged in misconduct from continuing to work in that state as an officer—that authority can be tightly limited. In some states, an officer can be decertified only after a criminal conviction for a felony or serious misdemeanor. Even in states that have more permissive decertification regimes, decertification is often used only sparingly. From the 1960s until 2017, only about 30,000 officers were decertified, and three states—Florida, Georgia, and North Carolina— make up about half of those. As the decertification expert Roger Goldman said in an interview for The Atlantic, that is not because those states have a higher proportion of bad officers; it is because those states "have very active decertification programs." States have good reason to strengthen their commitment to policing the police: according to a recent study by law professors Ben Grunwald and John Rappaport, officers who are hired by another police agency after being terminated or resigning in lieu of termination from a prior agency are more likely than other officers to engage in future misconduct.

A persistent culture of secrecy regarding personnel matters has not helped. Many states have sharply limited the public's right to access officers' disciplinary files or agency use-of-force investigations. Although there is, and must be, room for certain employee information to be kept confidential, an officer's actions while dealing with members of the community and the steps that an agency takes to investigate those actions are clearly matters of public interest. The states that have passed broad sunshine laws, such as Florida, have taught us that public access can be a crucial component of police accountability without impeding proper police action. States that allow agencies to shred disciplinary records after a set period, sometimes as short as six months, are effectively making patterns of misconduct by problem employees significantly more difficult to detect. States should follow the lead of Florida and, more recently, California in passing public-records laws ensuring that disciplinary records and reports pertaining to critical incidents such as police shootings or other serious uses of force cannot be hidden.

Finally, states can rethink their approach to criminalization. "Overcriminalization" has been broadly discussed; there are so many laws that violations are ubiquitous. If everyone is a criminal, officers have almost unfettered discretion to pick and choose which laws to enforce and whom to stop, frisk, search, or arrest. And, as the saying goes, when all you have is a hammer, every problem looks like a nail. For too long, the hammer of criminal law has been used against a wide array of social ills. The result is police overinvolvement in matters that would be far better left to other government institutions and social-service providers, including school discipline, poverty, homelessness, and substance abuse. The opioid crisis remains a stark reminder that the United States cannot arrest its way out of addiction. The troubling discrepancies between the way police have been cast as soldiers in the War on Drugs—a war that, despite almost identical drug-use rates between white and black Americans, is fought mostly in poor and minority communities—and the way police have been seen as an adjunct to the public health authorities addressing opioid abuse in suburban middle- or upper-class neighborhoods should be a stark warning for state legislators to rethink the scope of criminal law.

Local Intervention

Local agencies, for their part, have much they can do. To get started, they should focus on five specific improvements.

Many agencies have accountability systems—so-called early-warning or early-intervention systems—that look great on paper but are neither followed nor audited. Since the 1980s, these systems have had the potential to identify officers before they engage in misconduct and allow supervisors to step in to prevent bad outcomes. Unfortunately, many agencies ignore their own protocols—the early-warning system becomes a meaningless administrative task—or supervisors assume that officers do not need any intervention *unless* they are flagged by the early-warning system. Neither error is acceptable, and both can be corrected.

The hyperlocalization of policing in the United States has resulted in many agencies either creating their own policies and training from scratch, often without the benefit of research or broad experience, or simply purchasing them from private vendors. Agency policies and training should do more to incorporate industry best practices and generally accepted principles. For example, a 2017 Virginia Law Review study of use-of-force policies at the fifty largest agencies in the country—agencies that have the time, resources, and depth of experience to get it right—shows that they are all over the board. Some merely repeat the constitutional standard laid out by the Supreme Court. Others add little more than an interpretation of constitutional law and an aspirational instruction to safeguard the sanctity of life. But it is entirely possible to adopt policies that touch on tactics and provide meaningful guidance for officers to follow in the field; we know because some agencies have done exactly that. Some have adopted policies that instruct officers to use the least amount of force that can be safely employed, and others have provided specific tactical guidance for officers making traffic stops, effecting arrests, or interacting with people who are mentally ill.

Another crucial objective is that officers must also be trained—meaningfully so—on their agency's policies. The "read and sign" approach is an unfortunate reality; officers are expected to acknowledge that they have received new policies, but many agencies do nothing to ensure that they understand those policies. Sometimes agencies attempt to use technology to increase efficiency by, for example, having a command staff member read a policy aloud, posting the video online, having officers click the video link, and calling that "training." It is no surprise when such "training" is ignored. We have all read too many depositions in which officers testify that they were not familiar with the content of an essential policy. Policy manuals are too lengthy for anyone to realistically expect officers to memorize the whole thing—an entirely separate issue—but when it comes to use of force, emergency driving, and a few other areas of low-frequency, high-risk activities, a more robust effort is required.

Of course, the best policies and training in the world will not mean a thing if they are not enforced. When the Phoenix Police Department adopted a body-worn-camera system, for example, it had a broad mandatory recording policy that required officers to activate their cameras for almost all civilian interactions. A month after deployment, officers were recording only 42.2 percent of the incidents they were supposed to record; a year later, that number fell to 13.2 percent. The agency had the equipment and the policy; what it lacked was adequate supervision. Police reform lives or dies with first-line supervisors, and agencies need to ensure that corporals, sergeants, and lieutenants are doing the jobs they are paid to do. This, of course, requires agencies to train supervisors—a great officer does not always make a good supervisor—and to audit their decisions. In the same vein, agencies should invite external oversight. As government institutions in a democracy, police agencies must be responsive to community concerns, especially in the context of high-risk activities like the use of force and emergency-vehicle operations.

Police agencies also need to be much more transparent in the aftermath of high-profile incidents. Although certain information, such as body-worn-camera footage, may need to be withheld for a certain period to avoid contaminating crucial witness interviews, there is no legitimate justification for denying public access for months or years. The perception that police agencies are hiding embarrassing or inculpatory information is particularly destructive when agencies have readily shared video of interactions that reflect positively on the agency; nothing destroys public trust faster than a perceived double standard. As the authors of In Context: Understanding Police Killings of Unarmed Civilians, all officers or former officers, wrote, "Law enforcement agencies simply must find better ways to release more data, and to release it earlier." At a minimum, agencies can adopt policies that presumptively mandate the release of video or other information a set amount of time after an incident, as the Los Angeles Police Department has done with its forty-five-day commitment. Many members of the public may see that as too long, and perhaps it is; but having a certain date will help prevent perceptions of a police cover-up.

Perhaps most important, agencies need to create a culture that understands and values the importance of peer support and intervention. Officers, like everyone else, behave the way they think their colleagues and coworkers expect them to behave. Few things are more important to weeding out misconduct and creating a professional culture than peers sending the message that misbehavior is simply not acceptable. Agencies must put professionalism, including peer intervention, at the center of police culture. Following the example of the New Orleans Police Department's Ethical Policing Is Courageous (EPIC) program is an obvious first step that can protect officers and the public alike.

Meaningful police reform is possible, but it will require a coordinated effort from federal, state, and local government. It will require sustained pressure from the public to push elected officials to take action. This will not be straightforward, nor will it be fast. And as the protests of George Floyd's tragic, predictable death continue, it should be patently obvious that the country has no patience for the same old apologetic and halfhearted attempts at reform that we have seen previously. George Floyd and all of us deserve better.

BIBLIOGRAPHY

William Baude, "Is Qualified Immunity Unlawful?," *California Law Review* 106 (2018): 4590.

Ben Brunwald and John Rappaport, "The Wandering Officer," *The Yale Law Journal* 129, no. 6 (2020): 1676–1782.

Brandon L. Garrett and Seth W. Stoughton, "A Tactical Fourth Amendment," *Virginia Law Review* 103 (2017): 211–307.

Mark Iris, "Police Discipline in Chicago: Arbitration or Arbitrary," *Journal of Criminal Law and Criminology* 89 (1998): 215–244.

Candice Norwood, "Can States Tackle Police Misconduct with Certification Systems?," *Atlantic* (Apr. 9, 2017).

Nick Selby, Ben Singleton, and Ed Flosi, *In Context: Understanding Police Killings of Unarmed Civilians* (St. Augustine, FL: Contextual Press).

Introduction

What does a police officer in the United States look like? There is no way for us to foresee, as we write this months or years before you read it, the details of the officer you're imagining right now. They may be tall or short, male or female, white or black, uniformed or in plainclothes; there are an infinite number of variations. Yet we can confidently predict that the officer you're picturing is armed.[1] At a minimum, they have a handgun, but they may be wearing a duty belt or tactical vest outfitted with pepper spray, a baton, or a TASER; they may be carrying a shotgun, a rifle, or a transparent shield and a riot baton. You may even have pictured an officer using force, mentally replaying one of the many videos of police shootings or other uses of force that have been prominently featured in the news.

The fact—and we are confident enough in our predictions to call it a fact—that you pictured an armed officer demonstrates what academics and officers themselves have long recognized: the use of physical force is inherent in and inseparable from modern policing.[2] How could it be otherwise? Society invests officers with the legal authority to invade privacy and to restrict freedom, to deprive people of their basic liberties. Predictably, people do not always respond well to being deprived of those basic liberties. But police authority is backed by the threat of state-sanctioned violence; if an individual resists an officer's attempts to exercise their authority, the officer may well use physical force to fulfill their duties.

Police violence has proven to be a challenging and divisive issue in the United States, although the use of force, especially the use of deadly force, is relatively rare. Indeed, the vast majority of police–citizen encounters are insipid interactions that do not involve problematic coercion or result in complaints. According to the best available data—which admittedly is not as robust as we would prefer—only a small percentage (1.8 percent) of the more than fifty million police–civilian contacts every year involve a threat or actual use of force. Even in the context of interactions that involve the types of inherently coercive police action that are most likely to elicit civilian resistance, such as arrests, violence is the exception, not the rule. Studies have estimated that out of some thirteen million arrests, only about 4 percent involve the use of more force than necessary to handcuff a compliant subject.[3] And on those occasions when officers do use force, the vast majority of incidents involve low-level violence with little potential for injury: grabbing, shoving, and the like.

Why, then, should society care about the use of force? There are at least two different answers to that question: one philosophical, the other pragmatic. Philosophically, the use of government violence against civilians runs counter to our most basic democratic notions of individual freedom, liberty, security, and autonomy. Our system of democratic republicanism is premised on the belief that a non-tyrannical government can rule only with the consent of the governed. A sophisticated civilization must balance individuals' interest in liberty and privacy against society's interest in order and security, but if our democratic ideals are to mean anything that balancing must be carefully managed. The tension between the need for governmental infringement on freedoms and the need for protection from governmental abuse is particularly acute in the context of policing. Police agencies and officers are the paradigmatic public servants, the self-professed Thin Blue Line that stands between ordered society and criminal anarchy. Each use of force against civilians presents, at a microcosmic scale, a scenario that implicates longstanding fears of tyranny and government overreach. On a purely philosophical level, then, understanding and properly evaluating police uses of force against civilians is critical to properly maintaining the dynamic tension between security and liberty.

Pragmatically, there are several reasons to take police uses of force seriously. First, such incidents result in the injury or death of thousands of community members every year. Although the proportion of police–civilian interactions that involve violence are quite modest, the small percentage masks large absolute numbers. Even if force is used in only 1 percent of police–civilian encounters, the fact that there are, on average, more than sixty million such encounters every year would mean that there are at least 600,000 uses of force every year. That's more than one every minute in every hour of every day of the year. Most of the time, officers are not using force to defend themselves: over the last ten years, there have been, on average, about 56,000 incidents every year in which an officer was assaulted (just over a quarter of those assaults resulted in some type of injury to the officer). That leaves at least 544,000 occasions each year in which officers used force for reasons other than self-defense. That breaks down to almost 1,500 every day, which is still more than one per minute. Those numbers are at the low end of the spectrum based on data from the Bureau of Justice Statistics; if more than 1 percent of police–civilian encounters involve the use of force or if there are more than sixty million encounters in a given year, the absolute numbers may be significantly larger. The potential number of use-of-force incidents, then, make this an issue of public importance.

The use of force also plays an important role in shaping public attitudes toward government generally and policing more specifically. Police violence is among the most controversial uses of governmental authority. Community trust and confidence in the police is undermined by the perception that officers are using force unnecessarily, too frequently, or in problematically disparate ways. Over time, negative perceptions of the police can reduce civilian cooperation, making law enforcement and order maintenance significantly more difficult. Public distrust can also create dangerous situations for officers and community members. The use of force not only undermines public trust over time, it can also serve as a flashpoint, a spark that ignites long-simmering community hostility. Use-of-force incidents can have lasting reverberations, from the televised abuses of the Civil Rights Era to the beating of Rodney King in 1991, and from the shooting of Amadou Diallo in 1999 to the shooting of Walter Scott in 2015. Throughout the country, police uses of force have instigated violence or civil unrest.[4] Of the ten most violent and destructive riots in United States history, fully half were prompted by what were perceived as incidents of excessive force or police abuse.[5]

The central role that use-of-force incidents play in shaping public perceptions of policing is all the more critical in light of the limited information that most community members have about policing and the use of force. Traditional and social media shape public perceptions, but that coverage can lead to misperceptions about the frequency and substance of use-of-force incidents. Citizens often learn about police behavior from entertainment media—television, movies, video games, and so on—but such portrayals are rarely accurate. Even when news media provides more accurate reports of how force is used, the public can be left with an incomplete or inaccurate understanding about the use of force. During oral argument in a Supreme Court case involving officers who shot at a fleeing vehicle, for example, the late Justice Antonin Scalia asserted that officers shoot at moving vehicles "all the time"; this highly questionable statement was predicated not on data from academic studies or specific police agencies, but rather on "movies about bank robberies."[6]

In the aggregate, reporting on police uses of force naturally focuses on what are viewed as the most newsworthy events: particularly officer-involved shootings, brutal violence, or egregious misconduct. Because of a cognitive bias known as the "availability heuristic"—which causes us to make judgments about the frequency of an event based in large part on our awareness of other similar, recent, and significant events—such reporting can contribute to the false impression that such events are far more frequent than they actually are. A recent, high-profile incident of police violence in the news, then, can lead people to conclude that similar incidents of police violence are quite common even when that may not be the case.

Public misunderstandings about the use of force can also affect the way individual incidents are perceived. News reports, especially preliminary reports, are of limited value: inevitably, there is a significant amount of information the reporters—and, by extension, the public—simply do not have at the time. Many viewers, however, will come to a firm conclusion based on partial information, unconsciously relying on a host of cognitive biases to fill in the gaps. Worse, many viewers will have a high degree of confidence in their conclusions. As a result, a use-of-force incident may be judged by thousands of people who develop strong opinions based on weak and incomplete evidence.[7] And even when there is good information about a particular incident, most people simply do not apply any rigorous analytical framework to evaluate the use of force. That matters because police violence is just that: violence. Even when we are quite comfortable with the abstract proposition that officers use force, the actual use of force can be aggressive, brutal, and ugly. When force is, or appears to be, excessive or unnecessary, it can create the perception that a government official charged with ensuring public safety turned on a member of the public they are sworn to protect.

These philosophical and pragmatic rationales make it incredibly important for officers to use force appropriately and for officers and agencies to be held accountable when they do not. This book poses and responds to a question that is central to police accountability: how does society evaluate the propriety of an officer's use of force? That is, how do we tell whether any given use of force appropriately balanced the subject's interest in freedom against the social interests in order and law enforcement? We identify four different answers to that question, four evaluative standards that can be— and are—used in different contexts. Chapter 1 provides a detailed roadmap of constitutional standards, where the propriety of police force is regulated by the Fourth Amendment's prohibition of unreasonable seizures. Chapter 2 supplies an overview of state law, which sets out criminal and civil standards. Chapter 3 explores the administrative standards that individual police agencies create through policy, procedure, and training. Chapter 4 discusses what we term the "community expectations standard," an important, if informal, way to evaluate police uses of force through the lens of public expectations. In each chapter, we engage in a detailed discussion of one relevant standard, identifying the contexts in which that standard applies, describing the precise behaviors that each standard regulates, and exploring how each evaluative standard is used to assess the propriety of any given use of force.

In the final two chapters, we provide key information about the choices police make in use-of-force situations; understanding these choices is essential for applying any of the evaluative standards. In chapter 5, we discuss police tactics: the decisions that officers make and the actions they take as they approach and interact with civilians, both of which can contribute to whether and how force is used. In chapter 6, we explore the various ways officers use force, describing the role various techniques, tools, and weapons can play in use-of-force situations, and highlighting the continued development of tools and technologies that may shape when and how officers use force.

These discussions about the evaluative standards, and the additional information that is necessary to apply those standards effectively, are situated within a broader conversation about governmental accountability, the role that police play in modern society, and how officers should go about fulfilling their duties. We acknowledge the value of, but do not here explicitly engage in, those more extensive themes. This book does not claim to resolve, or even to address, all of the problems in policing; indeed, our focus on the evaluative frameworks that can be applied to use-of-force incidents is quite limited. This book explores how *individual* use-of-force incidents are evaluated, but we do not here examine how the use of force is or could be evaluated in the aggregate. That is to say, we explore different answers to the question, "How can society assess a particular shooting?" but not to the broader question, "How can society assess police shootings in the United States taken as a whole?"

We are cognizant that our focus on individual incidents excludes controversial and important aspects of police uses of force, including, for example, the racial dynamics of the criminal justice system generally, of policing, and of the use of force specifically. There is good reason to think that the use of force is not evenly distributed along racial lines. In a survey administered by the Bureau of Justice Statistics, 1.3 percent of white respondents reported being subjected to a use of force, compared to 3.3 percent of black respondents, which suggests that there exists, at a minimum, a racially disproportionate perception that officers have used force. While force was perceived as "necessary" by roughly the same percentage of blacks (32 percent) and whites (32.4 percent), the perception that force was "excessive" was reported more often by blacks (59.9 percent) than whites (42.7 percent). Further, data gathered by the FBI and various media outlets suggests that this is not just a matter of perception, at least in the context of officer-involved homicides: 13.4 percent of the US population, but more than 30 percent of individuals killed by police, are black.

These observations are deeply troubling, implicating longstanding concerns about racial equality—or, more accurately, the lack thereof—in the

United States and the manner in which policing as an institution has perpetuated inequity, both historically and today. They give rise to a series of challenging sociological quandaries. There is, of course, the very real possibility that individual officers act out of racial animus on at least some occasions. The picture is almost certainly more complicated than that, though. It is almost certainly the case that if officers are more likely to interact with black individuals, then, all other things being equal, we would expect them to use force at a higher rate against that population group. That, however, does nothing to explain *why* officers are more likely to interact with black individuals. The answer is likely systemic, reflecting the correlation between urban poverty and crime and a long, distressing history of race-conscious, and often overtly race-motivated, choices relating to education policy, housing policy, and economic policy, not to mention criminal justice policy. The looming role that race has played, and continues to play, in shaping how we define a "threat" or "threatening behavior" undoubtedly affects police uses of force. This is true at the wholesale level, where the identification of certain substances, but not others, as "illicit drugs" or the distinction between drugs and "hard" drugs is rife with racial overtones; consider the Federal Sentencing Guidelines' 100:1 disparity—later reduced to an 18:1 disparity—between crack cocaine and powder cocaine, in which possession of one gram of crack (a drug associated primarily with black users and dealers) was punished at the same severity as one hundred grams of powder cocaine (a drug associated primarily with white users and dealers). Or consider the difference in the law enforcement-oriented response to the crack cocaine epidemic of the 1980s and early 1990s, when the drug was largely confined to poor, inner city (read: predominantly black) communities and the public health–oriented response to the modern heroin epidemic, which has spread into middle- and upper-class suburban (read: predominantly white) communities.

It is impossible to entirely disaggregate the social dynamics of race and class from policing and the use of force, and we do not attempt to do so. We do, however, consciously avoid tackling head-on such complex and complicated issues: that discussion is very much needed, but it is simply outside the scope of what we set out to do in this book.

To reiterate, our focus in this book is narrow: we seek to explore how individual police uses of force are evaluated. Nevertheless, this book is both necessary and a significant contribution to public and academic debates about police violence. Police uses of force are the single most visceral and divisive aspect of contemporary policing. Police kill almost three people a day,[8] and people have responded with protests, civil unrest, and horrifying ambushes that have resulted in the murder of police officers in Texas, Pennsylvania,

Louisiana, and elsewhere. And yet, the public conversation about police uses of force has focused almost exclusively on whether individual officers who used excessive force in individual incidents should be criminally punished, without much, if any, broader discussion about how to determine whether the force used was excessive.

This is even more remarkable in light of the observation that the use of force by police has been studied for more than fifty years. There was only limited academic interest in the subject until the 1960s, when scholars like James Fyfe began conducting research and building a budding literature. Even then, the use of force was not the subject of sustained academic attention until 1980. That year, interest was energized by the publication of volume 452 of *The Annals of the American Academy of Political and Social Science*; that volume was a special edition that brought to the attention of a broad academic community the nature and scope of existing academic work on use-of-force issues.[9] Since then, there have been marked improvements in the academic literature.[10] Today, the use of force by police is an accepted topic for researchers and practitioners alike. Indeed, a volume of the *Annals* to be published in 2020 will be dedicated to research on fatal police shootings. These important research questions continue to develop, and interested scholars and practitioners investigate them and report their findings,[11] but scant attention has been paid to the analytical topics we address in this book: the various evaluative standards for use-of-force incidents and the tactics and tools of police violence.

PART I

Standards for Evaluating Police Uses of Force

In August 2014, an officer working for the municipal police department in the then-little-known St. Louis suburb of Ferguson, Missouri, shot and killed Michael Brown, an unarmed, black 18-year-old. The St. Louis County Prosecutor, Robert McCulloch, convened a grand jury to determine whether there was sufficient evidence to indict the officer. It was, by any measure, a complicated undertaking. The jurors met for months, heard hours of testimony from dozens of witnesses, and reviewed thousands of pages of documents. They also learned about *how* they should determine whether or not to indict the officer. The grand jury was first provided with a copy of a state statute that authorized the use of deadly force in certain circumstances, including to prevent the escape of a fleeing felon. Later, the grand jury was told about a Supreme Court case that held that officers can use deadly force only when they have probable cause to believe that the subject presents an imminent threat of death or great bodily harm.

What, then, should the grand jury have done if it concluded that, at the time of the shooting, Michael Brown was a fleeing felon, but did *not* present an imminent threat of death or great bodily harm? Applying the state statute, the officer's actions were lawful, and an indictment would be unwarranted. Applying the Supreme Court case, the officer's actions were unlawful, and an indictment would be entirely appropriate.

As that example demonstrates, the standard that is used to analyze a use of force is of tremendous practical importance. So which standard is the right one? Confusingly, there is no one "right" standard; it depends on context. More confusingly, there are at least four different standards that can be used to evaluate an officer's use of force in the United States: the constitutional standard, the state law standard, the administrative standard, and the community expectations standard.

The first three standards—constitutional law, state law, and administrative regulations—each play a formal role in the evaluation of use-of-force incidents. When an officer's use of force violates one or more of those standards, sanctions or remedies may be imposed. An officer who violates an administrative regulation, for example, can be disciplined or terminated by their agency, while a violation of the state or constitutional standards can result in civil liability or a criminal conviction.

For the other standard—community expectations—violations do not result in formal remedies. However, those standards remain important because violations can have significant, if informal, consequences: an officer, agency, or policing itself, as an institution, may be subject to public condemnation. In July 2017, for example, Minneapolis Police Chief Janeé Harteau resigned less than a week after Officer Mohamed Noor controversially shot Justine Ruszczyk, a woman who had called the police to report a potential assault near her home. Chief Harteau did not resign because the shooting was unconstitutional, illegal, or contrary to agency policy—at that early point, there had been no formal determination about any of those things. Instead, her resignation was driven in large part by the public pressure that resulted from the perception that the shooting had fallen far short of what community members expected. Despite its informality, community expectations may be the most potent of the various evaluative standards because, ultimately, they exert lasting influence on the other, more formal standards.

As that brief discussion suggests, the standards themselves are distinct, but they are all perfectly valid. They are not, however, perfectly interchangeable. The standards are context dependent. That is, the standard that we apply depends on the question that we are seeking to answer and the remedy that we may impose. Let us return to the grand jury in the Michael Brown shooting; should the prosecutors have instructed the jurors about the state standard or about the constitutional standard? The most obvious answer, one given by a number of legal scholars and other pundits at the time, is that the prosecutors should have instructed the jury about the constitutional standard. The Constitution sets the minimum level of protection, after all, so to the extent that state law purports to authorize the use of force in situations in which it would be constitutionally prohibited, it would appear that the state law was invalidated. That answer may be obvious, but it is also incorrect. The grand jury was called upon to determine whether there was probable cause to believe that, under *state law*, the officer's actions were criminal. In that context, the constitutionality of the officer's actions is irrelevant. It may be counterintuitive, but a state is not required to criminalize an unconstitutional use of force (nor, for that matter, is a state prohibited from criminalizing constitutional uses of force).

Understanding the evaluation of police uses of force, then, requires one to appreciate that any given use of force is subject to *different* evaluative standards. The first step in evaluating an incident is to identify which standard is being applied, what behavior that standard regulates, and how that standard regulates the use of force. The chapters in part I of this book provide a comprehensive look at those issues, with each one dedicated to a discussion of a particular standard. Chapter 1 provides a detailed roadmap of the constitutional standard that applies most frequently in federal court. Chapter 2 outlines the state law standard that applies to both civil and criminal claims. Chapter 3 explores the administrative standards that individual police agencies create through policy, procedure, and training. Chapter 4 is dedicated to a discussion of community expectations, which are less formal, but no less important for evaluating use-of-force incidents.

1

The Constitutional Law Standard

Police officers, like all government officials, are subject to the limitations imposed by the Constitution of the United States. The body of the Constitution largely sets out the structure of government: Articles I, II, and III lay out the framework for the legislative branch, the executive branch, and the judicial branch, respectively. Article IV explicates the requirements for state governments. Article V sets out the procedures by which the Constitution can be amended. Article VI establishes the Constitution as "the supreme Law of the Land." Finally, Article VII governs ratification of the Constitution.

The Constitution was first ratified in Delaware, on December 7, 1787, and, pursuant to Article VII, took effect on June 21, 1788, when New Hampshire became the ninth state to ratify it. Since it was first proposed and ratified, the Constitution has been amended twenty-seven times. The first twelve amendments, which include the ten amendments known as the Bill of Rights, were adopted on September 25, 1789, and were instrumental in convincing several colonies to ratify the Constitution and become states.

The Constitution, particularly the Bill of Rights and subsequent amendments, is centrally concerned with public and personal freedoms, which it protects by recognizing what one federal court referred to as "negative rather than positive liberties."[1] In short, the Constitution protects individual rights by limiting the ways the government can infringe on them, but generally does not lay out affirmative obligations that government officials must meet.[2]

Prior to 1989, there was no clearly defined constitutional standard under which the use of force was analyzed. Federal courts took different approaches, evaluating claims that officers' uses of force violated constitutional rights by applying the Fourth Amendment's prohibition of unreasonable seizures, the Eighth Amendment's prohibition on cruel and unusual punishment, and the Fifth and Fourteenth Amendments' prohibition on deprivations of liberty without due process of law. In 1985, the Supreme Court applied the Fourth Amendment in the context of a police shooting,[3] and, in 1989, the Court settled the issue by holding that the use of force against "free citizens"—that is, individuals other than incarcerated inmates—was to be analyzed under the Fourth Amendment.[4]

As it relates to police uses of force, the relevant text of the Fourth Amendment reads as follows: "The right of the people to be secure in their persons . . . against unreasonable . . . seizures, shall not be violated." In the body of this chapter, we will examine when this standard applies, what it applies to, and how it applies.

When Does the Constitutional Standard Apply?

The constitutional standard applies in at least three different ways: in civil litigation filed by a private plaintiff (or a class of plaintiffs) against an officer or agency; in civil litigation filed by the Department of Justice against an agency; and in federal criminal prosecutions against individual officers. Consider the following examples: A plaintiff files a lawsuit in federal court, alleging that an officer used excessive force in the course of making an arrest. A federal prosecutor files criminal charges against a police officer, alleging that the officer's use of force during the arrest constituted a crime. Attorneys in the Civil Rights Division of the US Department of Justice file a lawsuit alleging that officers at the police department have engaged in a pattern and practice of violating constitutional rights by using excessive force. In each case, the investigators, lawyers, judges, and jurors will be called upon to assess the use of force by applying the constitutional standard.

Civil "Excessive Force" Litigation under 42 U.S.C. § 1983 and Bivens

When an officer uses force against an individual, the subject can file a lawsuit alleging that the officer violated the Fourth Amendment. The Fourth Amendment itself sets out the substantive right to be free from unreasonable seizures, but it does not provide what is known as a "cause of action"—the basis of the legal argument that a plaintiff makes when filing a lawsuit. Instead, federal civil lawsuits are authorized by a federal statute and a Supreme Court case.

The federal statute, 18 U.S.C. § 1983, states, in relevant part:

> Every person who, under color of any statute, ordinance, regulation, custom, or usage, of any State or Territory or the District of Columbia, subjects, or causes to be subjected, any citizen of the United States or other person within the jurisdiction thereof to the deprivation of any rights, privileges, or immunities secured by the Constitution and laws, shall be liable to the party injured in an action at law, suit in equity, or other proper proceeding for redress[.]

That statute applies to state and local officials, including police officers, but not to federal officials. A Supreme Court case, *Bivens v. Six Unknown, Named Agents of Federal Bureau of Narcotics*,[5] held that federal officers were similarly subject to liability for constitutional violations, including Fourth Amendment violations. A complete discussion of the fascinating history and many nuances of § 1983 and *Bivens* is beyond the scope of this book. For our purposes, it suffices to say that, together, they potentially render liable any police officer who uses or abuses their authority in ways that violate an individual's constitutional rights, including uses of force that violate the Fourth Amendment.

Confusingly, a plaintiff can bring a § 1983 claim—that is, a claim brought under *federal* law—in either federal or *state* court.[6] Either way, the court will have to apply the constitutional standard to determine whether the officer's actions violate the Fourth Amendment. The plaintiff in such a suit, if successful, can ask the court to award different remedies. The three most common remedies are compensatory damages, punitive damages, and injunctive relief.

Compensatory damages are a monetary payment "intended to redress the concrete loss that the plaintiff has suffered by reason of the defendant's wrongful conduct."[7] Compensatory damages are awarded to cover the costs of physical injuries and psychological injuries as well as tangible harms (such as damaged property) and intangible, but quantifiable harms (such as lost earnings).

Punitive damages are intended to punish a defendant's misconduct and deter the defendant, and others in the defendant's position, from engaging in such actions in the future. Not every case in which compensatory damages are awarded will also result in punitive damages; the Supreme Court has strongly suggested that courts can award punitive damages only when an officer's conduct is malicious, intentional, or callously indifferent to the plaintiff's rights.[8]

In addition to monetary awards from compensatory or punitive damages, a plaintiff may also request injunctive relief. Under certain circumstances, a court can issue an injunction that prohibits an officer or agency from engaging in certain actions (such as an order to not use a particular weapon or technique) or, less frequently, an injunction that requires an officer or agency to engage in certain actions (such as an order for officers to go through particular training or adopt a particular use-of-force policy).

In short, 42 U.S.C. § 1983 and *Bivens* permit a private plaintiff—or, in rare cases, a class of plaintiffs—to bring a civil suit against local, state, or federal officers alleging violations of their constitutional rights, including the Fourth Amendment right to be free from unreasonable seizures.

"Pattern and Practice" Litigation under 42 U.S.C. § 14141

The Attorney General of the United States is authorized by federal law to sue police agencies that engage in a pattern or practice of constitutional violations. The statute, 42 U.S.C. § 14141, reads as follows:

(a) Unlawful conduct. It shall be unlawful for any governmental authority, or any agent thereof, or any person acting on behalf of a governmental authority, to engage in a pattern or practice of conduct by law enforcement officers or by officials or employees of any governmental agency with responsibility for the administration of juvenile justice or the incarceration of juveniles that deprives persons of rights, privileges, or immunities secured or protected by the Constitution or laws of the United States.

(b) Civil action by Attorney General. Whenever the Attorney General has reasonable cause to believe that a violation of paragraph (1) has occurred, the Attorney General, for or in the name of the United States, may in a civil action obtain appropriate equitable and declaratory relief to eliminate the pattern or practice.

Procedurally, the Department of Justice first conducts an investigation by reviewing police records, interviewing officers and civilian witnesses, and compiling data. Ultimately, the investigators can issue a report concluding that officers at the police agency being investigated have or have not engaged in a "pattern or practice" of constitutional violations. Frustratingly, there is no precise definition of "pattern or practice"; at best, it is clear that some degree of frequency is required—isolated acts are insufficient—although that degree may not be sharply defined. If the Department of Justice concludes that there *was* a pattern or practice of unconstitutional violations, it can file a federal lawsuit against the police agency.

Although it is theoretically possible for a police agency to litigate the issue, none actually do so. In practice, the police agency and the Department of Justice engage in bargaining that results in a negotiated settlement in which the agency promises to take certain, specified actions to end constitutional violations and to improve the delivery of police services. The settlement agreement can be submitted to the court for approval, and, if the court approves, the agreement is formalized as a consent decree. The court selects a monitor— typically a law firm or consulting group—to supervise and publish regular reports about the police agency's ongoing efforts to fulfill the requirements of the consent decree. If the monitor finds the agency is falling short or refusing to attempt to make progress toward satisfying the decree, the original litigation can be reinstituted or new litigation can be filed.

Fourth Amendment violations related to the use of excessive force are not the only predicate for a § 14141 lawsuit or consent decree, but they are a common factor. As law professor Stephen Rushin, who has studied § 14141 investigations and litigation extensively, has pointed out,

> Almost every single negotiated settlement signed by the DOJ pursuant to § 14141 addresses the policing agency's use of force. Some of these use-of-force stipulations regulated many different possible issues related to force. Others more narrowly targeted a particular type of force at issue in the case. In total, virtually all of the negotiated settlements that involved monitors included a section regulating the use of force.[9]

Criminal Prosecutions under 18 U.S.C. §§ 241, 242, and 245

Individual police officers can be prosecuted for violating the Fourth Amendment, although not every constitutional violation is inherently criminal. Although federal civil claims may be brought in federal or state court, a statute, 18 U.S.C. § 3231, establishes that federal courts are the exclusive forum for federal criminal prosecutions. Section 3231 states that federal courts "have original jurisdiction, exclusive of the courts of the States, of all offenses against the laws of the United States [that is, federal laws]." One of those laws of the United States, 18 U.S.C. § 42, is a criminal analogue to § 1983. It states:

> Whoever, under color of any law, statute, ordinance, regulation, or custom, wilfully subjects any person in any State, Territory, Commonwealth, Possession, or District to the deprivation of any rights, privileges, or immunities secured or protected by the Constitution or laws of the United States . . . shall be fined under this title or imprisoned not more than one year, or both; and if bodily injury results from the acts committed in violation of this section or if such acts include the use, attempted use, or threatened use of a dangerous weapon, explosives, or fire, shall be fined under this title or imprisoned not more than ten years, or both; and if death results from the acts committed in violation of this section or if such acts include kidnapping or an attempt to kidnap, aggravated sexual abuse, or an attempt to commit aggravated sexual abuse, or an attempt to kill, shall be fined under this title, or imprisoned for any term of years or for life, or both, or may be sentenced to death.

Both 18 U.S.C. § 242 and 42 U.S.C. § 1983, discussed above, have given rise to a substantial body of law and academic literature that we will not address in depth here. For our purposes, it is sufficient to know that the statute applies when (1) officers acting "under color of . . . law" (2) willfully (3) commit a constitutional violation.

With regard to the first prong, the Supreme Court has concluded that officers act under color of law when "clothed with the authority" of the state, even if the officer's actions are specifically prohibited by state law.[10] Thus, an officer who blatantly misuses the power they possess by virtue of their position can be liable under this statute because their actions were made possible by virtue of their state-granted authority.

The second prong—"wilfully"—relates to the officer's mental state, what criminal law calls *mens rea* (literally, "guilty mind"). Unfortunately, as legal scholar David Sklansky writes,

> [e]xactly what that means has never been clear. It doesn't mean that the officer had to be thinking about the Constitution, but it is not enough that the officer intentionally did something that a judge or jury later decides was unconstitutional. At a minimum, federal case law suggests that the officer must have acted in "open defiance or reckless disregard" of a clearly articulated constitutional prohibition. And even that may not be enough. Most federal courts require proof that the officer acted with a "bad purpose or evil motive," by which they mean some kind of an intention to deprive the victim of a constitutional right.[11]

On the one hand, an officer who uses force sadistically to punish a community member in the clear absence of legal authority easily satisfies the criminal standard. On the other hand, an officer who uses force in the good-faith but mistaken belief that force is appropriate is highly unlikely to have the requisite *mens rea*.

The third prong is the easiest to address in light of the earlier discussion of constitutionality: if the officer's actions were constitutional, then 18 U.S.C. § 242 is inapplicable. That is, without a constitutional violation, there can be no crime.

In addition, there are a range of other crimes in which the Fourth Amendment can play some predicate role. 18 U.S.C. § 924(c)(1)(A) criminalizes carrying, using, brandishing, or discharging a firearm using the commission of an act that is punishable by federal law as a crime of violence. Certain violations of 18 U.S.C. § 242—those in which "bodily injury results from the acts committed"—can constitute a crime of violence, which means that an officer may be criminally charged both for willfully violating someone's constitutional rights *and* for carrying or using a firearm while doing so.[12] If, on the other hand, the officer's actions did not constitute a Fourth Amendment violation, then there is no willful violation, which means there is no crime of violence, which means that the officer's carrying or use of the firearm is not a crime under federal law. The constitutionality of police actions may also be relevant in a more attenuated way; 18 U.S.C. § 241 criminalizes conspiracies—that is, agreements between two or more persons to "injure, oppress, threaten, or intimidate any person . . . in the free exercise or enjoyment of any right or privilege secured to him by the Constitution," which includes the Fourth Amendment right to be free from unreasonable seizures.

Thus, the constitutional standard applies in at least three different ways: in civil litigation filed by a private plaintiff (or a class of plaintiffs) against an officer or agency; in civil litigation filed by the Department of Justice against an agency; and in federal criminal prosecutions against officers.

What Does the Constitutional Standard Regulate?

The Fourth Amendment regulates *seizures*.[13] Thus, the Fourth Amendment only regulates the use of force to the extent that a use of force amounts to a seizure; a use of force that does not constitute a seizure is not constitutionally cognizable.

An individual is seized, the Court has held, when the circumstances are such that a reasonable person would not feel free to "disregard the police and go about his business."[14] The Court has held that this requires "an intentional acquisition of physical control."[15] The requisite acquisition of physical control can occur under two circumstances. First, when an individual submits to an officer's "assertion of authority," as when an officer initiates a traffic stop by activating their emergency lights and the target driver pulls over to the side of the road. Second, and more relevantly for purposes of this book, an officer acquires physical control by engaging in "mere grasping or [the] application of physical force."[16] Importantly, the nonphysical assertion of control constitutes a seizure only when the individual submits. In contrast, the physical assertion of control—that is, an officer's initiation of physical contact to control a subject's movement—constitutes a seizure regardless of whether the individual submits or resists.

There is a substantial overlap between seizures and uses of force, but the idiosyncrasies of constitutional law mean that they are not coextensive. Because an individual's submission to a nonphysical assertion of control can constitute a seizure, an officer can effectively seize someone without using force. If, for example, an officer tells a pedestrian to stop and the pedestrian stops, that interaction is highly likely to be deemed a seizure—which may comply with or violate the Fourth Amendment—even though the officer's verbal command did not involve the use of force as that term is generally understood.

At the same time, however, an officer can use physical force without that use of force being considered a seizure for constitutional purposes. If, for example, an officer fires their sidearm at a fleeing subject, but if the bullet misses and the subject continues running, there is neither submission to a show of authority nor physical contact. At most, there is an officer's *attempt* to make physical contact, but an officer's intentions alone are not sufficient to constitute a seizure for Fourth Amendment purposes. In that example, the Fourth Amendment simply is not a relevant standard that can be used to analyze an officer's use of force.

To be constitutional, seizures—including seizures involving uses of force—must be justified both at their inception and throughout their duration. The question in use-of-force cases is whether the application of force (or the threat of force against an individual who has been seized by submission to a show of police authority) exceeds the scope of what the situation allows. An officer can be legally justified in seizing an individual—for example, stopping a vehicle after observing a traffic infraction—without necessarily being justified in the use of force. In such a circumstance, the use of force will offend the Fourth Amendment's prohibition of unreasonable seizures even when the traffic stop itself did not.

In the remainder of this chapter, we will discuss how the Fourth Amendment standard is best understood in situations when it is applicable to an officer's use of force.

How Does the Constitutional Standard Apply?

In *Graham v. Connor*, the Supreme Court held that because the Fourth Amendment prohibits unreasonable seizures, the ultimate question in use-of-force cases is whether the officer's actions were "objectively reasonable" under the circumstances. That analysis requires, the Court said, "a careful balancing of the nature and quality of the intrusion on the individual's . . . interests against the countervailing governmental interests at stake." And that balancing, in turn, requires "careful attention to the facts and circumstances of each particular case." To guide the constitutional analysis, the Court set out three factors that are widely known as the "*Graham* factors." First, the *severity of the crime at issue* must be considered. Second, the *immediate threat* to officers and others posed by the subject must be evaluated. Third, whether the subject is *actively resisting or attempting to evade arrest by fleeing* must be taken into account. The Court added additional factors by recognizing the importance of the proportionality of the force used and the totality of circumstances. These considerations make the analysis of objective reasonableness more complicated by requiring the analyst to consider aleatory elements of the use of force. As the forgoing suggests, use-of-force investigations are "highly fact-intensive."[17]

To navigate the constitutional use-of-force analysis, this section offers an analytical roadmap broken down into the following three elements: (1) deference and the "reasonable officer," (2) governmental interests, and (3) proportionality. At each step, our roadmap addresses the three major tenants of the *Graham* decision, but where most accounts take the three *Graham* factors at face value, we illustrate how they are more properly viewed as three categories, each of which contains a number of subsidiary factors that can influence how any given use-of-force incident is analyzed. We also go beyond *Graham*, demonstrating that the factors that fit within the *Graham* categories are not the only relevant considerations. *Graham* itself suggests that the three identified categories were not intended to be exhaustive; they are "include[ed]" in "the facts and circumstances of each particular case" that evaluators must review, but they are hardly the only relevant factors to consider when determining whether a use of force was reasonable.

Fully analyzing a use-of-force incident under the constitutional standard, then, requires understanding and applying the full extent of the *Graham* factors as well as understanding what else in the totality of the circumstances can affect the conclusion. *Graham* and subsequent decisions have offered, at best, a partial view of the analytical process that should be applied to use-of-force incidents. Each case analyzed by the courts applies relevant portions of the test, emphasizing some factors over others and omitting some considerations entirely. This is as it should be; the facts of each case are unique, and a recitation of irrelevant considerations would be unnecessary. But while the fragmented application of the rules is appropriate when reviewing the specific facts of an individual case, we seek here to provide a more global perspective.

Deference and the "Reasonable Officer on the Scene"

In use-of-force situations, officers seldom have the opportunity to seek guidance from a peer, supervisor, or manual. Instead, they must apply their training, knowledge, and experience to a specific incident as one of an unlimited set of possible scenarios in which an error in judgment could have catastrophic consequences. The Supreme Court has adopted an objective analysis, a deferential approach that is perceived as necessary because of the inherent stressors in use-of-force situations and the resulting uncertainty. While deference to officer decision making is appropriate, we seek here to identify the contours and limits of that deference.

As the Court has said, analyzing whether a use of force was objectively reasonable requires "careful attention to the facts and circumstances of each particular case." But which facts? How are the operative facts and circumstances to be properly identified? After all, there is the potential for both factual and interpretive disagreements. Factual disagreements arise when individuals disagree about the underlying facts, as when two eyewitnesses report seeing two different things. Interpretive disagreements arise when individuals agree on the underlying facts, but disagree as to the conclusions that can be drawn from those facts. For example, two people can both see a subject make the same physical actions and still disagree about whether the subject's actions presented an immediate threat to the officers. In *Graham v. Connor*, the Court provided the touchstone for resolving both factual and interpretive disagreements, stating:

> The "reasonableness" of a particular use of force must be judged from the perspective of a reasonable officer on the scene, rather than with the 20/20 vision of hindsight. . . . The calculus of reasonableness must embody allowance for the fact that police officers are often forced to make split-second judgments—in circumstances that are tense, uncertain, and rapidly evolving—about the amount of force that is necessary in a particular situation.

Thus, the formula for determining the reasonableness of an officer's use of force has moved from what the Supreme Court had labelled a "purely objective" analysis to a more realistic, but more complex standard that has been called "subjective objectivity."[18] The operative facts, circumstances, and conclusions are those that a hypothetical "reasonable officer on the scene" would have perceived or come to if they had been in the position of the actual officer. In short, *Graham* instructs courts to rely on what the "reasonable officer" would have perceived, which is not necessarily what the officer actually perceived. To clarify this admittedly confusing point, consider the following examples.

First, consider a situation in which an officer *reasonably* perceives a threat. For example, an officer uses force against a subject who was aggressively waving a rigid, shiny object with a black handle. If, given the situation, the hypothetical "reasonable officer" would have perceived the object as a knife, then the courts applying the constitutional standard will analyze whether the officer's use of force was a reasonable response to a subject waving a knife, even if it later turns out (with the 20/20 vision of hindsight) that the knife was a harmless plastic toy.

Second, consider a situation in which an officer *unreasonably* perceives a threat. For example, an officer uses force against a subject who was standing quite still with their empty hands out at their sides, fully compliant with the officer's commands. The officer explains, quite truthfully, that they perceived that the subject had been aggressively waving a knife. Given these facts, the "reasonable officer" in this situation would not have perceived the subject the same way. Therefore, the courts will analyze whether the officer's use of force was a reasonable response to the compliant subject because that would have been "the perspective of the reasonable officer on the scene," even though that is not what the officer, in fact, perceived.

Reviewers can, and typically must, start their analysis by identifying the perspective of the officer in the moment. That perspective, however, is not in and of itself the source of the operative facts. In assessing the constitutionality of force, the officer's subjective observations must be filtered through the lens of the legal construct known as the "reasonable officer on the scene."

This should not be read to mean that the only party in a position to evaluate an incident was the specific officer who used force. There has been an unfortunate tendency to read *Graham* as forestalling *post hoc* review, especially within policing itself. Officers and police executives can be far too quick, in our view, to dismiss any review, especially any critical review, as inappropriate "Monday-morning quarterbacking." This defensiveness may be understandable, but it is misplaced; the Supreme Court's admonition to rely on "the perspective of a reasonable officer on the scene" and to avoid "the 20/20 vision of hindsight"[19] does not insulate officers' decisions from meaningful, even critical, review. Instead, the Court's admonition is a reminder that the review of an officer's subjective observations must be conducted using only the information that was reasonably available to the officer at the time force was used.

It is important to realize that information developed *after* the use of force can shed light on the information that was reasonably available *prior* to the use of force. For example, if an officer states that a subject was reaching for that subject's waistband and later investigation determines that the subject had a gun concealed in that waistband, the later investigation is probative as to the accuracy of the officer's observation. That is, the fact that the subject had a gun in that location makes it more likely that the subject was reaching for their waistband, and that, in turn, makes it more likely that the officer truly did see—and that a reasonable officer *would have* seen—the subject reaching for their waistband. In short, the information gathered after the use of force may suggest that the officer's observation *prior* to the use of force is more likely to have been accurate. If, on the other hand, subsequent investigation determines that the subject did not have a gun or other weapon, that finding calls the officer's statement into question, suggesting the potential for misperception, flawed memory, or deception. A subject with nothing in their waistband is less likely to reach for their waistband, which makes it less likely that the officer actually saw the subject reaching for their waistband, which in turn means that it is less likely that a reasonable officer could have seen the subject reaching for their waistband. Here, the information gathered after the use of force suggests that the officer's observations prior to the use of force are less likely to have been accurate. In either case, further investigation is required to identify whether the officer's perceptions were reasonable. Critically, the later findings are not dipositive—the subject with the gun may *not* have reached for their waistband and the subject without the gun may *have* reached for their waistband for other reasons—but they can help reviewers identify the questions that need to be answered to identify what a reasonable officer on the scene could have perceived at the time.

The officer's perceptions of the subject's actions are not the only aspect of a use-of-force encounter that must be viewed through the subjectively objective frame: reviewers must do the same with the use of force itself. The reasonableness of a use of force depends on the risk inherent in the type and manner of the force being used, not the ultimate effect of that force. For example, firing a gun at an individual is properly considered deadly force because of the potential harm the bullet is likely to cause, even if the bullet only grazes the person's leg, causing a superficial injury, or misses entirely. Similarly, using a closed fist to strike a subject in the face when the subject's head is on the ground is properly considered a serious use of force because of the potential for harm, even if the strike results in only a minor injury. In either of those two cases, predicating the reasonableness inquiry on the ultimate injury would lead reviewers to incorrectly ask whether the use of minor force was appropriate. Clearly, that is the wrong way to approach those examples. The correct question is whether the use of deadly force or serious force, respectively, was appropriate under the circumstances. In short, the reasonableness of any use of force depends on the foreseeable harms that arise from the officer's actions—that is, the harms that the "reasonable officer on the scene" would have anticipated—not the actual harms that result. As with other forms of evidence, of course, the actual injury that results can, in some cases, provide limited guidance as to what harms were foreseeable prior to the use of force.

Under Supreme Court precedent, then, reviewers must be able to identify the facts and circumstances as the reasonable officer on the scene could have perceived them, to draw the conclusions and to make the predictions that the reasonable officer on the scene could have drawn and made, and to analyze the resulting information. This has created at least three problems. First, the Court has provided no guidance as to how judges and other reviewers are to define the "reasonable officer on the scene," nor has the Court defined the extent to which the actual officer's individual characteristics—years of experience, training, and so on—should be imported into that analysis. Second, the Court has not provided any operational definitions of the *Graham* factors themselves. For example, how would the hypothetical "reasonable officer on the scene" assess the severity and likelihood of potential threats, and how exactly would they determine the immediacy of any given threat? Third, even if a reviewer is able to view the scene from the perspective of a "reasonable officer" and to apply the *Graham* factors, that assessment is best understood as answering the binary question of whether *some* amount of force was justified and not the more important, but more complicated question of *what type* or *how much* force was reasonable. Consider, for example, the arrest of a murder suspect: a physically diminutive and frail octogenarian who, while stark naked and unarmed, slaps at arresting officers. Taking the *Graham* factors at face value and applying them without additional analysis would lead inevitably to the conclusion that the crime is severe, there is an immediate threat to the officers, and the subject is actively resisting in an attempt to evade arrest, yet it would be patently absurd for officers to use more than a modicum of force, if any, to subdue the subject.

There are no perfect solutions to the problems identified above, but reviewers can subject use-of-force incidents to appropriate review when they know what features, characteristics, or categories of an event to examine, and how to examine and understand them. The use of force is messy, and evaluating uses of force after the fact can be just as messy. The purpose of this chapter is to operationally define relevant characteristics of a use-of-force incident and to provide a reliable framework that can be used to accurately determine whether a specific action was constitutionally reasonable. The following sections will untangle the contours of the *Graham* factors and give comprehensive (but not exhaustive) examples of how the facts of a use-of-force event may be evaluated under the Fourth Amendment.

Governmental Interest

Sociologist Egon Bittner famously identified the "unique competency of the police" as their ability to intercede to address "something that ought not to be happening and about which someone had better do something now."[20] Police, in other words, are uniquely trained and equipped to deal with situations in which the use of force may become necessary. And yet, it is inescapably true that not every aspect of policing will justify the use of force.

To understand this point, consider first the nature of the police function itself. That is, what is it that police *do* in a free, democratic society? Political scientist James Q. Wilson has offered perhaps the broadest and most useful taxonomy of the police function, which he describes as consisting of three types of tasks: officers engage in law enforcement, provide services, and maintain order.[21] Unfortunately, those tasks are not always clearly distinct; certain situations may require officers to engage in two or even all three of those tasks simultaneously, as with an officer who makes an arrest (law enforcement) to break up a house party (order maintenance) that has been the subject of a neighbor's complaint (service provision).

As that example suggests, it can be difficult to identify the police function with any precision precisely because the nature of the job requires officers to play a host of different roles. Officers detect, investigate, and apprehend law breakers, but decades of empirical study have established quite convincingly that only a relatively small percentage of most officers' time is dedicated to criminal enforcement.[22] Police officers are also called upon to perform a variety of services that do not in themselves constitute enforcement, even when there is a potential for enforcement activity. Officers provide at least rudimentary forms of marital, substance-abuse, and mental-health counselling; first aid; animal rescue; and auto-mechanical assistance and repair. They direct traffic, escort funeral processions, and manage crowd control during parades, sports events, rallies, and peaceful protests. They drive people from place to place, perform welfare checks, and convey death notifications to next of kin. They educate the public not just about criminal law and highway regulations, but also about personal safety, home security, and child-abduction prevention. They serve as community organizers, supporting neighborhood-watch groups and youth athletic leagues. They look into suspicious activity, suspicious persons, suspicious vehicles, suspicious packages, even suspicious smells[23] and an array of everyday items that have, at some point, struck someone as suspicious enough to call the police (including, according to news reports, a cucumber,[24] a burrito,[25] and a quarter[26]). And this only begins to scratch the surface of the nonenforcement services that police provide.[27]

Given this wide range of duties that officers perform, when can they legitimately use force? The answer to this question is of tremendous practical significance, but the question has rarely received an explicit answer. Clearly, officers cannot use force in every aspect of their jobs. Indeed, any number of commentators, including the Supreme Court, have lamented the use of force in situations that do not justify it. As far back as the 1968 case, *Terry v. Ohio*, the Court disapprovingly observed that force and intimidation were sometimes used to "maintain the power image of the beat officer, an aim sometimes accomplished by humiliating anyone who attempts to undermine police control of the streets."[28] The Supreme Court's lamentation is well-founded; officers may be within their rights to maintain a certain image, but clearly the need—real or imagined—to maintain "the power image of the beat officer" cannot justify the use of force.

That, however, is an easy case: establishing police dominance is not an independent, legally cognizable aspect of the police function. But even when officers are engaged in activities that are universally agreed to fall within the police function, they do not get *carte blanche* to use force. Officers are expected to engage in crime prevention, for example, and they indisputably have legal authority to do so. An officer may organize events for that purpose, such as educating community groups and neighborhood associations about how to reduce opportunistic crime. An officer may counsel someone at length about the perils of engaging in criminal activity, using a combination of promises and warnings. An officer may attempt to build a long-term relationship with an at-risk youth, encouraging them to join a sports team that the officer coaches. It would be inappropriate and deeply problematic, however, for officers to physically beat someone to deter them from breaking the law at some point in the future.

Similarly, officers have the legal authority to investigate crimes. Further, they clearly have the legal authority to *forcibly* investigate crimes. An officer with reasonable suspicion to believe that an individual committed a crime may detain that person; in the event that the person attempts to flee, the officer may use force to prevent that flight. An officer with probable cause to believe that an individual committed a crime may arrest that person; if the person physically resists, the officer may use force to effect the arrest. An officer who has arrested someone may interrogate that person. If the person refuses to cooperate with the interrogation, though, officers certainly cannot physically beat them to obtain an incriminating confession. In short, merely identifying that the police have the legal authority to take a particular action does not necessarily establish that the police can use force to realize that action.

Why not? In brief, society restricts the ability of officers to use force because the use of force itself infringes on the subject's individual interest in liberty, bodily autonomy, and personal safety; on the more generalized governmental interests in preserving legitimacy and public trust; and on the specific governmental interest in protecting the physical safety of its constituents. In other words, the use of force by police infringes on highly valued personal and state interests. Because the use of force is viewed—properly, in our view—as an infringement on individual and governmental interests, and because we do not allow the government to lightly infringe on such interests, the use of force is only permissible when it is specifically justified (as opposed to being generally permitted unless prohibited).

Having established that officers may only use force when it is justified, the question remains: what justifies police uses of force?

Perhaps the most conceptually sound answer to that question comes from law professor Rachel Harmon, who concluded that force can be legitimately used only when there is an "imminent threat" to certain pre-defined governmental interests.[29]

It is important to note at the outset that these three governmental interests that justify the police in using force are prospective. The use of force is required to achieve one of the identified goals *at some point in the future*. A use of force cannot be predicated on purely retrospective governmental interest. For example, it would be highly inappropriate for a police officer to use force to retributively punish a criminal suspect for a previously committed crime; the state's interest in punishing offenders is predicated on a formal adjudication of guilt, either through conviction by a jury or a guilty plea. Only once there is adjudication can the state impose punishment.[30] An officer may, however, use force to effect an arrest of a suspect who would otherwise escape; doing so is *prospective*, not retrospective, because the officer is acting pursuant to the state's interest in doing something in the future—here, subjecting the subject to a formal prosecution.

However, merely having a prospective interest is not sufficient to justify the use of force. The government has an interest in deterring future crime, for example, but it would be manifestly inappropriate for an officer to beat the individuals they come across as a way of encouraging them to avoid breaking the law in the future.[31] Some, but not all, prospective governmental interests can justify the use of force; Harmon has identified, and we endorse, only three.

First, the state has an interest in **law enforcement**: "facilitating [the government's] institutions of criminal law."[32] This interest can justify an officer's actions only *after* a crime has been committed—or, more accurately, is believed to have been committed—although force is used in such situations to ensure that they can satisfy the state's interest in law enforcement *in the future*. Officers cannot effectively investigate suspected crimes without the ability to detain persons whom they reasonably suspect to have committed those crimes, for example, and, in the event of a prosecution, the criminal justice system requires the presence of the individual who is charged with a crime, of witnesses, and of evidence. Through the application of certain legal processes, such as the issuance of an arrest warrant, a subpoena, or a search warrant, the state "expressly commands" individuals to comply by submitting to an investigation, or appearing, or testifying. As Harmon explains, these state commands can be implicit as well; when a state gives officers the authority to make an arrest or conduct a search *without* a warrant, implied in that authority is a command for the individual to comply. These commands implicate the state's interest in enforcing the law against those individuals who are believed to have violated it. "Police uses of force," Harmon writes, "are then justified to ensure that these commands are satisfied, that our criminal justice institutions function after a crime [is believed to have] occurred."

Second, the state has an interest in **order maintenance**: force can be justified "when it is necessary to eliminate a significant threat to public safety." As described above, this interest is prospective; it can justify an officer's actions only *prior* to the commission of a crime (or the infliction of harm on an individual) when the use of force is seen as a way of averting that crime (or harm). This interest can overlap to some degree with the government's interest in law enforcement. Harmon provides the example of officers breaking up a fight between teenagers. At the moment they forcibly separate the combatants, the officers may be acting both in their order-maintenance capacity, by using force to prevent harm to the combatants and bystanders, and in their law-enforcement capacity, by arresting the individuals so they may be charged criminally. It is equally possible, however, for officers to use force to maintain public order even without a criminal predicate. "Thus, a police officer may use force to stop a distraught person from committing suicide or to break up a rowdy crowd that could injure by riot or stampede, even though doing so entails applying force against someone who is not yet violating a criminal statute."[33] In other words, a use of force to prevent an individual's suicide may be entirely appropriate even though there is no crime on the statute books that would criminally punish the person's actions. (Although all United States jurisdictions have repealed statutes that criminally punish suicide and attempted suicide, some states continue to treat it as a common law crime.[34]) It can, in any individual case, be difficult to identify when the state's interest in order maintenance is fully manifested and when there is a threat that is sufficiently imminent so as to justify an officer's use of force. "But even though the edges of legitimate police efforts to protect the public are contested and blurry, the [immediate] prevention of crime and the maintenance of public safety remain central to contemporary policing."[35]

Third, the state has an interest in **officer safety**: force may be used to protect officers from physical threats to their safety. Notice, again, that this interest is prospective; it justifies force as a way to avert a physical hazard that would otherwise cause harm to the officer. The individual officer has a personal interest in their own safety, of course, but an officer has no greater interest in their own safety than anyone else does—if the individual interest in safety were the only interest at stake, we could simply apply the law of self-defense in situations in which officers used force to protect themselves.[36] The state, however, has a distinct interest in protecting officers. Without officers, the state's interests in law enforcement and order maintenance would be easily frustrated, leading Harmon to describe the interest in officer safety as "derivative" of the other two interests. "Because human police officers are the instruments by which the state pursues its interests in law and order, threats to those police officers often result in justified defensive force in excess of what would otherwise be required to serve the state's interests." It is for that reason that jurisdictions that have retained the common-law duty to retreat, which requires individuals who can safely retreat instead of using self-defense to do so, do not impose that requirement on police officers.[37]

Although the three factors are distinct, two or even all three may be present in any given case. This is particularly true when an officer has the legal authority to take a particular action or issue a particular order, when a subject attempts to impede that action or refuses to obey that order, and when the impediments or refusals constitute criminal violations. Consider a situation in which officers are authorized to enter a private home to check the welfare of a young child, but the child's father violently rebuffs their efforts to enter the home. Officers in that situation may well be authorized to use force to check on the young child (order maintenance), to apprehend the father for frustrating the government's interest in order maintenance by refusing to obey officers' lawful commands (law enforcement), and to defend officers from the father's attack (officer safety). Not all frustrations will amount to criminal activity, of course, but it is worth noting that any given situation may implicate more than one governmental interest.

To determine whether there was a legitimate governmental interest in any given case, reviewers should ask the following counterfactual question: if the officers had *not* used force, would one of the identified governmental interests have been thwarted or frustrated? At this point, the inquiry is somewhat abstract; if a governmental interest would have been thwarted or frustrated, *some* use of force *may* have been appropriate.

How, then, should we evaluate whether one of the requisite governmental interests existed, or could reasonably have been thought to exist, in any given situation? The Supreme Court itself has given us some guidance in the form of the *Graham* factors, but, as we will discuss, that guidance is incomplete.

Using the Graham *Factors to Identify Governmental Interests*

Here, we discuss how each of the *Graham* factors—the severity of the crime at issue, the immediate threat to officers and others, and whether the subject is actively resisting or attempting to evade arrest by fleeing—relate to the determination of whether there is a governmental interest in using force.

THE SEVERITY OF THE CRIME

In this context, the "severity of the crime" factor should be understood to pose three distinct, but interrelated questions about the nature of the officer–civilian interaction: First, did the officer have cause to believe that there was a crime? Second, if so, what is the relationship of the subject to that crime? Third, what is the nature of the crime? We address each question in turn.

First, did the officer have reasonable suspicion or probable cause to believe that there was a crime? Officers have the legal authority to arrest someone if they have probable cause to believe that the individual has committed a crime;[38] that authority reflects the government's interest in apprehending suspected criminals. It is difficult to describe the concept of probable cause with any precision. The Court has identified it as "a practical, nontechnical conception,"[39] "a fluid concept—turning on the assessment of probabilities in particular factual contexts—not readily, or even usefully, reduced to a neat set of legal rules."[40] The ultimate touchstone, as the Court has put it, is whether "a man of reasonable caution"[41] would have concluded from the available evidence that an offense had been or was being committed. This requires "more than bare suspicion," but "less than . . . would justify . . . conviction."[42] Within this fairly wide band, courts and commentators have come to inconsistent conclusions as to whether "probable cause" is, or should be, a "more-likely-than-not" standard.[43]

Officers also have the legal authority to detain someone so long as they have reasonable suspicion that the individual is involved in criminality;[44] that authority reflects the government's interest in, *inter alia,* investigating potential crimes. As with probable cause, the Court has rejected attempts to define reasonable suspicion with any degree of accuracy.[45] Instead, reasonable suspicion is typically compared to, but identified as *less than,* probable cause, with the Court writing:

> We have held that probable cause means "a fair probability that contraband or evidence of a crime will be found," *Illinois v. Gates,* 462 U. S. 213, 238 (1983), and the level of suspicion required for a Terry stop is obviously less demanding than that for probable cause, see *United States v. Montoya de Hernandez,* 473 U. S. 531, 541, 544 (1985).[46]

It is worth pointing out that there is disagreement among the various federal circuits as to whether the officer must have reasonable suspicion of a specific crime or whether it is sufficient for officers to articulate a more generalized reasonable suspicion that the person is involved in criminality of some type.[47]

Second, if there was a crime, what is the civilian's relationship to that crime? The fact that an officer is interacting with someone and that the interaction is related to a crime—or, more accurately, that the officer had reasonable suspicion or probable cause to believe that a crime occurred—does not necessarily establish a governmental interest that would justify the use of coercive authority against that person. Given that there is a clear governmental interest in the detection, investigation, and apprehension of criminals, an officer's coercive authority over an individual depends on the relationship of the individual to the crime. On one end of the spectrum, there is no governmental interest when the individual has no relationship with the crime. At the other end of the spectrum, there is substantial governmental interest in seizing individuals suspected of committing a crime. Officers can detain individuals whom they reasonably suspect of being involved in criminal activity and arrest individuals whom they have probable cause to believe committed a crime.

Between those two points, there may be a governmental interest when an individual has some relationship to a crime even if the individual is not suspected of committing the crime. For example, the individual may be the complainant, a witness, or a victim. As a constitutional matter, the Fourth Amendment provides limited authority for officers to detain individuals other than criminal suspects when "special needs" justify the detention—to somewhat simplify a complex area of law, "special needs" refers to a governmental interest *other than* the interest in stopping or arresting a criminal suspect. For example, officers serving a search warrant at a home may detain individuals inside the residence even when those individuals are not individually suspected of any wrongdoing. The "special needs" test defies easy application; it requires evaluators to balance the nature and degree of the government's interest in the seizure against the severity of the intrusion. However, for purposes of determining whether there is a governmental interest, it is sufficient to acknowledge that the government does have an interest in obtaining information from complainants, witnesses, and victims. Whether that interest justifies an intrusive government action, including the use of force, is a question of proportionality, which we discuss in the next section.

Third, what is the nature of the crime(s)? Assuming an officer had reasonable suspicion or probable cause that a crime was committed, the final aspect of *Graham's* "severity of the crime" factor is the nature of that crime. Under current law, the severity of the crime is not relevant to the presence or absence of a governmental interest; the government retains an interest in seizing suspected criminals even when the crime at issue is minor. It is important to reiterate that at this point in the analysis we are concerned only with the question of whether there is a governmental interest—we are not yet concerned with whether that interest justifies the use of force in any particular situation; we address that issue when we discuss proportionality.

In the context of determining whether there is a governmental interest, then, the nature of the crime is relevant only to the extent that it can establish whether the governmental interest is primarily or exclusively related to apprehension for criminal justice purposes or whether the government has an additional and distinct interest in maintaining public order or protecting officer safety. The essential question is whether the crime was violent or was otherwise so serious that it is reasonable to expect that the perpetrator will engage in future violence. If either of those conditions are met, then there is more likely to be a governmental interest in using force to protect officer and public safety. If neither of those conditions are met, the governmental interest is limited to detention or apprehension for criminal justice purposes.

For example, when an individual has shoplifted a pack of gum, there is a governmental interest in detection, investigation, and apprehension, but that incident simply does not involve the type of crime that would lead a reasonable officer to believe, without any additional information, that the subject was imminently dangerous to the officer or the general public. On the other hand, a known serial killer who is fleeing from officers implicates not only the governmental interest in apprehension, but also public safety interests. Between those two extremes, an individual who has committed a series of very serious, but nonviolent crimes may implicate the government's interest in officer safety because the severity of the punishment they face may make them more likely to violently resist than would the shoplifter.

When analyzing the nature of the crime, analysts must be cognizant that the relevant crime is not necessarily the crime that initially gave rise to the interaction. Instead, use-of-force determinations require analysts to identify all of the relevant crimes and, typically, to focus on the most serious crime or crimes in play. For example, the shoplifter who steals a single pack of gum commits among the pettiest of petty thefts. If, however, that shoplifter shoves the responding officer, the nature of the crime that establishes the government's interest in using force has shifted from petty theft to assault of an officer. If the shoplifting suspect draws a firearm and threatens to shoot the officer, the nature of the underlying offense shifts yet again to an aggravated assault. This is an extreme example, but the logic is equally applicable in more common situations: when a suspected criminal flees from an officer's command to halt, the relevant crime(s) may include resisting or obstruction (depending on state law) as well as the crime that originally gave rise to the officer's command.

IMMEDIATE THREAT

Where the first *Graham* factor, "severity of the crime," was primarily about identifying whether a use-of-force incident implicated the government's interest in detecting, investigating, and apprehending criminals, the second *Graham* factor, "immediate threat," is primarily about identifying whether the incident implicated the government's interest in safety.

We begin the discussion of this factor with the reminder that we are concerned at this point in the analysis only with the binary question of whether there was an immediate threat.[48] An officer's perception that an imminent[49] threat exists is reasonable when the officer has reason to believe that an individual has the ability, opportunity, and intent to cause harm.[50]

Ability means the individual's physical capacity to cause an identifiable type of harm. Ability in this context requires an explicit reference: the individual must be capable of taking an action that would cause some particular and identified type of physical harm. It is not sufficient to state that an individual has the ability to cause some undefined harm—identifying the presence of a governmental interest that permits officers to use force requires specifying the type or types of harm that the individual has the capacity to cause. A handcuffed individual, for example, lacks the ability to punch someone, although they may retain the ability to kick or ram someone with their shoulder. Similarly, an individual with a knife in their hand may have the ability to stab someone, while an individual without a knife does not. Articulating ability, then, requires officers both to identify what the individual was capable of at the relevant time and, for each type of harm identified, to explain how the officer came to that conclusion. In short, officers must not only identify that the subject was able to inflict some type of harm, they must identify that harm and explain why they concluded that the subject was capable of inflicting it. Relevant observations include, but are not limited to:

The subject's apparent physical condition (age, size, strength, apparent skill level, physical condition such as injury or exhaustion, etc.);

The subject's apparent mental condition (the apparent influence of mental illness, drugs, or alcohol, for example);

The proximity of weapons; and

The degree to which the subject has been effectively restrained at the relevant time and their ability to resist despite being restrained.

Opportunity refers to the environment and situation, specifically with regard to the individual's proximity to the potential target or targets. Even if an individual is physically capable of throwing a punch, they may not have any opportunity to cause harm by doing so because they are too far away for the punch to connect. Similarly, an individual with a knife who is a block away from the officer has the capability, but not the opportunity, to use the knife against the officer at the time; therefore, the knife should not be considered a threat to the officer in that moment (although it certainly may become a threat as the distance between the subject and the officer decreases). There is no set distance at which an individual does or does not have the opportunity to physically injure an officer; that determination depends on the relevant harms and the facts and circumstances of each case. Articulating opportunity requires officers to explain how the individual could cause an identifiable harm to a specific target at the relevant time. Relevant observations include, but are not limited to:

The physical proximity of the subject to potential targets;

The nature of the harm (e.g., an individual may be so far away as not have the opportunity to attack with a knife while still retaining the opportunity to attack with a firearm);

The subject's apparent physical condition and the speed at which they could close distance;

The reactionary gap (the amount of time that it will take for an officer to react to an individual's actions); and

The officer's ability under the circumstances to reduce or eliminate the opportunity for violent attack.

Intent refers to the individual's perceived mental state, their apparent desire to cause physical harm to the target or targets. Where ability and opportunity may be relatively easy for an officer to diagnose based on readily observable physical characteristics, intent is more complicated. Because officers, like everyone else, lack the ability to divine another's intentions by peering into their mind, officers must rely on behavioral indicators, physical manifestations indicative of intent. To take an obvious example, lunging at an officer with a knife is a clear physical manifestation of the intent to stab the officer. In contrast, an individual who is merely conversing with an officer while standing next to a knife block in the kitchen does not present any physical behaviors from which an officer could identify an intent to use the knife aggressively. It is important to avoid blurring the lines between intent and the other aspects of threat; an individual may be physically capable of causing harm and have the opportunity to do so, and yet not present any threat. For example, if an officer is standing next to a motorist who is changing a tire at the time, the motorist has the ability and opportunity to strike the officer with the tire iron they are holding. However, if there is no reason to believe that the motorist intends to strike the officer with the tire iron, there would be no threat in this situation. When that is the case, the use of force would not be justified at that moment.

Importantly, intent may be properly articulated through a combination of multiple factors even if no individual factor is sufficient on its own. To continue our previous example, merely holding a tire iron is not in and of itself indicative of the intent to cause harm. Nor is walking toward an officer. Nor is failing to obey an officer's commands. However, walking toward an officer while holding a tire iron and ignoring the officer's commands to stop or drop the weapon can be, in combination, indicative of the individual's intent.

It is worth emphasizing that officers must explain *why* they came to the conclusion that an individual had the intent to cause physical harm. This requires the articulation of specific, observable facts. It is not sufficient for officers to rely on unhelpfully generic descriptions such as an individual's "body language" or their "furtive movements" or the "look in their eyes." Officers must describe what the body language was, what the movements were, or the nature of the subject's facial expressions. Further, officers must explain why the body language, movement, or expressions were indicative of the intent to cause harm. Formulaic or boilerplate language is patently insufficient: officers must provide details.

As this suggests, some indications of threat should be treated with skepticism. In one case, for example, an officer struck a motorist with a baton because he thought the motorist was going to throw a piece of broccoli at him; although the officer claimed he feared that the subject was going to use the broccoli as a distraction before assaulting him, the court described the threat as "negligible."[51]

There has also been an unfortunate tendency for officers to articulate, and apparently to urge courts to rely heavily on, an individual's eye contact. In one case, for example, an officer expressed that she and another officer were being threatened because, "The stare the [subject was doing] was a stare to harm or hurt us."[52] Although an individual's facial expressions, tone of voice, or comments may be properly included in a combination of factors that would lead a reasonable officer to perceive that someone had the intent to cause harm, such factors are not sufficient in and of themselves.

Articulating intent requires officers to explain how the individual physically manifested their intent to cause an identifiable type of harm. Relevant observations include, but are not limited to:

The subject's conduct, including verbal statements and specific movements or
   body language;
The subject's apparent mental capacity, including the influence of drugs or
   alcohol;
The nature and seriousness of the suspected offense, if any; and
The nature of the subject's prior contacts with officers or any known violent
   history or known propensity for violence.

It is imperative for analysts to be aware that three aspects of threat—ability,
opportunity, and intent—must be supported by specific, articulable observations. An officer's conclusory statement that they feared for their safety or
for the safety of others is insufficient to establish a governmental interest.
Put differently, an officer's fear is not reasonable merely because the officer
was honestly afraid—an officer may honestly have been afraid of a perceived
threat in situations in which that perception or fear was unreasonable. An
analyst cannot conclude that there was a threat in the absence of articulated
details and circumstances that would have led a reasonable officer to conclude, at the time that force was used, that the individual against whom force
was used had the ability, opportunity, and intent to cause physical harm to
the officer or others.

It is also essential to distinguish the concept of "threat," meaning an imminent danger to a legitimate governmental interest, from the concept of "risk."
Risk is best described as a potential threat. More precisely, risk is the presence
of at least one but not all three of the prerequisites of threat (ability, opportunity, and intent) and the potential for the remaining factors to materialize.

While it may be wise, in many cases, for officers to mitigate risk in various
ways, the lack of imminent danger to a governmental interest makes it inappropriate to use force at that point. Consider again the example of a motorist
using a tire iron to change a tire; as the motorist is changing the tire, they have
the physical ability and opportunity to attack the officer with the tire iron,
which means that there is some risk to the officer. The officer could step farther away from the motorist (creating distance) or could move to a position
that keeps part of a vehicle between them and the motorist (using a physical obstacle to increase the amount of time it would take for the motorist to
reach them), but the officer would not be justified in using force at that point
because there was no perceptible intent to harm. Although there was some
risk, there was no apparent intent to cause harm, and therefore there was no
threat. And with no threat, there was no governmental interest at stake, and
no justification for using force. The same is true in other situations; the fact
that someone is capable of causing harm, has the opportunity to cause harm,

or has the intent to cause harm does not justify a use of force: all three factors must be present.

Understanding the difference between risk and threat makes clear that a use of force cannot be predicated on an officer's speculative articulation of what an individual *might* have done or the threat that *could have* existed *if* the individual were to have taken certain actions. Analysts must be alert to the problematic tendency of officers to rely excessively on hypotheticals. For example, an individual who is standing on loose rocks *could* reach down and pick up a rock and *could* attack an officer with that rock, but those possibilities do not by themselves justify the use of force. Even if the subject is refusing to obey an officer's commands at the time, it is not reasonable to conclude that merely standing in proximity to rocks creates a threat of being struck by a rock. Sometimes officers attempt to justify their actions on the basis of predictions that are even more far-fetched; vague pronouncements that the subject was threatening are insufficient, as are unreliable recitations of generic and worn indicators such as the look in a subject's eyes. Purely generalized concerns about a safety risk do not amount to an actual threat.[53] The existence of a bona fide threat must be predicated on an officer's articulation of details and circumstances that would lead a reasonable officer to conclude that the individual was physically capable of causing harm, was in a position to physically inflict that harm, and had manifested the apparent intent to do so. For a use of force to be constitutionally permissible, an officer must have an objectively reasonable belief that something *is happening*, not just that something *might possibly* happen.

That is not to say that officers must wait until they or another person are under attack. The threat must be immediate, but it need not have fully manifested into an actual assault. There is, for example, no requirement that a police officer wait until a subject shoots to confirm that a serious threat of harm exists.[54] The legal standard of "immediate threat" allows for situations in which an officer uses force to preclude an assault by reacting to a threat before it progresses into an assault.[55] As in other situations, of course, officers must be able to articulate *why* the situation presented a threat as that term is properly understood. Let us return to the example from the prior paragraph, of the subject who is standing in proximity to rocks. At that point, it would be inappropriate for officers to react as if they were threatened by a rock (although they are free to consider or use violence-reduction techniques, alternatives to force, or tactical options that may mitigate the risk and avoid a potential threat). If the subject ignored officers' verbal commands and reached for a rock, however, it would be reasonable to conclude that there was a threat of being struck even before the subject lifted the rock from the ground. At that point, the use of force may be objectively reasonable because delay or inaction on the officers' part may put them into the position of being unable to prevent the threat from manifesting into harm; once the subject throws the rock, it is too late for the officers' actions to make any difference.

ACTIVE RESISTANCE AND ATTEMPTS TO EVADE ARREST BY FLIGHT

Like the first *Graham* factor—the severity of the crime—the third factor implicates the government's interest in detecting, investigating, and apprehending criminals. The government has an interest in investigating individuals whom officers reasonably suspect are involved in criminal activity and in apprehending individuals whom officers have probable cause to believe committed a crime. Those interests are frustrated when an individual successfully resists or flees from officers. Thus, to protect the government's interests in investigation and apprehension, officers may use force to overcome resistance, including to prevent escape. The relevant question, then, is twofold: First, whether the government has an interest in detaining or apprehending the individual in question in relation to a crime. Second, whether the individual's actions create a realistic possibility that the subject will avoid detention or apprehension.

As with threats to officer safety, officers need not wait until a subject's resistance or flight is fully manifested before using force to address it. At the same time, however, the risk of resistance or flight by itself does not justify the use of force—there must at least be an articulate *threat* of resistance or flight, if not actual resistance or flight. In that vein, it is important to note that purely verbal resistance—statements indicative of noncompliance—do not constitute a threat of active resistance or attempts to evade arrest by flight. Such statements can indicate that there is a risk that the individual may resist or flee, of course, and officers are free to address that risk using a range of non-forceful options including conflict avoidance and violence-reduction techniques, alternatives to force, or tactical options that may mitigate the risk and avoid the potential threat of resistance or flight. They cannot, however, use force until there is a threat or manifestation of active resistance.

Articulating an individual's active resistance or attempt to evade arrest by flight requires officers to explain how the individual physically resisted or attempted to flee. Relevant observations include, but are not limited to:

The subject's conduct, including verbal statements and specific movements (body language);
The subject's apparent physical condition (age, size, strength, apparent skill level, physical condition such as injury or exhaustion, etc.);

The subject's apparent mental condition (the apparent influence of mental illness, drugs, or alcohol, for example);

The degree to which the subject has been effectively restrained and their ability to resist or flee despite being restrained;

The degree to which the subject's movement has been limited even when the subject has not been restrained (e.g., whether the subject is seated, surrounded by officers, etc.);

The environmental options that would enable or restrict flight; and

Prior contacts with the subject or awareness of any propensity for resistance or flight.

As a reminder, the sole focus at this point in the inquiry is the binary question of whether there is a governmental interest. Only when the presence of a governmental interest is confirmed does one continue the analysis by weighing the relative strength of the governmental interest against severity of the officer's use of force.

Additional Factors

The three *Graham* factors—severity of the crime, immediate threat, and flight—can help reviewers determine the existence of a governmental interest that can justify the use of force in any given encounter. Reviewers should be aware, however, that additional factors can establish the existence of a governmental interest, potentially justifying the use of force, even when the *Graham* factors seem inapplicable. This is the case because the *Graham* factors are primarily concerned with two governmental interests—facilitating the criminal justice process and protecting officer safety—but are less useful when it comes to determining whether the government has an interest in maintaining public order (which, as described above, includes preventing crime and preserving public safety).

Some courts have identified separate factors that apply when the *Graham* factors themselves do not. The Sixth Circuit, for example, has adopted what it described as "a more tailored set of factors to be considered in the medical-emergency context . . . [w]here a situation does not fit within the *Graham* test because the person in question has not committed a crime, is not resisting arrest, and is not directly threatening the officer."[56] Those factors are:

(1) Was the person experiencing a medical emergency that rendered him incapable of making a rational decision under circumstances that posed an immediate threat of serious harm to himself or others?

(2) Was some degree of force reasonably necessary to ameliorate the immediate threat?

(3) Was the force used more than reasonably necessary under the circumstances (i.e., was it excessive)?[57]

The first question posed by the Sixth Circuit addresses the issue of whether a governmental interest exists, while the second question addresses whether the governmental interest justifies the use of "some degree of force" and the third question addresses the extent to which force was permitted under the circumstances.

Other courts and commentators have identified two noncriminal governmental interests that can, at least in certain circumstances, justify the use of some force: community caretaking and involuntary commitment.

COMMUNITY CARETAKING

Police officers are charged not just with the enforcement of criminal law, but also with preserving the peace and security of their communities. As the Court has described, the community-caretaking function is "totally divorced from the detection, investigation, or acquisition of evidence relating to the violation of a criminal statute."[58] As federal judge and legal scholar Debra Livingston has written:

> "Community caretaking" denotes a wide range of everyday police activities undertaken to aid those in danger of physical harm, to preserve property, or to create and maintain a feeling of security in the community. It includes things like the mediation of noise disputes, the response to complaints about stray and injured animals, and the provision of assistance to the ill or injured. Police must frequently care for those who cannot care for themselves: the destitute, the inebriated, the addicted . . . and the very young. They are often charged with taking lost property into their possession; they not infrequently see to the removal of abandoned property. . . . Community caretaking, then, is an essential part of the functioning of local police.[59]

Not all aspects of the community-caretaking function will establish a governmental interest that justifies the use of coercive force, but some aspects of community caretaking implicate the government's interest in maintaining order. The preservation of public safety is one such example; although variations in state law and among the federal courts has shaped the community caretaking doctrine in different ways, all jurisdictions recognize that there is a governmental interest in protecting an individual from physical harm. The Fourth Amendment incorporates this concept by authorizing officers to use coercive authority to prevent imminent, serious physical harm by, for example, forcing entry into a private home or detaining one or more individuals.[60]

The governmental interest in order maintenance can justify the use of force even when the *Graham* factors do not appear or apply only weakly. Consider the facts of *Ames v. King County*: paramedics were attempting to render aid to an unconscious man who appeared to be overdosing as a result of a suicide attempt, but were being hindered by the man's mother. The *Graham* factors would not clearly justify a use of force. The crime, if there was one, was not very severe; Washington Criminal Code § 9.08.040 does criminalize resisting medics attempting to discharge their legal duties, but the statute makes such resistance a gross misdemeanor. There was no threat to the safety of officers, and the subject was not attempting to evade arrest through active resistance or flight. Despite the limited applicability of the *Graham* factors, there was an imminent threat to the governmental interest in order maintenance: the mother was preventing the medics from providing potentially life-saving aid. The United States Court of Appeals for the Ninth Circuit correctly held that the officer on scene was justified in using force to subdue the mother so that medical workers could treat her son.[61] In short, the need for officers to perform or facilitate a community-caretaking function established the existence of a governmental interest that served as a sufficient predicate for the use of force.

This does not mean that *any* use of force is permissible in community-caretaking situations—that question is best treated as an issue of proportionality, which we address later in this chapter. Our point here is more limited: a valid governmental interest can justify the use of force under the constitutional standard even when the *Graham* factors offer little guidance.

INVOLUNTARY COMMITMENT

While many different situations fall within the ambit of community caretaking, it is worth addressing one that officers encounter with some regularity: the involuntary evaluation or treatment for psychiatric/psychological issues or substance abuse. Officers frequently encounter individuals in situations in which there is a substantial threat of self-harm, either through an active suicide attempt or through the physical neglect that can accompany substance abuse, or a substantial threat of harm to others for similar reasons. In such cases, it is not at all unusual for the individual to refuse psychological, psychiatric, or medical evaluation and treatment. Depending on state law, officers may have the authority to initiate some form of involuntary evaluation process on their own, to seek judicial approval, or to enforce an involuntary commitment order initiated by a third party, such as a medical professional. "The government has an important interest in providing assistance to a person in need of psychiatric care," as the Ninth Circuit has written. Once the procedural requirements are satisfied such that officers have authority under state law to take someone into custody, the presence of that legitimate state interest can justify the use of force.[62]

The first step in analyzing any use of force is identifying whether there was a governmental interest at stake. This question may be framed as follows: did the governmental interests at stake justify *some* use of force? The answer to that question depends on whether a legitimate governmental interest would have suffered had officers *not* used force. The *Graham* factors and additional considerations discussed in the preceding pages can help answer that question. If the answer to that question is no—either because there is no legitimate governmental interest or because there is no threat to the government's interest that could be resolved with force—then, for constitutional purposes, the use of force was unjustified. If the answer to that preliminary question is yes, the analysis must continue by reviewing whether the actual force used was appropriate. We take up that question in the next section.

PROPORTIONALITY

Once a legitimate state interest has been identified, the next step of the inquiry is to determine whether the type and amount of force used was proportional to the apparent threat to the governmental interest. That is, after concluding that the subject's actions presented a threat to a governmental interest that justified *some* use of force, reviewers must determine whether the threat to the governmental interest justified the force that officers *actually* used. As the Supreme Court stated in *Graham v. Connor*, "Determining whether the force used to effect a particular seizure is 'reasonable' under the Fourth Amendment requires a careful balancing of the nature and quality of the intrusion on the individual's Fourth Amendment interests against the countervailing governmental interests at stake."[63]

This is the heart of analyzing any use-of-force incident: were the officer's actions appropriate to the situation? This analysis must be conducted while keeping the responsibilities of the officer in mind; officers are charged with enforcing governmental interests, as identified above, but they are also called upon to protect civilians from unnecessary indignity and harm.

It is also important to emphasize at the outset that uses of force are not single-event incidents. In every interaction that involves a use of force, officers will

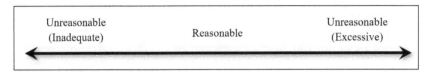

Figure 1.1. Simplified Spectrum of Reasonableness

make a number of choices and take a number of actions, including potentially using force multiple times. Each decision point and each use of force must be analyzed to determine whether it was reasonable in light of the information available to the officer at the time, including the decision points that preceded the initiation of violence by either the officer or the subject.

When determining whether an officer's use of force was proportional to the perceived threat, it is essential to keep in mind that the concept of reasonableness exists on a spectrum. Theoretically, at least, one end of that spectrum reflects uses of force that are unreasonable because they are inadequate to protect the governmental interest at stake: for example, an officer who verbally threatens to pepper spray someone who is actively shooting at the time, but takes no other action. That is highly unlikely to violate the constitutional standard—the Fourth Amendment protects individuals from having force used against them; it does not guarantee that a certain amount of force *will* be used—but the unreasonableness of the response is certainly relevant to fully evaluating a use-of-force incident.

More pragmatically, the other end of the spectrum reflects uses of force that are unreasonable because they are excessive: for example, an officer who shoots a passive protestor who refuses to stand up when ordered. Between those two extremes are uses of force that, in light of all the facts and circumstances, are proportional to the threat. This simplified spectrum is depicted in Figure 1.1.

The proportionality of a use of force presents a Goldilocks problem: reviewers must determine whether, in any given incident, officers used too little force, too much force, or just the right amount of force. Unfortunately, that analysis is easier to describe in the abstract than to apply to real-world incidents. Even when investigators have a firm factual understanding of an incident, it may be difficult to identify where a particular action falls on the spectrum. Not all incidents are difficult to assess, of course. Some incidents involve force that is clearly inadequate, clearly reasonable, or clearly excessive. But many other incidents will fall close to the line between inadequate and reasonable or reasonable and excessive, and those lines are impossible to draw in advance with complete clarity. Instead, they exist as grey areas, zones of

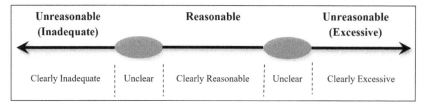

Figure 1.2. Analytical Spectrum of Reasonableness

uncertainty that require thorough investigation to resolve, to the extent that they can be clearly resolved at all. This analytical spectrum of reasonableness is depicted in Figure 1.2.

Exactly where a particular use of force falls will, of course, depend on the facts of the specific case. Reviewers are cautioned to avoid putting any weight on their initial impressions of an incident; preliminary information is almost always incomplete and is often simply wrong. Reliable determinations require thorough investigation and competent analysis.

Reviewers are also cautioned to avoid adopting an artificially narrow definition of reasonableness. For the constitutional analysis of any given use-of-force incident, the question is not whether the officer's choices and actions were the *only* reasonable options. Although there may be exceptions in unusual circumstances, there are typically some number of reasonable tactics and force options in any given situation. The question for reviewers is whether the officer's actual use of force is included in the array of options that fall within the "reasonable" portion of the spectrum.

In similar situations, then, it may be reasonable for different officers to use different force options. Officers should use only the amount of force necessary to address a threat to a governmental interest; however, so long as the force option they choose falls within the zone of reasonableness, they are not constitutionally required to use the least amount of force possible. Situation permitting, of course, officers should consider the available options, if any, and reviewers should take into account the clear availability of less intrusive alternatives that seem reasonably likely to address the threat when determining whether an officer's choice fell within the zone of reasonableness.[64]

In this section, we provide a detailed overview of the *Graham* factors and additional considerations that can affect the determination of whether a use of force was proportional to the apparent threat to the governmental interest.

The Proportionality of Deadly Force

The clearest application of proportionality comes from the 1985 Supreme Court case *Tennessee v. Garner*.[65] In that case, the Court articulated the circumstances under which officers could constitutionally use deadly force, concluding that the Fourth Amendment permits it when officers have "probable cause to believe that the suspect poses a significant threat of death or serious physical injury to the officer or others."[66] The Court explained that merely having sufficient legal justification to believe that an individual committed a crime, even a felony, did not automatically justify the use of lethal force to prevent the subject's escape:

> [N]otwithstanding probable cause to seize a suspect, an officer may not always do so by killing him. The intrusiveness of a seizure by means of deadly force is unmatched. The suspect's fundamental interest in his own life need not be elaborated upon. The use of deadly force also frustrates the interest of the individual, and of society, in judicial determination of guilt and punishment. Against these interests are ranged governmental interests in effective law enforcement. . . .
>
> Without in any way disparaging the importance of these goals, we are not convinced that the use of deadly force is a sufficiently productive means of accomplishing them to justify the killing of nonviolent suspects. The use of deadly force is a self-defeating way of apprehending a suspect and so setting the criminal justice mechanism in motion. If successful, it guarantees that that mechanism will not be set in motion. And while the meaningful threat of deadly force might be thought to lead to the arrest of more live suspects by discouraging escape attempts, the presently available evidence does not support this thesis. . . .
>
> Where the officer has probable cause to believe that the suspect poses a threat of serious physical harm, either to the officer or to others, it is not constitutionally unreasonable to prevent escape by using deadly force. Thus, if the suspect threatens the officer with a weapon or there is probable cause to believe that he has committed a crime involving the infliction or threatened infliction of serious physical harm, deadly force may be used if necessary to prevent escape, and if, where feasible, some warning has been given.[67]

In the aftermath of *Garner*, the rule governing deadly force appeared fairly straightforward: deadly force was a proportional response to a significant threat of death or great bodily harm, and was a disproportionate response to any lesser threat.

That straightforward reading was complicated in 2007, when the Court decided *Scott v. Harris*.[68] In that case, the Court reimagined the *Garner* holding, writing, "*Garner* did not establish a magical on/off switch that triggers rigid preconditions whenever an officer's actions constitute 'deadly force.' *Garner* was simply an application of the Fourth Amendment's 'reasonableness' test, to the use of a particular type of force in a particular situation." Instead of setting out the circumstances in which deadly force is constitutionally permissible, which is how *Garner* had been interpreted up until 2007, the *Harris* Court understood *Garner* to be an example of *Graham's* reasonableness test. This represented a rather tortured rewriting of *Garner*—the *Harris* Court was interpreting the *Garner* opinion, written in 1985, to apply a standard that would not be articulated until *Graham* was decided in 1989—but holes in the space-time continuum aside, *Harris* suggests that, for purposes of proportionality, there is no meaningful difference between deadly force and less-lethal force: "all that matters is whether [the officer's] actions were reasonable."[69]

This suggestion is called into question, at least to some degree, by the fact that *Scott v. Harris* itself appears to have followed the *Garner* rule. In *Harris*, an officer used his vehicle to ram a fleeing motorist, causing the fleeing vehicle to go into an uncontrolled spin and crash. The Court described the events leading up to the ram as "a dangerous high-speed car chase that threaten[ed] the lives of innocent bystanders." Indeed, the Court held that the fleeing motorist "posed a substantial and immediate risk of serious physical injury to others."[70] A simple application of the *Garner* rule to the facts as the Court understood them leads inevitably to the conclusion that the use of deadly force in that case was proportional.

After *Harris*, it is clear that deadly force is proportional when officers are confronted with a significant threat of death or serious bodily injury. What is unclear, at least at this point, is whether deadly force may be constitutionally proportional in *other* circumstances as well. Although *Garner* and *Harris* both represent useful touchstones in evaluating the constitutionality of deadly force, evaluators are cautioned that proportionality assessment in any context requires an extensive review of the pertinent facts and circumstances, including the factors laid out in *Graham*.

Graham *Factors*

In the following pages, we discuss how each of the *Graham* factors relate to the determination of whether an officer's use of force was proportionate to the apparent threat to a governmental interest.

THE SEVERITY OF THE CRIME

The severity of the crime is relevant to proportionality analysis in two distinct ways: as an indication of the strength of the government's interest in apprehension and, separately, as a measure of the potential for a physical threat, implicating the government's interest in safety. We address each in turn.

First, it is often taken for granted that the severity of the crime is a measure of the government's interest in facilitating the criminal justice process through apprehension. The assumption is that the government has less of an interest in seizing individuals who are suspected of low-level crimes than it does in seizing individuals who are suspected of more serious crimes. That assumption is logically translated into the use-of-force analysis, as reflected by the following syllogism: if the proportionality of a use of force depends on the strength of the governmental interest, and if the government has less of an interest in seizing individuals suspected of committing minor crimes, then officers are only justified in using lesser levels of force against such individuals. That conclusion grows out of the entirely intuitive perception of the relative strength of the government's interest in minor and serious crimes. As a strictly legal matter, the logic is flawed. However, it is quite relevant as a matter of policy.

Legal analysis commonly correlates the severity of the crime to the strength of the government's interest in criminal enforcement. In the context of searches, for example, the Fourth Amendment generally permits officers to force warrantless entries into private residences when there is an exigent need to preserve evidence of a crime, but the Supreme Court has held that officers may *not* do so when the crime is a minor offense.[71] The same thing is true when officers are in hot pursuit; officers can enter a private home when they are chasing a suspect who is thought to have committed a serious crime, but they cannot do so when the suspect has committed only a minor crime.[72] In both cases, the underlying logic is that the governmental interest in enforcing minor crimes is not strong enough to justify the intrusion, even though the interest in enforcing a more serious crime would be. Some courts have applied the same approach in the use-of-force context.[73]

We believe this association is misguided in the use-of-force context. In fact, the relative severity of the crime is of minimal use as a legal measure of the government's interest in apprehension. That assertion seems counterintuitive, as the government routinely dedicates more resources to investigating and apprehending an individual who commits a serious crime than it does for an individual who commits a minor crime. A police agency may be willing to extradite an armed robber from across the country, for example, and at the same time be unwilling to extradite a shoplifter from a neighboring county. Similarly, multiple police agencies may invest resources in a joint task force dedicated to apprehending wanted criminal suspects, but that task force may be directed to prioritize serious offenders and effectively ignore individuals who have warrants for minor crimes. Those are real world examples, but it is worth considering that agencies *could* extradite everyone or direct a fugitive-apprehension task force to go after suspects alphabetically, regardless of the severity of the underlying crime. Agencies have the *legal* authority to do so, but they do not always exercise their full authority for pragmatic reasons: often because they lack sufficient resources or are unwilling to spend political or social capital in particular ways. Further, it is worth remembering that, in the aggregate, agencies often dedicate substantial resources to the investigation and apprehension of individuals who commit what are, at best, minor crimes. As those examples demonstrate, the strength of the government's interest as a policy matter is quite distinct from the strength of the government's legal interests.

As in the context of extradition, the severity of the crime is legally irrelevant when it comes to using force to advance the government's interest in apprehension in order to facilitate the criminal justice process. That irrelevance can be demonstrated with a simple hypothetical. Consider two criminal suspects who are identical in all respects: age, physical condition, and so on. Assume that the suspects are being arrested by identical officers in identical environments—the middle of otherwise empty parking lots—and that both suspects resist officers in exactly the same way: by attempting to pull away and run. Officers, in turn, use exactly the same type and amount of force to subdue both suspects. The only difference is that the suspects are being arrested for two different crimes: one of the suspects committed the pettiest of petty thefts by shoplifting a single piece of gum from a convenience store, while the other committed a number of serious but nonviolent felonies by defrauding hundreds of elderly victims out of millions of dollars. Clearly, there is a substantial disparity in the severity of the crimes at issue.

In our view, that disparity will not affect the use-of-force analyses; if the officer who arrested the misdemeanant acted unreasonably, the same will be said for the officer who arrested the felon. Conversely, if the officer who arrested the felon acted reasonably, the same will be said for the officer who arrested the misdemeanant. The only explanation for that result, which we believe is an accurate prediction, is that the government's legal interest in apprehension is the same—or, rather, is not meaningfully different—in both cases.

An astute reader might ask at this point whether the officers in this example could perceive more of a threat from the subject who committed the more serious crimes because the severity of the punishment they are facing may motivate them to take more drastic action to avoid capture. This may be the case, but it only serves to prove our point: the government's interest in *apprehension* is the same, even if the government plausibly has asymmetric concerns about safety.

Although the severity of the crime is of little practical use in analyzing the government's legal interest in apprehension, it may still be relevant from a *policy* perspective. We address this point in chapter 3.

Second, separate and apart from the role it plays in establishing the government's interest in apprehension, the severity of the crime remains an important consideration in identifying the strength of the government's interest in safety—the safety both of community members and of the officer as a government agent. The interest in safety is a sliding scale, reflecting the different physical threats that the government seeks to protect against. In this context, the seriousness of the underlying crime the individual is suspected of committing serves as a proxy for how much of a threat to safety the individual is: the more serious the crime, the more dangerous the subject may be presumed to be. A violent crime may indicate that a subject has both the capacity and the willingness to engage in future violence. Separately, an individual who is suspected of committing a serious crime (even a nonviolent crime) may be more likely to violently resist officers in an effort to avoid a lengthy prison sentence than is an individual who is suspected of committing a minor crime and who therefore faces correspondingly minor punishment. The severity of the crime, then, can be a proxy for the danger that an individual may present to officer or others.

Importantly, assessments of individual dangerousness based on the severity of the crime are only valid in the absence of other, more reliable information. When, for example, an officer lacks reliable information about whether a subject is armed or dangerous, it is entirely logical to conclude that a robbery suspect is more likely to be armed and dangerous than a shoplifter. As the officer gathers additional information, however, the severity of the crime becomes less useful as an indicator of dangerousness. If an officer is approaching a naked robbery suspect whose hands are observably empty, for example, the severity of the crime is no longer an accurate proxy for any estimate about the safety risk that the subject presents. Instead, the severity of the crime as the basis of a threat assessment is supplanted by the officer's observations.

In sum, the severity of the crime is not a relevant consideration as to the strength of the government's interest in detaining or apprehending suspected criminals. The severity of the crime can be an important gauge for assessing an individual's dangerousness, but only insofar as other, more reliable information is not available.

IMMEDIATE THREATS, ACTIVE RESISTANCE, AND ATTEMPTS TO EVADE ARREST BY FLIGHT

Assessing whether a use of force was reasonable requires asking whether the "the nature and quality" of the use of force is proportional in light of the threat the individual presented to a governmental interest. This requires comparing the officer's actions to the suspect's actions. The second and third *Graham* factors—the immediate threat to officers or others and the suspect's active resistance or attempts to evade arrest by flight—are both concerned with the nature of the suspect's actions, which we address in this subsection. We discuss the officer's actions below.

When officers assert their authority by instructing a civilian to do something—to back up, stop, provide identification, exit a vehicle, or to put their hands behind their back, for example—the officer must assess the actions of the individual on the receiving end of that command. If the individual resists, the officer must assess both the nature of the threat and the severity of that threat.

THE NATURE OF THE THREAT

The most common method for determining the nature of the threat is by looking at the type of behavior that the subject is engaged in, but reviewers are cautioned against mechanically applying this approach. The question in any given case is not whether the officer's use of force was proportional to the suspect's physical actions *qua* behavior. Instead, the focus should be on whether the officer's use of force was proportional to the threat that the suspect's actions presented to the governmental interests identified in the first part of the analysis: facilitating the criminal justice process, maintaining public order, and preserving officer and civilian safety. The subject's behavior is pertinent, of course, but must be considered in light of the greater context of the interaction; focusing exclusively on the nature of the subject's behavior can lead to nonsensical results.

To see why, consider "active resistance." Mentioned specifically in *Graham*, active resistance is a widely used phrase within policing[74] that typically refers to nonaggressive physical actions taken by an individual to delay, defeat, or evade an officer's attempts to take them into custody, physical movements or actions (as distinct from inactions) that are unlikely to harm the officer or others.[75] An arrestee who pulls away from officers and begins to flee has taken two separate actions that both constitute active resistance (pulling away and running).

Unfortunately, however, that taxonomic approach does not provide a reliable foundation for constitutional analysis; focusing on the nature of the subject's behavior conflates a suspect's physical movements with a particular threat to a governmental interest. Rigidly applying this approach, for example, would suggest that active resistance threatens the government's interest in facilitating the criminal justice process, but not the government's interest in officer or public safety. Neither of those things is necessarily true. A hyper-obese octogenarian holding an oxygen tank may pull away from officers and begin to flee, and while their actions certainly constitute active resistance, the subject may well offer no actual threat to the government's interest in apprehension. Similarly, while a subject who pulls away from an officer and begins to flee after shoplifting a pack of gum threatens only the governmental interest in apprehension, a confirmed serial killer who engaged in the same behavior *also* presents a threat to public safety.

In short, the nature of the threat to a governmental interest cannot be reliably assessed by looking exclusively at the resistive behavior in which the subject is engaged. Additional context is necessary.

SEVERITY OF THE THREAT

Determining that the suspect's behavior poses a threat to a governmental interest is only part of the analysis. Reviewers must then determine the severity of the threat that the suspect's actions present. That is, having determined the nature of the threat, reviewers must determine the likelihood that the threatened harm was imminent. Note that this requires reviewers to engage in both a factual and counterfactual assessment of the timeline. Factually, reviewers must determine what happened and when it happened; doing so is necessary to assess the existence and severity of a particular threat at the time force was used. Counterfactually, reviewers must make at least some effort to assess what would likely have happened had the officer *not* used force at that moment.

As with the nature of the threat, a superficial assessment based exclusively on the subject's behavior is insufficient. Consider, for example, a subject who is kicking and punching an officer; clearly, that subject is engaged in assaultive resistance. A mechanical review of the subject's behavior would lead a reviewer to conclude that officers are justified in using force to protect themselves from assaultive resistance. If, however, the subject is an unarmed and physically diminutive ten-year-old, for example, the threat to officer safety is minimal; the use of severe force is inappropriate in that case even if it might be appropriate against a physically larger subject who was doing the same thing. Similarly, pulling away from officers or fleeing on foot is commonly classified as active resistance, presenting a potential threat to the government's interest in apprehension, but the same actions present very different levels of threat when the subject is a morbidly obese octogenarian (assuming such an individual presents *any* threat, as discussed above) as opposed to a young, athletically built subject wearing a t-shirt indicating that they are a member of the local college's cross-country running team.

As those examples suggest, it is not the suspect's behavior itself that drives proportionality analysis, it is the extent to which the suspect's behavior threatens a governmental interest. Reviewers can assess the severity of a threat by considering subject characteristics, officer characteristics, encounter characteristics, and environmental factors. The lists below are intended to provide useful, but not exhaustive guidance as to relevant factors.

SUBJECT CHARACTERISTICS

The subject's size;

The subject's apparent age and physical condition (level of fitness, strength, speed, exhaustion, etc.);

The subject's apparent psychological condition, including mental-health conditions and the influence of alcohol or drugs;

The subject's apparent knowledge of or training in martial arts;

The subject's conduct, including verbal statements and specific movements (body language) and their level of compliance or noncompliance at that point in the interaction;

The weapons held by or immediately accessible to the subject;

The subject's apparent interest or intent in using or immediately obtaining weapons;

Officer's prior contacts with or knowledge of the subject, including awareness of any prior history of weapon possession, violent resistance, or flight.

OFFICER CHARACTERISTICS

The number of officers on scene able to physically interact with the subject and their positioning;

The officer's physical size;

The officer's physical condition (level of fitness, strength, speed, exhaustion, etc.);
The officer's training in combative or defensive tactics;
The weapons held by or immediately accessible to the officer;
The weapons or physical techniques available to the officer at the time.

ENCOUNTER CHARACTERISTICS

The nature of the interaction, including the severity of the suspected offense, if any;
The physical proximity of the subject to officers and bystanders;
The degree to which the subject's movement has been limited even when the subject has not been restrained (e.g., whether the subject is seated, surrounded by officers, etc.);
The extent to which the subject has been effectively restrained and the extent of their ability to resist or flee despite being restrained;

ENVIRONMENTAL FACTORS

The nature of the immediate area, including the presence and reaction of bystanders, if any;
Environmental factors that could affect officer or subject sensory perceptions, including lighting, background noise, and so on;
Weapons potentially available to the subject and officers, including weapons of opportunity (e.g., a shovel laying on the ground) and weapons worn by the officers themselves;
The availability of obstacles that affect the suspect's or officer's ability to move freely or close the distance;
The availability of cover and concealment;
Any environmental options that would enable or restrict the subject's resistance or the officer's use of force.

ADDITIONAL FACTORS

The ultimate question in proportionality review is whether the force an officer actually used was appropriate under the circumstances. That requires reviewers to compare the nature and severity of the officers' actions against the presence, nature, and severity of an imminent threat to a governmental interest. A superficial description of an officer's use of force is an insufficient basis for this analysis; reviewers must be attuned to whether and how an officer's tactical decisions played a role in affecting the use of force, the mechanism by which a use of force is intended to address the threat to a governmental interest, the likely harm of the officer's use of force, and the availability of alternatives. We provide a brief overview of these topics here. We discuss tactics more fully in chapter 5 and explore the tools, techniques, and weaponry which with officers use force in chapter 6.

There are some situations in which a subject presents an imminent threat to a governmental interest only because of the decisions made and actions taken by the police officer. Imagine, for example, a paraplegic subject in a nonfunctional electric wheelchair who is aggressively brandishing a knife. It seems clear that if an officer walked up to within arms' reach of the subject, the subject's actions would present an imminent threat to the officer's safety and potentially to other governmental interests. It seems equally clear, however, that if the officer maintained a safe distance—perhaps taking cover behind their patrol car—the subject either would not present an imminent threat to a governmental interest or would not present a very significant threat.

Regrettably, the Supreme Court has never definitively explained whether an officer's decisions and actions *prior* to a use of force—sometimes referred to as "pre-seizure conduct" in the constitutional context—are relevant factors to consider when evaluating the reasonableness of the use of force. There is tension about this within *Graham* itself. On the one hand, the Court wrote that uses of force are to be reviewed under the "totality of the circumstances," which can certainly be read broadly enough to include pre-seizure conduct. On the other hand, the Court wrote that the constitutional standard of objective reasonableness "must embody allowance for the fact that police officers are often forced to make split-second judgments . . . in circumstances that are tense, uncertain, and rapidly evolving," which can be read to suggest what is referred to as "final frame" analysis: focusing exclusively on the moment at which force is used.[76]

The United States Courts of Appeals are split on this question. The First, Third, Sixth Circuit, and Tenth Circuits have held that pre-seizure conduct, including an officer's tactical decisions, is relevant to the determination of whether the ultimate use of force is objectively reasonable.[77] The Ninth Circuit had previously held that pre-seizure conduct is relevant if it involves an intentional and reckless provocation that amounts to an independent constitutional violation,[78] but that approach was overturned by the Supreme Court in 2017.[79] The Fourth and Seventh Circuits have held that pre-seizure conduct is irrelevant to the constitutional standard.[80] The United States Court of Appeals for the Eighth Circuit has provided inconsistent guidance, writing:

> Unreasonable police behavior before a [seizure] does not necessarily make the shooting unconstitutional; we focus on the seizure itself . . . and not on the

events leading up to it. But this does not mean we should refuse to let juries draw reasonable inferences from evidence about events surrounding and leading up to the seizure.[81]

We believe it is not only appropriate, but essential for courts to look beyond the "final frame" to determine whether a use of force was objectively reasonable. As we discussed earlier in this chapter, an officer's use of force inherently infringes on highly valued personal and governmental interests; it is therefore constitutionally justified only to the extent that those interests are outweighed by the state's interest in law enforcement, maintaining public order, and officer safety. It is conceptually and, we believe, constitutionally unsound for reviewers to overlook or ignore the extent to which officers contribute to the creation of a threat to one of those state interests.

We do not mean to suggest that an officer's use of force will always, or even generally, be unreasonable just because the officer put herself in harm's way; in a great many situations, officers are expected to do exactly that. However, when an officer fails to use reasonable tactics given the situation or otherwise contributes to the creation of a threat to a governmental interest in a way that violates professional norms—what some policing scholars have referred to as "officer-created jeopardy"[82]—the officer's role in unreasonably bringing about the threatening situation should generally be understood to render unreasonable an otherwise reasonable use of force.

When it comes to the actual application of force, there are effectively two mechanisms by which officers attempt to overcome resistance: pain compliance and mechanical disruption. Pain compliance refers to the intentional infliction of pain as a way of discouraging the subject from continuing to resist or, phrased differently, as a way of encouraging the subject to comply with an officer's commands. The paradigmatic example of pain compliance is a pressure point control hold, in which officers push on a sensitive spot on the body to inflict pain. Mechanical disruption, in contrast, works by physically overwhelming the subject's musculoskeletal system. There is perhaps no better example of mechanical disruption than when multiple officers "dog pile" on top of a subject, using their weight to prevent the subject from rising; although the subject may experience discomfort, it is the combined weight of the officers, not the discomfort they're inflicting, that prevents the subject from getting up. Unlike pain compliance, mechanical disruption does not depend on the subject's perception of pain to be effective. The application of pain compliance techniques and mechanical disruption techniques are not mutually exclusive; the two can be used congruently. For example, officers might use their body weight to hold a subject to the ground (mechanical disruption) while also striking a subject in the large muscles of the upper back (pain compliance). Indeed, the same technique or weapon can involve elements of both pain compliance and mechanical disruption, although it is almost always fair to describe any given technique or weapon as *primarily* dependent on pain compliance or mechanical disruption to induce compliances or otherwise overcome a subject's resistance.

The force option that officers apply should be assessed in terms of its potential harms, the harms that are reasonably foreseeable at the time force is applied. We discuss the gradations of harm more fully in chapter 6.

Conclusion

In this chapter, we reviewed the constitutional standard that applies in both civil and criminal cases brought in federal court. That standard, laid out most explicitly in *Graham v. Connor*, requires an officer's use of force to be "objectively reasonable." Determining whether a use of force is objectively reasonable requires "a careful balancing of the nature and quality of the intrusion on the individual's . . . interests against the countervailing governmental interests at stake." And that balancing, in turn, requires "careful attention to the facts and circumstances of each particular case," with special attention given to what have become known as the *Graham* factors: "the severity of the crime at issue, whether the subject poses an immediate threat to the safety of the officers or others, and whether he is actively resisting arrest or attempting to evade arrest by flight."

This chapter provided a detailed roadmap for constitutional analysis, demonstrating how the *Graham* factors and other considerations can be viewed through the appropriate lens to determine the existence of a governmental interest that justifies the use of force, the existence of any threat to that interest, and whether the force used was proportional to the severity of the threat.

As a threshold point, reviewers must carefully determine what the operative facts are by considering what the "reasonable officer on the scene" would have perceived and the conclusions they would have drawn.

With that perspective in mind, the first step in analyzing any use of force is identifying whether there was a governmental interest at stake. This question may be framed as follows: Without considering the force officers actually used in the incident under review, did the governmental interests at stake justify *some* use of force? The answer to that question depends on whether a legitimate governmental interest would have suffered had officers *not* used force. The *Graham* factors and additional considerations discussed in the preceding pages can help guide the analyst to an answer. If the answer to that question is no—either because there is no legitimate governmental interest or because there is no threat to the government's interest that could be resolved with force—then the analysis should be terminated: the use of force was unjustified. If the answer to that preliminary question is yes, the analysis must continue by reviewing whether the actual force used was appropriate.

2

The State Law Standard

Of the roughly 18,000 government entities in the United States that employ sworn officers, less than one hundred are federal agencies. The vast majority—over 15,000—are city police departments and county sheriffs' offices. The remainder are a mix of state police agencies and special jurisdiction agencies that provide either general policing services to specific geographic entities (e.g., hospital, university, or transit police) or state-wide policing services related to a specific activity or narrow set of activities (e.g., fish and wildlife, alcohol control, or gaming police). Of the roughly 900,000 sworn officers in the United States, more than 750,000 work for state and local police agencies.[1]

As those numbers demonstrate, the overwhelming majority of police agencies and the vast majority of officers derive their authority from state law. State law sets the criteria for who can be an officer, establishing, *inter alia*, age restrictions, minimum education prerequisites, citizenship requirements, criminal history limitations, and physical and mental health standards. State law creates a regulatory framework through which minimum training standards are set, professional licenses are issued, and, at least in forty-four states, police certifications can be revoked. State law determines how police agencies are funded, how they are permitted to procure equipment and services, and how they are to keep and disclose various records. State law also authorizes officers to use force and insulates them from civil or criminal liability for doing so.

In short, state law is an important and relevant standard under which the use of force can be analyzed. We provide in this chapter an overview of when state law applies, what it applies to, and how it applies. The Appendix of State Laws, set out at the end of this book, provides the relevant statutory provisions and, when statutes are lacking, judicial opinions regarding the regulation of police uses of force in all fifty states.

When Does the State Law Standard Apply?

A plaintiff sues an officer, seeking monetary damages for a use of force that they allege was an intentional battery. The plaintiff dies of their injuries, and their estate files a wrongful death lawsuit. A local prosecutor brings the case

58

to a grand jury to determine whether the officer committed a crime. The state Police Officer Standards and Training Commission opens an investigation to determine whether the officer's actions merit decertification. In each case, the officer's actions will be analyzed under state law.

Criminal Law

Officers, like anyone else, can be prosecuted for committing a crime if they engage in behavior that state law identifies as criminal. In most contexts, criminal cases start with a civilian complaint about, or an officer's firsthand observations of, suspected unlawful conduct. Police personnel will typically investigate and, if they develop probable cause to believe that a crime has occurred, make an arrest. After arrest, criminal cases are generally referred to the local prosecutor's office. A prosecutor reviews the existing information, sometimes works with officers to conduct additional investigation, and ultimately determines whether to pursue charges.

When the subject of the investigation is a police officer, however, different procedures might apply. In some jurisdictions, the agency that employs the officer will conduct the criminal investigation; in others, the agency may voluntarily request or be required to accept an external investigation. The local prosecutors' offices may be significantly more involved in the investigation than they are in most criminal cases. The prosecutor may decide to handle the case in-house, or the close working relationship between the local prosecutor and the police agency may lead the prosecutor to refer the case to the state attorney general or to a "special prosecutor" or an "independent prosecutor" to avoid the appearance of a conflict of interest. Concerns about potential conflicts and the potential appearance of conflicts has led some states to strip local prosecutors of their discretion to handle certain police use-of-force cases. In 2015, for example, New York Governor Andrew Cuomo issued Executive Order No. 147, appointing the state attorney general as the special prosecutor tasked with handling cases involving the use of lethal force by police officers "where, in [the attorney general's opinion], there is a significant question as to whether the civilian was armed and dangerous at the time of his or her death."[2]

The prosecutor can, depending on state law, either charge someone with a crime by filing an "information" or a "complaint" with the court (a process sometimes called "direct filing" or "charging by information") or by presenting the case to a grand jury. By rule or practice, some prosecutors' offices make it a habit to present all police shootings or serious uses of force to a grand jury, although that practice has been criticized because of the secretive nature of the grand jury process and the potential for grand juries to be used to insulate the prosecutor from political backlash. When the prosecutor direct-files a case or when the grand jury believes that there is at least probable cause to believe that an individual committed a crime and returns an indictment (technically a "true bill of indictment"), the officer formally becomes a criminal defendant and the prosecution can proceed.

After charging or indictment, the prosecutor typically engages in plea negotiations with the defendant or the defendant's attorney. The vast majority of criminal cases—at least 90 percent—are disposed of via plea deals;[3] the defendant either pleads guilty or *nolo contendere*,[4] often in exchange for less severe charges or a reduced sentence. If a case does not result in a plea deal, the case goes to trial. Criminal cases are typically tried before a jury (the "petit jury," as distinct from the "grand jury"), although a defendant can typically waive their right to a jury trial and have the case heard by a judge (a "bench trial"). State criminal law cases can only be heard by state courts, just as federal criminal law cases can only be heard by federal courts.

Although it is not uncommon for officers to be prosecuted for a variety of criminal acts—public corruption, sexual assault, and the like—they are only rarely prosecuted for duty-related uses of force. Bowling Green University criminologist Phil Stinson has collected extensive data on officers arrested, which reflects the fact that 7,518 state and local officers were arrested a total of 9,088 times between 2005 and 2013.[5] Of those, just shy of 1,600 arrests were for violent crimes:

1,364 officers were arrested for an assaultive crime
807 officers were arrested for aggravated or simple assault
557 officers were arrested for intimidation
234 officers were arrested for a homicide offense
152 officers were arrested for murder or nonnegligent manslaughter
82 officers were arrested for negligent manslaughter

The vast majority of those officers were arrested for violent acts that they took in their individual capacity rather than their official capacity, even defining "official capacity" broadly.[6] Officers are only very rarely arrested and prosecuted for duty-related uses of force. In Arizona between 2011 and 2018, for example, local prosecutors reviewed 523 officer-involved shootings, with another seventy-one shootings pending review, and prosecuted only one officer.

There are at least two interrelated reasons for the low rate of prosecutions. First, it is likely that most uses of force simply do not meet the criteria for a criminal act. Several studies have found that the single strongest predictor that an officer will use force is resistance, especially forceful resistance, by the subject.[7] As we will explain in detail below, state law typically authorizes officers to use force when and to the extent it reasonably appears necessary to overcome resistance, so the use of force under such circumstances is not necessarily criminal.

Second, even when a use of force may be a criminal act, proving beyond a reasonable doubt that the officer's actions exceeded the scope of what state law authorized—a question to which we return later in this chapter—can be a Herculean task. In part, that is because the use of force is unlike other acts for which an officer may be arrested. When an officer takes a bribe, for example, they are clearly acting outside the scope of their duties (except in truly exceptional circumstances). The same thing is true when an officer lies under oath or keeps seized money or drugs for themselves instead of properly impounding them. Such actions are *inherently* criminal; if a prosecutor can establish that the officer engaged in the underlying act, conviction should follow as a matter of course. Violence, in contrast, is a legitimate tool that officers can and do use in the course of their work. In light of the potential difficulty of distinguishing lawful from unlawful actions, prosecutors' ethical obligations to refrain from bringing charges unless the evidence both establishes probable cause[8] and is capable of proving guilt beyond a reasonable doubt[9] may dramatically restrict the likelihood of a prosecution in borderline cases.

The interplay between these two reasons means that criminal charges for duty-related violence remains the rare exception, even for the most committed prosecutors' offices. Additional reasons—including, for example, the manner in which police uses of force are typically investigated; prosecutors' conscious or unconscious reluctance to charge officers at a police agency that the prosecutor relies on and works closely with; the political fallout that can accompany the prosecution of a police officer; prosecutors' lack of familiarity with the subject matter (police tactics and techniques); and the longstanding observation that juries are reluctant to convict officers even in fairly egregious cases—also play a significant role in limiting the number of officers prosecuted for duty-related uses of force.

In short, the state criminal law standard applies to internal or external use-of-force investigations, to a prosecutor's decision to file charges or present the case to a grand jury, to a grand jury's decision to indict, to plea negotiations, and to the ultimate conclusion drawn by a judge or jury.

Civil (Tort) Law

Imagine a car crash. Vehicle 1 crashes into Vehicle 2, which was sitting stationary at a red light. The driver of Vehicle 2 sues the driver of Vehicle 1, demanding compensation for their personal injuries and damaged property. That lawsuit is civil, not criminal; it is brought by a private plaintiff, not by a prosecutor, and the goal is to compensate the victim for the harms they've suffered, not to criminally convict the at-fault driver. The driver of Vehicle 2 can file a civil lawsuit regardless of whether the driver of Vehicle 1 is criminally prosecuted. That civil lawsuit does not allege any breach of contract or, indeed, any pre-existing relationship between the drivers of Vehicle 1 and Vehicle 2. Instead, the underlying claim in the lawsuit is that the driver of Vehicle 1 has committed a "tort" (alternatively, a "tortious act"). According to Black's Law Dictionary, "tort" is used "to denote a wrong or wrongful act, for which an action will lie [that is, for which someone may sue], as distinguished from a contract."

State tort suits against police officers are civil allegations of wrongdoing, typically filed for the purpose of obtaining money damages as compensatory relief. Confusingly, issues of state tort law can come up in both state and federal courts. A litigant can file a lawsuit in federal court that alleges that a local police officer violated both state and federal law. If a litigant files a lawsuit in state court that lays out a claim under federal law—such as a violation of 42 U.S.C § 1983, discussed in chapter 1—the defendant officer can "remove" the case to federal court, bringing any state law claims along with it.[10] When a litigant sues a federal agent in state court alleging violations of state law, the federal agent can similarly remove the case to federal court.[11] Under either of the last two scenarios, the federal court will preside over both the federal and state law claims. Regardless of whether the case is heard before a federal or state judge, though, the court will rely on state law, including existing state precedent, to analyze the state law claims.

Regulatory Law

Like doctors, lawyers, and cosmetologists, police officers are, in most states, required to earn and maintain a state-issued certification (some states use the term "license"). According to Roger Goldman, the country's leading expert on police certification regimes, most states require most officers to be certified. State certifications are typically issued by a Police Officer Standards and Training Commission (a "POST Commission") or a Criminal Justice Standards and Training Commission (a "CJSTC"), although a few states, including Massachusetts and New York, do not have such commissions. With the exception of California and Rhode Island, all of the states that have a POST Commission—as well as New York, which does not—can revoke an officer's state certification for an officer's on-duty behavior, although when they can do so depends on the idiosyncrasies of state law.

As of 2018, every state now also sets minimum training standards for officers. Typically, state statutes do not set out specific requirements, instead delegating that responsibility to the POST Commission or CJSTC. Some states, however, have adopted specific training requirements as a matter of statute. In 2018, voters in Washington state approved Initiative 940, which amended state law by requiring "violence de-escalation training"[12] and "mental health training,"[13] both of which must be provided in an officer's first fifteen months of employment and periodically over the course of their careers. The exact content of that training was left to the state POST Commission, which, by statute, must "consult with law enforcement agencies and community stakeholders" and consider a range of what the legislature determined were relevant factors, including "[d]e-escalation in patrol tactics and interpersonal communication training, including tactical methods that use time, distance, cover, and concealment, to avoid escalating situations that lead to violence" and "[a]lternatives to the use of physical or deadly force so that deadly force is used only when unavoidable and as a last resort."[14]

Directly or indirectly, state law regulates police training—potentially including training on tactics and the use of force—as well as certification and decertification. Clearly, then, the state law standard that can be used to evaluate an officer's use of force can have regulatory ramifications.

What Does the State Law Standard Regulate?

While it is fairly clear that the Fourth Amendment regulates the use of force when that force amounts to a seizure, the state law standard is more complicated. Indeed, it would be more accurate to discuss the variety of state law *standards* because, unlike the solitary concept of "seizure," there is no one definition or single answer to the question of what state law regulates. State law may be best understood as regulating the infliction of various harms caused by the commission of different types of wrongdoing, potentially including the use of force. Understanding the scope of how state law regulates the use of force requires understanding how state law regulates criminal and tortious acts.

Criminal Law

What we commonly refer to as a "crime" is, in somewhat technical terms, the commission of a certain action or actions that, when performed under certain circumstances or when they result in certain consequences, have been identified as criminal. Criminal statutes identify the behaviors, circumstances, and consequences that are the "elements" of a crime: a crime is committed when all of the elements are satisfied.

Consider, for example, South Carolina Code § 16-4-600(E)(1), which states, in part, "A person commits the offense of assault and battery in the third degree if the person unlawfully injures another person. . . ." Parsing that clause into its constituent parts, we see that assault and battery in the third degree consists of three elements: it is a crime for someone to (1) unlawfully (2) injure (3) another person. If any of those three elements are lacking, then the crime of assault and battery has not been committed. If, for example, an individual unlawfully injures a toaster, they have not committed the crime of assault and battery because the third element—"another person"—is not satisfied (although they may have committed a crime other than assault and battery).

As that brief summary of statutory elements suggests, state criminal law regulates a range of behaviors, prescribing punishment for a variety of social harms. Providing a complete list of relevant behaviors is outside the scope of this book, especially given the potential for the criminal law to vary significantly from state to state. Nevertheless, we can offer some general guidance as to the behaviors that are both common in use-of-force situations and are commonly regulated by state criminal law.

Assault: threatening or attempting to physically touch someone else against their will;

Aggravated assault: making threats of physical harm with a weapon or in circumstances that suggest particularly severe harm;

Battery: touching or striking someone else against their will, offensive touching, or causing actual bodily injury;

Aggravated battery: causing serious injury or causing injury to particularly vulnerable victims such as children or the elderly;

Murder: the intentional killing of a human being in cold blood (often referred to as an "intentional" killing or a killing "with premeditation" or "with malice aforethought") or the unintentional killing of a human committed with callous disregard of the risk to human life (often referred to as "depraved heart murder");

Manslaughter: the intentional killing of a human being in hot blood (often referred to as a killing after "adequate provocation") or the unintentional killing of a human being resulting from recklessness or criminal negligence;

Kidnapping: restricting another person's movement or forcing them to move from one location to another against their will;

Attempt: intending and actually trying, unsuccessfully, to commit some underlying crime. For example, planning and attempting to kill another person would not constitute the crime of murder because it did not result in a death, but it could constitute the crime of *attempted* murder; and

Conspiracy: entering into an agreement to commit some underlying crime. For example, planning with another person to kill someone could constitute the crime of conspiracy to commit murder.

State criminal law could potentially apply to a range of actions that officers might take in a use-of-force situation: it is not at all uncommon, for example, for an officer to threaten to use force (assault), to tackle, handcuff, and search the subject (batteries), and to secure them in a police vehicle and transport them to a booking facility (kidnapping). Obviously, we use this example to demonstrate that state criminal law is *potentially* implicated when an officer uses force, not to suggest that an officer's actions, taken in the normal course of their duties, will amount to crimes. In this section, we are concerned only with identifying the type of actions regulated by state criminal law. Later in this chapter, we provide a more in-depth discussion of how to determine whether state criminal law applies in any given case.

Civil (Tort) Law

Like criminal law, there is no one action or set of actions that are regulated by state tort law. Instead, state tort law applies most clearly when there is cognizable harm to a person (emotional harms, personal injury, or death) or property. State tort law may be best understood by dividing it into *intentional* torts and *negligent* torts, both of which are potentially implicated by the use of force by police.

Intentional torts are harms resulting from actions that are purposefully performed. Here are some of the most common intentional torts in the police use-of-force context.

Trespass to chattels, which typically refers to damage done to personal property;

Battery, which typically refers to physically touching another person without their consent;

Assault, which typically refers to threatening to commit or attempting to commit a tortious battery;

False Imprisonment, which typically refers to restraining another person against their will; and

Intentional Infliction of Emotional Distress, which typically refers to intentionally engaging in conduct that reasonably results in outrage.

Some common negligent torts in the police use-of-force context include:

Negligence, which typically refers to the infliction of personal injury resulting from a failure to exercise reasonable care; and

Negligent Hiring, Training, or Retention, which typically refer to a police agency or political subdivision's failure to exercise reasonable care when hiring, training, or continuing to employ officers.

Some tort claims may involve claims of intentional or negligent conduct, depending on the specific facts. A wrongful death claim, for example, can be predicated on an allegation that an officer intentionally killed someone or that an officer's negligence resulted in someone's death.

Regulatory Law

As described above, almost all of the states require officers to earn and maintain professional certifications, and most states have the authority to revoke those certifications under certain circumstances. Sixteen states can revoke an officer's certification only after the officer is convicted of a crime, while other states can revoke an officer's certification if they find that the officer engaged in specified types of misconduct, independent of any other civil or criminal remedies.[15] Even in the states that either lack revocation authority or have only tightly limited revocation authority, state law allows for functional equivalents: in California and Massachusetts, an officer's certification is voided if they are convicted of a felony, while New Jersey has a robust "forfeiture of office" statute that strips public officials, including police officers, of their public office if they are convicted "of an offense involving dishonesty," of an offense of a certain level of severity, or "of an offense involving or touching [the official's] office, position or employment."[16]

In addition to police certification, state law can also regulate officer hiring. Connecticut law, for example, prohibits police agencies from hiring any individual who was previously employed as an officer and "(1) was dismissed for malfeasance or other serious misconduct calling into question such person's fitness to serve as a police officer; or (2) resigned or retired from such officer's position while under investigation for such malfeasance or other serious misconduct."[17] "Serious misconduct" is defined to mean "improper or illegal actions taken by a police officer in connection with such officer's official duties . . . including . . . repeated use of excessive force."[18]

How Does the State Law Standard Apply?

Imagine a random person—we'll call him John—who walks up to someone else in a shopping mall, tackles them, ties their hands together, carries them out to the parking lot, places them into a waiting vehicle, drives them across town, and locks them in a small room. In most contexts, John would be committing a series of serious crimes and opening himself to substantial civil liability. If John was actually *Officer* John, though, he may engage in functionally identical actions without running afoul of state law. Analysts must consider whether an officer's use of force is the type of action—or, more pertinently, caused the type of social harm—that state law regulates; that is, does state law apply to what the officer did? That is only the first half of the analysis, though. The second and equally important half of the analysis is determining whether state law authorized an officer to take the action or cause the harm under the circumstances. In other words, did the officer violate the applicable state law?

State statutes and common law doctrines can explicitly authorize police officers to engage in what would otherwise be criminal or tortious behavior.* They can also exempt police officers from otherwise applicable restrictions or provide officers with defenses to civil liability or criminal sanctions. For our purposes, there is no relevant distinction between authorizations, exceptions, and defenses; all three effectively allow officers to engage in what could otherwise be unlawful actions. Such authorizations, exceptions, and defenses can be police-specific—for example, authorizing officers, but not others, to act in particular ways—or more generally applicable, including officers within the scope of a broader legal rule.

In the remainder of this chapter, we first address the relationship between the constitutional standard and the state law standard. We then discuss police-specific state laws before broadening our perspective by briefly discussing more generally applicable state laws. Readers are advised that the

---

* To avoid overwhelming readers with endnotes, this section contains citations to state judicial opinions, but not to state statutory law except when a statute is directly quoted. The text of all relevant state statutes may be found in the Appendix of State Laws.

statutory analysis offered in the following pages is accurate as of the date of writing, but, as always, state law is subject to amendment.[19]

The Relationship Between the Constitutional Standard and the State Standard

The standard for analyzing the use of force under state law is distinct from the constitutional standard, although both are properly understood as *legal* standards. Without legal training or an unusually sophisticated understanding of the structures of American government, the distinction between state law and constitutional law can be difficult to grasp. Indeed, there is substantial confusion even among lawyers about the relationship between the constitutionality and the legality of a use of force. Strictly speaking, the constitutionality of an officer's use of force can be entirely distinct from the question of whether the officer violated state law. As Flanders and Welling put it, "The standards for criminal liability in a state criminal prosecution do not have to mimic the standards for a Constitutional tort."[20]

The relationship between constitutional law and state law is something like the relationship between the color of a car and the vehicle's speed. A car can be both red and fast, but a car can be red without being fast or be fast without being red. So it is with constitutional and state law: an officer's actions can be both unconstitutional and a violation of state law, but it is also true that an officer's actions can be unconstitutional without violating state law or be constitutional and still violate state law.

An officer's actions can be unconstitutional without violating state law because although the Constitution limits government authority, it does not require states to impose civil liability or criminal punishment on officials who exceed those limits. That is, states cannot authorize constitutional violations, but they are not required to civilly or criminally punish those violations, either.

An officer's actions can be constitutional and still run afoul of state law. The Fourth Amendment protects civilians' right to be free of unreasonable seizures, not officers' right to use force, which means that the states are free to pass laws that are more protective of individual rights than the Constitution itself by restricting the use of force. The California Supreme Court, for example, held that "state negligence law . . . is broader than federal Fourth Amendment law."[21] Thus, a use of force that may be objectively reasonable as a matter of constitutional law may still be negligent as a matter of state law.

Many states keep state law distinct from, and formally unaffected by, constitutional law. Indeed, many states do not even reference Fourth Amendment jurisprudence when applying or interpreting state law. Some states, however, have on at least one occasion implicitly or explicitly adopted part or all of the constitutional framework into state law. The following paragraphs identify, in both the less-lethal and lethal force contexts, cases in which state courts have incorporated or referenced constitutional law into the interpretation or application of state law. In our discussion, we are not concerned with cases involving the application of both constitutional law and state law, such as those in which the plaintiff brings both a § 1983 claim alleging a Fourth Amendment violation and, distinctly, a state tort claim. Further, we do not mean to suggest that a court that *has* incorporated constitutional law, at least in part and at some point, into state law will always do so. It is beyond the scope of this book to chart a definitive path of the evolution of state law in all fifty states. Here, we aim merely to provide examples of incorporation and reference. Finally, we note that this analysis is complicated by the fact that most states simply do not have very many, if any, judicial opinions interpreting state statutory or common law in the context of police uses of force. Indeed, in a handful of states, we were completely unable to find any judicial opinions applying or interpreting state law in the police use-of-force context.

In the context of less-lethal force, judicial decisions have incorporated at least some portion of the *Graham v. Connor* framework into state law in twenty-seven states: Alaska,[22] Arizona,[23] Arkansas,[24] California (in reference to an earlier version of state law),[25] Colorado,[26] Connecticut,[27] Delaware,[28] Florida,[29] Georgia,[30] Illinois,[31] Indiana,[32] Iowa,[33] Louisiana,[34] Maine,[35] Maryland,[36] Michigan,[37] Nebraska,[38] Nevada,[39] New Mexico,[40] Ohio,[41] Oklahoma,[42] Rhode Island,[43] South Carolina,[44] Vermont,[45] Virginia,[46] West Virginia,[47] and Wyoming.[48] Maryland offers perhaps the clearest example of this approach. In a state law tort case, the state Supreme Court described *Graham* as "the touchstone" for analyzing excessive force claims. It wrote that the principle of objective reasonableness, "announced in the context of a § 1983 claim for the violation of Federal Constitutional rights, is the appropriate one to apply as well to petitioner's claim under Article 26 of the Maryland Declaration of Rights and for the common law claims of battery and gross negligence."[49] Importantly, though, not every state that incorporates some aspect of constitutional law into state law goes so far as to incorporate every aspect of constitutional law into state law.

Four states—Idaho,[50] Kentucky,[51] Mississippi,[52] and New York[53]—have referenced *Graham v. Connor* without incorporating it, or at least without incorporating any aspect of its analytical framework into state law. Mississippi, for example, quotes *Graham* for the idea that "'[n]ot every push or shove, even if it may later seem unnecessary in the peace of a judge's chambers,' amounts to a constitutional deprivation,"[54] but it does not otherwise adopt Fourth Amendment jurisprudence as a matter of state law. New York provides less complimentary treatment, discussing and ultimately rejecting *Graham v. Connor* as an appropriate guideline for the state law framework.[55]

The remaining nineteen states—Alabama, Hawaii, Kansas, Massachusetts, Missouri, Montana, New Hampshire, New Jersey, North Carolina, North Dakota, Minnesota, Oregon, Pennsylvania, South Dakota, Tennessee, Texas, Utah, Washington, and Wisconsin—do not have any judicial opinions that reference or incorporate *Graham v. Connor* into the state law regulating the use of less-lethal force by police. Some of those states do have judicial opinions that separately address Fourth Amendment and state law claims, but they do not conflate the two standards or use the constitutional standard to interpret or apply state law.

A different picture emerges when it comes to the state law regulation of deadly force. Ten states have explicitly incorporated some aspect of *Tennessee v. Garner* or *Scott v. Harris* into state law: Colorado,[56] Georgia,[57] Iowa,[58] Michigan,[59] Nevada,[60] New Mexico,[61] New York,[62] Ohio,[63] Rhode Island,[64] and Wyoming.[65] The purpose for and extent to which states incorporate constitutional law varies. Michigan concluded that the Supreme Court had held unconstitutional the state's fleeing-felon rule,[66] for example, while Nevada followed a slightly different tack by adopting the Supreme Court's rejection of the fleeing-felon rule.[67]

Nine other states have referenced constitutional law in a case applying state law: Arizona,[68] California (in reference to an earlier version of state law),[69] Delaware,[70] Florida,[71] Kentucky,[72] Maryland,[73] Minnesota,[74] South Carolina,[75] and West Virginia.[76] A number of the states that have referenced Fourth Amendment jurisprudence have not done so in the context of evaluating a use of deadly force, though. Instead, their focus in on a distinct aspect of *Garner* or *Harris*. The Delaware Supreme Court, for example, discussed the *Garner* Court's conclusion that burglary was not a serious offense, ultimately disagreeing.[77] An Arizona appellate court relied on *Tennessee v. Garner* (in a footnote) for a different reason. The plaintiff in that case had argued that the officer could not invoke a state statute authorizing the use of force to effectuate an arrest because the officer was not "effectuating an arrest" at the time. Although concluding that the issue was not properly raised on appeal, the court noted that *Garner* had identified that the use of deadly force was a seizure, and therefore asserted that an officer who had used deadly force was necessarily seeking to effectuate an arrest.[78]

Thirty-two states, a significant majority, have simply not referenced constitutional law when interpreting or applying state law in the context of deadly force: Alabama, Alaska, Arkansas, Connecticut, Hawaii, Idaho, Illinois, Indiana, Kansas, Louisiana, Maine, Massachusetts, Minnesota, Mississippi, Missouri, Montana, Nebraska, New Hampshire, New Jersey, North Carolina, North Dakota, Oklahoma, Oregon, Pennsylvania, South Dakota, Tennessee, Texas, Utah, Vermont, Virginia, Washington, and Wisconsin.

Police-Specific Authorizations and Justification Defenses

Each state has its own statutes and common law doctrines that authorize officers to use force or protect officers from civil or criminal liability for doing so. Forty-two states regulate police uses of force by statute; thirty-six states have statutes that govern the use of both deadly and nondeadly force, while six states have statutes only for deadly force. The remaining eight states lack statutes to regulate police uses of force, doing so entirely through judicial decisions.

The forty-two states in which statutory law regulates at least some uses of force have a total of fifty-eight different statutes, with the earliest originally enacted in 1787 (Vermont), 1872 (California), 1858 (Tennessee), and 1863 (Georgia). Almost half of the statutes (twenty-eight, or 48 percent) were originally enacted in the 1970s; of the others, twenty (35 percent) were adopted prior to the 1970s and the remaining ten (17 percent) were enacted since 1970. The various states have taken very different approaches to amending these statutes. California's "justifiable homicide" law, for example, went unamended for almost 150 years—from the time it was enacted in 1872 until its amendment in 2019—while Georgia's law has been re-codified and amended some fifteen times since its original enactment in 1863. Of the fifty-eight total statutes, fifteen have never been amended, twenty-two have been amended only once, twelve have been amended two or three times, and nine have been amended more than three times.

In this subsection, we discuss several notable features of state law, focusing primarily but not exclusively on statutory law. We first explore the state statutes that set out the justifications for and limits of less-lethal force, then turn our attention to state statutes governing deadly force. In the Appendix of State Laws, we reproduce the text of state statutes and, when statutes are lacking, provide relevant quotations from judicial opinions regarding the regulation of police uses of force in all fifty states.

The Relevance of Assertive and Defensive Force: Applicability of Other State Laws

When applying state law to evaluate an officer's use of force, the characterization of that force as assertive or defensive is a relevant consideration. Assertive force refers to actions taken against a subject who is noncompliant or resisting, but whose resistance does not threaten the physical safety of the officer or others. Assertive force refers to situations in which an officer initiates violent action (typically as a response to a subject's failure to comply with orders or with nonviolent resistance). Defensive force, in contrast, refers to actions taken against a subject who has initiated violence by physically threatening the officer or others.

In the state law analysis, this distinction can be critical. Some states provide specific limits to the exemptions from civil or criminal liability that officers can otherwise claim, and those limits depend on whether the officers' use of force was assertive or defensive (although the state laws do not use that terminology explicitly). In Alabama, for example, the statute that regulates the use of both deadly and nondeadly force states explicitly: "Nothing in [the subdivisions regulating the use of assertive force] constitutes justification for reckless or criminally negligent conduct by a peace officer amounting to an offense against or with respect to persons being arrested or to innocent persons whom he is not seeking to arrest or retain in custody."[79] That statute does not allow officers to claim that their reckless or criminally negligent use of assertive force was justified, but appears to allow exactly such a claim in the context of defensive force.

Even without explicit limits like those set forth in Alabama law, the assertive/defensive typology can help analysts determine whether they need to review and apply *other* aspects of state law and, if so, which other aspects. When officers use assertive force to make an arrest, for example, analysts may have to establish that the arrest was, in fact, lawful. This threshold determination is often easily satisfied, as when officers make an arrest pursuant to a valid warrant, but reviewers cannot take for granted that such is the case, especially in the context of warrantless arrests. Some states authorize officers to make warrantless arrests for all felonies, but only for certain misdemeanors (e.g., misdemeanors that are committed in the officer's presence, amount to a breach of peace, or are specifically designated by statute[80]). Other states restrict the severity of force that officers can use to effect misdemeanor arrests. The Virginia Supreme Court, for example, has adopted a common-law restriction on the use of assertive force, holding almost one hundred years ago that "officers have no right to inflict serious bodily harm upon one who is simply fleeing arrest for a misdemeanor."[81] If an officer uses force assertively to effect an arrest, then analysts may have to review state law to determine that the arrest was lawful, which may require, *inter alia*, assessing whether the underlying offense was a misdemeanor or a felony.

Similar review may be necessary when officers use defensive force. In such cases, analysts must be prepared to determine whether the subject who threatened the officer (or others) was acting lawfully. This analysis requires a more robust review of state laws authorizing private persons to use force than this text can provide; it is sufficient for our purposes to note that some states authorize private persons to use force to resist unlawful arrests or to resist the use of excessive force in the course of a lawful arrest. An officer's use of force to protect themselves from a subject's violent actions may violate state law if the subject is lawfully resisting the officer's efforts. An officers' use of defensive force, in short, may require analysts to review the propriety of the subject's actions. That determination will often be straightforward, but reviewers must be attuned to such rarer circumstances that demand a more searching inquiry.

State Law Justifications for Less-Lethal Force

Thirty-seven states have a total of forty statutes that regulate, to at least some extent, the use of less-lethal force by police. Although these state statutes vary significantly in their particulars, many of them share certain common features. Indeed, many states share almost identical wording, at least in part.[82] Most obviously, the state statutes that authorize the use of force have commonalities in the purpose(s) for which force may be used (including to make an arrest, to prevent an arrestee from escaping, and to defend the officer or others) and in how much force may be used (from reasonably necessary force to force perceived as necessary). The following paragraphs discuss each of those dimensions in detail.

TO MAKE AN ARREST

All thirty-seven states with statutes governing the use of less-lethal force authorize officers to use force to make an arrest (five states explicitly include detentions). In this context, there are a variety of different requirements that apply in different states.

Reasonable Belief in the Lawfulness of Arrest. Ten states—Alaska, Arizona, California, Connecticut, Minnesota, Missouri, New York, North Carolina,

Texas, and Wisconsin[83]—allow officers to use force to effect an arrest that they reasonably believe is lawful. States provide differing degrees of guidance for determining when such a belief is reasonable. Most states do not provide extensive guidance. Alaska is instructive; the statute states that officers can only use force to make an arrest when they "reasonably believe[] the arrest . . . is lawful."[84] Connecticut, on the other hand, provides far more extensive guidance; the statute in that state authorizes the use of force to "[e]ffect an arrest . . . of a person whom [the officer] reasonably believes to have committed an offense, unless [the officer] knows that the arrest is unauthorized," and it defines the phrase "reasonable belief that a person has committed an offense" to mean "a reasonable belief in facts or circumstances which if true would in law constitute an offense."[85] The statute goes on to make clear that while a reasonable but mistaken belief of the facts can support the use of force to effect an arrest, a mistaken understanding of the law will not: "If the believed facts or circumstances would not in law constitute an offense, an erroneous though not unreasonable belief that the law is otherwise does not render justifiable the use of physical force to make an arrest."[86]

Subjective Belief in the Lawfulness of the Arrest. Nine states—Alabama, Arkansas, Colorado, Delaware, Kentucky, Maine, Nebraska, New Hampshire, and Oregon—permit the use of force to make an arrest when the arresting officer subjectively believes the arrest is lawful. Most of those states do so by authorizing the use of force "unless the officer knows that the arrest is unlawful." A few states make substantially the same point in another way. Delaware, for example, authorizes arrests pursuant to a warrant when "the warrant is valid or believed by the [officer] to be valid," and warrantless arrests when the officer "believes the arrest to be lawful."[87] Kentucky, in contrast, provides a justification defense for the use of force in the arrest context only when the officer "[b]elieves the arrest to be lawful."[88] (Although several states that use this formulation have a separate statutory provision defining "believes" to mean "reasonably believes," Kentucky does not have such a law.) Two states—Nebraska, and New Hampshire—provide a justification defense for uses of force when officers believe, even mistakenly, that they are making a lawful arrest, unless that belief is based on a mistake of law.

Actual Lawfulness. A few states have statutes authorizing the use of force to make lawful arrests without any indication that a reasonable or subjective belief in the lawfulness of the arrest is sufficient. Florida law states that officers "need not retreat or desist from efforts to make a lawful arrest."[89] Louisiana allows force for the purpose of making "a lawful arrest."[90]

South Dakota permits the use of force "in the performance of any legal duty."[91] While it is not clear that such statutes adopt an "actual lawfulness" standard, the statutes suggest as much. It is also worth noting that some states—including Massachusetts,[92] Michigan,[93] and Nevada[94]—that lack statutory law provide a common law authorization for or defense of the use of force to effect a lawful arrest.

Importantly, six states—Hawaii, Illinois, Indiana, Iowa, Kansas, and Pennsylvania—have adopted an "actual lawfulness" approach for warrantless arrests, meaning that officers are authorized to use force to a make a warrantless arrest only when the arrest is actually lawful. For arrests pursuant to a warrant in those states, however, the use of force is permissible unless the officer knows that the warrant is invalid (that is, the use of force is permissible so long as the officer subjectively believed that the warrant was valid). New Jersey takes a very similar approach, but requires that officers reasonably believe that the warrant was valid. More confusingly, Idaho authorizes the use of force for warrantless arrests when they are lawful (i.e., when there is "probable cause to believe that the person has committed an offense") and for any arrest "under the authority of a warrant."[95]

Further, it is worth pointing out that some states authorize private persons to use self-defense to protect themselves against *unlawful* arrests. In Georgia, for example, the state Supreme Court has held, "Where an arrest is not lawful, the person sought to be so arrested, contrary to his right if the arrest had been lawful, has the right to resist."[96] This approach does not definitively answer the question of whether state law authorizes officers to use force to make arrests only when those arrests are lawful, of course; it is possible for state law simultaneously to give the subject a right to resist an unlawful arrest and to insulate the officer from civil or criminal liability for using force to make that unlawful arrest. Nevertheless, it provides some evidence of the legal value that the state puts on the actual lawfulness of the arrest underlying a use of force.

Without Regard for the Lawfulness of Arrest. Four states—Montana, Tennessee, Utah, and Washington—have statutes that authorize officers to use force to effect an arrest without specifying whether the arrest must be lawful, or whether the officer must reasonably or subjectively belief that the arrest was lawful.

Identification or Information-Forcing Requirements. Six states—Arizona, Delaware, Hawaii, Kentucky, Nebraska, New Jersey authorize the use of force to make an arrest only if (1) an officer makes known the purpose or fact of arrest, (2) the purpose or fact of arrest is known or reasonably appears to be known by the subject, or (3) the purpose or fact of arrest cannot reasonably be made known under the circumstances. Texas has the same provisions, but also requires officers to identify themselves. Other states have adopted similar, though less nuanced, approaches. Minnesota law appears to permit the use of force only after "a peace officer has informed a defendant that the officer intends to arrest the defendant."[97] Tennessee authorizes force in the arrest context only after officers identify themselves.

Resistance to Arrest. Most statutes authorize the use of force to overcome a subject's resistance to an arrest without qualifying the nature of resistance. Some states, however, take what appears to be a more limited approach. Idaho, Minnesota, Washington, for example, authorize the use of force if the subject flees or forcibly resists; there is no explicit statutory authorization to use force to overcome passive resistance.

TO PREVENT AN ARRESTEE FROM ESCAPING

Twenty-four states explicitly authorize the use of force to prevent the escape of an arrestee or other person in custody. The majority of these states have a single statutory provision that authorizes the use of force to effect an arrest or to prevent an arrestee's escape: Alabama, Alaska, Arizona, Arkansas, California, Colorado, Connecticut, Idaho, Maine, Minnesota, Missouri, New Hampshire, New York, North Carolina, and Oregon. Most of the remainder have a separate subdivision that authorizes the use of force to prevent escape (or to recapture an escaped arrestee) to the same extent that force could have been used to effect the initial arrest: Delaware, Hawaii, Indiana, Kentucky, Montana, Nebraska, New Jersey, and Pennsylvania. Florida law authorizes the use of force when "retaking felons who have escaped,"[98] but has no provision specific to escaped misdemeanants.

Two more states appear to implicitly authorize the use of force for such purposes. North Dakota law sets out that the use of force is justified when "required or authorized by law,"[99] which conceivably extends to preventing escape. South Dakota, meanwhile, permits the use of force "in the performance of any legal duty."[100]

This is not to suggest that the other states would not allow officers to use force to prevent an arrestee from escaping. Retaining an arrestee in custody is as important to the governmental interest in criminal justice as taking the arrestee into custody is in the first place, so we do not read the lack of clear statutory authorization to preclude officers from using force to prevent escape.

TO DEFEND THE OFFICER OR OTHERS

Eighteen states authorize the use of force to protect the officer or another person. Fifteen of those states countenance the use of defensive force in the context of making an arrest or preventing escape: Alabama, Arkansas, Colorado, Connecticut, Florida, Illinois, Iowa, Kansas, Maine, New Hampshire, New York, North Carolina, Oregon, Pennsylvania, and Utah. Alabama's law is representative, authorizing an officer to use force "[t]o defend himself or a third person from what he reasonably believes to be the use or imminent use of physical force while making or attempting to make an arrest for a misdemeanor, violation or violation of a criminal ordinance."[101] Delaware takes a similar, but more limited, approach by authorizing the use of force when a would-be arrestee "has taken a hostage" and the officer "believes that the use of force is necessary to prevent physical harm to any person taken hostage" or has been ordered to use force "by an individual the [officer] believes possesses superior authority or knowledge."[102]

Four states use almost identical statutory wording to explicitly authorize the use of defensive force in other contexts, including to prevent the subject's suicide; to prevent the self-infliction of serious injury; or to prevent the commission of a crime involving actual or threatened physical injury, damage to or loss of property, or a breach of the peace: Delaware, Nebraska, New Jersey, and Pennsylvania.

The surprising lack of any police-specific authorization for officers to use force to defend themselves or others outside of the context of an arrest may be explained, at least in some states, by generally applicable legal principles that allow everyone, including officers, to use force for self-defense or the defense of others. Some states make this point explicitly; Indiana, for example, does not have a specific statutory authorization for officers to use force defensively. However, the state does have a statute that establishes that officers have "has the same right as a person who is not a law enforcement officer to assert self-defense under" the generally applicable self-defense statute.[103] We discuss potential conflicts between police-specific use-of-force statutes and generally applicable use-of-force statutes later in this chapter.

Beyond the circumstances that can justify the use of force, most state statutes also identify, at least at a certain degree of abstraction, the degree of force that officers can use when force is authorized: reasonably necessary force, reasonable force, and necessary force.

Reasonably necessary force. With regard to how much (less-lethal) force officers may use, the prevailing approach by far is the adoption of a "subjective objectivity"[104] standard, discussed at length in chapter 1, that authorizes force to the extent that it is reasonably necessary or that it is reasonably perceived by the officer as necessary. Twenty-seven states do so by statute: Alabama, Alaska, Arizona, Arkansas, Colorado, Connecticut, Delaware, Hawaii, Idaho, Illinois, Indiana, Iowa, Kansas, Kentucky, Missouri, Montana, Nebraska, New Hampshire, New Jersey, New York, North Carolina, Oregon, Pennsylvania, Rhode Island, Tennessee, Texas, and Utah. Eight of the states without statutes typically follow the same approach via judicial decision: Georgia,[105] Massachusetts,[106] Michigan,[107] Mississippi,[108] Nevada,[109] New Mexico,[110] Ohio,[111] and South Carolina.[112]

Rhode Island takes a prohibitionist approach by precluding "unnecessary or unreasonable force."[113] Most states, in contrast, affirmatively authorize the use of force when reasonably necessary or when perceived as such. Oregon's law is representative: "a peace officer is justified in using physical force upon another person only . . . to the extent that the peace officer reasonably believes it necessary."[114] Four states—Arizona, Missouri, New Jersey, and Texas—appear to take a restrictive approach, authorizing the use of force only when it reasonably appears to be "immediately necessary."

A few states have statutes that appear to adopt a purely subjective approach, but the standard is clarified either by another statutory provision or by case law. Pennsylvania's law authorizes force when an officer "believes [it] to be necessary,"[115] but an earlier statutory provision defines "believes" to mean "reasonably believes."[116] The same is true in Hawaii.[117] Delaware has a similar law, permitting the use of force when the officer "believes that such force is immediately necessary to effect the arrest,"[118] but a separate provision denies a justification defense to anyone who "is reckless or negligent in having such belief or in acquiring or failing to acquire any knowledge or belief which is material to the justifiability of the use of force."[119] Nebraska appears to adopt a purely subjective approach by statutorily authorizing force to the extent that the officer believes it to be necessary and *not* having any provision that defines "believes" to mean "reasonably believes," but that statute has nevertheless been interpreted to allow only reasonably necessary force.[120] Kentucky's statute has been interpreted in the same way.[121]

Florida authorizes force to the extent that the officer "reasonably believes [it] to be necessary to defend himself or herself or another from bodily harm while making the arrest," but does not use the same language in the other contexts in which force is authorized.[122]

Reasonable Force. Four states—California, Louisiana, Maine, and Wisconsin—have statutes that authorize force to the extent that it is reasonable. A few states do the same by common law, including Maryland,[123] Oklahoma,[124] Vermont,[125] Virginia,[126] and West Virginia.[127]

Necessary Force. Two states—South Dakota and Washington—have statutes that authorize the use of force to the extent it is necessary, but do not explicitly define how necessity is to be determined. Florida permits officers to use physical force "[w]hen necessarily committed in retaking felons who have escaped" and "in arresting felons fleeing from justice."[128]

OTHER LIMITS ON THE DEGREE OF FORCE

Minnesota authorizes reasonable force in one statute and necessary force in another, leaving the statutory standard somewhat unclear. North Dakota, meanwhile, is something of an outlier, having adopted a statutory tautology by authorizing force in circumstances and to the extent it is "required or authorized by law."[129]

No overview or summary can capture all of the nuances in the various statutes, of course, so it is worth noting that, beyond the justifications for and limits to the use of force, some statutes have idiosyncratic features. We discuss just a few here:

Georgia precludes police agencies from adopting "any rule, regulation, or policy which prohibits a peace officer from using that degree of force to apprehend a suspected felon which is allowed by the statutory and case law of this state."[130]

New Hampshire and Maine both reject the exclusion of evidence or the invalidation of an arrest as consequences for an unlawful use of force, stating in identically worded statutory provisions: "Use of force that is not justifiable under this section in effecting an arrest does not render illegal an arrest that is otherwise legal and the use of such unjustifiable force does not render inadmissible anything seized incident to a legal arrest."[131]

Regrettably, there is no reliable source of information about the frequency or severity of police uses of force in the various states. The lack of reliable data about officers' uses of force makes it impossible, at this point, to evaluate the relationship between statutory authorizations of force and how officers actually use force. We discuss this in more depth in the conclusion of the book.

State Law Justifications for Threats of Force

In most states, an individual commits the crime of assault by, *inter alia*, "intentionally placing another person in reasonable apprehension of imminent physical injury."[132] That means that it is not only the use of force that potentially runs afoul of state criminal or tort law; threats of force are also potentially subject to sanction. An officer's threat to use force, then, may need to be assessed even if the situation is resolved without the actual application of force.

Most states do not have any statutory provisions related specifically to threats of force, but a few do. In those statutes that do explicitly regulate threats of force by statute, threats of less-lethal force are regulated in the same way as the use of less-lethal force. In Arizona, for example, state law uses the same statutory language to authorize "threatening or using physical force against another."[133]

To the extent that state law regulates threats of lethal force, however, they are typically regulated rather differently. Our analysis has identified three distinct approaches. First, some statutes appear to regulate threats of deadly force implicitly. Statutes in Idaho, Minnesota, Washington, and Wisconsin authorize officers to use "all . . . means" to effect an arrest, a phrase that we read to include threats of lethal force.[134] Idaho's law, for example, authorizes "all reasonable and necessary means to effect the arrest" without distinguishing between the use of force and the threat of force.[135]

Second, statutes in Alaska, Arkansas, South Dakota, and Tennessee explicitly regulate threats to use deadly force, equating such threats with the use of less-lethal force and regulating them in exactly the same way. Arkansas is representative of this approach, stating: "A law enforcement officer is justified in using nondeadly physical force or threatening to use deadly physical force upon another person" when certain statutory conditions, discussed above, are met.[136]

Third, Arizona takes a unique approach, regulating threats of deadly force differently, at least to some extent, than either the use of less-lethal force or the use of lethal force. Under Arizona law, officers may threaten to use less-lethal force, but not deadly force, to apprehend a fleeing misdemeanant. At the same time, they may threaten to use deadly force in situations in which the actual use of deadly force would not be justified, such as to prevent the escape of a fleeing, nonviolent felon.

State Law Justifications for Deadly Force

Forty-two states have statutory law governing the use of deadly force, and the remainder set out the standard in judicial decisions. In this section, we adopt the prevailing definition of deadly force: deadly force is that which is likely to cause death or great bodily harm.[137]

Prior to 1985, twenty-three states retained some version of the common-law "fleeing felon" rule that authorized officers to use deadly force to prevent the escape of a fleeing felon.[138] That year, the Supreme Court decided *Tennessee v. Garner*, which held that the Fourth Amendment limited the use of deadly force to situations in which an officer had probable cause to believe that the subject presented a risk of death or great bodily harm to the officer or another person.[139] Over the next thirty years, other states followed suit, often limiting the common-law rule by statute or state-level judicial decision. In a 2016 article, Chad Flanders and Joseph Welling counted twelve states that retained the common-law rule, thirty-seven states that rejected it, and one state where the law governing the police use of deadly force remained unclear. As they put it, "There is only the one question: Are you sticking with the common law, or are you following *Garner*?"[140]

While we appreciate and respect Flanders and Welling's work, our review of the state statutes suggests the need for a more nuanced taxonomy. State statutory law is better divided into three nonexclusive categories, which we present from most permissive to most restrictive: the "fleeing felon" approach, "partially restrictive" approaches, and the *Garner* approach.[141] Additionally, some states adopt one of the preceding frameworks, but also apply some number of additional restrictions atop those frameworks that are more restrictive, in some ways, than the *Garner* approach. Importantly, a state may fall into more than one category, as their statutes authorize the use of deadly force in a variety of different circumstances. Beyond setting out the circumstances that justify the use of lethal force, state laws also vary when it comes to the quantum of proof that officers must have before using deadly force; most states, for example, authorize the use of deadly force when it is reasonably necessary for the identified purposes, while others require it to be necessary to overcome actual resistance.

THE "FLEEING FELON" APPROACH

These statutes maintain the common-law rule that allows officers to use lethal force to prevent the escape of a felon. Four states still codify this rule: Alabama, Florida, Mississippi, and South Dakota. Florida law provides a justification defense to criminal charges related to the use of deadly force to arrest a fleeing felon, but imposes additional restrictions on officers who seek to invoke a justification defense against civil claims; we discuss that dichotomy in our discussion of liability rules, later in this chapter. Oregon appears to adopt a version of the fleeing-felon rule, authorizing the use of deadly force against subjects who have committed or attempted to commit a felony when "the use of such force is necessary" under the totality of the circumstances, although the statute does not clearly set out the purpose for which the use of force must be "necessary."[142]

Separately, though relatedly, a number of states have, by statute or common law, explicitly precluded the use of deadly force for the purposes of arresting a misdemeanant. In 1936, for example, the West Virginia Supreme Court held that "[a]n officer may not wound or kill a fleeing misdemeanant."[143] The Georgia Supreme Court followed suit in 1943, adopting the fleeing-felon rule (which has since been abrogated in that state) in an opinion that made a point of saying, "But where the arrest is only for a misdemeanor, such extreme and deadly force merely to effect the arrest and prevent escape is not justified."[144] The Michigan Attorney General came to the same conclusion in 1976, writing, "A peace officer may not use deadly force when attempting to stop or arrest a person who has committed a misdemeanor."[145]

"PARTIALLY RESTRICTIVE" APPROACHES

The partially restrictive approach falls between the fleeing-felon rule and the *Garner* rule, requiring more than merely the suspected commission of a felony, but less than an imminent threat of death or great bodily harm. The states take a variety of different approaches in what exactly is required.

Violent Felonies/The Use or Threatened Use of Deadly Force. Most commonly, such statutes authorize the use of lethal force to effect the arrest of a subject who is believed to have committed a violent felony, a felony involving the use or threatened use of deadly force, or a felony involving physical injury, great bodily injury, or death. Under this type of statute, for example, officers could hypothetically use deadly force against a ninety-year-old suspect of an armed robbery committed seventy years prior. Twenty-four states have statutes that follow this approach: Alaska, Arizona, Arkansas, Colorado, Connecticut, Delaware, Georgia, Hawaii, Illinois, Kansas, Maine, Minnesota, Missouri, Nebraska, Nevada, New Hampshire, New York, North Dakota, Oklahoma, Oregon, Pennsylvania, Texas, Tennessee, and Utah. Indiana takes a slightly narrower approach, permitting the use of deadly force when an officer has probable cause that it is necessary to prevent the commission of a forcible felony, a term that is defined by statute as "a felony that involves the use or threat of force against a human being, or in which there is imminent danger of bodily injury to a human being."[146]

Certain Crimes. Three states—New Jersey, New York, and Oregon—allow deadly force to be used to effect an arrest or prevent escape, but specifically identify certain predicate crimes. New York and Oregon, in identical statutory provisions, identify "kidnapping, arson, escape in the first degree, burglary in the first degree or any attempt to commit such a crime."[147] New Jersey identifies substantially the same crimes (substituting "burglary of a dwelling" for "burglary in the first degree"), but adds homicide, robbery, and sexual assault crimes to the list.[148]

Future Threats. Nineteen states permit the use of deadly force against individuals who may present a threat of death or great bodily harm unless apprehended without delay: Alaska, Arizona, Colorado, Delaware, Hawaii, Illinois, Iowa, Kansas, Maine, Minnesota, Missouri, Nebraska, New Hampshire, Oklahoma, Pennsylvania, Tennessee, Texas, and Utah. We read this to imply a risk of future harm, rather than an imminent threat as that term is properly understood.*

Escaping, Armed Subjects. Six states authorize deadly force to address armed subjects who are attempting to escape, but there are different iterations of this approach. Pennsylvania allows officers to use deadly force to prevent the escape of a subject, without further clarification, who is armed with a deadly weapon. Arkansas does the same, but limits it to preventing the escape of a felony suspect who is armed or dangerous. Georgia, Maine, and New York do so when the escaping felony subject is armed with a dangerous or deadly weapon. Alaska takes a narrower approach, allowing deadly force when the subject has escaped or is attempting to escape while armed with a firearm.

Information Forcing. Rhode Island goes beyond the fleeing-felon rule in a very different way; that state authorizes the use of deadly force to make an arrest for a felony consistent with the fleeing-felon rule, but requires the officer to reasonably believe that "the person to be arrested is aware that a peace officer is attempting to arrest him or her."[149]

Convicted Felons. North Carolina permits the use of deadly force to prevent the escape of a convicted felon (but not, it appears, a suspected felon).

Combinations. Some states combine some of the partially restrictive approaches discussed above. Kentucky, for example, permits the use of deadly

---

* We discuss "imminent threat" at length in chapter 1.

force when making an arrest only "for a felony involving the use or threatened use of physical force likely to cause death or serious physical injury"
and the officer "believes that the person to be arrested is likely to endanger
human life unless apprehended without delay."[150] California's recently
amended law takes a similar approach, but also requires officers to attempt
to identify themselves and warn the fleeing subject that deadly force may
be used.

THE "*GARNER RULE*" APPROACH

As in *Garner*, these statutes permit officers to use deadly force when the
subject presents a threat of death or great bodily harm to the officer or others. Twenty-five states permit the use of deadly force under such conditions:
Alabama, Arizona, Arkansas, California, Colorado, Connecticut, Georgia,
Idaho, Illinois, Indiana, Kansas, Maine, Minnesota, Nevada, New Hampshire, New Jersey, New Mexico, New York, North Carolina, North Dakota,
Oklahoma, Oregon, Pennsylvania, Utah, and Washington.

California, like many of these states, limits the use of deadly force to "imminent threats," but is unique in that it provides a statutory definition of
that term:

> A threat of death or serious bodily injury is "imminent" when, based on
> the totality of the circumstances, a reasonable officer in the same situation
> would believe that a person has the present ability, opportunity, and appar-
> ent intent to immediately cause death or serious bodily injury to the peace
> officer or another person. An imminent harm is not merely a fear of future
> harm, no matter how great the fear and no matter how great the likelihood
> of the harm, but is one that, from appearances, must be instantly confronted
> and addressed.[151]

Seven states—Arizona, Illinois, Kansas, Missouri, New Hampshire, North
Carolina, and Oklahoma—specifically authorize the use of deadly force when
the subject is escaping or attempting to escape by using a deadly weapon or
dangerous instrument, a particular subset of cases in which the subject may
present an imminent threat of death or great bodily harm.

Additionally, eight states—Connecticut, Florida, Indiana, Nevada, New
Mexico, Tennessee, Utah, and Washington—require officers to give a warning, when feasible, before using deadly force. As the Court made the same
suggestion in *Garner*, we include this "requirement" as a component of the
Garner rule.

ADDITIONAL RESTRICTIONS

Some statutes adopt the basic framework from one of the "partially restrictive" approaches or from *Garner*, but add additional restrictions. There are a few different types of restrictions:

Risk to Innocent Persons. Four states—Delaware, Hawaii, Nebraska, and New Jersey—have statutes that permit the use of deadly force only when there is "no substantial risk of injury to innocent persons." Massachusetts does the same by judicial decision.[152] Pennsylvania takes a similar approach, but only with regard to deadly force used to prevent suicide or the commission of a crime.

Suicidal Subjects. Six states—Delaware, California, Nebraska, New Jersey, Pennsylvania, and Tennessee—prohibit officers from using deadly force against suicidal subjects who pose an imminent threat of death or great bodily harm only to themselves.

Actual Resistance. Three states—Idaho, Mississippi, and Washington—authorize the use of deadly force under certain circumstances only when that force was used to overcome "actual resistance."

Exhaustion Requirements. Three statutes, two in Tennessee and one in Delaware, have exhaustion requirements; in both states, deadly force is permitted only when "all other reasonable means of apprehension have been exhausted." Iowa allows the use of deadly force "only . . . when a person cannot be captured any other way."[153] New Hampshire allows for deadly force only when "there is apparently no other possible means of effecting the arrest."[154] California law includes a legislative declaration instructing officers to "use other available resources and techniques [instead of deadly force] if reasonable safe and feasible to an objectively reasonable officer."[155]

Information-Forcing Requirements. Three states—Maine, New Hampshire, and Tennessee—have notification or information-forcing requirements of various types. Tennessee requires that officers to inform the subject of their identity when it is feasible to do so. Maine and New Hampshire go further, requiring officers both to inform the subject of their identity and their intent to make an arrest, although both states waive that requirement when the officer has reason to believe that the subject is already aware of those facts.

Limitations on Predicate Crime. Colorado, which has essentially codified the *Garner* rule, does not permit officers to use lethal force when the only indication that the subject presents a threat of death or serious bodily harm is the subject's commission of "a motor vehicle violation."[156]

Two states, Montana and South Carolina, defy the above categorization, leaving the standard for deadly force unclear. In Montana, the statute permits "all reasonable and necessary force . . . in making an arrest," but does not specify any rules for deadly force.[157] In South Carolina, a confusing state supreme court case cited *Tennessee v. Garner* for the proposition that "an officer may use whatever force is necessary to effect the arrest of a felon including deadly force to effect that arrest," leaving the disconnect between the *Garner* rule and the fleeing-felon rule unresolved.[158]

We would be remiss if we did not mention a few notable idiosyncrasies. Some statutes that appear to authorize the use of force in situations that are even more permissive than the common law's fleeing-felon rule. Nine states— Arizona, Delaware, Idaho, Mississippi, Nebraska, Pennsylvania, South Dakota, Vermont, and Washington—authorize the use of deadly force to suppress a riot or mutiny that, at least in certain circumstances, may not present an immediate threat of death or great bodily harm. Here, too, there is some variation. Arizona and Washington permit the use of lethal force only if the subject or another person participating in the riot "is armed with deadly weapon,"[159] while Delaware and Nebraska both authorize the lethal force "after the rioters or mutineers have been ordered to disperse and warned, in any manner that the law may require, that such force will be used if they do not obey."[160] The remaining states authorize the use of lethal force to suppress a riot, but do not set out any other explicit requirements or limitations for that context.

Illinois and Colorado have adopted statutory restrictions on certain types of force: chokeholds. Illinois restricts chokeholds, which it defines "direct pressure to the throat, windpipe, or airway of another with the intent to reduce or prevent the intake of air" to circumstance where deadly force is justified.[161] Colorado, meanwhile, defines chokeholds as a restriction on breathing, and it limits them in the same way and using the same statutory language that it uses to restrict deadly force.

As with less-lethal force, most state statutes also identify the relevant quantum of proof that must exist before lethal force is permitted: when lethal force is reasonably necessary, when it is necessary, when the officer reasonably believes that certain conditions exist, and when the officer believes that certain conditions exist (apparently without regard for the reasonableness of that belief).

REASONABLY NECESSARY/REASONABLE BELIEF

Thirty-four states have statutes that adopt a "subjective objectivity"[162] approach by authorizing lethal force when it is reasonably necessary or reasonably perceived as necessary for at least some statutory purpose, or when the officer reasonably believes that certain statutory justifications are present (e.g., that the subject presents an imminent threat of death or great bodily harm): Alabama, Alaska, Arizona, Arkansas, California, Colorado, Connecticut, Delaware, Florida, Georgia, Hawaii, Idaho, Illinois, Indiana, Iowa, Kansas, Kentucky,[163] Maine, Missouri, Montana, Nebraska,[164] New Hampshire, New Jersey, New Mexico, New York, North Carolina, Oklahoma, Oregon, Pennsylvania, Rhode Island, Texas, Tennessee, Utah, and Washington. (As with less-lethal force, a few states have statutes that appear to adopt a purely subjective approach in the context of deadly force, but either another statutory provision or case law clarifies that the standard is actually reasonable belief. This is the case in Delaware, Hawaii, Kentucky,[165] Nebraska,[166] and Pennsylvania.)

Three states—Indiana, New Mexico, and Oklahoma—specify that the officer must have probable cause that lethal force is reasonably necessary.

Two states—Missouri and Texas—appear to take a restrictive approach, authorizing the use of deadly force only when it reasonably appears to be "immediately necessary."

Idaho law states that deadly force must be reasonably necessary to overcome "actual resistance."[167] Washington has adopted a similar approach, holding that deadly force is authorized only when the officer, in good faith (a test that has both objective and subjective elements), uses force to overcome "actual resistance."[168]

NECESSARY

Five states—Minnesota, Mississippi, Nevada, North Dakota, and South Dakota—have statutes that authorize deadly force when it is "necessary" or when it is "necessarily committed" for identified purposes. Nevada permits deadly force when necessary to prevent escape only if there is "probable cause to believe" that certain conditions exist.[169]

The relationship between the legal regulation of deadly force and the actual application of deadly force is more nuanced than it might first appear. We reviewed the US Census Bureau's state population data and the number of lethal police shootings in the four-year period from 2015 to 2018 as collected by the *Washington Post*. Readers should note that the available data suffers from serious limitations. First, it captures only actual deaths; it does not include any uses of force, including shootings, that do not result in death. Second, even with regard to actual deaths, the data is both under- and overinclusive. The *Washington Post* methodology includes "only those shootings in which a police officer, in the line of duty, shoots and kills a civilian" and specifically excludes "deaths of people in police custody, fatal shootings by off-duty officers or non-shooting deaths."[170] Thus, the data fails to include fatalities resulting from uses of force other than a shooting. Despite its many limitations, the information reflected in this chart is the best available data to date.

Figure 2.1 depicts the number of lethal police shootings in the relevant period per 100,000 residents of each state and the District of Columbia. The rates range from a high of 0.982 per 100,000 people in New Mexico to a low of 0.086 per 100,000 people in New York. The "National Rate" reflects that there were 0.304 lethal police shootings per 100,000 people in the population of the country as a whole, while the "Average State" rate shows that a hypothetical average state—with an average population and an average number of police shootings—would have had 0.307 lethal police shootings per 100,000 people.

State-level legal regulation is, of course, only one of many factors that likely affect the rate of officer-involved homicides. Those rates are almost certainly affected by the pre- and in-service training provided to officers, agency policies, the quality of supervision, the delay before medical first responders arrive, the proximity to trauma-care facilities, and a host of other factors. Consider, for example, that the average rate of lethal police shootings in the twelve states with a population of more than eight million—California, Florida, Georgia, Illinois, Michigan, New Jersey, New York, North Carolina, Ohio, Pennsylvania, Texas, and Virginia—was 0.255 per 100,000 people, significantly lower than the national rate of 0.304 per 100,000. In fact, only two of those states were above the national rate: Georgia, which was marginally above the national rate at 0.309 per 100,000 people, and California, which was substantially above the national rate at 0.384 per 100,000 people.

Indeed, the relative permissiveness or restrictiveness of a state's statutory and common law regulation of police uses of deadly force are not necessarily reflected clearly in the number of lethal shootings in the state. Florida, for example, provides broad statutory authorization for officers to use deadly force when it is reasonably necessary to prevent the escape of a fleeing felon. Tennessee, in contrast, has a restrictive statute that requires officers to have probable cause, does not allow officers to use deadly force unless all other reasonable means of apprehension have been exhausted or are infeasible, and requires officers to inform subjects of their identity when feasible. Yet the available data suggests that officers kill many more people per capita in Tennessee (0.355/100,000) than in Florida (0.292/100,000).

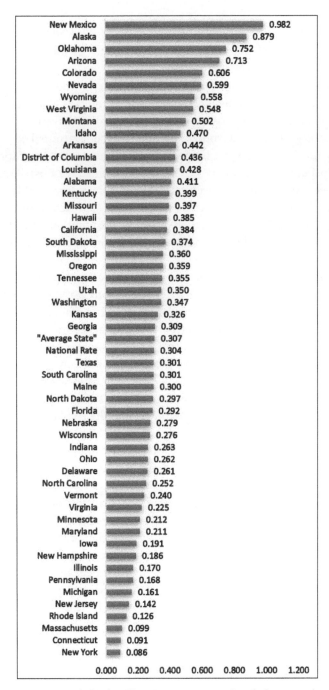

Figure 2.1. Lethal Police Shootings per 100,000 People (2015–2018)

State Law Limitations on Police-Specific Justification Defenses

Some of the same statutes that authorize police to use force also limit the liability defenses that officers can raise.

Three states deny a justification defense to officers who act culpably. Alabama does not allow a justification defense for officers who recklessly or criminally negligently use assertive force ("[t]o make an arrest . . . or to prevent . . . escape") against anyone, either "persons being arrested or . . . innocent persons."[171] Hawaii and Nebraska both authorize the use of force that officers believe to be necessary (for statutorily defined reasons), but officers whose belief was reckless or negligent remain liable for such recklessness or negligence. North Carolina takes an even broader approach, with the statute reading, "Nothing in this subdivision constitutes justification for wilful, malicious or criminally negligent conduct by any person which injures or endangers any person or property."[172]

Six states do not allow officers to invoke a justification defense against claims brought by innocent persons (that is, persons that the officer was not attempting to arrest or prevent from escaping). Minnesota takes the broadest approach, disallowing officers from claiming a statutory justification to use less-lethal or deadly force "in a civil action brought by an innocent third party."[173] Maine and New Hampshire follow suit, but only in the context of deadly force, rejecting the justification defense in cases where officers used deadly force against anyone whom the officer "is not seeking to arrest or retain in custody."[174] New York does not extend the justification defense to officers who recklessly use deadly force in a way "amounting to an offense against or with respect to innocent third persons whom [the officer] is not seeking to arrest or retain in custody." Oregon takes a very similar approach, disallowing any justification defense for the use of deadly force that amounts to "reckless or criminally negligent conduct . . . against or with respect to innocent persons whom the peace officer is not seeking to arrest or retain in custody."[175] Colorado precludes officers from claiming justification after recklessly or negligently using deadly force assertively ("to effect an arrest, or prevent . . . escape") in claims brought by innocent persons.[176]

Further, states do not necessarily adopt the same approach to justification defenses in the civil and criminal contexts. Florida Statute § 776.05(3), for example, states that officers making a lawful arrest are "justified in the use of any force . . . when necessarily committed in arresting felons fleeing from justice." As indicated above, this statute authorizes officers to use deadly force (and thus precludes them from being prosecuted for using deadly force) even in situations in which the use of deadly force would run afoul of the constitutional limitations set out in *Tennessee v. Garner*. This is not the end of the statutory story, though. The law continues:

> However, this subsection shall not constitute a defense in any *civil action for damages* brought for the wrongful use of deadly force *unless* the use of deadly force was necessary to prevent the arrest from being defeated by such flight and, when feasible, some warning had been given, and
> A. The officer reasonably believes that the fleeing felon poses a threat of death or serious physical harm to the officer or others; or
> B. The officer reasonably believes that the fleeing felon has committed a crime involving the infliction or threatened infliction of serious physical harm to another person.[177]

Thus, under Florida law, an officer may be civilly liable, but not criminally liable, for shooting a fleeing, nonviolent felon who is not believed to present any risk of death or serious physical harm to anyone.

The laws that specifically authorize officers' uses of force or limit officers' liability for using force can vary significantly from state to state, making universal declarations largely inaccurate. See the Appendix of State Laws for the text of state statutes and relevant quotations from state judicial opinions.

State Law "Mistake of Fact" Defenses

The preceding discussions focused on state laws that authorize—or, phrased differently, provide a justification defense for—the use of force by officers. Even when an officer's actions are not authorized, however, the officer may avoid criminal liability if state law provides a "mistake of fact" defense. Essentially, a defense of this type can partially or completely exculpate a criminal defendant who successfully argues that they acted the way they did based on a misunderstanding of the facts and, had the facts been what they thought, their actions would have been appropriate. Law professor Paul Robinson and attorney Tyler Williams have concluded that states take three different approaches to this type of defense.

The first category consists of states that follow a Model Penal Code approach to *mens rea*: the extent to which an officer's mistaken belief that force is justified will be exculpatory will depend on the culpability of the mistake. As Robinson and Williams write,

> If the officer has made an honest but a reckless mistake as to the necessity for the use of force, then he or she may have a defense to offenses requiring [in-

tent] or [knowledge], such as murder, but would have no defense to an offense that requires only recklessness, such as manslaughter. Similarly, if the officer is negligent in mistakenly believing that the use of force is necessary, then he or she can be held liable for an offense requiring negligence, such as negligent homicide, but would get a defense to offenses requiring recklessness, knowledge, or intention, such as manslaughter or murder.[178]

Robinson and Williams count five states that follow this approach: Delaware, Hawaii, Kentucky, Nebraska, and Pennsylvania.[179]

The second category provides a complete defense for officers who reasonably, if mistakenly, believe that their conduct is justified, but no defense for officers whose mistake was negligent, reckless, or otherwise unreasonable. They count twenty-nine states that take this approach to mistake: Alabama, Alaska, Arkansas, California, Colorado, Connecticut, District of Columbia, Florida, Georgia, Illinois, Indiana, Iowa, Kansas, Maine, Michigan, Missouri, New Hampshire, New Jersey, New York, North Carolina, Ohio, Oregon, South Carolina, Tennessee, Texas, Utah, Virginia, Wisconsin, and Wyoming.[180]

The third and final category consists of states that authorize the use of force only when it is necessary, but provide a mistake defense to officers who use force when they mistakenly believe that it was necessary. As Robinson and Williams put it, these states "provide a mistake as to justification defense or mitigation but do so in a separate mistake excuse provision apart from their objective justification defense."[181] They count seventeen states that take this approach: Arizona, Idaho, Louisiana, Maryland, Massachusetts, Minnesota, Mississippi, Montana, Nevada, New Mexico, North Dakota, Oklahoma, Rhode Island, South Dakota, Vermont, Washington, and West Virginia.[182]

General Exceptions and Defenses

In addition to laws that specifically authorize the police to use force or exempt officers from liability for using force, state laws also provide for more generic rules that regulate the use of force, such as the laws governing self-defense, defense of others, defense of habitation, and defense of property. The potential availability of these non-police-specific authorizations to use force raise the question of whether officers can claim *both* a police-specific authorization and a general authorization in any given situation. Indiana resolves this issue by stating explicitly that "a law enforcement officer who is a defendant in a criminal proceeding has the same right as a person who is not a law enforcement officer to assert self-defense,"[183] but other states are less clear on that point.

To see the potential relevance of these more generalized laws to police uses of force, consider two cases from Florida. While working in plain clothes and driving an unmarked car, former Palm Beach Gardens Officer Nouman Raja pulled over to investigate what he apparently thought was an abandoned vehicle. The owner, Corey Jones, a legal concealed-weapons permit holder, was in the vehicle at the time; it had broken down and he was waiting for assistance. Although Raja later said he identified himself as an officer, a recording of a phone call between Jones and a roadside assistance company suggests otherwise. As Raja approached Jones' vehicle, Jones exited and, perhaps thinking that Raja was a potential assailant, pointed a gun at him. Raja responded by fatally shooting Jones. The local prosecutor charged Raja with manslaughter by culpable negligence, among other crimes, stating that he "chose to approach Corey Jones' vehicle in a tactically unsound, unsafe, and grossly negligent manner." Because he approached the vehicle in that manner, the prosecutor believed, he was criminally liable for creating the situation and ultimately killing Jones.[184]

In a separate incident, former Broward County Sheriff's Deputy Peter Peraza responded to a call about a man who was walking through a neighborhood with a rifle. Peraza and other deputies found the subject, Jermaine McBean, who was carrying what looked like a rifle, but was in fact a pellet gun that he had just purchased from a nearby pawn shop. Peraza and several other deputies ordered him to put the weapon down, but he didn't do so. Peraza fatally shot McBean; he was the only officer to open fire, and he later claimed that McBean appeared to be raising the weapon threateningly. The investigation ultimately revealed that McBean probably did not hear the deputies' orders; he had earbuds in and may have been listening to music at the time. Peraza was charged with manslaughter.[185]

Both Raja and Peraza argued that they could not be prosecuted. Their arguments were not based on state law related to an officer's ability to use deadly force, but rather upon Florida's "Stand Your Ground" law. Passed in 2005, that law states that an individual who is in a place where they have a legal right to be does not have to retreat before using deadly force in self-defense; they can instead stand their ground. In essence, Raja and Peraza claimed that even if they were not authorized to use deadly force as officers, they *were* authorized to use deadly force in the same way any civilian would have been under the circumstances. In both cases, the prosecutors objected, arguing that laws that specifically regulate police uses of force take precedence over the more general law governing civilians' use of force. At least one state appellate court agreed with that position; former Haines City Officer Juan Caamano, who was prosecuted for attempted battery relating to an on-duty use-of-force incident, was not allowed to assert a "Stand Your Ground" defense for exactly the reasons argued by the prosecutors in the Raja and Peraza cases.

That position was ultimately rejected by the Florida Supreme Court, which held in late 2018 that "law enforcement officers are eligible to assert Stand Your Ground immunity."[186] That holding was predicated on the statutory language of the Stand Your Ground Act, which granted the defense to "any person." That expansive phrase was read to include officers, who are, after all, persons.

As the Raja, Peraza, and Caamano cases demonstrate, an officer's use of force may implicate state law beyond the police-specific laws discussed in the preceding section. While a complete review of such laws is beyond the scope of this text, we briefly describe the more relevant laws here:

Self-Defense. By statute or common law, every state in the country authorizes the use of physical force in self-defense, including the use of deadly force in certain circumstances. When the elements of a self-defense claim have been satisfied, the defense precludes criminal liability for violent actions. When some, but not all, of the elements of a self-defense claim have been satisfied, an "imperfect" self-defense claim may serve as a partial excuse that reduces, but does not completely eliminate, criminal liability (e.g., by reducing the relevant crime from murder to manslaughter). State laws vary in several ways, including whether they recognize imperfect self-defense claims and whether, when, and how an individual loses the right to use self-defense by becoming an "aggressor." State laws also vary with regard to whether individuals have a duty to retreat; no state imposes an unqualified duty to retreat in one's own home, and about half the states do not require retreat from a public place before using deadly force.

Defense of Others. State laws typically authorize one person to use force to protect another person when that other person had the right to use self-defense. States follow one of two different approaches: under the "reasonable perception" rule, Person A is authorized to use force to defend Person B if it reasonably appears to Person A that Person B had the right to use self-defense. Under the "alter ego" rule, Person A is authorized to use force to defend Person B only when Person B actually has the right to use self-defense, regardless of how the situation appears to Person A.

Defense of Habitation. State laws typically authorize individuals to use force to prevent someone from committing a felony inside their home or to prevent someone from entering their home for the purposes of committing a felony.

Defense of Property. State laws typically authorize individuals to use force to protect property—their own or others—from being stolen or damaged. Most states do not allow for the use of deadly force to protect property.

Arrest and Prevention of Escape. In addition to the laws that authorize police officers to use force for the purposes of making an arrest or preventing an escape, most states also permit private persons to use force for those purposes. Often, although not always, the state laws regulating what is often known as "citizen's arrests" are more restrictive than the laws that govern arrests by officers; some states do not allow civilians to make arrests for misdemeanors, for example, while others hold that civilians are liable for arresting persons who turn out to be innocent even in situations in which officers would *not* be liable because there was probable cause to believe the subject committed a crime. In some states, however, the state law may provide more leeway to civilians than to officers. As mentioned above, the South Carolina case law regarding officers' use of deadly force is unclear, but the state law governing civilians' ability to use deadly force is readily understandable. South Carolina Code § 17-30-20 states:

A citizen may arrest a person in the nighttime by efficient means as the darkness and the probability of escape render necessary, even if the life of the person should be taken, when the person:

(a) has committed a felony;
(b) has entered a dwelling house without express or implied permission
(c) has broken or is breaking into an outhouse with a view to plunder;
(d) has in his possession stolen property; or
(e) ... flees when he is hailed [under circumstances which raise just suspicion of his design to steal or to commit some felony].

Thus, a civilian may use deadly force even in situations in which an officer would almost certainly be prohibited from doing so—such as when a fleeing person is in possession of five dollars of stolen property, a misdemeanor under state law.

These state laws, and perhaps others, leave open an interesting and important issue: when an officer's use of force is *not* authorized by "police law," can the officer invoke more generally applicable law as a defense to civil or criminal liability? Unfortunately, we cannot provide any clear and universal answer; analysts and policy makers must be attuned to the issue and aware of the relevant law in their jurisdiction.

Conclusion

In this chapter, we reviewed the various state law standards that can apply in criminal, civil, and regulatory dimensions. Confusingly, there is no one "thing" that state law regulates in the use-of-force context; instead, state law regulates a range of behaviors that may or may not be implicated in any given use of force. For example, state criminal and civil tort law may both generally prohibit individuals from making threats, touching another person against their will, and inflicting physical injury. In many cases, however, officers are authorized by statutory and common law to engage in conduct that would, for anyone else, constitute a crime or tort. In other cases, officers may be protected by the laws that authorize any civilian to use force in the situation. Determining whether an officer's use of force was a criminal or tortious act, then, may require applying both police-specific laws and laws that are more generally applicable, including laws related to self-defense, defense of others, and defense of property.

Although a complete and nuanced discussion of the laws of all fifty states are beyond the scope of this text, this chapter offered an overview of how state law regulates police uses of force. An Appendix of State Laws, set forth at the end of this book, provides the text of police-specific state statutes and, when statutes are lacking, relevant quotations from state judicial opinions regarding the regulation of police uses of force.

3

The Administrative Standard

The use of force is regulated not just by the constitutional and state law standards, but also by police agencies themselves in the form of written policies and training. As of 2000, the most recent year for which data is available, the Bureau of Justice Statistics estimated that over 93 percent of police agencies had written rules related to the use of deadly force and 87 percent had written rules related to the use of less-lethal force.[1] These written rules—typically referred to as policies, directives, general orders, procedures, or formal guidelines—are collected into voluminous texts known variously as a "Book of General Orders" or a "Policy and Procedure Manual." Additional guidance comes in the form of training; of the roughly 650 police academies in the country, 98 percent provide firearms training and 99 percent provide training related to other uses of force.[2]

If one were to compare all of the administrative standards—both the written rules and the live training—at all of the approximately 18,000 different police agencies in the United States, one would find notable consistencies and broad, though not universal, agreement on certain shared principles.[3] When it comes to the details of how agencies draft their internal policies, however, there can be significant variation. A 2011 study of over 1,000 agencies across the country found that "it was difficult to identify a standard practice" in terms of how the administrative guidelines are articulated and presented to officers.[4]

It is far beyond the scope of this text—or any single text—to provide a detailed analysis of the various use-of-force policies in place at each of the 18,000 police agencies in the country. Indeed, such an effort would be almost immediately outdated, as agencies periodically review and revise their administrative standards. Instead, we offer in this chapter an overview of when the administrative standard applies, what it applies to, and how it applies, including a discussion of how it has evolved and of common, valuable features of agency policy.

When Does the Administrative Standard Apply?

The constitutional and state law standards discussed in the previous chapters may be applied by supervisors within a police agency, but they are more pertinent in the context of *external* review by lawyers and judges. The administrative standard, in contrast, may be addressed by external reviewers, but is more salient to *internal* review. When a supervisor in an officer's chain of command, an Internal Affairs investigator, or an instructor assigned to the Training Section reviews a use of force, they are tasked, in large part, with analyzing the officer's actions under the administrative standard. That is, they must determine whether the officer did what the *agency*—as opposed to any other sources of authority—has told the officer to do and, if so, whether the officer did so in the manner that the agency has told the officer to do it. In short, they are analyzing whether the officer's actions were consistent with the agency's policies and training.

We will not, in this text, discuss administrative investigations in any depth. Here, we limit ourselves to briefly explaining the way internal investigations into alleged misconduct are typically classified. An allegation may result in one of four findings:

Unfounded, which typically means that the officer did not act in the way alleged. In the use-of-force context, a complaint against an officer would be unfounded if the investigation resulted in the discovery of reliable information that shows that the officer did not use force or did not use the force alleged.

Exonerated, which typically means that the officer did act in the way alleged, but that the officer's actions were within policy and consistent with training. In the use-of-force context, an officer would be exonerated if the investigation resulted in the discovery of reliable information that shows the officer used force appropriately.

Sustained, which typically means that the officer did act in the way alleged and that the officer's actions were a violation of policy or inconsistent with training. In the use-of-force context, a complaint against an officer would be sustained if the investigation resulted in the discovery of reliable information showing that the officer used force inappropriately.

Not Sustained, which typically means that there is insufficient information to come to one of the preceding conclusions.

Agency policy cannot create binding legal obligations or requirements. For that reason, an officer's failure to comply with the administrative standards will not, in and of itself, expose the officer to civil or criminal liability, nor will an officer's compliance with the administrative standards, in and of itself, protect the officer from civil or criminal liability. Even without carrying independent legal significance, however, an officer's failure to comply with the administrative standards can have serious repercussions. An officer who violated policy or training can expect some combination of retraining, counselling, or disciplinary sanctions that can range from the least punitive measure (typically an oral reprimand) to the most punitive (termination).

That is not to say that the administrative standard is irrelevant in legal arenas. External reviewers, including attorneys in civil and criminal litigation, can and do rely, at least to some extent, on the administrative determination that an officer's actions were consistent or inconsistent with agency policy, although their reliance is more because of the persuasive and rhetorical force of that determination than for its legal value. Rhetorically, it can be advantageous for an attorney to describe an officer's actions in relation to agency policy and training. An attorney defending an officer's actions might emphasize that the officer was within policy and acted pursuant to their training to show that the officer acted professionally, appropriately, and reasonably. Similarly, an attorney suing over an officer's actions might emphasize that the officer violated policy or acted contrary to their training to show that the officer was out of control, a loose cannon whose willful abandonment of professional norms resulted in an unreasonable use of force. Such arguments can be powerfully persuasive even when they lack the weight of legal authority.

What Does the Administrative Standard Regulate?

As with the state law standard, there is no one answer to the question of what actions and behaviors are regulated by the administrative standard. Individual police agencies are free to define for themselves which behaviors constitute "force" and are therefore regulated by the agency's use-of-force policy.

To understand what the administrative standard typically regulates, it may be useful to consider the concepts of coerciveness and physicality as two axes on a chart. An officer can act coercively or noncoercively and, separately, an officer can take physical action or nonphysical action. Those concepts are presented in Table 3.1.

This two-axes approach is useful because it provides a sense of how police agencies regulate the use of force. Actions that are both noncoercive and nonphysical are typically subject to little, if any, detailed regulation. Non-coercive physical actions and coercive nonphysical actions are subject to relatively more. Coercive physical uses of force are typically subject to the most regulation under the administrative standard.

Not all coercive physical actions are regulated as a use of force, though, largely because of the lack of any standardized definition of what constitutes "force." Defining "force" is far more challenging than it may first appear. The difficulty comes from the entirely understandable desire for a definition that is

TABLE 3.1. Administrative Regulatory Considerations

	Physical	Non-Physical
Coercive	The application or attempted application of physical contact intended to induce a subject's compliance or overcome a subject's resistance through the infliction of pain (pain compliance) or by physically limiting or overwhelming the subject's musculoskeletal system (mechanical disruption). Examples include, but are not limited to, handcuffing a subject, employing a takedown, swinging a baton (even if the swing does not make contact), and discharging a firearm at a subject (even if the shot misses).	The invocation of an officer's authority, which a reasonable person would interpret as a command, without making or attempting to make physical contact. This can include verbal (explicit) and nonverbal (implicit) threats to use physical force intended to induce a subject's compliance. Examples include, but are not limited to, using overhead lights to initiate a traffic stop, verbal commands for a subject to do something (e.g., "Get on the ground!") or to refrain from doing something (e.g., "Don't stand up!"), verbal warnings that force will be used, and drawing and presenting a firearm or other weapon.
Non-Coercive	The application or attempted application of nonviolent physical contact that is not intended to inflict pain or disrupt the subject's musculoskeletal system. Examples include, but are not limited to, shaking hands, casual physical contact incidental to conversation, and using a light "guiding touch" to direct the subject's movements.	Verbal and nonverbal communications that are not reasonably interpreted as commands, explicit or implicit threats. Examples include, but are not limited to, casual conversations and voluntary interviews with complainants and witnesses.

neither overinclusive (that is, a definition that includes behaviors that should be excluded) nor underinclusive (that is, a definition that excludes behaviors that should be included). The actual application of physical violence—say, a takedown or baton strike to the subject's leg—clearly falls within any reasonable definition of "force," but not all cases are so readily subject to easy answers. Consider, for example, the following questions:

Is an officer drawing a weapon properly considered a use of force if the officer never presents it, threatens to use it, or attempts to make physical contact with it?
Is an officer's presentation of a weapon (e.g., pointing a firearm or raising a baton into a striking position) properly considered a use of force if the officer never attempts to actually use the weapon?
Are the answers to the two previous questions consistent for each weapon?
Is, for example, drawing a canister of pepper spray treated the same way as

drawing a pistol from a holster or deploying a rifle or shotgun from a car-mounted rack?

Does the answer change depending on civilians' awareness or ignorance of the weapon being drawn or presented?

Is an officer's express verbal threat to use force (e.g., "You are going to get shot!") properly considered a use of force?

Is an officer's attempt to use physical force (e.g., swinging a baton) properly considered a use of force if it misses and there is no physical contact?

What if civilians, including the subject against whom force was attempted, are unaware of the attempt?

Are all instances of physical contact related to detention or arrest properly considered uses of force?

What about light touches intended to direct a fully compliant subject?

What about the application of handcuffs to a fully compliant subject?

Various police agencies have answered these questions, and a host of others, in very different ways. Most agency policies identify a subset of coercive physical actions as reportable events that require the completion of a "Use of Force" or "Response to Resistance" report, while other applications of coercive physical force are considered non-reportable events. We are not aware of any police agencies, for example, that require officers to report the application of handcuffs to a compliant subject as a use of force, despite clearly being a coercive physical act. Beyond that, there are a variety of different standards for reporting. The police department in Arlington, Texas has adopted a broad reporting policy, requiring officers to submit a "Use of Force" report after using force or after pointing (or, in some cases, even drawing) a firearm.[5] The Atlanta Police Department, in contrast, has adopted a more limited reporting policy that requires officers to report any use of force that (1) results in, or is alleged to have resulted in, a physical injury or death, (2) involves the use of weapons, (3) involves "weaponless control techniques" that are likely to cause "physical injury, a claim of injury, or an allegation of excessive force," or that (4) results in property damage.[6] Thus, the use of empty-hand control techniques that neither cause injury nor are likely to cause any complaint would be considered reportable in Arlington, but not in Atlanta. We discuss this aspect of use-of-force reporting at greater length below, when we discuss policy definitions.

How Does the Administrative Standard Apply?

Discussions involving the administrative standard—from determinations of whether a particular use of force was consistent with agency policy to broader discussions about the type of policies that agencies should have in place—require an overview of both the history and important features of that standard. In this part, we first explore the relationship between the administrative standard and the legal standards discussed in the previous two chapters: the constitutional and state law standards. We then review the evolution of the administrative standard through the creation of various "models" that have been used as training and policy guides, before identifying some common and important features of use-of-force policies.

The Relationship between the Administrative Standard and the Constitutional and State Law Standards

The administrative standard is a distinct evaluative framework; at each police agency, uses of force must be assessed for compliance with policy and training. The relationship between the legal standards addressed in the two previous chapters (the constitutional and state law standards) and the administrative standard is complex. As a rule, police agencies have policies, procedures, and training that are based on constitutional and state law, even when there are no clear formal requirements for that to be the case.

With regard to constitutional law, the "anti-commandeering doctrine" articulated by the Supreme Court in a series of cases dating back to 1842 is a constitutional rule that sharply limits the federal government's ability to impose affirmative obligations on state or local executive entities or officials, including police agencies and officers. In short, police agencies are typically not required to adopt or reject any particular approach to regulating police uses of force. There are, however, some exceptions. An agency that adopts a policy that results in a constitutional violation may expose itself (or, technically, the municipality or other political subdivision under which it is organized) to civil liability; the adoption of the policy itself can be a cognizable constitutional harm.[7] In that way, the constitutional standard exerts a real, but sometimes subtle, influence on the administrative standard. More directly, a federal statute, 41 U.S.C. § 14141, gives the Attorney General of the United States the authority to sue police agencies that have been found to engage in a "pattern or practice" of constitutional violations; such lawsuits almost always result in the police agency agreeing to make a series of changes, including revising its use-of-force policies, procedures, and training.[8] The constitutional law standard, then, sets something of a floor, a minimum level of protection for civil rights that police agencies are required to meet, at least in some sense, but also one that they are free to exceed.

State law, in contrast, clearly *could* require police agencies to adopt a particular administrative standard. As the preceding chapter demonstrates, however, most do not. As a result, the relationship between the state law standard and the administrative standard mirrors the relationship between the constitutional law standard and the administrative standard: state law creates another floor that police agencies are free to exceed. Our review identified only one state with a law directly related to the administrative standard: Georgia. By statute, police agencies in Georgia cannot adopt "any rule, regulation, or policy" regarding the "degree of force to apprehend a suspected felon" that is more restrictive than that "which is allowed by the statutory and case law of this state."[9] Georgia is unique in that state law creates both a floor and a ceiling for the administrative standard, at least in one narrow context.

Where the constitutional standard is intended to protect Fourth Amendment rights and the state law standard is intended to protect civilians from criminal or tortious harms, the administrative standard is intended to serve officers as a guide to rules that govern the use of force, including the constitutional and state law standards. There is a running and contentious debate about how the administrative standard can best accomplish that goal. As we discussed in chapters 1 and 2, the constitutional and state law standards generally authorize officers to use only the type and amount of force that is "reasonable" under the circumstances, but the legal standards do not define that concept at an easily applicable level of specificity. Some police agencies have addressed this by adopting administrative standards that lay out a more detailed prescriptive approach—for example, by identifying the circumstances in which officers may use a series of different force options. This detail can help inform the constitutional and state law standards; as the United States Court of Appeals for the Eighth Circuit wrote, "Although these police department guidelines do not create a constitutional right, they are relevant to the analysis of constitutionally reasonable force."[10] However, this approach has also been criticized as being more restrictive than necessary, limiting officers by narrowing the range of force options that are legitimately available. That criticism has given rise to a contrary approach; the abandonment of detailed use-of-force policies in favor of a more free-form approach that instructs officers to be "reasonable" without much, if any, additional guidance.

In the past decade, this argument has become particularly heated. Criminologist Lorie Fridell and police executives Steve Ijames and Michael Berkow brought the issue to a head in an article published in *Police Chief*.[11] They identified the one position as "continuum" advocates, who believe that officers need detailed use-of-force policies or a graphical guide (referred to as a "continuum" or "matrix"), and the other as advocates of a "just be reasonable" model, who believe that officers do not need any guidance beyond the titular instruction. In that article, the authors work through the arguments and counter-arguments, a presentation that is particularly notable for the way it explains the real-world adaptations of the various force models discussed below. Ultimately, they contend that the argument itself may be misplaced: regardless of whether an agency falls into the "continuum" camp or the "just-be-reasonable" camp, the goal of administrative regulation should be to train officers to make decisions on uses and types of force by looking at the totality of circumstances to analyze and appropriately address the threat. Separate and apart from the applicable administrative standard, they argue, officers consider individual, situational, and organizational factors in their use-of-force decision making.

Regardless of the formal relationship between the constitutional and state law standards and the administrative standard, it is clear that the administrative standard remains heavily informed by both. Garrett and Stoughton's review of use-of-force policies at the largest fifty police agencies in the country found that "some policies simply ape the Fourth Amendment standard."[12] And almost all of the agency policies that we have reviewed explicitly incorporate the constitutional and state law standards indirectly by requiring officers to act lawfully; thus, an officer who violates state or federal law *also* violates agency policy.

THE RESOURCE-ALLOCATION APPROACH

Police agencies continually make decisions about how to best allocate their available resources. Some resources are easily identifiable as allocable assets: the amount of money an agency has and the number of officers who are available to provide policing services, for example. Well-run agencies will only allocate financial or human resource assets to extradition or a fugitive apprehension task force when they can afford to do so after sufficient resources have been allocated to higher priorities. To any agency manager, that statement is almost painfully obvious.

What may be less obvious is that there are other, less tangible, resources that can be appropriately viewed as allocable assets. For example, there are occasions in which officers are expected to put themselves in harm's way, which is to say that the agency is willing to "spend" officer safety—or, perhaps, to risk spending officer safety—in some situations to accomplish certain goals. However, almost all police agencies also have any number of policies and procedures that are intended to limit officers' exposure to harm, which is to say that the agency is *not* willing to "spend" officer safety in some situations. In this way, officer safety may be viewed as an asset, which means that agencies can make resource-driven decisions about allocation. The same may be said for the public's perception of police legitimacy, a blend of political and social capital. Agencies may be willing to spend that asset (potentially reducing public perceptions of police legitimacy) to accomplish some goals, but not others.

Although it has not traditionally been thought of in this way, the administrative standard may be conceptualized as a method of allocating officer and public safety. Viewing officer and public safety as a resource that can be spent or preserved, and using agency policy to regulate how that resource should be spent or preserved, is a radical concept in the use-of-force context, but not in policing. Agencies have followed just such an approach in the context of vehicle pursuits for decades. Vehicle pursuits are dangerous to the officer and the public, including the fleeing driver, any passengers in the fleeing vehicle, and innocent bystanders. Approximately a third of vehicle pursuits result in property damage, injury, or death. The best data we have, which is almost certainly underinclusive, suggests that police pursuits result in the death of over one hundred innocent bystanders every year.[13] By any measure, pursuits present significant dangers to officers and civilians alike. To mitigate those dangers, many police agencies have adopted restrictive pursuit policies, such as those that permit officers to pursue a fleeing vehicle only when they have probable cause to believe an occupant of the vehicle committed a violent felony. Agencies with a restrictive pursuit policy have chosen—wisely, in our view—to prioritize how they allocate officer and public safety, only "spending" those resources when the situation justifies it.

USE-OF-FORCE MODELS

In this subsection, we explore the evolution of the administrative standard, providing an overview of how agencies have and continue to approach the regulation of force. For more than fifty years, the central feature of the administrative use-of-force guidelines has been the conceptual model provided as a visual reference for officers about how and when to use various force options. These references fall into three different categories: the incremental model, the situational tactical options model, and the situational behavior model.

THE INCREMENTAL MODEL

The oldest and most popular use-of-force model is the "continuum" or "matrix." The development of a force matrix depends on the arrangement of two components: a resistance continuum and a force continuum. Both continua categorize behavior—civilian behavior in a resistance continuum and officer behavior in a force continuum—by relative severity. A force matrix correlates the force continuum with the resistance continuum, creating a formalized representation of how the gradations of force can be applied in response to various types of resistance. A stand-alone force continuum, in other words, tells an officer what force they can use (what use-of-force options are available to them), but a force matrix incorporates a resistance continuum to tell them when they can use each option. Figure 3.1 offers a simplified visual depiction of this concept.

The incremental model has been presented in several different ways, but its conceptual underpinnings remain static: it is designed to illustrate the incremental relationship that exists between the levels of subject noncompliance

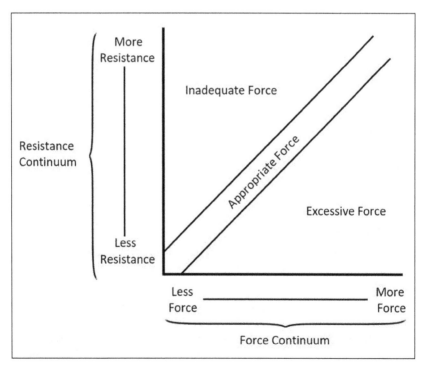

Figure 3.1. Conceptual Force Matrix

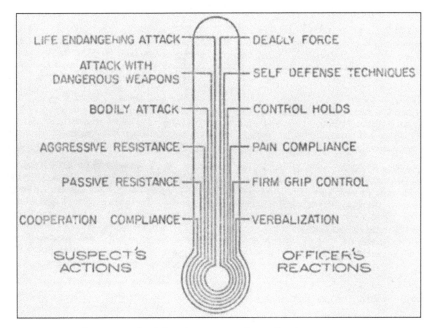

Figure 3.2. Early Los Angeles Police Department Force Continuum

or resistance on the one hand and officer responses on the other. Incremental models thus match levels of subject resistance to what are viewed as appropriate levels of force. Precisely because they illustrate the relationship between force and resistance and provide a hierarchy of force, they have proven to be useful references for assessing whether and explaining why certain levels of force were appropriately used in any given encounter.

The earliest known force-matrix model was a barometer-style visualization introduced by the Los Angeles Police Department in the late 1970s. As the suspect's actions escalated from "cooperation [and] compliance" toward "life endangering attack," the barometer indicated that officers could respond with force that escalated from "verbalization" to "deadly force."

The first modern matrix was developed at the Federal Law Enforcement Training Center (FLETC).[14] The continuum model quickly became a very popular way to explain to officers, courts, and others how police use force in relation to subject actions and why officers might use different force options over the course of a single encounter. The FLETC model was widely adopted by agencies when it was first introduced, and it continues to exert a substantial influence on police policies and training. Although many trainers and police managers have changed the way they think about the

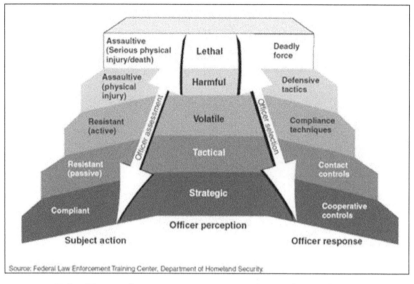

Figure 3.3. Federal Law Enforcement Training Center (FLETC) Use-of-Force Model

use of force, a majority of police agencies continue to rely on some version of the FLETC model.[15]

The FLETC Model uses five categories or levels to explain how a "reasonable" officer will perceive a subject's response to an officer during an encounter, and it prescribes a range of responses for each level of perceived response:

Compliant: the subject complies with the officer's requests or commands. When a subject is compliant, there is no justification for the use of force beyond "come-along" holds or strong direction.

Resistant (Passive): the subject does not follow the officer's commands or directions, but nor do they physically resist the officer. Officers may use some force against passive resistance, such as directing the subject through the use of "contact controls" or pain compliance techniques.

Resistant (Active): the subject has physically resisted the officer in a nonaggressive way. At this level, an officer is authorized to use a number of compliance techniques, which may include pain compliance, takedowns, or other techniques in which they are trained.

Assaultive (Physical Injury): the subject is physically attacking the officer or another individual in a way that is likely to cause some bodily harm. This type of attack justifies officers in using strikes with hands, fists, elbows, kicks, or less-lethal weapons, to get the subject under control.

Assaultive (Serious Physical Injury/Death): the subject is physically attacking the officer or another individual in a way that is likely to cause serious bodily injury or death. This level is the least frequently encountered, but presents the most serious threat to an officer's safety. The appropriate officer response at this level would be deadly force.

More recently developed iterations of the incremental model still bear a strong resemblance to their progenitor, although there can be significant variation in the number and exact definitions of the different levels of force and resistance.[16] Figure 3.4 depicts the model previously used in Florida, reflecting another common approach to visualizing the incremental model.

Perhaps the most sophisticated example of an incremental model comes from John Desmedt, a former Assistant Special Agent in Charge of the Office of Training of the United States Secret Service, whose work on the pedagogy of teaching psychomotor (that is, conscious movement) skills to officers has remained influential. Like the other incremental models, Desmedt's "Transactional Use of Force Paradigm," shown in Figure 3.5, sets out categories of subject resistance and officers' force options, but it seeks to be far more granular in its application, reflecting "the actual degree of reasonableness of government actions in response to subject behaviors." According to Desmedt:

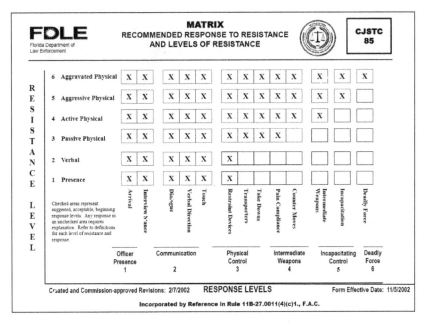

Figure 3.4. (Former) Florida Force Matrix

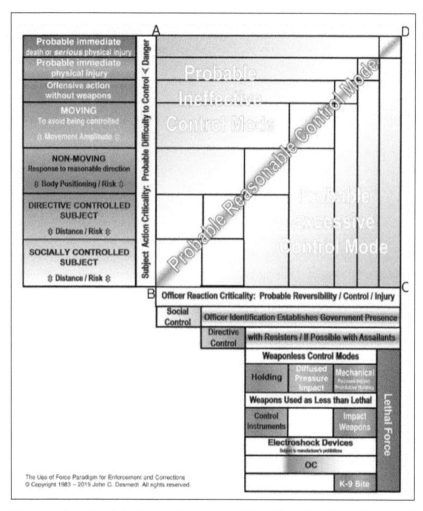

Figure 3.5. Protective Safety Systems Transactional Use of Force Paradigm. Courtesy of John Desmedt.

The [Transactional] Use of Force Paradigm does not show absolutes, but rather the intersecting degree of probable appropriateness of treatment modalities as applied to qualitative and quantitative subject action modes. The goal of this paradigm is to map the probable appropriateness of individual officer reactions in relation to each corresponding subject action during an actual specific event. The "subject action continuum" is set in categories, but each category contains subcategories, which each, in turn, contain embedded ranges, that are equal to continuously smaller categories. This conforms to the actual definition of continuum. The officer reaction continuum is ordered by probability of control, probability of injury, and probable reversibility.[17]

Incremental force-continuum models have been criticized on a number of grounds. They have been criticized on tactical grounds for implying a sequential approach to the use of force; the linear layout of most force-continuum models, or so it is argued, suggests that officers must move through each category of force as they transition to higher or lower levels of force. That is, a literal view of a linear force continuum (especially those with stepped depictions) suggests that an officer cannot use deadly force without first attempting to use every force option that falls lower on the continuum (e.g., defensive tactics, compliance techniques, contact controls, and cooperative controls).

This is, in our view, a misunderstanding of force continuum models; a linear approach may have some superficial appeal, but neither the creators nor the police agencies that have adopted the incremental model would be surprised by the assertion that a linear progression will often prove wildly inappropriate. Consider officers who are faced with a subject who is actively shooting at them; it would be imbecilic to require officers to first attempt empty-hand techniques and then use intermediate weaponry before utilizing deadly force. A strictly linear approach would likewise suggest an absurdity as officers transitioned to lower levels of force; faced with a subject who had been actively shooting but who then became fully compliant, it would be inappropriate to require officers to use intermediate weaponry and empty-hand techniques before applying handcuffs. This point, we think, is so patently obvious that the argument against "linear progression" is properly understood as a straw man, as Fridell and her co-authors argued, rather than a valid criticism.[18] It is well known that an officer may enter a situation which has already developed, is serious, and requires an immediate physical response to control a subject or protect a life. In the same vein, it is well known that a situation may escalate, de-escalate, remain stable, or fluctuate quickly and with little warning. An officer must be prepared to enter and respond to dynamic situations using the appropriate type and amount of force, without progressing linearly through the various "levels" of response.

A more nuanced criticism of the incremental model is that, regardless of how the graphical representation *should* be read, officers *may* interpret it as imposing a linear progression requirement. That is, the graphical method by which the information is presented creates an unacceptably high potential for misinterpretation, especially by officers at smaller agencies who lack the regular access to sophisticated training and use-of-force instructors that larger agencies enjoy. As Fridell, Ijames, and Berkow have pointed out, however, that criticism rather misses the point: "[I]f an agency's officers cannot assimilate these concepts (for example, 'you can start in the middle,' 'you can jump levels'), the agency's problems are severe and relate to hiring and training, not to whether they should retain or eliminate the linear continuum."[19]

A more powerful criticism of the incremental model relates to the limited range of information that force-continuum models deem relevant: while incremental models correlate levels of force to subject resistance, most versions do not provide a threat assessment mechanism or encourage officers to consider contextual issues in use-of-force situations. Criticisms on this ground have focused on both pragmatic and conceptual shortcomings. Pragmatically, the focus of incremental models on subject behavior—that is, the nature of the resistance itself—fails to take into account relevant personal characteristics or context. Consider, for example, two suspects who are attempting to flee on foot. One subject is young and athletic. The other is morbidly obese and toting a portable oxygen machine. On their face, most incremental force continuum models would appear to classify their behaviors as the same category of behavior—active resistance—and would indicate to officers that the same type of force—say, baton strikes to the upper legs—is an appropriate option for both subjects. This obviously overlooks the very clear differences in the two scenarios: only one of the subjects presents any appreciable risk of evading apprehension. Desmedt's "Transactional" paradigm (Figure 3.5) goes further; while both subjects would be considered "moving," the obese subject would have a lower "movement amplitude," and would thus present a lower threat profile than the athletic subject. Thus, a particular use of force might be permissible against the higher-range subject, but impermissible against the lower-range subject. Most incremental models, however, lack this level of nuance.

Conceptually, the incremental model has been criticized because it governs the officer's response to resistance during the interaction without reference to the underlying justifications for the officer–civilian encounter or the relative importance of the state interest at issue. Force continua, in other words, are merely overlaid onto the underlying justifications for coercive state action without taking into account any normative considerations of the relative strengths of those justifications. For example, a force continuum that authorizes baton strikes to the upper legs as a response to attempted flight on foot does not, on its face, distinguish between a fleeing jaywalker and a fleeing murder suspect.

As those criticisms suggest, the most popular iterations of the incremental model do not accurately account for or explain the reality of modern police work; such depictions typically provide weak and imperfect guidance for deciding whether force is appropriate and, if so, which level of force is appropriate in any given situation. More comprehensive models, such as Desmedt's "Transactional" paradigm (Figure 3.5), may be too complicated to serve as a reference to officers in the field, even if they can be highly useful when evaluating a use of force after the fact. Those observations have led a number of police trainers to call for the abolition of linear force matrices altogether. There has not, however, been a universal movement toward eliminating graphical models to provide guidance to officers and reviewers; indeed, a number of alternatives have been suggested. Those alternatives fit into two categories: situational tactical options models and situational behavior models.

SITUATIONAL TACTICAL OPTIONS MODELS

Situational tactical options models conceptualize the range or array of tactical options in a circular format in which the tactical options are arranged randomly. Such models do not emphasize one option over another, and there is no entry point and no indication of a linear progression in levels of force. The point of the situational tactical options model is to encourage officers to consider all available tactical options as the encounter develops and changes, keeping in mind that the fluidity of confrontational encounters may make it necessary to utilize different options over the course of the interaction. The need for constant assessment and re-assessment of the situation is at the heart of this model and is critical to the success of the encounter.

The situational model stresses both officer and public safety, as well as tactical communications. Some models have a police officer in the middle of the circle to show that officers can select any of the options, including nonviolent options, at any time during the encounter. In this way, both escalation and deescalation techniques can be used when appropriate. Tactical communication is specifically integrated into the model—often at the center of the model—as opposed to being a separate category; doing so recognizes that almost every police–citizen encounter begins with and includes through its duration some level of communication, and it emphasizes the critical importance of communication in any interaction.

The situational tactical options model includes a variety of weapons and nonviolent options arranged in no particular order. That arrangement is intentional; it is intended to serve as a reminder that officers should not rely on any incremental steps, but should instead focus on safety, communication, and training. Most models, including the one pictured in Figure 3.6, include options that are shared with most incremental models, such as officer pres-

Figure 3.6. Queensland Police Service, Situational Use-of-Force Model (2016). Courtesy of State of Queensland (Queensland Police Service, 2019).

ence and the use of empty-hand tactics or firearms. Many situational tactical options models go beyond incremental models, though, by also including tactical disengagement, negotiation, and "situational containment" as options for officers to consider. Instead of referring to the model to make use-of-force decisions, the situational tactical options model is used to teach officers to continually assess the risk in each encounter, to come up with a plan,[20] and to take appropriate action. An example of this type of model, shown in Figure 3.6, is the use-of-force model adopted by the Queensland, Australia, Police Service.

Situational tactical options models are designed to balance simplicity with the many options available for a comprehensive approach to the use of force. As Michael Williams and Jenny Lloyd have describe them, "Situational Tactical Options Models allow flexibility of force option choices rather than a prescriptive approach that sees force matched with like or greater force."[21] The model encourages officers to consider a wider variety of options, responses, and tactics than they would by referring to an incremental model, including "tactical disengagement" and "tactical withdrawal." The strength of the situational tactical option model is the diversity of options that officers are encouraged to consider, although we should acknowledge that some of the terminology may prove difficult to import. Policing in this country often exhibits a strong cultural resistance to anything that smacks of retreat, although the tactical concepts that underlie disengagement, withdrawal, reposition, and restraint are familiar to officers in the United States.[22] Semantic concerns aside, because they do not provide potentially misleading proportional force-resistance guidance, these models may better prepare officers to justify their selection of tactical options among the universe of different situations.

But the strength of this model is also its weakness: the model does little to define what "appropriate situations" are for the many tactical options it presents. The long menu of tactical options fails to provide officers with any easily applicable framework or direction, which can contribute to hesitation, putting officers at a disadvantage. Using this decision-making model as a training tool may be more difficult than training under an incremental model, largely because officers must quickly recall their possible options and apply their decisions in real time, under pressure, with no guidance from the model itself. Further, the lack of guidance may fail to properly constrain officers' use-of-force decisions. Unlike incremental models, the situational tactical options model does not specify or categorize subject resistance beyond the generic instruction that officers should assess, plan, and act with an eye to the specific dynamics of the encounter, making it difficult or impossible to refer to the model to explain why a use of force was inappropriate under the circumstances.

The situational behavior model addresses this absence by including the behavior of the subject as a guide for the officer to determine the appropriate response to the situation.

SITUATIONAL BEHAVIOR MODELS

A logical progression from the situational tactical options model, situational behavior models incorporate the subject's behavior. Use-of-force instructors in Canada, frustrated by the artificial limits of shoot/don't shoot training scenarios, developed situational behavior models in the 1990s. The early situational behavior models linked the separate academic and physical defensive tactics training skills in order to improve officers' decision-making and assessment skills. These models, as with the incremental and situational tactical options models, have also been used in court proceedings to explain why certain levels of force were used against suspects. As a result of the changes,

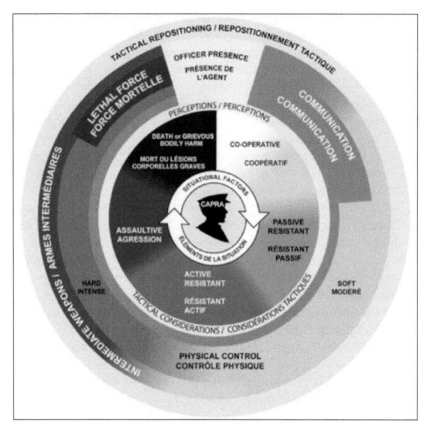

Figure 3.7. Royal Canadian Mounted Police Incident Management/Intervention Model. Courtesy of the Royal Canadian Mounted Police (2019).

the Canadian National Use of Force Framework (NUFF) was developed to provide a common approach to the use of force for police agencies across Canada. The Royal Canadian Mounted Police (RCMP) Incident Management/Intervention Model (IMIM) serves as a good example of a situational behavior model. It is shown in Figure 3.7.

Situational behavior models draw from both incremental models and tactical options models to assist officers in choosing the appropriate option. Like incremental models, situational behavior models include the subject's behavior and level of resistance as a primary referent. But they also explicitly include other circumstances, such as officer perceptions and tactical considerations not contemplated by most incremental models. As with tactical options models, the circular format reflects the fluid and ever-changing nature of encounters, and encourages officers to adjust their selection of tactics and force options as the encounter evolves. Situational behavior models provide guidance for officers on appropriate tactics relative to subject behavior, but they are not prescriptive in the sense that they recognize that every encounter may be perceived differently by different officers depending on individual characteristics or other factors that influence the perceived threat.

Situational behavior models provide a comprehensive analytic framework for explaining the justification for various force options. The situation models provide more guidance than the static or incremental models, as they integrate behavioral issues and personal characteristics, such a mental illness, into the decision-making process. For example, if a subject is known or observed to have a mental disorder, a de-escalation option may be a more appropriate tactical choice than using force, even if the subject's belligerence or aggressive actions could be perceived as "assaultive resistance." Such decisions are more difficult to explain in static models that simply associate a high level of resistance with a corresponding level of force.

As with situational tactical options models, the complex design of situational behavior models makes the options and choices difficult to recall under pressure. However, having a limited range of situations and tactical options may potentially simplify the way an officer plans to resolve a conflict or encounter.

A SUMMARY OF THE MODELS

Use-of-force models were developed to augment training and to be a visual guide to officers making decisions about when to use various force options. Over time, they have also been used to justify uses of force by serving as a reference to explain the relationship between force, resistance, and other factors to laypersons and in judicial proceedings. The models started as a simple continuum, moved to a correlated comparison of resistance and force, and have changed over time in an effort to address more complex questions and situations. Ironically, the continued evolution of force models—each driven by the incessant need to improve on the previous model's oversights and shortcomings—has led to the development of models that are so complex that their real-world usefulness is now being questioned.

When considered as an incident management tool, the various models all serve a similar purpose: agency heads use force models as a simple and flexible way of communicating to officers the concept of "reasonableness" without unduly restricting them in high-pressure situations. As we have seen, there are divergent views on how the use-of-force models can be optimally constructed.

What is missing from the debate is evidence. No one has conducted a proper study of the relative effects of the various types of use-of-force policies.[23] As passionate as their advocates may be, it is not clear whether any one model serves that purpose more effectively than the others. The argument that one model or another has more appeal in litigation remains unanswered as well. Each side has an answer, but as several commentators have pointed out, the quality of the subject matter expert explaining the use of force to the factfinder will often prove far more important than the language or configuration of the model.[24]

Every police agency must make a series of decisions about how to prepare officers for encounters that can result in the use of force. The debate surrounding use-of-force models is an important and powerful one that can increase public awareness of the difficulties faced by officers and can help create new initiatives and partnerships. Hopefully, empirical evidence will shed some light on the effectiveness of the different models, but until the evidence is convincing, the debate will persist and officer actions will continue be subjected to ongoing scrutiny under the existing models and rules.

Use-of-Force Policy Components

Like force models, use-of-force policies seek to guide officers' use-of-force decisions toward reasonable options and away from unreasonable uses of force. Some variation is to be expected, as is a substantial overlap between the different approaches. While different communities have unique social and cultural drivers that shape the mechanisms by which the reasonable use of force is determined, there appear to be more commonalities than differences. Nevertheless, those differences can be substantial. In a stratified, random survey of 1,000 different police agencies, criminologists William Terrill, Eugene Paoline, and Jason Ingram concluded that "it was difficult to identify a standard practice that is used by police departments across the country." The vast majority, over 80 percent, used some type of graphical force model, but there was no "typical" formulation for how force options were represented: the authors identified a "total of 123 different permutations" of force progression with between three and nine levels. Agencies, the authors report, "pick and choose, tweak and adapt, in a multitude of ways—all, unfortunately, with no empirical evidence as to which approach is best or even better than any other."[25]

A more recent survey by Garrett and Stoughton reviewed the fifty largest police agencies in the country. Such large agencies might be expected to have the resources to research and implement best practices through the adoption of more consistent and detailed policies. The reality did not live up to those expectations. The fifty largest agencies had "widely varying force policies, many of which were quite minimalistic." Just over half (31, or 62 percent) used a continuum, with six (12 percent) including a graphical representation. The agencies' policies differed on whether officers must use the minimum amount of force that can safely address the situation, whether officers were required to provide verbal warnings (when feasible), or whether there were specific guidelines to be followed in situations involving emotionally disturbed persons and, if so, what those guidelines were. "About half of the policies," the authors report, "did not discuss tactics or provide officers with guidance on how to approach a situation, nor did they discuss de-escalation or other techniques that could be used to diffuse a violent situation or avoid the need to use force."[26]

As these analyses suggest, there are plenty of models and examples of a range of different use-of-force policies. The following subsections identify twelve common and, in our view, necessary elements in use-of-force policies.

MISSION STATEMENT

The mission statement incorporates the mission of the agency and its most highly regarded values. Although a use-of-force policy need not have its own mission statement, it should refer explicitly to the agency's mission statement as a backdrop for the values that underlie the guidance given to officers in the use-of-force context, keeping in mind that the ultimate goal of policing is to protect civilians from unnecessary indignity and harm. A mission statement should reflect the idea that the mission of the police is to work cooperatively with the civilians they are sworn to protect, upholding the Constitution and protecting life, dignity, and property. Specifically, the mission statement should explain that officers are sworn to preserve the peace, enforce the laws, reduce fear, and provide a safe environment while engendering public trust and confidence by being fair and just to all members of the community. Although it is often overlooked, assessing whether a particular use of force is consistent with the agency's overarching mission is an important component of applying the administrative standard.

POLICY STATEMENT

The policy statement should acknowledge that the reasonable use of force is a necessary part of law enforcement, and it should state clearly that the use of force will be used only when necessary to advance or protect a governmental interest. The policy statement should also acknowledge that community support is the ultimate source of police authority. This is important because the use of force is one of the most intrusive and controversial government actions;

officers are empowered by the community, which means that unreasonable or excessive force undermines legitimacy and police authority. For that reason, the general policy statement should explain that the life, liberty, and dignity of community members are of the utmost importance, and that the police officer's main goal is to protect civilians from unnecessary indignity and harm. If force against an individual is necessary, officers should strive to use the minimum amount of force that is likely to safely address the situation.

DEFINITIONS

It is helpful to define the principal terms, especially those that may not be common knowledge, either to the police or to the general public. We have provided a list of terms and general definitions in alphabetical order that is neither exhaustive nor extensive, but exemplifies the types of terms that need to be defined:

Levels of Resistance are the different categories of resistance, typically grouped by severity, that a subject may offer. Different agencies may adopt different terminology or define their adopted terms differently, but each term should be clearly defined.

Levels of Force are the different categories of force, typically grouped by severity, that an officer can use to address resistance. As with levels of resistance, there may be substantial differences from agency to agency in terminology and definition, but it is important for each term to be clearly defined. Typically, agencies should categorize the various force options by referring to the likely consequences; some common levels of force include low-level force, intermediate force, and deadly force. More broadly, less-lethal force is that which does not create a substantial risk of serious bodily harm or death, while lethal force is that which does. We discuss various categories of force options in more depth in chapter 6.

Force Transition is the escalation/de-escalation to different force options, transitioning from the application of one force option or level to another.

Imminent Threat is the characterization that a reasonable officer would give an action marked by the ability, opportunity, and intent to cause harm that is more than likely to cause a particular harm if not adequately addressed.

Officer-Involved Shooting is an officer's intentional or unintentional discharge of a firearm at a person or other target.

Reportable Force is any use of force the agency requires to be reported. Different agencies have taken different approaches; at a minimum, agencies should require officers to report uses of physical force that are likely to result in an injury as well as uses of force that actually result in an observable injury or the complaint of pain or injury.

THE LEGALITY OF FORCE

This section should be a brief discussion of the constitutional and state law standards in the jurisdiction. While there are valid concerns about policies that simply mirror the constitutional law or state law standards, we believe that it is appropriate for agencies to inform officers about how their actions will be evaluated under governing law. This discussion may differ depending upon the type of policy, but will typically draw on *Graham*'s "objectively reasonable" standard, describing the "totality of the circumstances" review as assessed from the perspective of a reasonable officer on the scene and without the benefit of hindsight.[27] The policy should explain that an officer's reasonable perceptions are a consideration, even if those perceptions are factually erroneous. Courts will refer to an officer's reasonable perceptions and a range of other factors to determine the reasonableness of force. Policy may identify those factors, which may include, but are not limited to, the *Graham* factors, subject and officer characteristics, and encounter and environmental characteristics described in chapter 1.

DUTY TO REPORT

Officers should be instructed that they have a duty to report uses of force. Policy must identify reportable force events; that is, those that require the completion of a "use of force" or "response to resistance" form. This section of the use-of-force policy will include the specific types of information required to be included in the form, how to complete the form, and why the information is necessary. As noted above, all uses of coercive force beyond physical contact with a compliant subject must be reported. The degree of detail that is required will vary among agencies, but agencies and executives should keep in mind that these data can help analyze policies and training. The more information they have about the individuals involved and the specific situation, the better the analysts will be able to discern practices, patterns, and trends, and the more feedback trainers, instructors, and supervisors will have. If the agency requires the officer to complete the "use-of-force" or "response-to-resistance" form, all officers who were involved as an actor or observer of the event must complete the form, and they must do so without collaborating. If the agency requires the supervisor to complete the form, then they will separately interview the officer(s), suspect(s), and any civilian witness(es).

The form may include checkboxes or, on electronic forms, dropdown boxes, but it must include a narrative section in which each force option used in each encounter is specifically justified. The data included on these forms should also be fed into early warning systems. Separately, policy should require officers to promptly report to a supervisor any potentially improper uses of force that they observe or become aware of.

DUTY TO INTERVENE

Agency policy should state explicitly that any officer who observes another officer using force or other tactics that, under the circumstances, are clearly unsafe, unlawful, or outside of policy shall intercede safely to prevent the unnecessary creation of danger or the use of excessive force. Such events should be reported as described above.

USE-OF-FORCE MODEL

The use-of-force model is the explanation of the type of continuum or options model used by the department (as discussed above). This section may include a comprehensive explanation of the levels and types of force that the agency has adopted. It should include instructing officers to assess risks, develop plans, and take appropriate actions. Depending on the model the agency selects, force options, responses to resistance, and types of force will be described and explained. This section can serve as a training guide for academy and in-service training.

CONFLICT AVOIDANCE

Conflict avoidance is a tactical approach through which officers minimize the potential for a situation to require the use of force. This section should identify the importance of dignity and require officers to conduct themselves in a procedurally just manner that reduces the potential for interpersonal conflict. Agencies may include a discussion of tactical communication concepts to describe how communication skills can be used, when appropriate, to reduce the risk of violent encounters.

DE-ESCALATION

De-escalation refers to a reduction in the level of conflict that exists at the time. Agency policies should define de-escalation as a process through which an officer attempts to verbally reduce the level of force needed, or which may be needed in the immediate future, to control a suspect. For example, an officer who would need to use force to bring an actively resisting subject under control would de-escalate the situation by verbally communicating with the subject until the subject is passively resisting or compliant. It is important for policies to emphasize that de-escalation is a tool that, like any other force option, may be appropriate or inappropriate depending on the circumstances. Agency policies should require officers to engage in de-escalation when it is reasonably safe for them to do so. The process of de-escalation requires a continual risk assessment that takes into account the individual and environmental characteristics, including the knowledge of ready resources. Whether there is a safe opportunity for de-escalation depends on the suspect's behavior in light of the tactical situation. For example, it may be appropriate to attempt to de-escalate a subject who is aggressively moving toward officers if the officers can maintain a safe position by using distance or obstacles. In the same vein, it may be inappropriate to attempt to de-escalate a passive protestor who is lying across the driveway of a hospital as an ambulance is trying to pull in with a critically injured patient on board. We discuss de-escalation in more depth in chapter 5.

TACTICS

Tactics, in the use-of-force context, are the actions that officers use to manage the risk profile of an encounter by providing them with, or depriving the subject of, advantageous physical positioning. Agency policies should explain that tactics are important because they allow officers to minimize both their own exposure to physical danger as well as the need to use force.

Policies should identify time as a core tactical concept, and they should describe ways officers can maximize the amount of time they have to make use-of-force decisions, including the use of distance, cover and concealment, tactical restraint (when an officer maintains a stable position without moving forward), and tactical disengagement, repositioning, or withdrawal (when an officer moves from a disadvantageous position to a more advantageous position). Officers must decide how to perform their work in a safe manner, avoiding poor tactical decisions that may put their safety or the safety of others at risk. This includes avoiding "officer-created jeopardy," or officers putting themselves into unnecessarily dangerous situations, which dramatically increases the potential for officers to resort to the use of force to address a threat that a more tactical approach could have avoided. We discuss tactical concepts, including officer-created jeopardy, in more depth in chapter 5.

AUTHORIZED TOOLS, TECHNIQUES, AND EQUIPMENT

This section of policy serves to remind officers that only agency-approved tools, techniques, or equipment are authorized, except as specifically provided. Approved firearms, less-lethal weapons, ammunition, and other items can be listed here, as can a general proviso that addresses the *ad hoc* use of other tools and weapons (sometimes referred to as "weapons of opportunity" or "weapons of necessity"). This can be an essential component of an agency's policy, as it explains the use of police tools, techniques, and weaponry and provides examples of approved uses, tactical considerations, and supervisory responsibilities.

USE-OF-FORCE INVESTIGATIONS

Policies should clearly state that use-of-force investigations can or will be conducted on all reportable uses of force to determine whether or not the force and tactics employed are consistent with governing law, applicable policy, and relevant training. This investigation will also be used to identify policy or training deficiencies. Officers who become involved in reportable use-of-force incidents will immediately notify a supervising officer. Investigations on use-of-force incidents require a thorough and detailed evaluation of the tactics used, the types and levels of force selected, and the actions of all persons involved.

Conclusion

Use-of-force policies set parameters for officer use-of-force decision making and the various models are used to train officers to apply policies to field situations. Regardless of the training model—whether incremental, situational tactical, situational behavioral, or "just be reasonable"—officers must be trained to make decisions on uses and types of force based on the totality of circumstances, the threat analysis, and how best to address the threat. The goal of all police agencies is to form policies and provide training to assist officers in making critical and sometimes life-and-death decisions in the field—without the opportunity to seek advice, consult a manual, or ask a supervisor. While police officers are tasked with making these decisions, they are prepared to do so through training and policy and for the most part are quite capable of engaging in reasonable decision making that does not violate an individual's constitutional rights.

4

The Community Expectations Standard

The preceding three chapters have each explored either a *legal* standard (constitutional law and state law) or a *legalistic* standard (administrative policies) under which an officers' use of force can be evaluated. An officer's use of force can be entirely lawful and within policy, but still fall far short of public expectations about how officers should behave; incidents that fit that description are often referred to as "lawful but awful." This chapter discusses community expectations, which are far less formal, although no less important, than the other evaluative standards.

Public confidence and trust in policing are exceptionally important for at least three pragmatic reasons: the impact they can have on crime rates, police effectiveness, and safety. With regard to crime rates, there is good reason to believe that positive perceptions of the police reduce crime. As the President's Task Force on 21st Century Policing wrote in its final report, "decades of research and practice support the premise that people are more likely to obey the law when they believe that those who are enforcing it have the legitimate authority to tell them what to do."[1] Unfortunately, it is also the case that people are *less* likely to obey the law when they perceive the police as illegitimate.[2]

Beyond its effects on crime, community expectations also have important implications for police effectiveness. Every aspect of policing depends, to a significant extent, on the assistance or cooperation of community members. Consider, for example, the many anecdotes involving a daytime shooting in a populated area that none of the many bystanders admits to actually witnessing; such anecdotes are used by officers to express frustration at a lack of cooperation precisely because of the impact that such cooperation can have on the investigation. It is worth pointing out that while such anecdotes are common, the dynamics they represent are the exception, not the rule. Imagine the impossibility of performing even basic police services if motorists *typically* refused to pull over or provide their documentation during a traffic stop, if tow truck drivers *typically* refused police requests to remove crashed vehicles from the roadway, if crime victims *typically* did not call the police, if witnesses *typically* refused to provide any useful information, if hotels and other businesses *typically* required the police to get a warrant before allowing them onto the property or sharing any information, and so on. To the extent that perceptions of police legitimacy shape people's willingness to report to and cooperate with the police, public distrust can cripple the effective delivery of police services.

Public distrust can also create dangerous situations for officers and community members alike. People's reactions are based on their perceptions, and people's perceptions are colored by distrust. An officer who sees a subject's lack of deference as a challenge may be motivated to assert their authority in a way that can provoke, rather than prevent, resistance. A young man who sees the police as a threat may be motivated to assert his own authority by defying officers' attempts to control a situation. In the ambiguous environment of a police encounter, officers and community members who distrust each other are more likely to perceive each other as a threat and to react accordingly, increasing the potential for violence.

At a broader level, too, public distrust can jeopardize safety. Perhaps the best modern example is the public reaction to the shooting of Michael Brown in Ferguson, Missouri. In the aftermath of that shooting, two narratives emerged. In one narrative, Mr. Brown had violently attacked an officer who was sitting in his patrol car at the time, then walked away, and was then shot while aggressively approaching the officer for a second time. In the other narrative, Mr. Brown was shot with his arms raised as he surrendered to the officer. In the immediate aftermath of the shooting, people were confronted with both narratives, but the one that they believed had very little to do with the shooting itself—the various witnesses' grand jury testimony and the results of the Department of Justice's investigation would not be available for months. Instead, people believed the narrative that confirmed their pre-existing perceptions of police. Individuals who tended to trust the police believed the first narrative, while individuals who tended to distrust the police believed the second. The resulting protests, which endangered hundreds of officers and thousands of community members, were a direct result of that distrust.

As that example demonstrates, the use of force and how it is perceived in the community can not only undermine public trust over time, it can also serve as a flashpoint, a spark that ignites long-simmering community hostility. Use-of-force incidents can have lasting reverberations, from the televised abuses of the Civil Rights Era to the beating of Rodney King in 1991 or the shooting of Walter Scott in 2015. Throughout the country, there have been multiple incidents in which police uses of force have instigated violence or civil unrest.[3] Of the ten most violent and destructive riots in United States history, fully half were prompted by what were perceived as incidents of excessive force or police abuse.[4]

Clearly, then, it is important to understand the standards that community members apply to evaluate whether any given use of force meets their expectations. Of course, the concept of "community" is inherently overly simplistic; as individuals, we each exist in multiple communities simultaneously based on geographic location, age, race, ethnicity, political and religious identification, and so on. We cannot, in a single chapter, hope to address every aspect of what every community expects from officers in the context of violent encounters. We can, however, offer an overview of how use-of-force incidents are evaluated under the community expectations standard without attempting to comprehensively discuss every possible permutation. We do so by first addressing the question of when the community expectations standard applies. We then discuss which police actions are subject to analysis under the standard of community expectations. Finally, we explore the application of the community expectations standard through two different dimensions; one that views police in a negative light, and the other, which views the police more positively.

When Does the Community Expectations Standard Apply?

In the context of the legal and legalistic standards discussed in the previous chapters, the use of force itself is not sufficient to trigger the application of the evaluative standard. That is, there can be a use of force *without* any formal evaluation of the incident that applies one of those standards. To understand why, consider the context in which those standards apply. The constitutional law standard, for example, applies in excessive force lawsuits brought under § 1983. The state law standard, in contrast, applies in civil or criminal litigation in state court. The administrative standard, meanwhile, applies in the course of an agency's internal investigation. In each case, there is some formal triggering event—the filing of a lawsuit or the initiation of an internal investigation—that makes it necessary to apply a particular evaluative standard.

The community expectations standard, however, is far less formal: it does not require any triggering event beyond the public perception that there has been a use-of-force incident. The emphasis on *perception* is intentional: the public can, and has, reacted to what is believed to be a violent incident even when there is no underlying use of force or when the underlying use of force is very different from the way the incident was perceived. In 1965, the highly destructive Watts riots in Los Angeles, California, were kicked off when officers were believed to have used force to arrest a drunk driver (true) and to have kicked a pregnant woman (not true). Two years later, two white officers in Newark, New Jersey, were believed to have arrested and beat a black taxi driver (true) to death (not true), leading to six days of rioting. Both of those examples, of course, come from the Civil Rights Era, and history makes clear that, by the 1960s, the many decades of disparate and racist treatment of individuals of color at the hands of government agents had led large swaths of urban communities to lose any faith they might have otherwise had in public institutions. But not all examples are drawn from what were already among the most contentious periods in American history. The aftermath of the Michael Brown shooting, discussed above, provides a more recent example of how community members react to their perceptions of what happened during a police encounter, rather than the reality of the encounter itself.

As the incidents in Watts, Newark, and Ferguson suggest, the community's understanding of an encounter or a use of force will often be based on limited, and sometimes entirely inaccurate, information. Historically, the limited expectations about the release of materials by police and the pace at which people could share information gave police agencies the leeway to refuse to publicly share information, at least until the conclusion of an internal investigation. In the modern era of the 24-hour news cycle, press releases, and social media, however, the demands and expectations are higher and information, misinformation, and emotion can be transmitted instantly to local, national, and even international audiences. To their detriment, most police agencies have not kept pace with technological evolution and social change.

The common failure to provide timely information increases the potential that the community's understanding of an event will be based on limited or inaccurate perceptions. Yet that understanding is no less powerful for being flawed. As French artist Robert Delaunay is credited with saying, "Our understanding is correlative to our perception." In the context of police uses of force, as in other areas of life, people draw conclusions about an incident based on their perceptions with little regard for the possibility that their perceptions are or may be inaccurate. As NFL quarterback Steve Young said, "Perception is reality. If you are perceived to be something, you might as well be it because that's the truth in people's minds."[5]

Maximizing the potential for community reaction to be based on the best facts available at the time, then, requires police agencies to release information faster than has previously been necessary. There is broad, although not universal, agreement that police agencies need to improve in this regard. As documented in the book *In Context*, for example, the authors' review of every officer-involved homicide of an unarmed civilian in 2015 led them to a set of key findings. Their very first finding was that "police must release more data, and do it sooner." They write:

Law enforcement agencies simply must find better ways to release more data, and to release it earlier. There is a significant public interest in this data, and the public has a legitimate right to understand how it is being policed. . . . Police agencies failing to release information look like they're hiding something, and alternatively, agencies that release what they have, when they have it are invested with the trust of their communities.

It has been shown in agencies across the country that substantial portions of the known material can be placed in the public domain early, and updated as necessary, without negatively affecting the integrity of the investigation. . . . Release early, release often, put a face to the investigation, and don't even appear to be hiding.[6]

In short, the community expectations standard is implicated when community members believe there has been a relevant event during the course of a police encounter, and the standard is used to analyze the facts available to the public at the time. In the next section, we describe the type of events that may be deemed relevant. We then discuss what the community expectations standard can entail.

What Does the Community Expectations Standard Regulate?

The community expectations standard applies to the actual use of physical force, of course—a topic that needs little in the way of explanation—but that is not all it applies to; community members, for the most part, do not care *only* about the use of force during a police encounter. Other aspects of the encounter that are related to, but that do not themselves involve, the use of force can affect the way community members evaluate use-of-force incidents.

Most, if not all, of these concerns arise from the asymmetric power dynamic inherent in police encounters. As armed agents of the state, officers have tremendous authority to interfere with people's privacy and freedom. Officers, after all, can require someone to submit to a search of their body or property. They can detain or arrest someone with the full power of the state behind them. They can use force. They can use lethal force. Individuals who interact with the police, on the other hand, are sharply limited in what the state permits them to do in that encounter. It can be a crime to refuse an officer's commands or to fight back, even if the individual honestly or reasonably thinks that officers are exceeding their authority. This lopsided allocation of power can arouse great skepticism, which should be no surprise given the longstanding American tradition of suspicion about governmental intrusions into people's private lives.

The community expectations standard applies to the use of physical force, of course, but it also applies more broadly. In the following subsections, we explore two areas in which public concern seems particularly relevant to the evaluation of use-of-force incidents: procedural injustice and the failure to protect.

Procedural Injustice

A substantial body of research has found that people care at least as much, and often more, about *how* they are treated in a police interaction than they do about the actual outcome of the encounter.[7] Two terms are used to distinguish between treatment and outcome: "procedural justice" and "substantive justice." Procedural justice refers to the fairness of the process by which a particular issue or dispute is resolved. Substantive justice, in contrast, refers to the fairness of the resolution to the dispute itself.

To illustrate this difference, imagine two people are driving their cars to the hospital, each having received a call about a family member's serious injury. Both are stopped by the police. Consider the officer's statements during the two encounters:

OFFICER 1: Where are you speeding off to? You know what, I don't even care. There's no excuse for driving like an asshole. Give me your driver's license, registration, and proof of insurance. Now stay here so I can check you for outstanding warrants.

You didn't have any warrants in the system, but if you keep speeding like that you're going to, and you're going to get someone killed. I'm about to get off shift and don't want to deal with having to write a ticket, so I guess it's your lucky day. Now get the hell out of here and don't let me catch you driving like that again.

OFFICER 2: G'morning, I'm Officer Smith, and I pulled you over for speeding today. Is there any reason you were going so fast? The hospital, huh? Oh, I'm sorry to hear that; I'll get you on your way as soon as possible. Can I see your driver's license, registration, and insurance, please? Thank you. Give me just a minute and I'll get you out of here, I promise.

Okay, here are your documents back. I did write you a ticket this morning; this is a pedestrian-heavy area, and we've been having a lot of problems with speeding cars, including a couple of close calls with some kids on bikes last week, so we're really trying to get the speeds down to keep everyone safer. I know it sucks to get a ticket while you're on your way to the hospital, but it'd be worse to have hit someone or crashed and end up in the hospital yourself.

The instructions are on the ticket; I know you're in a hurry, so I won't go over them right now. Do you have any questions for me? Okay, here's my card with my voicemail number on it if you have any questions later. Please drive safe, and I hope everything works out at the hospital.

Which of the two traffic stops was the better example of policing? As we—and the motorists—assess the two traffic stops, we unconsciously apply the concepts of substantive and procedural justice. We care, of course, about substantive justice; the ultimate resolution of the issue in these two encounters is the issuance of a warning and a ticket, respectively. But we also care, and most people tend to care more, about procedural justice, the nature of the interaction that led to the issuance of the warning or the ticket.[8] Most readers will have concluded that the second traffic stop was "better" than the first: Officer 1 mistreated the motorist before issuing a warning, while Officer 2 treated the motorist fairly even though that traffic stop resulted in a ticket.

The hypothetical traffic stops highlight the distinction between procedural justice and substantive justice, but they do little to explain exactly what people care about when they assess whether an encounter was procedurally just. Although one might fairly presume that people care about the legality of the traffic stops—that is, whether officers actually had the legal authority to initiate the encounter—it turns out that legality either does not matter at all or does not matter very much to most people's assessments. Research by Tracey Meares, Tom Tyler, and Jacob Gardener has found that most people are not cognizant of the legal standards that regulate police behavior and, for that reason, "the actual lawfulness of police action has at best a minor influence on public evaluations of appropriate police behavior."[9] More directly, "[p]eople do not automatically approve of [police stopping someone] just because an officer is legally entitled to [do so]."[10] Instead, their approval or disapproval is based on four key components of procedural justice:

Dignity and Respect. Police encounters are more likely to be viewed as procedurally just when officers treat individuals with dignity and respect. Police officers are professional public servants, and individuals who interact with the police expect officers to behave accordingly.
Voice. Police encounters are more likely to be viewed as procedurally just when the less-powerful individuals in the interaction (e.g., the civilians) have been given the opportunity to participate in the decision-making process by, for example, explaining their actions, perceptions, or reasons for desiring a particular outcome.

Neutrality. Police encounters are more likely to be viewed as procedurally just when officers are perceived to be acting for valid reasons and without bias. In many situations, the perception of neutrality can be bolstered by officers explaining the reasons for their actions.

Motivation. Police encounters are more likely to be viewed as procedurally just when officers are perceived to be acting out of a sincere interest in performing their public duties.[11] As with neutrality, officers can, in most cases, establish the perception of acting with benevolent intentions by explaining the reasons for their actions.

To see why the concept of procedural justice affects the community's assessment of police uses of force, go back to the two hypothetical traffic stops and change the facts slightly: both officers now decide to issue a ticket, but the motorists refuse to sign the tickets (which they are legally obligated to do). Officer 1 angrily places the motorist under arrest and uses force when the motorist refuses to submit to handcuffing. Officer 2 listens to the motorist's objections, patiently explains that refusing to sign the ticket will result in arrest, encourages the motorist to sign the ticket, and offers several opportunities for the motorist to do so. Only afterward does Officer 2 place the motorist under arrest, using force when the motorist refuses to submit to handcuffing. In both cases, the motorist's physical resistance and the officer's use of force are identical.

Looking only at the actions surrounding the attempted arrests, the motorists' resistance, and the officers' uses of force, there is little to distinguish the two traffic stops. However, the public evaluation of the two use-of-force incidents under the community expectations standard is likely to be very different precisely because of Officer 2's exhibition of procedural justice and Officer 1's failure to do so.

The potential for perceptions of procedural (in)justice to affect community members' use-of-force assessments was amply suggested in two studies. The first study found, unsurprisingly, that an officer's use of profanity can negatively affect the perception of the officer, making them appear less professional and unfair.[12] The second study asked two groups of respondents, put in the role of "bystanders" to a use-of-force incident, to evaluate a use of force. One group saw officers use profanity in the context of using force, while the other group saw the same events, but without any profanity. The "bystanders" who heard officers use profanity were substantially more likely to view the use of force as excessive or unjustified.[13] This finding provides some support for the relevance of procedural justice to the evaluation of use-of-force incidents under the community expectations standard.

The Failure to Protect

It is not just police actions that are evaluated under the standard of community expectations, but police *inactions* as well. Community members expect that officers will protect them, to the extent possible, from unnecessary indignity and harm. This expectation is hardly novel; it has been reinforced by police agencies across the country for more than half a century. In 1955, the Los Angeles Police Department solicited officers for suggestions about a motto for the police academy.[14] Officer Joseph S. Dorobek's winning entry—"To Protect and to Serve"—soon became a mantra for police agencies across the country.[15] Versions of that mantra have appeared printed on police vehicles, featured in swearing-in ceremonies, included in agency mission statements, and repeated in articles written by and for officers.[16] It should come as no surprise, then, that community members respond negatively when they perceive officers as failing to live up to that promise.

In the use-of-force context, there are two distinct situations that implicate community expectations related to officers' duties to protect the public: the failure to intervene and the failure to render aid.

The failure to intervene relates to an officer failing to protect an individual from a third party. Officers only rarely have a constitutional obligation to protect individuals from third-party harms,[17] a topic that is outside the scope of this book, but they are certainly subject to public expectations that they will do so. Consider, for example, the events that occurred in Caldwell Woods, a park on the northwest side of Chicago, in June 2018. Mia Irizarry was preparing for a birthday party in the park when Timothy Trybus walked into the gazebo she had reserved. He aggressively questioned Irizarry's citizenship and demanded to know why she was wearing a shirt fashioned after the Puerto Rican flag. Cook County Forest Preserve District Officer Patrick Connor was nearby, and the video of the incident—shot on Irizarry's cell phone—shows him ignoring multiple requests for assistance even as several bystanders took it upon themselves to step between Trybus and Irizarry.[18] Officer Connor was roundly, and properly, criticized for failing to intervene.

While that incident did not involve a use of force, it takes no great imagination to realize that it *could* have and, if it had, that Officer Connor's reluctance to intervene would affect the way members of the public evaluated any resulting use of force. Not stepping in increases the risk of escalation, and officers may put themselves in the position of using more force to address the situation than they would have had to use if they had intervened earlier. More troubling, though, is the risk that the situation will evolve in a way that requires officers to use force against the individual at the receiving end of the harassment. If, for example, the encounter between Trybus and Irizarry had become physical and Officer Connor had used pepper spray on them both, his failure to step in earlier would, in all likelihood, taint the public perception of his use of force.

More directly, the community expects officers who use force to render aid, when necessary, to the very individuals against whom force was used. Public criticism of multiple high-profile police homicides—including Walter Scott,[19] Eric Garner,[20] Tamir Rice,[21] Akai Gurley,[22] and Terrence Crutcher,[23] just to name a few—has focused not just on the use of force, but also on the officers' failures to provide what might have been life-saving aid. Although it may seem counterintuitive, a person's later actions can influence how we perceive and assess their earlier actions. This is known as "hindsight bias."[24] In the use-of-force context, an officer's later failure to render aid may lead a reviewer to conclude that the officer's actions earlier in the encounter displayed a disregard for the subject's life. Such a conclusion has obvious implications for how the public will assess the propriety of the use of force.

How Does the Community Expectations Standard Apply?

The prior section explored how community expectations about fair treatment and the provision of medical aid can, along with expectations about the use of force itself, affect the public evaluation of a use-of-force incident. In this section, we discuss aspects of the evaluation itself. Unfortunately, as important as community expectations are, it can be much more difficult to define and apply the community expectations standard than it is to apply the standards discussed in previous chapters. That is because—unlike the judicial opinions that articulate the constitutional standard; the statutory laws and cases that articulate the state law standard; and the policies, procedures, and training that articulate the administration standard—there is no definitive expression of what community expectations are. It may never be possible to provide a universally satisfying explanation of community expectations because there is no universally satisfying definition of what the relevant "community" is. Within a single city, community members may have wildly different opinions about a specific use-of-force incident, and those differences may reflect variations in neighborhood characteristics, history, socio-economic status, race, age, and other factors. Just as the existence of over 18,000 separate police agencies in the United States[25] makes it a mistake to speak of "the police" as a monolithic entity, the innumerable diversity of the American populace makes it unwise to think of "the public" in the singular, capable of developing a consistent and coherent perspective.

There are, however, some broad commonalities, including identifiable variations in how people of different races view the police. According to a survey conducted by the Pew Research Center in 2016, 75 percent of non-Hispanic white respondents believe that police in their community do an excellent or good job "using the right amount of force for each situation" and "treating racial and ethnic groups equally." When the same questions were asked of non-Hispanic black respondents, however, only 33 percent and 35 percent, respectively, reported that police did an excellent or good job. When asked about officers being held "accountable when misconduct occurred," 70 percent of non-Hispanic white respondents reported that police in their community did an excellent or good job, compared to only 31 percent of non-Hispanic black respondents. These results correspond with overall confidence in the police; 42 percent of non-Hispanic white respondents reported having "a lot" of confidence in the police department in their community, but only 14 percent of non-Hispanic blacks shared that confidence. In contrast, only 18 percent of non-Hispanic white respondents had only a little or no confidence at all in the police, while 44 percent of non-Hispanic black respondents reported having one of those views.[26] While Gallup polls have consistently found that the police, as an institution, tend to generate among the highest reports of confidence—57 percent of the public expressed confidence in policing in 2018, putting it behind only the military, 72 percent, and small businesses, 70 percent—it is clear that community expectations about police uses of force are more complicated than those simple national numbers suggest.

At the risk of oversimplification, we will split our discussion of the community expectations standard into two components: common perspectives critical of the police, which tend to focus on the perceptions, actions, and motivations of officers themselves; and common perspectives that are favorable toward the police, which tend to focus on the characteristics of officers generally, the environment, or the subject's actions. For both critical and favorable perspectives, we identify common threads in public discussions about use-of-force incidents, exploring the various perspectives in some detail.

Importantly, our selection of the topics is based on the frequency with which they appear in public discourse; we do not intend to endorse or reject any of the arguments we discuss. Regardless of whether they criticize or support a use of force, community members often lack a sophisticated or even rudimentary understanding of police tactics or best practices, risk and threat assessment, perceptual distortions that can affect human decision making, the precepts of verbal communication, and so on. In short, community members are often deeply ignorant of some or all of the factors that a fully informed evaluation of any given incident can require. Our discussion of the various critical and complementary perspectives should not be read to suggest that any or all of them will ever or always provide a valid basis for criticism or support in any given case, nor that these perspectives are the only foundations for public criticism of or support for a use of force.

This should not be taken as condemnation, and our discussion of the weaknesses and oversights in the various arguments should not be read to mean that such arguments should be dismissed. Most community members are not, and should not be expected to be, technical experts, but the community expectations standard is no less important for that. It is essential for policy makers, police officials, and students of policing to understand and appreciate how the public evaluates use-of-force incidents, even when that evaluation is flawed. That understanding is necessary to bolster effective communication and facilitate positive police-community relations both leading up to and following a use-of-force incident.

The cases that we refer to—all of them real use-of-force incidents that resulted in significant public attention and criticism—are intended to provide examples of how the various perspectives and criticisms play out in the real world. Our application of the various criticisms to the cases we discuss should not be read to signal that we agree or disagree with any of the perspectives we describe.

Critical Perspectives

Community members have criticized, and will almost certainly continue to criticize, police uses of force, for a number of different reasons.

Here, we discuss three perspectives that are frequently incorporated into the community expectations standard: evaluations based on the underlying governmental interest, evaluations based on the necessity of force, and evaluations based on officer motivation.

EVALUATING FORCE BASED ON THE UNDERLYING
GOVERNMENTAL INTEREST

When evaluating a use of force, it is common for community members to measure the officer's actions against the original justification for the police encounter. Under this approach, the use of force is appropriate when, and only when, it is proportionate to the importance of the governmental interest that gave rise to the initial encounter.

Public criticism based on the importance of the underlying governmental interest commonly plays out in two slightly different ways. First, community members can conflate the original justification for police action with the immediate cause of police violence, treating the two as one and the same for purposes of determining whether force was appropriate. Second, community members can simply weigh the use of force against the underlying justification for the encounter without conflating them. Either way, an officer's use of force during an encounter predicated on a minor infraction may fall short of community expectations precisely because the interaction is the result of a low-level offense.

CONFLATING THE JUSTIFICATIONS FOR THE ENCOUNTER AND THE USE OF FORCE

In July 2014, Eric Garner was detained by officers with the New York Police Department, apparently after he had helped break up a fight, because they suspected him of selling loose cigarettes. Mr. Garner did not comply with officers' attempts to place him under arrest. Officers then used force to take Mr. Garner to the ground; Officer Eric Panteleo put Mr. Garner in a chokehold and partially laid on him as he was handcuffed. Mr. Garner lost consciousness and died. According to a report by the New York City Medical Examiner's Office, Mr. Garner died as a result of "compression of neck (choke hold), compression of chest and prone positioning during physical restraint by police."[27]

The conflation perspective is reflected in public discussion of how the underlying crime was the principal cause of officer's actions and Mr. Garner's death. As a major online media publication stated in a headline, "Eric Garner Was Choked to Death for Selling Loosies."[28] This conflation sets the stage for significant public criticism precisely because of the relatively weak governmental interest in prohibiting the sale of loose cigarettes. Pursuant to NY Tax Law § 1814(b), the possession for sale of unstamped (and thus, untaxed) packages of cigarettes is a crime, but as far as crimes go it is a fairly minor one: a first offense is a misdemeanor. Clearly and inarguably, no misdemeanor should be punished by death.

In practice, community members who adopt the "conflation" perspective may overlook, intentionally or unconsciously, the potential presence of any factors beyond the underlying reasons for the encounter. In the case of Mr. Garner, for example, some community members entirely ignored the relationship between Mr. Garner's actions and the use of force. We do not mean to suggest that the use of force in that case was appropriate, but it nevertheless represents how a conflation approach shifts the terms of the discussion away from whether the officers' reactions were a proportionate response to a subject's behavior.

COMPARING THE JUSTIFICATIONS FOR THE ENCOUNTER AND THE USE
OF FORCE

The second perspective provides a more nuanced basis for public criticism: it does not ignore additional factors, but it contends that the government's interest in enforcing low-level infractions is simply too weak for any additional factors to make a difference. Put differently, the interest in personal autonomy and freedom from government interference outweighs the government's interest in enforcing low-level offenses. To return to the tragic case of Eric Garner, the fact that Mr. Garner's resistance frustrated the officers' attempt to arrest him did not justify the use of force because the governmental interest in enforcing such a low-level infraction (selling loose cigarettes) outweighed by the strong interest in preserving Mr. Garner's life.

This perspective raises questions about the actions that police can take to enforce minor offenses; would they be permitted to make arrests that do not require the use of force or prohibited from making arrests in the first place? Some commentators have argued—erroneously, in our view—that the government has no interest in using force to effect a seizure of an individual suspected of committing only a minor crime. Yale Law School professors Ian Ayres and Daniel Markovits have argued that

> [a] police officer confronting someone suspected of only a minor crime should not be permitted to arrest the suspect by force. In most cases, the police should simply issue a ticket. If the police wish to take someone into custody, they should not use force but instead issue a warning, like the *Miranda* warning, backed by a sanction. The text might say something like: "I am placing you under arrest. You must come with me to the station. If you don't come, you're committing a separate crime, for which you may be punished." If the person complies upon hearing the warning, that ends the matter. If not, then the police can obtain a warrant from a judge and make a forcible arrest for both the old crime and the new. Similar rules of engagement should govern searches based on suspicion of petty crimes.

It is not clear that Ayers and Markovits' proposed solution actually addresses the perceived problem. Specifically, it is not clear why the governmental interest in making the arrest would be any stronger after officers obtain a warrant (which would allow them to make a forcible arrest) than it was beforehand (when a forcible arrest would not be permitted), and thus why it would afford officers any additional leeway to use force.

University of Virginia law professor Rachel Harmon has suggested that there may be some merit to the second approach—prohibiting officers from making arrest for minor offenses altogether—by calling into question the underlying justifications for custodial arrests, particularly for minor violations.[29] This approach would address public concerns about the weakness of the underlying governmental interest: if officers could not make arrests for low-level infractions, there would be no civilian resistance and thus no justification for using force.

Differences in Assertive and Defensive Force

It is worth noting that both approaches to this argument—the conflation approach and the comparison approach—are most clearly applicable when officers use force assertively, and potentially inapplicable in the context of defensive force. As we have discussed, assertive force refers to actions taken against a subject who is resisting, but whose resistance does not threaten the physical safety of the officer or others; typically, officers use force assertively when they respond to a subject's nonviolent resistance or refusal to comply. The use of force against Eric Garner is a textbook example of assertive force.

Defensive force, in contrast, refers to actions taken against a subject who has initiated violence by physically threatening the officer or others. It is far less common for community members to weigh an officer's use of defensive force against the original justification for the encounter than it is in the context of assertive force. This is almost certainly because the intervening events—namely, the threat posed by the subject—is both salient and too significant to ignore. For example, it seems fair to say that few community members would criticize the police for using force, even deadly force, against an individual who, upon being stopped for a low-level infraction, drew a firearm and began shooting at officers.

EVALUATING THE NECESSITY OF FORCE

When community members evaluate a use of force, they also question whether it was necessary. In this context, the concept of "necessity" is deceptively multi-faceted. We believe it can be broken into three distinct types of criticism based on, respectively, perfect information, force avoidance, and force minimization. We discuss each of those components, and their various constituents, in turn.

Criticisms Based on Perfect Information. When evaluating use-of-force incidents, one critical threshold issue involves identifying which facts reviewers should take into account for the purpose of analysis. As discussed in prior chapters, the constitutional law standard, the state law standard, and the administrative standard generally adopt some variant of the perspective of the reasonable officer on the scene. Under those standards, reviewers take into account those facts which a reasonable officer would have been aware of at the time. Community members, however, can look at use-of-force incidents through a different lens, one that takes into account *all* of the information about the incident, including information that no officer on the scene could have been aware of, such as information that developed after the use of force itself. In practice, this leads to criticisms based on perfect information about the situation, or at least more and better information than that which was available to the "reasonable officer on the scene."

Consider, for example, the tragic shooting of Tamir Rice in Cleveland, Ohio, in 2014.[30] A complainant called the police to report an incident in a park, saying, in relevant part:

> [A] guy holding a pistol, you know. It's probably fake, but he's like pointing it at everybody. . . . The guy keeps pulling it in and out of his pants. It's probably fake, but you know what, he's scaring the shit out of people. . . . He has a camouflage hat on . . . he has a grey, grey coat with black sleeves and grey pants. . . . He's black. . . . He's sitting on the swing right now. See, he's pulling it in and out of his pants. And pointing it at people. He's probably a juvenile, you know. . . . He's right here by the, by the youth center or whatever and he's pulling it in and out of his pants. I don't know whether it's real or not.[31]

Tamir Rice was, as the complainant suspected, a juvenile; he was only twelve years old. And the pistol he had was, in fact, a toy gun; it resembled a real firearm but had a neon orange tip. The responding officers were not aware of either fact: the dispatcher who gave them information about the call did not mention the complainant's suspicions that the gun was "probably a fake" or that the subject was "probably a juvenile." As far as the officers were aware, the caller was reporting a grown man threatening people with a firearm. Within two seconds of Officers Frank Garmback and Timothy Loehmann arriving on scene, Officer Loehmann fatally shot Tamir Rice.

Given the dispatcher's failure to provide salient information to the officers, their perception of Tamir Rice's age and the nature of the "weapon" were arguably reasonable, if erroneous. Through the lens of perfect information, however, what matters is whether the situation as it actually existed justified the use of force. Tamir Rice was a boy with a toy gun, a situation that clearly does not justify the use of deadly force.

The same criticism—that the use of force was inappropriate because a subject perceived as armed was not actually armed—is a common refrain in public discourse about other high-profile shootings as well, from Amadou Diallo to Stephon Clark and beyond. Although an academic study concluded that media framing in the immediate aftermath of a critical incident tends to reflect the "official police narrative,"[32] it is worth pointing out that media reports—such as an ABC News headline that reads: "Video of Police Shooting Boy Holding Toy Gun Is Released"[33]—can also reflect and reinforce the evaluation of use-of-force incidents through a lens of perfect information.

Criticisms of Avoidable Force. Use-of-force incidents can also arouse community criticism when the conflict or the use of force itself is perceived as avoidable, particularly in the context of deadly force. A use of force may be viewed as avoidable if community members perceive that it was possible for officers to prevent the subject from presenting a threat, to resolve ambiguous situations by gathering additional information before using force, or to address an existing threat without the use of force. In all three contexts, the underlying criticism is that officers were simply too quick to use force.

First, force is avoidable when it could have been prevented. The public generally understands that the nature of policing occasionally requires the use of force. However, the public also expects that police agencies will seek to minimize the use of force by hiring good officers and that individual officers will not put themselves in harm's way when it is professionally irresponsible to do so.

With regard to agency hiring practices, there has been significant public criticism of use-of-force incidents—particularly questionable use-of-force incidents—involving officers who, arguably, should never have been employed as officers at the time. To return to the shooting of Tamir Rice, for example, the Cleveland Police Department was criticized for hiring Officer Timothy Loehmann in light of his history of poor performance at both the Cleveland Heights Police Academy and at a previous job at the Independence Police Department. Written reviews of Officer Loehmann's performance indicate that, among other things, he had twice gotten "distracted" and "weepy" during firearms training, that he "could not follow simple directions," and that he did not "show[] the maturity needed to work in" policing. A supervisor with the Independence Police Department recommended that the agency terminate Officer Loehmann, writing, "I do not believe time, nor training, will be able to change or correct the deficiencies."[34] In the aftermath of the shooting of Tamir Rice, the public criticism of the Cleveland Police Department was grounded in part on the perception that Officer Loehmann's deficiencies contributed to the shooting and that the shooting could have been avoided if the agency had employed a qualified officer.

The public also condemns individual officers for using force when the threat to officers is perceived as avoidable. When, for example, officers unreasonably create or exacerbate a danger to themselves or others—implicating the concept of "officer-created jeopardy"—the use of force to address the threat that results from the officer's actions is likely to be subject to public criticism. We discuss officer-created jeopardy in more detail in chapter 5; for our purposes here, it is sufficient to illustrate this concept by returning again to the Tamir Rice shooting.

Security video of the incident shows that after the officers were provided information by dispatch, Officer Garmback drove the police vehicle into the park and onto the grass near the gazebo where Tamir Rice was sitting, coming to a stop with the front passenger door less than ten feet away. Officer Loehmann, who was sitting in the front passenger seat, exited the car as it was coming to a stop and, within two seconds, fatally shot Tamir Rice.[35] One justification offered for the shooting was the imminent threat that Officer Loehmann faced upon exiting the vehicle in such close physical proximity to a man who had reportedly been pointing a gun at bystanders. This justification, and the shooting itself, was criticized on the grounds that Officer Garmback should have parked the vehicle some distance away and the officers should have taken advantage of cover and concealment to communicate with Tamir Rice from a (relatively) safe distance. Officer Garmback's approach, which was contrary to longstanding and well-known tactical norms, needlessly thrust Officer Loehmann (and himself) into that dangerous position; adopting a different approach, one that minimized rather than exacerbated the threat to the officers, may have prevented the shooting entirely.

In short, public criticism can be predicated on the perception that agencies or officers unnecessarily and unreasonably created the circumstances that gave rise to the use of force.

Second, force may be viewed as avoidable in ambiguous situations. Another aspect of public criticism relates to the perception that officers are too quick to perceive a threat or to use force in ambiguous situations. Phrased differently, the criticism asserts that officers are inappropriately jumping to the application of force rather than taking the time to properly assess the situation. This criticism is often asserted after officers shoot someone whom they believed had a weapon when, in fact, the subject had an entirely innocuous item or nothing at all.

There are multiple examples of use-of-force incidents that have aroused criticisms on these grounds—the shootings of Stephon Clark, Terence Crutcher,

John Crawford, and Charles Kinsey are just a few of the available examples—but perhaps the clearest example is the 2014 shooting of Levar Jones by South Carolina Highway Patrol Trooper Sean Groubert. Trooper Groubert pulled behind Mr. Jones' vehicle in the parking lot of a gas station after apparently observing a seatbelt violation, but by the time the trooper initiated the stop, Mr. Jones had already exited his vehicle. As Trooper Groubert approached Mr. Jones, he asked Mr. Jones for his driver's license; video from the in-car camera system shows Mr. Jones patting his back pocket, then reaching into his vehicle. Believing that Mr. Jones was reaching for a weapon, Trooper Groubert fired four shots, striking Mr. Jones once in the hip.[36] The trooper was criticized for his perception that Mr. Jones, who was doing exactly what he had been asked to do, presented a threat and for his decision to use deadly force to address that threat rather than take the time to properly assess Mr. Jones' actions.

While most community members accept the idea that taking the time to gather additional information leaves the officer exposed to the risk of harm if the subject *does* have a weapon, this perspective is often grounded in a belief about the appropriate allocation of risk. Specifically, the foundational belief is that officers are paid public servants who are armed, equipped, and expected to know that their jobs require them to accept a certain level of personal risk and that it is professionally inappropriate for officers to shift that risk to community members by using force in ambiguous situations.

Third, force may be viewed as avoidable when there were nonviolent alternatives. In some circumstances, the public may accept that a subject is unambiguously resisting and that the situation is one that officers could not have prevented. In such a situation, the use of force may still be subject to criticism if community members perceive that officers could have attempted to resolve the situation without resorting to physical force. It is this criticism that has given rise to many of the public demands for officers to receive mandatory de-escalation training and for agencies and supervisors to require officers to attempt to de-escalate situations prior to using force.

Criticisms of Excessive Force. When community members accept that force was both justified and unavoidable, the perception that officers used more force than necessary can give rise to significant public criticism. In other words, even when there is broad agreement that officers need to use force, community members expect them to use no more force than the situation is believed to require. As with the criticisms of avoidable force, this perspective has at least two aspects: one that focuses on police agencies and one that focuses on individual officers.

Police agencies may be subject to public criticism for failing to provide officers with the training or equipment that they need to minimize the severity of force in various situations. This criticism is particularly common when officers who use lethal force did not have ready access to less-lethal options that could have addressed the situation. In 2015, for example, almost a dozen San Francisco Police Department officers responded to a reported stabbing and encountered Mario Woods, who was holding a knife. Mr. Woods was standing next to a wall, so officers formed a semicircular perimeter around him. Officers gave verbal commands and used both pepper spray and less-lethal projectiles, to no avail. As Mr. Woods moved along the wall, he came to within about ten feet of one of the officers; multiple officers opened fire, fatally wounding him. In the aftermath of the shooting, the agency was criticized for failing to equip officers with TASERs, which could have allowed officers to incapacitate Mr. Woods and take him into custody instead of using lethal force.

Individual officers, similarly, are subjected to criticism when community members perceive that they used more force than the situation demanded. There is significant variability in how such criticisms are presented. Some are based on perceptions about police training or officers' abilities; for example, officers, who are trained to aim primarily at the chest because it offers the most reliable target, may be criticized for not shooting someone in the arm or leg.[37] Some are based on perceptions about the respective size and physical ability of officers and the subjects; for example, community members may accept that an officer has to physically control or take into custody a middle school girl, but criticize the officer's decision to use a forcible takedown to do so. San Antonio Independent School District Officer Joshua Kehm, for example, was criticized (and ultimately terminated) for "body-slamming" a 12-year-old girl. The Superintendent released a statement that perfectly encapsulated the criticism of excessive force, saying, "We understand that situations can sometimes escalate to the point of requiring a physical response; however, in this situation we believe that the extent of the response was absolutely unwarranted."[38]

EVALUATING OFFICER MOTIVATION

Community members also evaluate use-of-force incidents by weighing officer's motivations or, perhaps more accurately, the motivations that officers are perceived or presumed to have. An otherwise acceptable use of force can result in outrage if officers are believed to have instigated the encounter or initiated the use of force for unacceptable reasons. As we discussed earlier in this chapter in the context of procedural justice, community members care deeply about the perception that officers are acting without bias and out of the sincere desire to perform their public duties. Criticisms of use-of-force incidents based on officer motivations are commonly grounded in perceptions or presumptions about an officer's reactions to the personal characteristics of the subject (race, ethnicity, gender expression, age, sexual orientation, or social status, to name the most obvious examples) or on whether the officer is properly wielding public authority.

Criticisms relating to the personal characteristics of the subject are rooted in perceptions of disparate treatment. When officers are believed to use more force, or use force more often, against young men of color than they would in situations that are identical apart from the race of the subject, then what might otherwise have been an unremarkable use of force becomes a focal point for public criticism. The perception that race, or some other personal factor, played a role in any given incident may be driven by public knowledge of other, similar cases rather than anything inherent in the incident being evaluated. In a 1997 study of college students, for example, participants watched a grainy video that depicted two police officers making an arrest.[39] The study participants could tell that the subject was black, and they could identify the officers by race, but the quality of the recording was too poor to provide other details.[40] On the video, the subject was shown offering a low level of resistance, and the officers responded with a moderate amount of force. The study participants were then asked "to estimate the degree of violence and illegality (i.e., brutality) employed by police in the arrest they had viewed."[41] Though the participants did not know it, the arrest was staged; one set of participants saw a video of two black officers, another set saw two white officers, and a third set saw one black officer and one white officer.[42] Although the officers' actions were identical in the three videos, participants reported "significantly greater violence and illegality" when the arresting officers were both white than when one or both of the arresting officers were black.[43] This study demonstrates that at least some audiences' evaluations of a use-of-force incident may depend on *who* does the policing and *who* is being policed.

There is, unfortunately, no shortage of evidence that the perception of disparate treatment is well founded. Consider that, if officers used force equally, roughly the same percentage of people should report being subjected to police uses of force within each race or ethnicity. That is not the case. According to survey data collected by the Bureau of Justice Statistics, only 1.3 percent of white respondents reported being subjected to a use of force, compared to 3.4 percent of black respondents. Such survey data should not be taken as definitive, but it does reinforce the fact that there is at least a disproportionate perception that officers have used force.

Further, non-survey data reinforces the evidence that officers do not use force proportionate to population. According to the US Census Bureau, approximately 13.4 percent of the population identifies as black and 76.6 percent of the population identifies as white. If the use of force were proportionate to population, about 13.4 percent of uses of force would be against black subjects and about 76.6 percent would be against white subjects. That is not the case. According to data maintained by the FBI as well as data collected by aggregating and coding media reports about fatal police shootings, more than 30 percent of individuals killed by police have been black.[44]

We would be remiss if we did not point out that it is, in all likelihood, a mistake to evaluate proportionality based solely on representation within the greater population. The belief that police uses of force should be proportionate to various groups' representation in the population assumes that everyone in the population has a roughly equal chance of being involved in a police encounter, including the types of encounters in which force is most likely (e.g., arrests). That assumption, while common, rests on a flawed premise. Young men, particularly young black men, are significantly more likely to come into contact with the police, especially in the law enforcement context. There are multiple reasons for this, the majority of which are systemic rather than individual. They include the relationship between youth and risk-taking behavior and the correlations between race and urban poverty and between urban poverty and crime, not to mention our country's long, often distressing history of race-conscious and, at times, explicitly racist public policy choices relating to education, housing, land use, economics, and criminal justice. We do not mean to dismiss or downplay the importance of the underlying reasons by emphasizing that what matters for purposes of identifying racial disproportionality in police uses of force is one's relative likelihood of interacting with an officer, rather than one's representation in the country's population.

Reliable analysis of police uses of force in society, then, requires recognizing and controlling for differences beyond the prevalence of races or ethnicities in the population. Unfortunately, there is no universally accepted way to take those differences into account: the various studies that have done so have taken different approaches, and no one approach is without its advantages and limitations. Regardless of the variation, the majority of the studies have found that officers *do* use force, or certain types of force, against people of color at a disproportionate rate.

Of course, the question of whether there is a racial disparity in how force is used is distinct from the question of whether community members *believe* that such a racial disparity exists. For purposes of the community expectations standard, it is the perception of disparity, not the actual existence or the exact quantification of any disparity, that matters. When the public evaluates a use of force under the community expectations standard, what matters is whether or not there is a public perception that an officer treated a subject differently at some or multiple points during an encounter, and ultimately used force, because of the subject's personal characteristics.

Criticisms related to the officer's use of public authority, in contrast, tend to be based not on other, similar cases, but rather on an officer's behavior in the incident under evaluation. The community expectations standard can find fault with an officer for being unnecessarily or inappropriately aggressive or assertive. To put it simply, the perception that an officer is being a bully can lead community members to criticize the use of force even in the face of actual resistance. In 2015, for example, Orlando Police Department Officer James Wilson approached Terre Johnson, who was sitting on a curb with his legs in the street. During the ensuing interaction, an internal investigation found, Officer Wilson "repeatedly used insolent language in a mocking manner toward Mr. Johnson."[45] A video of the incident shows Mr. Johnson ultimately attempting to walk away, prompting Officer Wilson to use force to take him into custody. Although the officer's use of force was in response to the subject's resistance, community members evaluating the incident may well see Officer Wilson's use of force as a continuation of his deeply disrespectful treatment of Mr. Johnson. Under that perception, Officer Wilson was not using force because he was sincerely engaged in law enforcement activity; instead, he used his law enforcement authority to verbally bully a civilian, and that bullying transitioned into physical abuse.

An officer need not be verbally abusive for their motivations to affect the evaluation of a use of force under the community expectations standard. Perhaps the clearest example comes from Texas, where State Trooper Brian Encinia stopped a vehicle driven by Sandra Bland for changing lanes without signaling. Once he re-approached the vehicle—to deliver what was later determined to be a warning ticket—Trooper Encinia asked Ms. Bland if she was okay, saying that she "seem[ed] very irritated." She explained that she was; she had changed lanes (without signaling) only to move out of the way of Trooper Encinia's vehicle, which had been accelerating behind her. Trooper Encinia paused for several seconds before asking dismissively, "Are you done?" The trooper then asked Ms. Bland to put out her cigarette. She questioned this request, saying, "Why do I have to put out my cigarette? I'm sitting in my car." Trooper Encinia then put his pen back in his pocket, placed his ticket book on Ms. Bland's car, and commanded Ms. Bland to get out of the car. Ms. Bland refused, leading Trooper Encinia to threaten and ultimately use force to extract her from the vehicle and take her into custody. Video of the interaction, taken by Trooper Encinia's in-car camera system, strongly suggests that the trooper had been prepared to issue a warning ticket while Ms. Bland was seated in her car, but changed his approach when she challenged his request to put out her cigarette.[46] The public evaluation of the ultimate use of force, then, was heavily affected by the perception that Trooper Encinia was not motivated by his desire to enforce the law, but rather was using his authority (to enforce the law) as an excuse to exercise his dominance over a civilian.

Favorable Perspectives

The previous section discussed three different, but common, perspectives that affect the critical evaluation of use-of-force incidents under the community expectations standard: evaluations based on the underlying governmental interest, evaluations based on the necessity of force, and evaluations based on officer motivation. Not all community members criticize police for use-of-force incidents. Many, in fact, tend to evaluate police uses of force through a favorable lens, one as rooted in trust of the police as the critical perspectives can be rooted in distrust of the police. In this section, we turn to common perspectives that affect the favorable evaluation of use-of-force incidents. We discuss two such perspectives: one that focuses on an officer's "split-second" decision making and one that focuses on a subject's noncompliance.

EVALUATING FORCE AS THE PRODUCT OF THE SUBJECT'S RESISTANCE

Community members who take a more favorable view of the police can focus on a subject's resistance, asserting that the use of force is justified *because* the subject was resisting. Under this perspective, the subject could avoid having force used against them by doing what the officer is telling them to do. As an anonymous police officer posted in relation to a story about the death of Eric Garner (discussed at greater length above):

> It's sad that he died, but that blame goes to he and he alone. The police generally don't show up ten deep at your door just to say hey. This pervasive mentality that these assholes seem to have about not listening to the lawful orders of the police is what leads to these deaths and injuries. All he had to do was comply and he would not be dead. Tough shit and too damn bad.[47]

Another officer expressed a similar sentiment more eloquently in a *Washington Post* opinion piece:

> Even though it might sound harsh and impolitic, here is the bottom line: if you don't want to get shot, tased, pepper-sprayed, struck with a baton or thrown to the ground, just do what I tell you. Don't argue with me, don't call me names, don't tell me that I can't stop you, don't say I'm a racist pig, don't threaten that you'll sue me and take away my badge. Don't scream at me that you pay my salary, and don't even think of aggressively walking towards me.[48]

There is some truth to this perspective; most of the controversial use-of-force incidents that provoke public controversy would have been avoided had the subject complied. There are, however, notable exceptions. Levar Jones, for example, was shot during a traffic stop while reaching into his car to retrieve the license an officer had just asked him for, and video of the John Crawford shooting suggests that he may not have ever realized officers were there. As those examples demonstrate, not all subjects can be faulted for failing to comply with, or for resisting, officers' commands.

In many cases, perhaps even most cases, however, it is likely correct to say that the subject's resistance was a "but for" cause of the officer's use of force. That is, the use of force would not have occurred had the subject complied. By focusing exclusively on the subject's resistance, though, this perspective tends to approach the evaluation of use-of-force incidents as a binary determination: either force was used to overcome resistance or it was not. That determination is a component of competent use-of-force analysis, of course, but it fails to address another critical issue: whether the officer's use of force was appropriate to the situation. In short, this perspective relies solely on the answer to one question—"Was the subject resisting such that the officer needed to use some amount of force?"—without considering the relevance of the follow-up question: "If so, was the officer's use of force proportionate to the subject's resistance?"

Evaluating the use of force solely as the product of resistance suffers from the same shortcomings as the critical perspective that conflates the use of force with the underlying justification for the stop: both approaches focus exclusively on one component of the interaction (the presence of resistance and the reason for the encounter, respectively) and overlook the presence of additional information that, when properly considered, could affect the evaluation of use-of-force incidents.

EVALUATING FORCE AS THE PRODUCT OF A HIGHLY
DANGEROUS ENVIRONMENT

Community members who take a favorable perspective can also be highly deferential to officers because they view the use of force as a product of the highly dangerous environment in which officers operate. This perspective can both take the officer's subjective perceptions at face value and focus on factors that are indicative of threat, while minimizing or ignoring other interpretations. In that way, this approach to evaluation is similar to the critical perspective that views use-of-force incidents through the lens of perfect information, except that the favorable perspective focuses on the facts that can be interpreted to indicate that the officers are in danger instead of the facts that can be interpreted to indicate that the officers are *not* in danger the way the critical perspective does.

This approach is reflected in how some community members evaluated the actions of McKinney Police Department Corporal Eric Casebolt, who responded to a scene involving a large group of kids at a pool party. Cell phone video of that incident shows Corporal Casebolt harshly ordering several kids to the ground, using a painful joint manipulation on one subject, and pointing a large flashlight at others. During the interaction, Corporal Casebolt sought to take 15-year-old Dejerria Becton into custody. When he did so, a group of bystanders approached to angrily protest the officer's actions, including two young men, leading Corporal Casebolt to unholster his firearm. Corporal Casebolt's actions were widely criticized, including by one of the authors of this book.[49]

Some commentators approved of the way Corporal Casebolt handled the situation, focusing primarily on the potential danger he faced. As one author wrote for *PoliceOne*, an internet-based publication intended primarily for a police audience:

> When the officer arrived on scene, it was one against many. Even when backup arrived, the angry crowd outnumbered the responders trying to restore order to the suburban scene. What's more important—and what has been ignored wholesale in the mainstream coverage of this incident—are the actions of those two young men in the video, and how those actions can be perceived by the officer on the street.
>
> An officer (or a number of them) engaged with a subject on the ground is highly vulnerable to an unprovoked attack by a third party. In that position, the officer occupies a position of disadvantage in comparison to an oncoming ambush attacker (or, in this case, a number of them). . . .

As [the two young men] quickly closed in on the officer, they made themselves appear bigger by taking up more space in the officer's field of view. They did this by both closing distance as well as spreading their arms and legs apart—classic indicators of threatening intent. . . .

If all that wasn't enough, one of the young men appeared to be reaching into his waistband with his left hand. The split-second decision the officer made may have been out of policy by the judgement of the administration, but it was understandable to anyone who has studied human factors in rapidly unfolding, high-stress encounters.[50]

The favorable perspective focuses heavily on the officers being outnumbered and on the one young man who "can clearly be seen in the video reaching toward his waistband,"[51] concluding that Corporal Casebolt either was in a highly dangerous situation or that it was entirely reasonable for him to *perceive* that he was, even if that perception was ultimately mistaken. Under this perspective, the decision to deploy the firearm was appropriate because it—the decision itself—was the product of a highly dangerous environment.

The problem with this perspective is obvious: the presumption that every environment in which officers operate is a highly dangerous one is factually questionable and exists as a perpetual justification for actions that would otherwise be properly considered misconduct. In the context of the McKinney pool party, for example, the commentator either plays down or overlooks the fact that the "angry crowd" was comprised primary of teenagers who were largely following the various officers' instructions. The two young men who approached Corporal Casebolt were wearing swim trunks and carrying towels. At that point, Corporal Casebolt abandoned his attempt to take Dejerria Becton into custody and approached the two young men, who began backing away. Approximately two seconds after the young men had begun backing away, Corporal Casebolt unholstered his firearm.[52] While teenagers wearing bathing suits certainly *can* present a threat, the circumstances of this particular case do not support the presumption that the operational environment was highly dangerous at the time. Generic presumptions of danger are of dubious value when assessing an officer's use of force; reviewers should instead seek to identify risks and threats of particular harms.

Conclusion

In this chapter, we described the community expectations standard, explaining first why it is important for policy makers, police officials, and students of policing to understand and appreciate how community members evaluate use-of-force incidents. We then described the various officer behaviors that are subject to evaluation under this standard, including both the use of force itself and proximate behaviors—those actions that do not themselves involve the use of force, but which affect how community members evaluate the use of force in a given situation. The bulk of the chapter was dedicated to an overview of how use-of-force incidents are evaluated under the community expectations standard, discussing two sets of common perspectives: those that are critical of the police and those that are favorable toward the police. As this chapter made clear, the community expectations standard is significantly less formal and more susceptible to widely varying interpretations than are the constitutional, state law, or administrative policy standards. It is, however, significantly more potent; when community members protest a police use of force, or riot in the aftermath of an officer's acquittal, or demand legal reform through the political system, they do so because an officer failed to live up to the standard of behavior that the community expects officers to meet. While the significant variation in what exactly community members expect from the police makes the standard difficult to define with any precision, the importance of community expectations in shaping public debates about the use of force generally, or of any use-of-force incident specifically, means that scholars, police leaders, and elected officials and other policy makers should be attuned to this important evaluative standard.

PART II

Police Tactics and Force Options

In part I, we laid the groundwork for the evaluation of police uses of force by discussing four distinct standards that can be applied to any given incident: constitutional law, state law, administrative policy and procedure, and community expectations. Reliably evaluating a use-of-force incident, however, requires more than familiarity with or even expertise in the standards themselves. Applying the analytical frameworks also requires a sophisticated understanding of the fundamental principles and concepts that can be implicated in use-of-force situations. Without a thorough understanding of what the various options are and when each may be reasonably employed, though, what ought to be an informed, methodical determination is doomed to be little more than ad hoc guesswork, idiosyncratic conclusions draped in a mantle of misplaced confidence. Reviewers cannot assess whether the officer approached the scene appropriately, in a way that was likely to minimize the need to use force, without understanding police tactics. They cannot evaluate the application of a particular force option, or determine whether other options were reasonable alternatives under the circumstances, without understanding how officers use force.

We address these essential issues in part II. This part provides a thorough grounding in those fundamental concepts. In chapter 5, we discuss police tactics; the decisions and actions that officers take leading up to the use of force, which often contribute to whether and how force is used. In chapter 6, we explore a variety of force options, discussing the most common, and many of the less common, tools, techniques, and weaponry that officers are trained in or to which they have access. These chapters, and the concepts discussed therein, are indelibly intertwined with the evaluative frameworks discussed in part I; reviewers cannot begin to apply one of the evaluative frameworks in the absence of information about police practices, nor can they apply that information, in and of itself, to assess a use of force in the absence of an evaluative framework.

5

Tactical Considerations[1]

Officers do not use force in a vacuum. Any given use of force is the result of an iterative process, an interaction or, more often, a series of interactions between an officer and a subject. For decades, scholars of policing have recognized that the use of force is not the result of a single decision, but rather the result of, as criminologists Arnold Binder and Peter Scharf have described it, "a contingent sequence of decisions and resulting behaviors—each increasing or decreasing the probability of an eventual use of . . . force."[2] Very often, evaluating a use of force requires assessing what happened in the seconds or minutes before the moment when the officer swung the baton or pulled the trigger, the effect that the officer's decisions and behaviors had on the probability that force would be used as well as on the ultimate severity of any force used. In this chapter, we discuss such decisions and behaviors through the framework of police tactics.

The Merriam-Webster dictionary defines "tactics" as "the art or skill of employing available means to accomplish an end."[3] In policing, the "ends" are the strategic goals that agencies and officers work toward, while "tactics" refers to the tools and techniques that agencies and officers employ to advance those goals.

Police leaders and rank-and-file officers must balance multiple strategic goals that can be in tension with each other. For example, crime reduction and building or maintaining public trust are two distinct strategic goals, and the tactics that could advance one of those goals may undermine the other, at least to some extent. It is beyond the scope of this book to address all of the many strategic goals that police agencies may have. Indeed, even in the limited context of police interactions involving a use of force, multiple strategic goals may run uncomfortably into each other: the goal of accomplishing the police mission, for example, may be in tension with the goals of respecting individual rights, building or maintaining public trust, and protecting community members from indignity and harm.

Most of the time, there are few, if any, obstacles to the government's interest in achieving the desired end. In the vast majority of police interactions, individuals comply with officers in every meaningful respect. However, the nature of policing is such that officers work in environments and around people who can, and regularly if infrequently *do*, present risks and threats[4] to one or more of the governmental interests discussed in chapter 1: law enforcement, public safety and order maintenance, and officer safety.

Tactics are the techniques and procedures that officers use to protect themselves and community members by reducing risks, mitigating the likelihood that risks will become threats, and preventing threats from manifesting into harms. In the police use-of-force context, tactics may be defined as "a sequence of moves that limit the suspect's ability to inflict harm and [that] advance the ability of the officer to conclude the situation in the safest and least intrusive way."[5]

In many cases, the safety of the officer and the subject alike are path-dependent on police tactics. An officer who successfully manages potential threats early in an encounter is less likely to be physically threatened—and thus less susceptible to harm—later in the encounter. In the same vein, the officer is also less likely to perceive any need to use force to address a threat of harm, which increases the *subject's* physical safety. The opposite is also true; an officer's poor tactics can expose them to an otherwise avoidable threat, which increases the likelihood that they will use force to address that threat.

In short, reviewers cannot determine whether officers minimized the potential need to use physical force, or whether officers had reasonable alternatives to physical force, without considering relevant tactical concepts. In this chapter, we first provide a conceptual framework for analyzing tactics, then offer an in-depth discussion of tactical concepts. We conclude by exploring three situations that call for very different tactical approaches: custodial arrests, crisis intervention response, and active shooters.

A Conceptual Framework for Analyzing Tactics and "Officer-Created Jeopardy"

In the early 1980s, Binder and Scharf posited that every lethal-force situation—which we suggest can be extended to any use-of-force situation regardless of the severity of force—involves four distinct phases: *anticipation*, *entry*, *information exchange*, and *final frame decision*.[6] The phases are sequential; each depends and builds on the phase preceding it.

The initial phase, "anticipation," begins when officers realize that they will be or are likely to be interacting with a civilian in the near future. At this point, officers gather information about the location, the individuals they may be interacting with, the context of the interaction, and so on. This information can come from their own observations or from other officers, dispatchers, or civilians. During this phase, officers filter the information they receive; their decisions are likely to be influenced by the source of the information and by how credible they believe the information to be. When time permits, officers can consult with each other or otherwise create a general plan of how to respond when they begin the interaction itself. This first phase continues until officers arrive on scene.

As officers arrive on scene, the "entry" phase of the encounter begins. In this phase, officers must make decisions about how to approach the subject or other civilians. Obviously, if an emergency exists, the options are limited. As officers assess the scene, they can confirm and consider or disregard the information they received during the anticipation phase.

Once the officer makes contact with a civilian, they engage in the "information exchange" phase, in which the officer and civilian continue to gather information about each other from verbal and nonverbal cues, and react according to their perception of those cues. In some circumstances, such as when the officer must react immediately to the situation, the officers will skip this phase altogether. In other circumstances, this phase will last for hours. Typically, this is the most critical phase of the encounter; the officers' decisions and actions during the "information exchange" phase heavily influence the ultimate use-of-force decision.[7]

At some point, the officer will make a decision about whether to use force, which type of force to use, and how to deploy it. When that happens, the use of force has entered the "final frame" phase of the interaction.[8]

Other policing scholars have characterized use-of-force situations in different ways, simplifying[9] or expanding[10] on Binder and Scharf's four-phase approach. One aspect has remained remarkably consistent: the observation that an officer's ultimate use-of-force decision is affected by decisions and actions that occur well before the use of force itself, including the decisions that officers make and the actions they take to manage the risks and threats of any given situation.

As officers manage those risks and threats, they may expose themselves to potential harm, increasing the likelihood that they will use force to address the threat of harm. At times, this exposure can be warranted under the circumstances. On other occasions, however, an officer's decision to affirmatively create or passively accept a particular threat is unjustified in light of the availability of other tactical options that would avoid or minimize the threat. "Officer-created jeopardy" refers to situations in which officers affirmatively create or passively accept unjustifiable risks or threats that could have, and should have, been avoided.

As that definition suggests, culpability is inherent in the concept of officer-created jeopardy. There are many situations in which officers create or accept a certain degree of risk or threat, but that do not constitute officer-created jeopardy because the officers' actions are justified under the circumstances. The oft-used phrase that "officers run toward the sound of gunfire," for example, reminds us that officers may well be called upon to put themselves in harm's way and that their doing so is not inherently problematic.[11] Indeed, it reminds us that officers are professionally, if not legally, required to accept, even create, certain risks and threats in the course of their work. For example, former Broward County Deputy Scot Peterson, a school resource officer at Marjory Stoneman Douglas High School in Parkland, Florida, was roundly criticized for standing outside the school while an active shooter killed seventeen people inside. There is no doubt that entering the school and confronting the gunman would have exposed then-Deputy Peterson to the threat of being shot and killed, a threat from which he was insulated while waiting outside. However, the circumstances were such that then-Deputy Peterson should have entered the school, meaning that doing so would not have constituted officer-created jeopardy.

Officer-created jeopardy is, in essence, a manner of describing unjustified risk-taking that can result in an officer using force to protect themselves from a threat that they were, in part, responsible for creating. Consider one unfortunately common example: officers who step in front of vehicles. In the late 1990s, Officer Kimberly Raso was working in an off-duty security capacity for a local mall when she attempted to arrest Robert Abraham for shoplifting. She followed Abraham as he left the mall and got into his vehicle. As Officer Raso commanded him to stop, Abraham pulled out of his parking spot, backing into another vehicle as he did so. Officer Raso then stepped in front of his car. Abraham first began inching forward, then suddenly accelerated toward Officer Raso. Officer Raso fatally shot Abraham. She later testified that she fired at him because "[i]f I didn't, I was going to be killed."[12]

In that case, Officer Raso was confronted with a legitimate threat at the time she used force; Abraham had the apparent ability to strike her with the car (he was sitting in the driver's seat of a running vehicle), the opportunity to run her over (she was standing immediately in front of the car), and the intent to do so (he was intentionally accelerating toward her). However, Officer Raso's actions had contributed to the existence of that threat; had she stayed to the side of the vehicle rather than stepping in front of it, Abraham would not have had any opportunity to strike her with the car. Further, her risk-creating behavior was not justified by the situation. Officer Raso stepped in front of Abraham's car as a way to prevent it from leaving, but it was patently obvious that she could not have physically prevented the car from moving forward. At best, she may have hoped to dissuade Abraham from driving away. The potential benefits of persuasion in that situation fall far short of justifying the potentially lethal risk of being struck by a vehicle. Further, the relatively low-level offense that Abraham was suspected of committing—a nonviolent property crime—is not serious enough to justify accepting a potentially lethal risk. Under the circumstances, then, Officer Raso's actions were tactically unsound and amounted to officer-created jeopardy.

Stepping in front of vehicles is only one example. Officer-created jeopardy also includes the actions of officers who, without sound justification, willingly fail to take advantage of available tactical concepts like distance, cover, and concealment (discussed later in this chapter), willingly abandon tactically advantageous positions by moving into disadvantaged positions without justification, or act precipitously on their own without waiting for available assistance from other officers.

Just as unjustified risk-taking is taken into account in other legal contexts, so too is it a relevant concept in the evaluation of police uses of force. While it should be remembered that a subject certainly bears significant responsibility for the threat they pose to officers—such as the threat that Abraham would strike Officer Raso with his vehicle—that observation should not insulate officers from responsibility for contributing to avoidable harm. Officers' tactical decisions can be relevant evidence in the determination of whether officers violated the applicable legal standard, civil or criminal; indeed, multiple federal circuits and state courts have done exactly that.[13]

It is also appropriate for agency policy and training to emphasize the need to avoid officer-created jeopardy. From an administrative perspective, it is appropriate for agencies to adopt policies that instruct officers to use sound tactics. The operations manual of the Denver Police Department offers one such example, stating, "Officers should ensure that they do not engage in unreasonable actions that precipitate the use of force as a result of tactical, strategic, and procedural errors that place themselves or others in jeopardy."[14] With regard to training, agencies should avoid exclusively using drills that focus on the mechanics of a particular use of force (such as drawing and firing a sidearm) or scenarios that artificially limit an officer's options to the binary choice of using or not using force. While such training has its place, agencies should provide, and even emphasize, training that more closely simulates operational realities by presenting officers with a variety of decisions that they must make even before they initiate an encounter. Such training is valuable precisely because it can reinforce how, in many circumstances, sound tactical decision making early in an encounter can minimize threats and therefore reduce the need for officers to use force to address those threats.

In the next part of this chapter, we discuss the concepts that inform sound tactics.

Tactical Concepts

In this section, we discuss tactical concepts, as well as some of the techniques and procedures that officers use to operationalize those concepts in real-world situations. It is worth noting at the outset that we discuss the relevant concepts at a relatively high level of generality, providing examples when appropriate but without making any attempt to provide a comprehensive discussion of all of the many situations in which a particular concept, technique, or procedure may be properly used. Our discussion here is intended to identify the building blocks of police tactics; it is outside the scope of this text to provide an exhaustive list of exactly how those building blocks can be assembled in every variety of police–civilian encounter.

Time

Time is the single most important tactical concept in policing. This is the case because of the impact that time has on the accuracy of officers' perceptions and the quality of their decisions.

Tactical training is intended to be put to use in real-world operational environments, which can involve circumstances that the Supreme Court described as "tense, uncertain, and rapidly evolving."[15] In stressful environments, human decision making suffers. Officers may experience distorted sensory perceptions, including visual distortions (e.g., "tunnel vision"), auditory distortions (e.g., "auditory blunting"), and temporal distortions (perceiving events as occurring more quickly or more slowly than they actually are).[16] In a time-compressed, high-stress situation, officers may also suffer from cognitive impairments, such as slowed reaction time; and physiological deficiencies, including a reduction in manual dexterity and motor skills.[17] In short, even the best-trained officers may make mistakes, exercise poor judgment, and perform deficiently in high-stress environments, especially when they are forced to make truly split-second decisions.

The reality, however, is that "there are very few instances where police officers have only a split second to make a significant use of force determination."[18] This is particularly true when officers use sound tactics. To a significant extent, the field of police tactics was designed to protect the safety of officers and community members alike by minimizing the extent to which officers must make truly split-second decisions.

To understand the foundational importance of time as a tactical concept, one must understand the Observe, Orient, Decide, and Act ("OODA") Loop model of human response time that the field of police tactics has been built on, as well as modern behavioral economics research related to human decision making. We discuss each in turn.

The OODA Loop

The OODA Loop—sometimes referred to as "Boyd's Cycle"—was first developed by Colonel John Boyd, a Korean War-era Air Force pilot whose theories and strategies enabled the pilots he trained to consistently out-fly technologically superior enemy aircraft.[19] Over the last fifty years, the OODA Loop has been enthusiastically embraced in the policing context. As one author put it in an article published in *Police Magazine*:

> Every law enforcement officer needs to understand the OODA loop because it explains how people act and react in a demanding, evolving, and highly charged situation. This decision-making model can be used to deconstruct verbal and physical confrontations.[20]

The OODA Loop is a descriptive model; it seeks to categorize the psychological steps that must be taken for someone to respond to stimulus. That is, it attempts to explain the psychological processes that take place from the moment that someone becomes aware of a stimulus to the time that they can begin to react to that stimulus.

The OODA Loop consists of four stages:

Observe. In this stage, individuals actively and passively gather information about the world around them. When an officer sees a motorist reach into the glovebox, feels an arrestee pull away from them, or hears a loud noise, they are in the observation phase of the OODA Loop.

Orient. In this stage, individuals process the information they have gathered, interpreting that information in the current context to draw conclusions about what is happening. When an officer determines that the motorist is reaching into the glovebox to get their registration and insurance paperwork, or for a gun, or that there is insufficient evidence to make a determination one way or another, they are in the orientation phase of the OODA Loop.

Decide. In this stage, individuals determine how they are going to react to the conclusions they have drawn about their observations. This will often require selecting from among a range of available responses. When an officer has concluded that a motorist's actions are ambiguous, for example, they may wait for additional information or react in a particular way; that determination happens in the decision phase of the OODA Loop.

Act. In this stage, individuals put their decision into motion, actually responding to the conclusions they drew about the stimulus they observed.

The OODA Loop is not a singular event; it is instead a continuous process; individuals, including police officers, are constantly taking in new information, processing that information, making decisions on the basis of that processing, and implementing those decisions. Further, there is no clear temporal separation between the steps in the OODA Loop process because they overlap; even while an individual is in the midst of reacting to stimuli, they are taking in new information that will shape their continued response.[21]

The OODA Loop is an important foundation for police tactics precisely because it explains the amount of time it takes for officers to respond to an emergent situation. An officer who sees a motorist reaching into a glovebox will not be able to react to that stimulus *until* they make it through the OODA Loop process. With that emphasis in mind, it is easy to see the impact of the OODA Loop model on police tactics and training, which are often intended to reduce the amount of time that officers need to make it through the OODA Loop process.

With regard to the "observe" phase, for example, officers are taught to be alert to body language and physical movements, especially what the subject is doing with their hands. Officers learn to pay close attention to whether someone's hands are empty or not, whether their hands are open or balled into fists, and whether someone's hands are reaching somewhere that the officer cannot see. An officer who is alert to the movements of someone's hands will observe relevant events faster, which enables them to complete the OODA Loop and respond more quickly than an officer who was inattentive.

Because the "orient" phase involves the application of pre-existing mental models, which are used to interpret the stimuli that has been observed,[22] tactical training often focuses on teaching officers to properly interpret their observations. To continue with the same example, officers are often taught that balled fists are indicative of aggression and that areas that officers cannot see, such as a subject's pocket or a vehicle glovebox, may conceal a weapon. When an officer observes someone ball their fist or reach toward a glovebox, then, they have a pre-existing mental model that enables them to more quickly interpret that observation than they could without that pre-existing model.

Other aspects of tactical training focuses on the "decision" phase. Experiments by psychologists William Edmund Hick and Ray Hyman suggest that the amount of time it takes to make a decision increases as the possible options increase.[23] In short, the more options a person has, the more time it takes for them to select from among those options. In the policing context, tactical training can seek to narrow the options that officers should consider; by *not* considering certain actions, officers may complete the OODA Loop process more quickly. Take an overly simplified example: an officer confronted by an aggressive subject brandishing a knife from about fifteen feet away. The officer is wearing standard duty gear, which includes a firearm, pepper spray, baton, TASER, and handcuffs. Someone without tactical training may consider each option. Standard police tactical training, however, would rule out most of the available options; in most circumstances, it would be contrary to generally accepted police practices for an officer to attempt to handcuff or use a baton on the subject at that point, which immediately narrows the scope of options that the officer must consider before coming to a decision.

Finally, a significant amount of police training focuses on implementation, which relates to the "act" phase of the OODA Loop. Officers, for example, receive training in how to draw, aim, and fire their sidearms, and many agencies require officers to demonstrate a minimum level of competency by completing a qualification course annually (or more often). To satisfy the requirements of a qualification course, officers must establish that they can shoot accurately (that is, that they can hit the target a minimum number of times at different distances) and efficiently (that is, that they can draw, aim, and fire within an acceptable amount of time).

Police tactical training not only emphasizes maximizing accuracy and efficiency in every stage of the OODA Loop model, it can also emphasize *disrupting* the subject's OODA Loop process as a way of increasing the amount of time it takes for a subject to react to an officer's actions. As one firearms instructor wrote:

> The really great thing about understanding the O.O.D.A. Loop is the realization that everybody has one and their O.O.D.A. Loop is affected by the same factors that yours is. This is one of the reasons why . . . nearly every drill we teach . . . incorporates moving. [Your movement] has the effect of resetting your opponent's O.O.D.A. Loop and giving you still another advantage.[24]

Movement, in that example, serves to introduce something that forces the subject to do something other than what they were already doing. It is not the movement itself that is important, but rather the unexpected nature of that action. As one tactical text puts is, surprise is the best "method of depriving the suspect of time"; because human beings "are handicapped by an inability to instantly process and react to a new stimulus, surprise deprives a suspect of the ability to react to new circumstances effectively."[25]

Perhaps no tactic better exhibits the intention to disrupt a subject's OODA Loop process than dynamic entries, in which officers rapidly enter a residence, business, or other location "using specialized battering rams or entry explosives," potentially including the use of diversionary "flash-bang grenades designed to temporarily disorient the occupants."[26] A dynamic entry involves officers "go[ing] in hard and fast, relying on speed, surprise and radical tactics" that are intended to create a situation in which, from the suspect's perspective, "one second there is nothing happening and the next all hell breaks loose."[27] The goal is not to maximize the time officers have to make decisions, but rather to deny the occupants the time they need to properly assess the situation and mount any effective resistance.

That is not to suggest that such tactics are clearly preferable; a time-pressured environment dramatically increases the potential for mistakes by officers and subjects alike, making dynamic entry "infinitely more dangerous" than other entry tactics. Indeed, there are any number of examples where a dynamic entry has had tragic results, resulting in a death or serious injury that another entry tactic might well have avoided.[28] The potential for catastrophic error has been well known for decades, leading reputable police agencies and instructors to recognize that the proper use of such tactics is "very limited."[29] Nevertheless, dynamic entries serve as a valuable example of the central importance of time as a tactical concept.

Importantly, the simplified OODA Loop model does not make any attempt distinguish between conscious and unconscious thought processes; any of the stages in the OODA Loop, or the OODA Loop as a whole, may involve either or both depending on the situation. The next model we discuss, in contrast, draws exactly on that distinction.

System 1/System 2 Thinking

The OODA Loop process is the model of human decision making that is most widely accepted, by far, within the field of police tactics, but it is not the only model. Nobel Prize-winning behavioral economist Daniel Kahneman popularized a dual-process theory of human thought that posits that decisions are not based exclusively on conscious deliberation and rational consideration. Kahneman instead categorizes cognition into two different types of thinking: "System 1" and "System 2."[30]

System 1 thinking is fast, and it is fast because it is subconscious. "System 1 operates automatically and quickly, with little or no effort and no sense of voluntary control." Emotional judgments, reflexive assessments, and responses to sudden stimuli are examples of System 1 thinking. System 2 thinking, by contrast, is slower, and it is slower because it requires conscious deliberation. Deliberative contemplation or the use of logic are examples of System 2 thinking.[31] If, for example, a red-faced stranger were aggressively to scream a math problem at you, your perception of him as angry or threatening would be the result of System 1, while actually solving the math problem would require System 2.[32]

As that example suggests, the different systems may be preferable in different types of situations. In some circumstances, a System 1 reaction based on the gist of the situation may be preferable; indeed, Kahneman suggests that System 1 serves an evolutionary function by decreasing our reaction time in threatening situations.[33] With decreased reaction time, of course, comes a reduction in the quality of decision making. Police tactics are intended, in part, to decrease the need to use System 1 thinking in officer–civilian encounters. By reducing immediate threats to the officer, good tactics create more opportunities for officers to engage in System 2 thinking.

Further, System 1 reactions pose special problems in the use-of-force context. Substantial research suggests that, while moderate levels of stress may enhance sensory perception and attention, people faced with more serious perceived or actual physical threats, particularly deadly threats, may experience stress reactions that make sound decision making far more challenging.[34] The so-called "fight or flight" response can result.[35] This response can be an effective System 1 reaction, a biological response designed to ensure safety of an individual, but it does not necessarily comport with law enforcement goals to protect the public and minimize loss of life or injury, both to officers and the public.

This is particularly true in light of the cognitive challenges associated with high-stress environments, discussed above. In light of the heavy, if not exclusive, reliance on System 1 thinking in dangerous environments, police tactics can create space for System 2 thinking by reducing the risk to the officer. By providing more time for officers to both gather and process information before responding, police tactics serve to improve the quality of decision making.[36]

Under both the OODA Loop framework and the System 1/System 2 thinking framework, time is the single most important concept in the field of police tactics. Tactics are designed to maximize the amount of time an officer has to more accurately assess a situation, make more informed decisions, and better implement a response.

The Tactics of "Creating" Time

Having established that time is the central concept around which police tactics are built, this subsection discusses the tactical procedures that officers use to ensure that they maximize the time available to them. Within policing, this is often referred to as "creating" time. Officers use four basic tactical concepts to create time: tactical awareness, distance, cover, and concealment. We discuss each in turn.

TACTICAL AWARENESS

"Tactical awareness," sometimes called "situational awareness," refers to being alert to the risks inherent in a given situation. Even before officers find themselves in a situation, they are taught to manage risk by predicting the risks that the situation *may* present. There are two distinct but interrelated aspects to tactical awareness: tactical approach and pre-planning a tactical response.

Tactical Approach. Tactical considerations come into play even before an officer arrives on scene or begins interacting with someone. An officer who is exercising tactical awareness by thinking about the risks (*qua* potential threats) presented in any given encounter puts that awareness to use by approaching the encounter, when possible, in a way that minimizes the likelihood that the risks will evolve into threats.

We do not mean to suggest that officers will always be able to approach a situation safely. As discussed above, the nature of policing requires officers to operate in tactically uncertain situations and, in many cases, to accept certain risks or threats. However, when officers are in danger—when there is a threat, as that term is properly understood—they have less time in which they can assess the situation and respond appropriately. Creating time, then, requires officers to avoid putting themselves into time-pressured situations whenever it is reasonably possible to do so; to do otherwise may be to engage in officer-created jeopardy.

To that end, an officer will take steps to manage risk well before a threat manifests. When approaching a door, for example, officers typically pay attention to whether the door will open out (as is the case in most nonresidential buildings) or in (as is the case in most residential buildings), as well as which direction it will swing. An officer who is knocking on a door will stand, when possible, slightly to the side of the door, on the door knob side and opposite of the hinges, making it marginally more difficult for someone to open the door and surprise them. In certain situations, such as clearing a building (walking through to either apprehend a building occupant or to ensure that the building is unoccupied), officers will move quickly through, without lingering in, narrow areas such as doorways, stairwells, and hallways. Such choke points are "fatal funnels"; they force officers to move through a predictable location that dramatically limits officer movement (the narrowest part of the funnel) while at the same time offering any would-be ambusher a wide range of positions from which to attack (the widest part of the funnel). In other words, an ambusher's fire can easily be concentrated in a location where officers are most likely to be and least able to avoid attack. To avoid this risk, officers are taught to approach fatal funnels by "clearing" them as expeditiously as possible; for example, an officer will step through the doorway and quickly move to one side, while the next officer will follow but move to the other side.

Another familiar example of a tactical approach comes in the form of the humble traffic stop. In that context, an officer may begin managing risk prior to making contact with the subject by following the target vehicle until they reach an area that provides the officer with some tactical advantage or which neutralizes some disadvantage from which the officer would otherwise suffer. Importantly, the subject of the encounter is not the only relevant source of risk. Traffic stops conducted on the shoulder of the highway carry a risk that a passing vehicle will strike the officer or the officer's vehicle; an officer may use a tactical approach that mitigates that risk by delaying the initiation of a traffic stop until the motorist is in a well-lit area or near the entrance to a parking lot.

The subject of the stop itself does present some risk, of course. As one tactical trainer warns, "Dangerous motorists and passengers cannot always be identified in advance. That is why it is so critical to *control* your stop."[37] That includes using cover and concealment, including the "wall of light" discussed below. It also includes making sure that officers can get help should it become necessary. Generally, officers notify their dispatcher—and other officers on the same radio channel—of the make, model, and license plate number of the stopped vehicle and of the location of the stop either prior to initiating the stop itself or after initiating the stop but prior to approaching the vehicle.[38] This aspect of tactical approach seeks to mitigate the risk that other officers will not be able to respond to the stop (if they do not know the location) or locate the subject (if they do not have a description) in the event that the subject of the stop either violently engages the officer or disables the officer and flees.

Traffic stops are not the only context in which officers use a tactical approach, of course. Officers are trained to approach pedestrian stops in a similar manner, selecting the location and environment, so far as possible, before commanding a civilian to stop, and taking steps to mitigate the risks of the situation.[39] Further, suspicion is not reserved for the subjects of vehicle or pedestrian stops or the suspects of criminal investigations; officers are trained to practice tactical awareness and use tactical approaches in their interactions with witnesses and victims as well.[40]

Pre-Planning the Response to Threat. In addition to approaching each encounter in a way that mitigates the potential for risks to become threats, officers are also trained to pre-plan their response to the threats that may manifest. One of the most popular police training texts instructs officers to make tactical thinking a constant part of their working lives by considering, as they approach each encounter, how they would respond to different types of resistance. The goal of such thinking is to reduce officers' response time should they be faced with a threat. "As you approach any situation, you want to be in the habit of looking for cover, so you can react automatically to reach it should trouble erupt."[41] To that end, officers are taught:

> [Y]ou can turn "routine" observation into a survival-oriented game. As you watch people in a crowd or on the sidewalk, pick out certain ones at random and assume that they are armed suspects. How would you deploy to approach them? What cover might you use? How could you best protect yourself and/or shoot back if they suddenly displayed aggressive behavior?[42]

By reducing the amount of time they need in order to react in a particular way, officers effectively extend the amount of time that they have to observe and assess the situation.

DISTANCE

Officers also use distance to create time and manage risk. The relationship between distance and threat depends on the situation, as does the determination of whether an officer should seek to reduce the distance from the subject, maintain a steady distance from the subject, or increase the distance from the subject.

Generally speaking, the distance between the officer and the subject is inversely correlated with the threat of physical harm. In most cases, that is, the further an officer is from a subject, the safer they are. To use the terminology of risk and threat, the opportunity that an unarmed subject or a subject armed with an edged weapon (e.g., a knife) or blunt instrument (e.g., a hammer) has to attack an officer depends entirely on the distance between that subject and the officer. When the distance between them is such that the officer is not immediately threatened, the lack of imminent danger gives officers the time to continuously evaluate the situation, coordinate with each other, and plan and implement a response.

It is also typically the case, however, that the distance between the officer and the subject is correlated with the threat of escape. In most cases, for example, the closer an officer is to a subject, the less opportunity the subject will have to flee on foot.

As with the other tactical concepts we discuss in this chapter, it is not possible to mechanically define a tactically ideal distance. The "right" distance—or, more accurately, the range of distances that are fairly considered "reasonable"—will depend on the situation, environment, and individuals. To fully explore the tactical implications of distance, we address three related concepts: reactionary gap, unholstering or aiming a weapon, and tactical positioning.

Reactionary Gap. In the tactical context, the term "reactionary gap" is often used to describe distance as it relates to threats to officers. Introduced by Charles Remsberg in the 1980s, reactionary gap originally referred to the amount of time that an officer needed to become aware of and react effectively to any given threat.[43] Today, it is more common to see "reactionary gap" used as a measure of distance; specifically, the distance that a subject can cover in the time that it takes an officer to react effectively.[44]

It is important to recognize that the reactionary gap is context-specific; it is not a measure of the average distance that an average subject can cover before an average officer can react in some undefined way. Rather, it is a measure of the approximate distance that a specific subject can cover in a specific situation before a specific officer can react in a specific way. As that definition suggests, there is no universal "reactionary gap" that applies equally to all actions.

One of the most perennially misleading ways of thinking about the "reactionary gap" is reflected in what has become known as the "21-Foot Rule." In 1983, John Tueller, a lieutenant and firearms instructor with the Salt Lake City Police Department, created a drill in which a "suspect" armed with an edged weapon would stand approximately twenty feet from where an officer would stand, firearm holstered. Tueller described the results of what became known as the "Tueller Drill" in the March 1983 issue of *SWAT Magazine*:

> How long does it take for you to draw your handgun and place two center hits on a man-size target at seven yards? Those of us who have learned and practiced proper pistolcraft techniques would say that a time of about one and one-half seconds is acceptable for that drill.
>
> With that in mind, let's consider what might be called the "Danger Zone" if you are confronted by an adversary armed with an edged or blunt weapon.

At what distance does this adversary enter your Danger Zone and become a lethal threat to you?

We have done some testing along those lines recently and have found that an average healthy adult male can cover the traditional seven yard distance in a time of (you guessed it) about one and one-half seconds. It would be safe to say then that an armed attacker at 21 feet is well within your Danger Zone.[45]

Tueller's goal was to demonstrate the reactionary gap concept. With that concept in mind, Tueller encouraged officers to take steps either to increase the amount of time they had to assess and respond to the situation ("A tactical withdrawal . . . may be your best bet") or to decrease the amount of time they needed to respond effectively ("draw your weapon as soon as the danger clearly exists").

In practice, however, the Tueller Drill and his article have given rise to the so-called 21-Foot Rule, which erroneously posits that a subject with a knife (or other edged weapon) presents a threat of death or great bodily harm whenever they are within twenty-one feet of an officer. In other words, the 21-Foot Rule suggests that officers can use deadly force against any subject who has an edged weapon and is within twenty-one feet.

This is exactly how the reactionary gap concept was misapplied by the State Attorney's Office in West Palm Beach, Florida, in the review of the 2009 shooting of Jamil Murray by off-duty Deputy Donald Smith of the Palm Beach County Sheriff's Office. While shopping at a local supermarket, Deputy Smith was approached by someone who said that Murray "was walking around with a gun." Deputy Smith approached Murray and, from about 20 to 25 feet away, asked him if he had a gun. Murray said he did not have a gun. Deputy Smith ordered Murray to lift his shirt, which he did. According to the deputy himself, Murray "pulled a knife out and in the process of doing that, he said 'I don't have a gun.'" A witness later stated that Murray began to say, "This is what I have," as he withdrew the knife. There was no indication that Murray was holding the knife threateningly or moving toward Deputy Smith. Nevertheless, Deputy Smith shot Murray twice, killing him.[46] In 2010, the incident was reviewed by Investigator Glenn Wescott of the Palm Beach County State Attorney's Office, who wrote, in a paragraph of his memorandum titled "Facts Drawn from This Investigation":

There are numerous studies regarding the distance at which an assailant can injure or kill an officer while armed with a bladed instrument and this distance has been determined to be 21 feet. At the time of the [shooting] of Jamil Murray, he was armed with a bladed instrument, he failed to comply with the verbal instructions of [Deputy] Smith and he was approximately 25 feet from [Deputy] Smith when [Deputy] Smith fired.

On that basis, the Palm Beach County State Attorney's Office released a memorandum in 2012 concluding that no further review was necessary because "Deputy Smith was reasonably in fear for his safety at the time he discharged his firearm."

A mechanical application of the 21-Foot Rule fails to appreciate that there are no set rules; the size of the reactionary gap depends on the individual physical characteristics of the officer and the subject, their relative postures, and the environment in which they are acting.[47]

Relevant physical characteristics include the condition and capabilities of the officer. In a deadly force situation, for example, an officer who is highly proficient at shooting will require less time to draw, aim, and fire a weapon than an officer who is minimally competent. The proficient officer has a shorter reactionary gap because the subject will be able to cover less distance before the officer can react effectively.

The subject's condition and capabilities are similarly relevant. A morbidly obese octogenarian will take more time than an athletic college-age subject to cover the same distance. An officer interacting with the octogenarian, then, has more time than would be the case with the college athlete. Stated differently, the octogenarian will be able to cover less distance before the officer can react effectively than the athlete could, which reduces the reactionary gap.

The reactionary gap is also affected by the relative posture of the officer and the subject. "Posture," in this context, refers to the actions, mental awareness, and physical positioning of the subject vis-à-vis the officer and vice versa. For example, in the context of a subject who is threatening to strike an officer with their fists, the reactionary gap distance will be different if the subject is sitting down (because the seated subject can cover less distance in the time it takes the officer to respond) than if the subject is standing and moving toward the officer (because the standing, moving subject can cover more distance in the time that it takes for the officer to respond).

Similarly, the reactionary gap will be smaller if the officer is already aware of the subject or has taken steps to prepare an effective response. When that is the case, the officer will need less time to react, which means the subject will be able to cover less distance before the officer can react. In many cases, it is especially important to consider the posture of the officer. The reactionary gap between an officer who has already drawn and aimed a firearm at a knife-wielding subject, for example, may be much shorter than the reactionary gap of an officer who has not yet realized that the subject has a knife or who is aware of the knife but has not yet drawn a firearm or otherwise prepared a response.

The environment, too, can affect the reactionary gap. When an object, such as a police vehicle, is interposed between the subject and the officer, that obstacle can dramatically impact the reactionary gap. An individual who would have to climb over or go around a vehicle, for example, will take more time to reach the officer, so the amount of time that an officer has to react is correspondingly longer. We more fully discuss the tactical implications of obstacles in the environment when we address cover and concealment, below. Beyond obstacles, characteristics of the environment can also expand or contract the reactionary gap. For example, imagine that a subject is only fifteen feet away from an officer, but that the subject is at the bottom of a steep, rough embankment, while the officer is at the top. In that case, the reactionary gap is fairly short; the subject would not be able to cover much distance before the officer could react. On the other hand, if the subject was at the top of the embankment and the officer was at the bottom, the reactionary gap may be much wider; coming downhill, the subject could cover more distance in the amount of time that it would take the officer to react.

Unholstering or Aiming a Weapon. The decision to unholster and ready a weapon has time-related tactical implications. Most obviously, drawing or aiming a weapon can reduce the reactionary gap in some contexts, decreasing the amount of time that an officer will need before responding to the subject's actions by using the weapon (and thus decreasing the total amount of distance the subject can cover before the officer responds).

However, recall that the reactionary gap is referential; it is a measure of the time that it will take for an officer to respond (or the distance that a subject can cover before the officer can respond) in a *particular* way. Drawing or aiming a weapon can *increase* the reactionary gap—allowing the subject to cover more distance before the officer can respond appropriately—if the relevant response is something other than the use of the weapon itself. For example, it will take an officer more time to deploy a baton if they have their firearm out than if they do not, because the officer must properly holster the firearm before drawing the baton. Tactically, then, the drawing of a weapon creates an issue of path dependence, limiting an officer's ability to use *other* force options and making the use of the drawn weapon more likely as the situation progresses. We discuss other implications of drawing and presenting a weapon in chapter 6.

Tactical Positioning, Restraint, Repositioning, and Withdrawal. Tactics are, in some sense, like a game of chess: officers seek to outmaneuver the subjects they interact with. Unlike chess pieces, of course, officers are not passively moved into various positions; they can move as freely as the situation, environment, and their physical abilities allow. Even when officers have little or no ability to control the subject's movements, they typically retain the ability to control their own movements. Depending on the situation, officers may actively reduce, maintain, or increase their distance from the subject regardless of whether the subject is standing still or moving toward or away from them. To create time, officers can take a particular position ("positioning"), stay in that position (sometimes known as "tactical restraint"), move from one location to another ("tactical repositioning"), or move away from the subject ("tactical withdrawal" or "tactical retreat").

As officers approach an encounter or take their initial positions, they should be attuned to the tactical advantages and disadvantages of different options. In the context of a traffic stop, for example, officers must decide how to park their own vehicle in relation to the stopped vehicle: in-line (parking directly behind and facing the same direction as the subject vehicle), offset (parking behind and to the side of, but facing the same direction as, the subject vehicle), angled (parking behind and to the side of the subject vehicle, but at an angle to the subject vehicle), or some other variant. They must also decide whether they are going to approach the stopped vehicle on the driver's side, approach on the passenger's side, or call the stopped driver back. Each option has potential benefits and drawbacks that may make it more or less appropriate in any given situation. The same thing, of course, is true in contexts other than traffic stops.

Further, the approach and initial positioning of two or more officers can be interdependent; one officer can take advantage of the tactical opportunities that are created by another officer's actions. Consider, for example, the common "contact and cover" tactic: when two officers are interacting with an individual, one will take on the role of a "contact" officer and interact with the subject while the other takes the role of a "cover" officer. The cover officer takes up a tactically advantageous position, perhaps taking an "L" position (where the officers are the two endpoints and the subject is the point of intersection) with the contact officer directly in front of the subject and the cover officer a little farther away and off to the side. That positioning gives officers time-related advantages; officers can see each other in a way that facilitates their communication while limiting the ability of the subject to focus on both of them simultaneously. It also puts the officers outside of each other's line of fire, reducing the amount of time they maneuver before employing deadly force, should it become necessary.[48]

Tactical restraint serves as a reminder that aggressing—that is, moving toward the subject—is not always the safest or most appropriate option. In some situations, advancing toward the subject is tactically sound. In many others, though, it will be preferable for officers to maintain a position that provides at least some tactical advantage rather than forsake that advantage by moving out of that position. Consider a simplified example: an officer interacting with a wheelchair-bound paraplegic who is aggressively wielding a knife in an otherwise empty parking lot. One need not have the tactical instincts of Napoleon to appreciate that an officer who rushes in to apprehend the subject risks putting themselves into a dangerous situation, one in which they could be cut or stabbed. Aggressing in that situation is likely to be considered officer-created jeopardy; the officer would be better served by keeping some distance away from the knife-wielding subject.

Tactical repositioning, similarly, comes from the observation that it is not always better to stand one's ground than it is to relocate. In most situations, officers should continually assess the situation and seek positions that either provide some advantage or reduce a disadvantage. Whether a particular location is suitable depends on, and can shift during, the dynamic nature of an encounter. For example, the driver's side of an officer's car may provide cover or concealment (terms we discuss below) from the knife-wielding paraplegic subject on the passenger side of the vehicle. If the subject were to move around the front of the vehicle to the driver's side, of course, the driver's side would become less advantageous and the passenger's side would become more advantageous. An officer in such a situation may engage in tactical repositioning by mirroring the subject's movements—moving around the back of the vehicle as the subject moves around the front and moving to the passenger's side as the subject moves to the driver's side—keeping the vehicle interposed between them.

This is not to suggest that every situation will be such that officers *can* safely engage in tactical repositioning or tactical withdrawal. In some situations, the act of relocating can itself create an unacceptably high-risk situation. In the example of the otherwise empty parking lot, for example, it may be appropriate for the officer to walk backwards away from the knife-wielding subject because the flat, level surface makes that withdrawal relatively safe. However, on rough, unfamiliar terrain, the risk that walking backwards may result in tripping and falling may outweigh the risk of staying still or moving in another direction.

Tactical restraint, repositioning, and withdrawal are, in essence, techniques that officers can use to control or influence the distance between themselves as the subject. That, in turn, can reduce the opportunity that the subject has to cause a particular harm, which can give officers more time to assess and react to the situation.

COVER

Cover is another tactical concept that officers can use to affect distance and time. Cover refers to a physical obstacle that can prevent a particular attack from ever reaching the officer.[49] Importantly, the characteristic of cover is context-dependent; whether any given obstacle constitutes cover depends on the nature of the threat under consideration. A polycarbonate riot shield or a wooden door serving as a barrier may protect an officer against a blunt or edged weapon, for example, providing cover by preventing the attack from ever reaching the officer on the other side of the obstacle. However, the same shield or wooden door would not stop a bullet and so could not be considered cover against a firearm. Similarly, a tree or wooden telephone pole may provide cover from handgun fire, but not from bullets fired from a rifle.

Cover can be full or partial. An officer has full cover from an attack when the obstacle shields the officer's entire body. Partial cover, in contrast, leaves some portion of an officer's body unshielded. Even in situations where officers have full cover available, they may use the obstacle as partial cover so that they can maintain visual contact with the subject and potentially respond to attack. For example, an officer who takes a position behind a thick concrete wall might have full cover from a subject with a handgun, but may stand near the edge of the wall or attempt to look over the wall; doing so does expose the officer, but it also allows the officer both to keep the subject in sight and to return fire.

Officers can use cover to effectively change the distance between themselves and a subject; the subject does not have the opportunity to attack an officer behind cover until the subject maneuvers around the obstacle itself. Officers can thus create time by taking advantage of cover, which offers a position of relative safety.

CONCEALMENT

Like cover, concealment refers to an obstacle that officers can interpose between themselves and a subject. Unlike cover, however, concealment does not physically prevent an attack from reaching the officer. Instead, it breaks or obstructs the subject's line of sight to the officer, reducing or eliminating the subject's ability to accurately target the officer. Concealment can include tangible obstacles, such as foliage or a wall, but can also include intangible obstacles, such as fog or smoke (e.g., from a smoke grenade), or even light. In the context of a traffic stop, for example, the officer who has initiated the stop may activate their vehicle's high-beam headlights, "takedown" lights, and spotlight to create what is known as a "wall of light." The amount of light coming from the police vehicle serves to conceal the officer's vehicle—specifically the officer's location in or near the vehicle—from the occupants of the stopped vehicle, whose vision cannot penetrate the wall of light. In pedestrian stops, officers may use their flashlights similarly, directing the light near or even at a subject's face to obscure the details of their own position and movement, although some agencies have specifically prohibited the practice for most encounters.

Regardless of the nature of the obstacle, concealment is intended to reduce the subject's opportunity to accurately target officers, which creates time for officers to assess and react to the situation.

Using Time to Minimize the Potential Need for Force

Expanding the amount of time that officers have to assess a situation and react appropriately is one tactic that can reduce the need to use force, but officers can also use that time to employ additional tactics to mitigate risks and avoid threats, including conflict avoidance, de-escalation, and the issuance of verbal commands. Each of those tactics, and some others, is worthy of at least a chapter, if not an entire book, in their own right. Here, we discuss them at a relatively high level of generality so as to provide sufficient context for the evaluation of a use-of-force incident.

CONFLICT AVOIDANCE

Conflict avoidance is the term given to a set of tactics that recognize that officers can approach most situations in a way that is likely to diminish the potential for conflict, reducing the likelihood that the individuals they interact with will resist in some way.

Conflict avoidance represents a departure from one common approach to police interactions: the "command presence" model. That term was developed in the military to describe someone who displays the qualities of a leader; such a person was said to have command presence. In the policing context, officers are typically taught that their mere presence can be a means of establishing control over a situation, and that they can maximize that effect by having command presence. That entails adopting an approach that displays or reinforces their authority. In practice, command presence is a somewhat nebulous term that can describe, among other things, an officer's appearance and demeanor, including tone of voice, body language, and eye contact. An officer has command presence when the individuals with whom the officer is interacting perceive that the officer is capable, competent, and in charge. Command presence has traditionally been justified by the assertion that it encourages lawful behavior and protects the officer by deterring subjects who might otherwise attack the officer.[50] This belief led to the widespread adoption within policing of the command presence concept. Police training at the Los Angeles Police Department, as described by legal scholar Erwin Chemerinsky in the early 2000s, is representative; officers were taught, "You are in charge, you have to show everyone that you are in charge. Be decisive. Have command presence."[51] To the extent that command presence has been used to encourage officers to assert their authority and demand compliance from the individuals with whom they are interacting, the concept has been criticized for its tendency to be equated with masculinity or traditionally masculine traits such as assertiveness and a physically imposing presentation.[52]

Of more relevance to the purpose of this book, the command presence concept has been criticized as contributing to, rather than mitigating, the risk that an encounter will turn confrontational.[53] Both the Christopher Commission, which investigated the LAPD in the aftermath of the Rodney King beating, and the LAPD's post-Rampart investigation explicitly tied command presence to unnecessary aggression by officers.[54] As one scholar has argued, "The police are trained to believe that they must always be in control and that they must win in every encounter."[55] To the extent that the vast majority of police–civilian interactions require a degree of mutual cooperation and compromise, the mindset that one must "win" an encounter can prove counterproductive.

Officers trained under the command presence model have been trained, *inter alia*, to demonstrate and exercise their control by using an "Ask, Tell, Make" approach. Officers are to first ask a civilian to do something. If the civilian does not do as requested, the officer will then order the civilian to comply. If the civilian does not comply with the order, the officer then physically coerces the civilian to comply, using force if necessary. Under the command presence model, the officer is an authority figure who is to be obeyed out of respect or fear.[56] An individual who does not accept the police officer's understanding of the interaction is, in John Van Maanen's classic taxonomy, an "asshole."[57] "Assholes" must be taught the consequences of "contempt of cop."[58] "When police officers believe that a citizen has a bad attitude because he/she is openly defiant or disrespectful, they may resort to some form of abuse in order to 'correct' the attitude problem. It is a way for the police to take control of the situation, to show that they are in charge, and to ensure that the citizen will act 'respectfully' toward the police in future encounters."[59]

The problem with the command presence model, which the conflict avoidance model recognizes, is that an officer's attempt to establish control over a situation exhibits the expectation that community members can and should defer to them on account of what is, in essence, the civilian's lower status in the interaction. That expectation, and the approach and actions that accompany it, can come across as domineering, disrespectful, or entitled. Further, it may fail to align with the civilian's expectation that their own status will be recognized and respected by officers. Sociologists Richard Sykes and Edward Brent termed this an "asymmetric deference norm," and described how it can lead to conflict. "Because the actors are not responding [to each other] as expected [by either party to] the encounter, the defiance between them escalates. As both actors discredit each other, they exchange roles as threatening and threatened."[60] Instead of deferring to the officer, the civilian becomes *more* likely to push back against the officer's attempt to dictate their relative social standing. "Because few people like being humiliated or gratuitously ordered about, an officer's expectation of and insistence on deference increases the potential for conflict. This may be particularly true in times of tension between the police and the community."[61]

Conflict avoidance tactics, in contrast, seek to minimize the potential for interpersonal conflict by recognizing and respecting the status of all parties to the encounter. By interacting with civilians in a way that acknowledges their social status and by recognizing a civilian's need to maintain "face" in front of the officer and other members of the community, officers can avoid the conflict that a different attitude can create. According to one study of military officers:

> [W]hen officers ignored the questions or other actions that civilians posed they were much more likely to use force. By contrast, where officers responded to or simply acknowledged civilian actions, civilians were much more likely to cooperate and officers were much more likely to complete their projects cooperatively. All of this suggests that . . . unilaterally asserting authority generates more problems than it solves.[62]

There is, for example, a meaningful distinction between how an individual will respond to an officer who makes an effort to earn their cooperation and an officer who demands their compliance.

The distinction between the way people respond to attempts to demand compliance and how they respond to attempts to earn cooperation may be demonstrated with a simple drill that we have used before a variety of audiences: grand juries; officers at the Federal Law Enforcement Training Center;

the command staff of the Bureau of Alcohol, Tobacco, Firearms, and Explosives; attendees at a National Association of Women Law Enforcement Executives conference; and attendees at a TEDx talk delivered by one of the authors of this book.[63] In this drill, the audience is divided in half. The first half is given something like the following instructions: "Would you guys mind standing up for me? Great, thanks. Yeah, everybody stand up for me here. I know, this is odd, but bear with me. Okay, we're all standing. Great!" The half of the audience that is now standing is asked to perform several intentionally silly actions, such as striking various poses, turning in a circle, or standing on one foot. After three or four such actions, the first half of the audience is asked to sit back down and their efforts rewarded with a round of applause. Once the applause dies down, the other half of the audience is addressed and issued a series of simple shouted commands: "Stand the fuck up! Do it now! Stand up! Stand the fuck up, damn it!" In doing this drill multiple times in front of audiences that range from a dozen or so to several hundred people, we have never had more than a very few people in the second half of any audience stand up. That is the only instruction directed at the second half of the audience. The audience as a whole is then asked to reflect on what just happened: half of the audience stood up and performed a series of embarrassing actions that they would certainly have not performed in public, and maybe not even in private, on their own. But almost everyone in the other half of the audience refused to even stand up, an action that is not only much simpler and unembarrassing, it is also an action that they *inevitably* would have engaged in at some point in the very near future entirely on their own. Further, those few audience members who do stand up often exhibit some face-saving behaviors, delaying or talking or laughing to each other as a way of communicating, to each other and to themselves, that they are choosing to humor an odd request, not abdicating their own social status by complying with an order. The point of the compliance/cooperation drill, of course, is to demonstrate that the manner in which officers approach someone, not just the things that they ask someone to do, can increase or decrease the likelihood of resistance.

Conflict avoidance techniques, then, can be used to encourage cooperation in situations in which a more adversarial or commandeering approach can generate resistance.[64] These techniques include verbal and nonverbal communication tactics employed to establish a dynamic exchange of status and deference during an encounter; an officer avoids conflict—or, more accurately, reduces the likelihood of conflict—by recognizing and respecting the status of the individuals they interact with.

DE-ESCALATION

De-escalation refers to a range of techniques that can be used to reduce an existing conflict. Unlike conflict avoidance, which seeks to avoid conflict before it arises, de-escalation techniques are intended to nonviolently, or less violently, resolve conflict that has already manifested. Most de-escalation techniques serve a dual purpose: they seek to convince the individual with whom the officer is interacting to voluntarily reduce their level of resistance while at the same time helping officers maintain their equilibrium when their own status is challenged.

Tactical communication, the cornerstone of de-escalation, consists of physical positioning (in a way that properly manages the risks and threats of the situation) and verbal and nonverbal communication. De-escalation techniques consistently emphasize slowing the pace of the encounter to the extent possible by maintaining a certain distance from the subject (both as a matter of officer safety and to avoid provoking a physical response by invading the subject's personal space) and speaking with appropriate tone (calmly), volume (quietly), and cadence (slowly and concisely) while engaging in active listening, paying more much attention to the motivation for the subject's statements rather than the content of those statements. Challenges or insults should be ignored or deflected. "Verbal Judo," an early iteration of tactical communication training that was popularized in the 1990s, suggested that officers acknowledge insults or curses by deflecting them, but avoid engaging with or responding to them.[65] For example, an officer who had been insulted might be trained to respond with a "strip phrase," a statement described as "a deflector that strips the insult of its power" in a way that allows the officer to refocus the conversation.[66] For example, an officer who was insulted during the course of a traffic stop might respond, "Well, I 'preciate that, sir, but I need to see your license."[67]

Where Verbal Judo training emphasized deflecting aggression, more recent tactical communications training has drawn from procedural justice concepts to emphasize positive engagement as a way to reduce conflict. For example, Sue Rahr, a member of President Obama's Task Force on 21st Century Policing, Seattle Police Chief John Diaz, and Joe Hawe, then-Director of the Washington State Criminal Justice Training Commission, laid out four pillars of "Justice Based Policing" by using the acronym "LEED," for "Listen and Explain with Equity and Dignity."[68] Although not presented specifically as a de-escalation model, the principles are certainly applicable to resolving conflict nonviolently:

Listen. Allow people to give their side of the story; give them *voice*, and let them *vent.*

Explain. Explain *what* you're doing, *what* they can do, and *what's* going to happen.

Equity. Tell them *why* you're taking action. The action must be *fair and free of bias*, and show their input was taken into consideration.

Dignity. Act with dignity and leave them with *their* dignity.[69]

There are innumerable other de-escalation models that emphasize tactical communications, most of which include a range of techniques intended to develop rapport and build goodwill that can, it is hoped, reduce the need to use force to resolve a given conflict.

That said, it is inappropriate to think of de-escalation as a replacement for physical responses to resistance. Instead, it is a complementary option, a tool that can be used when it is appropriate, in exactly the same way that pepper spray, a TASER, or a baton are tools that can be used when appropriate. As with those other force options, de-escalation is not always feasible or appropriate; when officers have used sound tactics to reduce the threat they face and to expand the amount of time they have to address the situation, however, they may be able to use de-escalation techniques in an attempt to avoid kinetic alternatives.

VERBAL INSTRUCTIONS

The term "instructions," in this context, refers to information that the officer provides to the subject, such as a characterization of the interaction (e.g., "You are under arrest.") or predicative information about what the officer is about to do (e.g., "I'm now going to frisk you."). To take a common example, it is tactically preferable, in most cases, for officers to inform someone that they are under arrest prior to attempting to make physical contact with them. That is true for at least two reasons.

First, in the absence of the clear communication of the fact of arrest, an individual who pulls away or otherwise resists may avoid being criminally charged for their resistance. In Connecticut, for example, state law reads, in relevant part: "A person is guilty of interfering with an officer when such person obstructs, resists, hinders or endangers any peace officer . . . in the performance of such peace officer's . . . duties."[70] This statute has been interpreted to apply only when the subject acts with the specific intent to interfere with the performance of an officer's duty,[71] which means that the subject must know that the officer is engaged in the performance of their official duty, such as attempting to make an arrest. Informing a subject that they are under arrest thus serves to put the subject on notice that the officer is engaged in their duties such that resistance is subject to criminal sanction.

Second, and more pertinently, announcing that a subject is under arrest prior to physically engaging or applying handcuffs can not only reduce resistance, but can also mitigate the risk to officers by allowing them to both more efficiently identify indicators of resistance and to more effectively address any resistance offered. Having informed the subject that they are under arrest, the officer can then assess the subject's compliance from a position of relative safety—if the officer is more than arm's length away, for example, then there is no threat of physical assault because the subject lacks the opportunity, in that moment, to touch the officer. If the subject tenses, pulls away, looks around for escape routes, or engages in other physical movements, it can serve to indicate to the officer that the subject may resist. With this information, the officer may then take steps to preempt such resistance by, *inter alia*, verbally de-escalating, stepping in front of the subject to cut off a path of escape, or issuing appropriate verbal commands.

Failing to inform the subject that they are under arrest, in contrast, can increase the potential threat to both the officers and the subject. A subject who is not aware of an officer's intent to arrest them is more likely to be surprised than a subject who has been informed that they are under arrest. That surprise can lead the subject to pull away, not in an attempt to avoid arrest but in honest confusion about what the officer (who may be behind them) is doing. Officers, in turn, may interpret that reaction as resistance and use force in response. In short, the failure to inform the subject that they are under arrest can contribute to a use of force that might have been avoided had the subject been informed by an officer that they were under arrest.

VERBAL COMMANDS

Officers use verbal commands that can, if understood and obeyed, eliminate or reduce the need to use force. Verbal commands are directives, orders for someone to take a specific action ("Put your hands up!") or to refrain from taking some action ("Don't move!"). The failure to obey verbal commands, let alone more expressive acts of defiance in the face of verbal commands, can be interpreted as noncompliance at that moment and as an indication of future resistance. In evaluating a use-of-force incident, reviewers should be attuned to whether verbal commands were issued and, if so, whether they were reasonably comprehensible and whether the subject could reasonably comply. These points of analysis are critical because the conclusions drawn from the failure to obey verbal commands are only valid if the subject actually *heard* and *understood* the verbal commands and *chose* not to comply.

In assessing comprehensibility, reviewers should determine the volume at which an officer issued verbal commands, the distance between the officer and the subject, environmental conditions that could affect auditory perceptions (such as background noise or high windspeed), and whether verbal commands were issued once or repeated. Further, reviewers should determine how many officers issued verbal commands at various points, recognizing that multiple officers yelling commands simultaneously can inhibit, rather than facilitate, the comprehensibility of those commands.

Reviewers must also determine whether compliance was possible under the circumstances. In an arrest situation, for example, an officer may command a subject who is lying face down on the ground with their hands under their chest, "Give me your hands!" That command may be contextually appropriate in that officers want to prevent the subject from accessing a weapon and to secure them by handcuffing them with their hands behind their back. However, it may be impossible for the subject to comply if multiple officers are lying or kneeling on the subject's back; in that case, the officers' weight—which is presumably being used to prevent the subject from getting up—may also prevent the subject from complying with the command. In such circumstances, the subject's failure to comply is effectively involuntary. In the same vein, it can be impossible for a subject to comply with inconsistent verbal commands. For example, on March 11, 2018, officers from the Oakland, California Police Department encountered Joshua Pawlik after being called about an armed man who was lying down, unconscious, between two houses. Pawlik was apparently asleep with a gun in his hand. Body-worn camera footage shows that, as the officers approached Pawlik, one officer yelled, "Don't move! Get your hands up!"[72] A similar issue arose several years earlier, on June 6, 2015, when Oakland officers approached Demouria Hogg while she was sleeping in a car with a pistol on the passenger seat. After breaking the car window and deploying a TASER, shouts of "Get your hands up!" were intermingled with shouts of "Don't move!"[73] There is, of course, no way for a subject in that situation to comply with both commands: complying with either one necessarily means not complying with the other. The subject's failure to comply with (at least one) command may be interpreted as resistance, and an officer may respond to that resistance with force. Inconsistent verbal commands, then, not only do not serve the tactical purpose of reducing the potential need to use force, but may prove affirmatively counterproductive. That is, inconsistent verbal commands can increase the likelihood that an officer will use force.

One tactical approach that could potentially preclude both the problem of multiple officers yelling commands simultaneously and the problem of inconsistent verbal commands is for one officer to be designated as the person giving verbal commands. This is consistent with, although not identical to, the "contact and cover" tactic described above; one officer directs most of their attention to a particular aspect of the encounter—giving verbal commands—while any other officers are free to focus on continually assessing the situation and responding appropriately.

While it is important for officers to communicate their verbal commands clearly and in a manner that is likely to be both understood and obeyed by the subject, there is significant variation in how they may choose to do so. In this context, for example, it is not uncommon for officers to use profanity. Indeed, police trainer and author Jim Glennon has written that, while officers should "absolutely . . . treat the vast majority of people . . . with dignity and respect," it is also the case that "a well-placed profanity is sometimes necessary. It may actually save lives."[74] The common argument is that profanity can serve to emphasize the seriousness of the situation and the officer's insistence on compliance. Some police trainers, including Gary Klugiewicz and Dan Marcou, have argued that the use of profanity is potentially provocative; that it is reasonably foreseeable that profanity will make an individual *less* likely to obey an officer's commands, or even make them more likely to resist. Profanity, in short, can escalate an encounter, increasing the likelihood that officers will need to use force.[75] Separately, researchers have shown that an officer's use of profanity can negatively affect the perception of the officer, making them appear unfair and unprofessional,[76] and can increase the likelihood that bystanders will view the use of force as excessive.[77]

Profanity is not the only possible tactical error that could exacerbate a situation. On May 19, 2018, while conducting a high-risk traffic stop, Houston, Texas, Police Department officers were issuing verbal commands for a passenger to exit a vehicle. The subject was instructed by an officer using a police vehicle's public-address system to put her hands up. The subject raised her arms to the point where her palms were at approximately the height of her face. The officer's next verbal command was, "Over your head. Pretend like we're going to shoot you."[78] The subject of that command was apparently taken into custody without incident, but that statement could easily have provoked unnecessary confusion and fear, if not outrage, by the subject. It did provoke a negative reaction from a bystander: immediately after the officer's command, the woman recording the encounter angrily said, apparently to herself, "No! Why would you say that?!"

Profanity and inappropriate comments are not only arguably profession-ally unacceptable—a topic that is outside the scope of this book—they may also be tactically counterproductive and could affect how the use of force itself is evaluated.

DRAWING A WEAPON

Some police agencies consider the drawing, displaying, or aiming of a weapon to be, essentially, a communication technique. Documentation from the New York Police Department's Police Academy, for example, states that "drawing and displaying [a] firearm often is a deterrent to violence[] because it lets suspects know that they are very close to a much higher degree of force."[79] However, a review of the New York City Police Department by the RAND Center on Quality Policing found that drawing and pointing a weapon can have less desirable tactical implications.

First, the presentation of a weapon could escalate the encounter. A subject who is threatened with a drawn weapon may lash out at the officer *because* of the weapon. When Fort Wayne, Indiana, Police Officer Bob Abels responded to a domestic disturbance call, he drew both his firearm and his TASER dur-ing the course of his interaction with Izaiah Galvan and Galvan's father. Al-though Galvan's video recording of the incident began in the middle of the encounter, it is clear that he and his father reacted negatively in part *because* the officer drew his weapons, at one point saying, "Put your . . . gun down and talk to me, then." Even overlooking the tactical mistake of holding *two* weapons simultaneously, it is clear in that case that the subjects perceived the officer's choice to deploy his weapons as exacerbating the encounter.

Second, an officer who is holding a drawn weapon is limited in their ability to use force options *other than* that weapon. The NYPD study guide, quoted extensively in the RAND study, offers relevant examples:

> If an offender who is being held at gunpoint by an officer who has come too close to him or her decides to forcibly resist the officer, he or she has great advantage over the officer. Such an offender has both hands free to overpower the officer, but one of the officer's hands—almost always the stronger hand—is tied up in trying to safe-guard the weapon. It is nearly impossible for officers who are handicapped in this way to overcome such a suspect, and, if they fail to overcome them, either officer or suspects become victims of shootings that should not have happened. Such situations—a suspect is being held at gun point—greatly increase the chances of accidental or unintended shootings. Should suspects make some unanticipated movement—like turning to explain

themselves, reaching for their identification, slipping, or tripping—officers are likely to be startled and to pull their triggers. Should suspects try to forcibly resist, the chances of an accidental shooting that will strike the suspect, an officer, or a bystander are increased significantly.[80]

Third, the unholstering of a weapon can increase the danger, or the perceived danger, to the officer or others. In a physical altercation, an officer is far more likely to lose control, or *fear* losing control, of a weapon in their hand than a weapon that is securely holstered. Drawing or presenting a weapon, then, can lead officers to use more force because of the perception that the threat is more serious than it would have been had they left their weapon holstered.

ADDITIONAL RESOURCES

Officers who have "created" time can also use that time effectively to obtain additional resources, including situationally appropriate tools and weapons. Officers can, for example, use sound tactics to give themselves time for an officer to arrive with a TASER, police canine, or other equipment that is not immediately available on scene. Other officers can also be a valuable resource in a potential use-of-force situation. Having multiple officers present may have a moderating effect on a subject's behavior; a subject who may be inclined to physically resist a single officer's attempt to place them into handcuffs may not be inclined to resist multiple officers. It is also the case that having multiple officers on scene may decrease the risk or threat of resistance; the threat presented by a physically resistant subject to two officers may be significantly less than the threat the same actions would present to an officer acting on their own.[81] Because the threat of harm is reduced, the amount of force that officers need to address that threat of harm is correspondingly reduced.

With that said, it is worth noting that empirical research has found that having more officers on scene may actually be a sociological factor that increases the likelihood that officers will use force.[82] Tactically, it is sufficient to say that the presence of multiple officers may decrease the potential threat even while acknowledging the potential incentive for officers to use force to maintain their professional image in front of their colleagues.

Applying Tactical Concepts

The field of police tactics has seen the development of generally accepted practices, although it is widely recognized that there is no way to mechanically predetermine which tactics, if any, will prove to be the most effective in any given incident. The exigencies of the situation; the officers' training, resources, and capabilities; the environment; and the subject's characteristics and actions will all play a role in shaping the range of reasonable tactics. Still, it is worth describing three very different tactical scenarios, even in a somewhat abstract manner, as a way to demonstrate the potential application of police tactics to manage risk and threat. Below, we describe generally accepted tactical approaches to arrests, crisis intervention incidents, and active shooter incidents. Tactical concepts like time, distance, and risk/threat reduction techniques are salient in each context, but they apply very differently from one context to another.

Arrests

Few actions are more closely associated with the police than arrests. There is, of course, some variation in how officers are trained and how arrests are actually made, but describing one generally accepted approach to arrests can serve as a useful demonstration of the tactical concepts discussed above.

Arrests are not necessarily, or even frequently, spontaneous events. An arresting officer is under no obligation to reach for their handcuffs immediately after determining that probable cause exists and an arrest is appropriate. Instead, officers approach physical arrests tactically, choosing where the arrest is to be conducted and, to the extent possible, maximizing their own advantages and minimizing the subject's advantages in the situation. For example, officers routinely ask the individuals they intend to arrest to move to a neutral or officer-controlled area. Thus, they move a suspected shoplifter from the aisles of a department store to a security office, persuade a domestic battery suspect to leave their house and stand in the yard, and ask an apparently impaired driver to step away from their vehicle in a parking lot. A number of police departments prefer officers to delay making an arrest until multiple officers are present.[83]

After determining that a particular location is appropriate, the officer informs the arrestee that he is under arrest. As described above, this helps protect the governmental interest in law enforcement by increasing the likelihood that a subject who resists at this point will be criminally culpable. It also helps protect the governmental interest in officer safety. The officer can gauge the subject's compliance, monitoring their behavior before and throughout the physical arrest process so as to be maximally responsive to resistance.

After informing the arrestee that they are under arrest, the officer commands them to face away—so he cannot watch the officer—and assume a position that puts the subject in some disadvantageous position, such as standing with their hands behind their back or on their head, or kneeling. The arresting officer keeps their own hands free during this phase of the arrest; that is, the officer does not yet have a pair of handcuffs in hand. If the arrestee complies, the officer moves in from behind the arrestee and "tests the waters" by lightly touching the arrestee on the back or shoulder with one hand. The rationale for this action is to gauge the suspect's "fight or flight" response on the understanding that some arrestees will begin to resist only after the officer makes physical contact with them or after handcuffs are partially applied.[84] By making physical contact with the arrestee before retrieving the handcuffs, the officer is prepared to respond to resistance without having to first secure the handcuffs or put them beyond the reach of the combative arrestee.

If the arrestee remains compliant, the officer will establish control over the arrestee's hands, for example by sliding their "testing" hand down the arrestee's arm and grabbing both of the arrestee's thumbs. Only if the arrestee continues to remain compliant will a well-trained officer then use their free hand to remove their handcuffs from a belt pouch or handcuff holster and apply them to the arrestee's wrists. Officers are trained to be particularly wary during the actual application of handcuffs. Not only is an officer's attention drawn momentarily away from the arrestee's behavior to the mechanics required to apply the handcuffs, but the handcuffs themselves are a potential weapon that the arrestee could use against the officer. There are multiple examples of an arrested subject using handcuffs as a weapon to attack or threaten the arresting officer.[85] In the event that an initially compliant arrestee resists at some point, officers are trained to forsake any attempt to wrestle the arrestee into handcuffs. Instead, they are instructed to subdue the arrestee to a point where handcuffs can be applied with minimal effort. As Charles Remsberg put it, "[I]f [a suspect] is still fighting and is not stabilized, you should not be attempting to handcuff him. . . . It's control first, then handcuffing."[86]

Properly applied, handcuffs hold the subject's arms behind their back with the backs of their hands facing each other.[87] Law enforcement training emphasizes that threats originate from the hands—hands can wield a weapon or be used themselves as weapons—so behind-the-back handcuffing is preferred because it minimizes the arrestee's range of motion, reducing the threat posed by a secured arrestee by limiting their ability to grab or use a weapon or throw a punch.[88] In some circumstances, especially those involving pregnant subjects or subjects with medical limitations, the subject may be handcuffed with their hands in front of them. In other circumstances, especially those involving subjects who remain combative after being handcuffed, officers may apply four-point restraints or hobbles to further limit the subject's movement.

Crisis Intervention Response

Perhaps the clearest modern example of time as a tactical concept comes in the form of Crisis Intervention Team (CIT) training, which has established a strong track record of improving the ability of officers to safely deal with individuals in the midst of a mental health crisis.[89] Prior to the 1970s, officers were taught to quickly and aggressively establish control over suspects, especially those with apparent mental illnesses. In the 1970s, this training began to shift, becoming in the 1980s what modern policing knows as the CIT model. Our focus here is on the tactical applications of a crisis intervention approach, but it is worth noting that crisis intervention itself goes well beyond the street-level interaction between rank-and-file officers and persons in crisis. A broader approach to crisis intervention may include partnerships between the medical mental health community and the police agency to provide a range of support services after the initial interaction with an officer. The "Memphis model" of crisis intervention, for example, includes tactics and techniques within a broader approach that emphasizes pre-arrest jail diversion and post-event treatment continuity.[90] The "Illinois model," in contrast, emphasizes adaptive problem-solving.[91]

For purposes of this discussion, "crisis intervention" is an umbrella term for a series of tactics and techniques that are intended to enable officers to avoid force when interacting with someone in the midst of crisis. Although crisis intervention training and CITs are most closely associated with mental health issues, the nature of the "crisis" is effectively irrelevant: The core principles are applicable whether someone is emotionally distressed because of a mental health issue or because of events in their personal life. CIT training typically includes multiple dimensions, including how officers can recognize a person in crisis and the tactics and techniques that officers can use to avoid violence by communicating effectively.[92]

The tactical component of CIT training incorporates conflict avoidance and de-escalation, but enhances those concepts with specialized guidance. Officers are instructed to maintain a safe distance to slow the pace of the encounter so that they can use tactical communication and verbal de-escalation.[93] Although empirical evidence about police uses of force is notoriously spotty, several studies suggest that officers who use the tactics they learn from CIT training are injured less often and use less force than officers who have not had such training.[94]

Although more a strategic concern than a tactical one, it is also worth noting that officers who use CIT techniques also engage in more treatment-oriented responses, potentially using their enforcement authority (i.e., arrest powers) less often with regard to individuals with mental health issues,[95] which may contribute to the reduction in uses of force.

Active-Shooter Response

Where crisis intervention training serves to demonstrate how some aspects of police tactics have evolved to emphasize slowing the pace of an encounter, active shooter response shows exactly the opposite evolution.

In the late 1990s, the conventional belief about hostage situations was that trained negotiators or well-equipped entry teams were in the best position to maximize positive outcomes. The patrol officers who typically arrived first on scene were to take tactically advantageous positions and then exercise restraint until additional resources arrived in the form of a well-trained and specially equipped SWAT team.[96] But in April 1999, two seniors at Columbine High School went on an hour-long rampage, killing thirteen people and injuring thirty-five more before taking their own lives. Pursuant to their training, and consistent with the prevailing approach at the time, the first officers to arrive on scene set up a perimeter during the shooting and waited for the SWAT team to respond. Almost two hours after the shooting started, SWAT finally entered the school. Later investigation determined that multiple victims were killed in the time between officers' initial arrival and the SWAT entry.

After Columbine, police agencies and trainers were faced with the unpleasant reality that, in some cases, waiting for additional resources simply gives a hostage taker more time to kill victims. Establishing a perimeter and waiting for specialized units remains the appropriate tactic in some cases, such as static hostage situations or barricaded subjects without hostages, but active shooter situations, it was determined, require a different approach. Officers are now taught that the first officer or officers on scene should aggressively search for active shooters with an eye to eliminating the threat in the shortest possible time.[97] This shift in policy and tactics has required a change in equipment and training. As Professor J. Pete Blair told the Police Executive Research Foundation in 2014, "We have seen attackers barricade themselves in, so we need police to have the skills and techniques and equipment to get in and stop the killing."[98] Today, it is common for rank-and-file officers to be given at least some of the dynamic entry and rapid room-clearing training, described above, that had previously been reserved for SWAT units.[99]

Active shooter response tactics increase the potential for officers to encounter the gunman, which obviously carries a significant risk, if not an actual threat. It also carries other risks. Officers are typically trained to focus on finding and eliminating the threat, even if that means ignoring or stepping over injured persons who may die without prompt medical attention. Further, because of the rapid entry, officers do not form a perimeter, which carries the risk that the shooter will evade officers and escape, potentially moving on to a new location and continuing to shoot. Under the tactical calculus, the risk that the officers' rapid entry will result in harm to the government's interests in officer safety and law enforcement are outweighed by the need to protect the interest in public safety by addressing the shooter as promptly as possible. In short, those risks are justified by the exigencies of an active shooter situation.

Conclusion

There is more to evaluating an officer's use of force than assessing the potential harms of the officer's actions and determining whether they were justified in the moment. An officer's decision to approach a situation in a particular way, to stand in a particular location, to speak to the subject in a particular manner, and a number of other decisions that occur prior to the actual use of force can all affect the analysis. This has been well recognized within the policing field, which has developed tactics that officers employ to reduce or mitigate physical risks and threats. Poor tactics can expose an officer to danger—and result in the officer using force to address that danger—that another course of action would have avoided, making tactics a critical component of evaluating police violence.

This chapter provided a detailed overview of the techniques and procedures that officers use to protect themselves and community members, identifying time as the core tactical consideration because of the impact that time can have on officer decision making. It outlined the tactics that officers use to "create" time, and described how, circumstances permitting, officers can use that time to reduce the potential need to use force. Using three scenarios—arrests, crisis intervention response, and active shooter response—it demonstrated how the same tactical concepts can be implicated in very different ways. No single chapter can capture the full and nuanced range of tactical options that can be applied in the universe of officer-civilian encounters, of course, but a working knowledge of the tactical concepts discussed in this chapter is essential for accurate evaluation of use-of-force incidents.

6

Force Options

Tools, Techniques, and Weaponry

An officer is arresting a suspected shoplifter and, when the subject begins to pull away, uses a supinating wrist takedown. In reviewing that use of force, it would be impossible to determine whether the officer's actions were constitutional, or authorized by state law, or consistent with agency policy without also knowing something about supinating wrist takedowns—the nature of the technique, its attendant risks, and how it is generally taught and used in the policing context. Applying any of the evaluative standards discussed in part I requires more than an advanced working knowledge of the relevant analytical framework; it also requires at least some familiarity with the actual use of force that is to be evaluated as well as potential alternatives.

This chapter provides an overview of the most common, and many of the less common, tools, techniques, and weaponry that officers employ in use-of-force situations. Our goal is not to provide a comprehensive description of every conceivable force option and its variants, but rather to provide information sufficient to allow readers to better appreciate the limits of their own knowledge.

As a threshold matter, there are two particularly relevant characteristics of the various force options: the means by which they work and their likely effects. With regard to means—that is, how a use of physical force is intended to actually overcome resistance—the various force options can be placed into two categories: pain compliance and mechanical disruption.

Pain compliance refers to the intentional infliction of pain as a way of discouraging the subject from continuing to resist or, phrased differently, as a way of encouraging the subject to comply with an officer's commands. Effectively, the officer uses pain as an incentive to convince the subject to do what the officer wants them to do or to stop doing what the officer wants them not to do. The paradigmatic example of pain compliance is a pressure-point control hold, in which officers push on a sensitive spot to inflict pain. At the risk of stating the obvious, pain compliance relies on the subject's perception of and reaction to pain. Techniques and weapons that rely on pain compliance may prove unreliable when applied to a subject who is experiencing what police training typically refers to as a "mind-body disconnect." Highly agitated subjects, mentally ill subjects, or subjects under the influence of drugs or alcohol may not perceive, process, and respond predictably to pain, reducing the value of techniques that rely on pain compliance.

Mechanical disruption, in contrast, works by physically overwhelming the subject's musculoskeletal system. There is perhaps no better example of mechanical disruption than when multiple officers "dog pile" on top of a subject, using their weight to prevent the subject from rising; although the subject may experience discomfort, it is the combined weight of the officers, not the discomfort they're inflicting, that prevents the subject from getting up. Mechanical disruption is not just a matter of strength or weight, of course; officers are commonly trained in leverage-based mechanical disruption techniques. An officer who applies a leg sweep, for example, relies primarily on leverage to mechanically disrupt the subject's balance, taking them to the ground despite their desire to remain standing. It is important to recognize that mechanical disruption may result in pain to the subject; such a consequence is incidental to, rather than the goal of, mechanical disruption. Unlike pain compliance, mechanical disruption does not depend on the subject's perception of pain to be effective.

Importantly, the application of pain compliance techniques and mechanical disruption techniques are not mutually exclusive. For example, officers might use their body weight to hold a subject to the ground (mechanical disruption) while also striking the subject in the muscles of the upper back (pain compliance). Indeed, the same technique or weapon can involve elements of both pain compliance and mechanical disruption, although it is almost always fair to describe any given technique or weapon as *primarily* dependent on pain compliance or mechanical disruption to induce compliance or otherwise overcome a subject's resistance.

With regard to potential effects, the types of harms that can result from the various force options can be divided in a number of different ways. The following four categories accurately and comprehensively reflect the universe of likely physical harms:

Non-Physical Force. Officer actions that do not involve physical contact and cannot cause bodily injury.

Low-Level Force. Officer actions involving physical contact that may cause temporary discomfort or low-level pain but is unlikely to cause more serious harm.

Intermediate Force. Officer actions involving physical contact that are likely to cause more than low-level harm, but that do not create a substantial risk of death or serious bodily harm. Intermediate force is the broadest of the categories, and consists of a spectrum ranging from moderate pain or minor harm—such as contusions (bruising), abrasions, short-term impairment of movement, or superficial wounds (of a type that do not require suturing)—to what one court has termed "serious" harm, which would include force that results in wounds that require stitches, but not extensive suturing, or that involve the infliction of a high level of pain for a limited period of time.

Deadly Force. Officer actions involving physical contact that carry a substantial risk of causing death or serious bodily injury. Serious bodily injury is defined in federal law as (1) a substantial risk of death, (2) extreme physical pain, (3) protracted and obvious disfigurement, or (4) protracted loss or impairment of the function of a bodily member, organ, or mental faculty.[1] The Model Penal Code adopts a similar approach, defining the term as "bodily injury which creates a substantial risk of death or which causes serious, permanent disfigurement, or protracted loss or impairment of the function of any bodily member or organ." Reviewers should be mindful that state law may adopt a different definition of serious bodily injury. For example, the California Penal Code defines serious bodily injury as a "serious impairment of physical condition, including, but not limited to, the following: loss of consciousness, concussion, bone fracture, protracted loss or impairment of function of any bodily member or organ, a wound requiring extensive suturing, and serious disfigurement."[2]

Critically, this classification requires reviewers to identify the *foreseeable* harms of the officer's actions, not (just) the actual harms that result from an officer's actions. Firing a handgun at a subject, for example, creates a substantial risk of causing serious bodily injury or death and is thus properly considered a use of deadly force even if the bullet misses the subject completely or only grazes the subject's leg, causing a superficial injury that does not even require suturing. Under any of the evaluative frameworks, it is the likely nature and quality of the force—that is, the consequences that were reasonably foreseeable *at the time that force was used*—that matters.

In assessing the likely harms of the various force options, there are a few generally applicable rules that permit few, if any, exceptions; for example, firing a handgun at a subject should always be considered deadly force. Most force options, however, can present different harm profiles depending on the circumstances. A baton, for example, may be classified as a low-level force option when held horizontally and used to hold back protestors on a skirmish line, as an intermediate force option when swung laterally into the large muscles of the thigh, and as a deadly force option when swung or jabbed at a subject's head or face. We describe the most salient factors for assessing foreseeable harm in our discussion of the various force options, but it is also worth noting that the foreseeability of harm to the subject can depend on a number of generic factors, including:

The subject's size;

The subject's apparent age and physical condition, including any known medical issues;

The subject's apparent psychological condition, including mental health conditions and the influence of alcohol or drugs;

The subject's physical positioning;

The subject's apparent knowledge of or training in martial arts;

The degree to which the subject's movement has been limited;

The number of officers on scene and their respective characteristics and actions;

The officer's size;

The officer's physical condition;

The officer's training in combative or defensive tactics;

The tool, technique, or weapon being used by the officer and the manner in which it is being used; and

Environmental factors that could mitigate or exacerbate the harm to the subject.

In the remainder of this chapter, we provide a detailed discussion of an array of force options, organizing our approach by separately addressing police tools, techniques, and weaponry. These categories are principally a matter of convenience, and we are cognizant that the inclusion of certain force options in one category, rather than another, is subject to reasonable debate. Nevertheless, we believe that the categories we adopt here are useful ways of classifying force options for purposes of discussion. After we discuss the various tools, techniques, and weaponry, we turn to two force options that defy even our flexible approach to categorization: police canines and police vehicles.

It is worth noting at the outset that we exclude nonphysical options from our discussion of force options. While concepts like "officer presence" and verbal communication are key considerations in evaluating use-of-force incidents, the lack of potential for physical harm leads to the conclusion that they are better conceptualized as tactical considerations than as force options in their own right. We discussed a variety of tactical options and considerations in chapter 5.

Tools

In use-of-force situations, officers use a variety of implements that are not themselves traditionally considered to be weapons. These tools are typically proximate to a use of force, employed to preclude a subject's resistance or to improve the tactical situation, but the tools themselves are not used offensively to overcome resistance through pain compliance or mechanical disruption. Nevertheless, some of these tools can cause physical injury, which merits including them in a discussion of force options.

Restraint Devices: Handcuffs, Flex Cuffs, Leg Restraints, Four-Point Restraints, and "Hog-Tying"

Restraint devices are used to restrict the movement of a subject; reducing the likelihood of physical resistance allows for a safer means of controlling and transporting the subject. Restraint devices include handcuffs, flex cuffs (heavy-duty plastic straps with a built-in ratcheting system), and leg restraints. Handcuffs are the most common restraint device. Handcuffs are essentially a pair of metal bracelets held together by a short length of chain or, less commonly, by a single hinge. They are secured by a ratcheting lock system that requires a key to open. All reputable handcuffs have a double-locking mechanism which can be engaged to prevent the handcuffs from ratcheting tighter. Flex cuffs, sometimes sold as "disposable handcuffs," are heavy-duty plastic devices that resemble "zip-ties." Like handcuffs, flex cuffs are secured by a ratcheting lock system, but most designs lack a double-locking mechanism and must be cut off instead of being unlocked by a key.

Handcuffs or flex cuffs are most frequently applied when officers make custodial arrests and are engaged in prisoner transport, but they may also be used when officer safety concerns make their application appropriate during investigatory detentions (*Terry* stops).[3] Both types of restraints are generally applied with the suspect's hands behind their back, with their palms either apart (facing outward, with the backs of the hands together). After an officer applies any restraint device, it should be inspected by the officer to ensure it is properly applied. Handcuffs should be double-locked, and both handcuffs and flex cuffs should have approximately one finger's width of room between the restraint device and the subject's wrists. An improperly lax application of handcuffs or flex cuffs can allow the subject to extricate themselves from restraints by sliding their hands out of the metal or plastic loop that secures their wrists, but an overly aggressive application can cause the subject discomfort, pain, or injury. As the First

Circuit has held in the context of a subject who was handcuffed while being searched:

> If the search extends to the point when the handcuffs can cause real pain or serious discomfort, provision must be made to alter the conditions of detention at least long enough to attend to the needs of the detainee.... The restraint should also be removed if, at any point during the search, it would be readily apparent to any objectively reasonable officer that removing the handcuffs would not compromise the officers' safety or risk interference or substantial delay in the execution of the search.[4]

In evaluating whether restraint devices were applied too tightly, reviewers should be attuned to (1) whether the subject complained about the tightness of the restraints, and (2) whether the officer ignored the complaints or appropriately checked the fit of the restraint device.[5]

Leg restraints are metal or nylon shackles that are used to bind a subject's ankles together, typically to prevent the subject from kicking or running. As with handcuffs, leg restraints should be inspected after they are applied to ensure that the restraints are not too tight. As with handcuffs and flex cuffs, it is generally appropriate to leave about one finger's width of space between the restraint device and the subject's ankles.

The term "four-point restraints" refers to the application of both wrist restraints and leg restraints, and may involve binding the subject's ankles to their wrists behind their back with twelve inches or less of separation, a position colloquially known as "hog-tying." Putting a subject in such a position for a prolonged length of time can create a serious risk of asphyxiation (positional and compression asphyxia), especially if the subject is obese or has a diminished capacity due to severe intoxication, use of controlled substances, discernible mental impairment, or other conditions.[6]

Noise-Flash Diversionary Devices: Flashbangs and Blast Balls

Noise-flash diversionary devices—also known as diversionary devices, distraction devices, or light-sound distraction devices, and colloquially called flashbangs, concussion grenades, or stun grenades—detonate to create a loud report; more than 170 decibels at the source is standard. For purposes of comparison, the Centers for Disease Control and Prevention estimates that "shouting or barking in the ear" is 110 decibels, while "standing beside or near sirens" is 120 decibels. "Loud noise above 120 dB," the Centers warns, "can cause immediate harm to your ears."[7] Some models also produce a brilliantly blinding light. Flashbangs are most often used as a tactical tool to disorient or confuse a suspect.[8] Because flashbangs create an explosion to generate noise and light, they can severely burn or otherwise injure someone who is too close to the detonation. Manufacturers generally warn that the improper use of a flashbang can result in death or serious bodily injury.[9]

Proximity to the flashbang detonation can be dangerous, so it is highly recommended that officers visually ensure that the immediate deployment area is clear of people. Further, the device should be delivered in a way that ensures that the ports—the parts of the device that channel the explosive force—are free from obstruction. The devices are designed to route the explosive in such a way that they stay stationary upon detonation, but if a port is obstructed the device may move in unexpected ways. Ideally, flashbangs should be deployed in areas that are clear for five to six feet around where the device is expected to come to rest. Thus, officers should not engage in "blind deployments" (e.g., blindly throwing the device around a corner), "window drops" (e.g., throwing or pushing the device through a window that officers cannot see through), or deployments immediately following a breach (prior to visual inspection). Officer should avoid deploying the flashbang any closer than five feet from any individual.

Courts have held that officers can be civilly liable for failing to ensure that the detonation area was clear. In one case, a SWAT team served a search warrant related to an armed robbery at an apartment where, they had learned, up to eight people could be sleeping. After the officers announced their presence, one officer reached inside the door of the dark apartment and, without looking, tossed a flashbang near the front wall of the residence. The flashbang detonated near an individual who was sleeping on the floor, causing serious burns to her forearm. The court found no reasonable officer could have believed it was appropriate to deploy a flashbang—an explosive, incendiary device—without either looking or providing a warning under the circumstances.[10]

In some circumstances, officers can mitigate the risks of deploying a flashbang through the use of a "bangstick." A bangstick is essentially a pole with a coupling on one end to which the flashbang can be secured. The operator attaches the flashbang to the bangstick, then holds the opposite end, deploying and detonating the flashbang—by, for example, pushing it into an open door or through a closed window—without releasing physical control of the device. The use of a bangstick minimizes the potential for an unintentional contact injury to an officer or a citizen.[11]

One variant of noise-flash diversionary devices comes in the form of "blast balls." Blast balls are ball-shaped, rubber-coated, less-lethal hand-thrown devices that, like a flashbang, emit a loud noise and bright light. Some models also disperse a chemical irritant[12] or small rubber projectiles; we discuss chemical munitions and kinetic energy weapons later in this chapter. Blast balls are typically used in crowd-control situations that involve the active destruction of property or which create a threat to public safety. There are three primary objectives of a blast-ball deployment: to move a crowd or to keep a crowd moving; to create space between the officers and a crowd; and to disrupt a crowds' ability to commit acts of violence.

When deploying blast balls, officers generally use an underarm low deployment—that is, throwing the blast ball underarm at a trajectory that keeps it low to the ground—to avoid the potential for the device to detonate at torso level. The target area for deployment is typically an open space between the officers and the crowd, but it is impossible to predict the exact spot of the deployment because the environmental conditions and the rubber exterior cause the ball to bounce unpredictably.

Detonation of a blast ball occurs in two stages. In the first stage, the metal fuse of a blast ball separates from the rubber base. Once the fuse has separated, the blast-ball sphere breaks apart at its equator and the second detonation occurs, simultaneously emitting a bright light and a loud noise. The second (and larger) detonation can cause burns, and the separation of the components of the blast ball, caused when the flash powder inside explodes and the two halves of the base fly apart, can propel pieces of the base toward nearby individuals, causing blunt force trauma. While there are no lingering effects of a blast-ball, unlike those found with a chemical spray or an impact weapon, and no prolonged shock like what may be caused by a TASER, there is potential for anyone in close proximity to be injured by the metal fuse or rubber shrapnel from the ball breaking apart. Indeed, the product safety warning included in literature provided by the manufacturer states that blast balls "may cause serious injury or death to you or others." Absent a situation in which officers were facing the immediate threat of death or serious bodily injury, officers should not intentionally target a blast ball at a specific person.

Techniques

The most common uses of force do not involve or require external implements such as tools or weapons.[13] Instead, they rely entirely on officers' bodily weapons: grabbing, pushing, striking, and so on. In this section, we describe an array of such techniques.

Empty-Hand Techniques 1: "Soft Hands"

Empty hand techniques are traditionally divided into two categories: "soft hands" and "hard hands." Soft hand techniques are designed to address or control noncompliance or passive resistance (when a subject does not comply with an officer's verbal direction, but does not offer physical resistance), or low-level active resistance (when a subject physically pulls away from an officer but does not put much effort into it). A variety of different methods of subject control fit into the "soft hands" category, including:

Guiding movements, such as placing an encouraging hand on the subject's back;

Escort holds, such as putting one hand on the subject's wrist and the other on the elbow in a position that is not itself painful, but which officers can use to rapidly transition to more forceful techniques;

Come-along holds or pain-compliance holds, which include a range of low-impact joint locks, such as the "chicken wing" or "goose neck" hold (in which the officer puts steady pressure on the subject's wrist joint by pressing the subject's knuckles down toward the inside of their forearm); and

Pressure-point control holds, in which officers use their fingers to put pressure on sensitive spots such as the mandibular nerve (behind the ear lobe), the infraorbital nerve (under the nose), the hypoglossal nerve (under the jaw), or the clavicle notch (at the side of the neck).

Soft-hand techniques can be nonviolent, as with guiding movements and escort holds, or can rely on pain compliance. They are intended to set up or establish officer control over a subject or to move an individual in a controlled manner.

Empty-Hand Techniques 2: "Hard Hands"

"Hard hands" refers to strikes with the open hand, closed fist, forearm, knees, and feet as well as high-impact joint locks and takedowns. Hard-hands control techniques are typically used to gain control over a subject engaged in active resistance.

Distraction Blows. When the situation allows, officers can use empty-handed strikes to cause a short burst of pain for the purpose of causing surprise and the loss of physical or mental balance; the temporary disruption, it is hoped, will divert the suspect's attention and create an opportunity for the officer to use another technique to gain control of the suspect. A distraction blow is generally applied to the large muscles of the subject's arms or legs and followed immediately with a control technique (distinct from the strike itself) to take the subject into custody. For example, if a subject is actively pulling away from an officer's efforts to put them in handcuffs, the officer might use a knee strike to the subject's thigh followed by an armbar takedown. The head, neck, throat, spine, heart, kidneys, groin, and joints should not be intentionally targeted for a distraction blow due to the heightened risk of injury to these areas of the body.

On occasion, the classification of a strike as a "distraction blow" has caused substantial confusion. Because the purpose of a distraction blow is to divert the suspect's attention while the officer applies a control tactic, strikes and techniques that are intended to independently cause the subject to submit are not properly considered distraction blows. For example, it is common for officers to use repeated blows against a subject who is lying face down on the ground refusing to be handcuffed by holding their arms underneath their body; such blows are frequently, but improperly, described as "distraction blows." The potential for confusion has led some police agencies to eliminate the phrase "distraction blows" from use-of-force reports. In November 2006, then-Los Angeles Police Chief Bill Bratton banned the term after concluding that its ambiguity had led to its misuse by officers.[14] Importantly, the ban did not prohibit officers from using any particular technique; instead, it required them to provide more descriptive accounts of their actions instead of merely stating that they employed a distraction strike.

Whether they are referred to as "distraction blows" or not, such techniques must be justified under the circumstances, just like any other strike or technique. There is no exception or lesser standard that would permit distraction blows when any other similar strike or technique would be prohibited.

Strikes. Strikes may be delivered by various parts of an officer's body. In rough order of severity, the following body parts can be used to deliver a strike: an open hand (e.g., a slap or strike with the "knifehand," or meaty outer edge of the palm beneath the pinky finger), the bottom of the closed fist (i.e., a "hammerfist"), the knuckles of the closed fist (i.e., a punch), the forearm (e.g., a brachial stun), the elbow, knee, or feet (e.g., a kick or stomp). The safest targets for strikes are the large muscles of the arms, legs, and upper back. The risk of injury increases with other targets, particularly with strikes of any type to the face, head, hands, feet, spine, and joints, and with knee strikes, kicks, and stomps to the chest and ribs.

Strikes to the face and head present a special risk. They are unreliable as pain compliance techniques. As a *PoliceOne* article put it: "Remember the last time you were punched in the face? Were you a bit livid at the person throwing the punch? The resulting effect may be that the person will now fight even more strongly against your efforts to control him."[15] They are also unreliable as mechanical disruption techniques; it is possible, but unlikely, for an individual to be rendered unconscious with a punch or strike to the head or face. Further, under some circumstances strikes to the head or face can be reasonably expected to risk causing death or serious physical injury. There is a substantial likelihood, depending on the type of strike and where the strikes connect, that a strike will damage the eyes, nose, orbital bone, cheekbone, or jaw through blunt trauma; cause permanent scarring by, for example, tearing skin or damaging the outer ear; cause the head to twist beyond normal rotation in a way that injures the cervical spine or associated muscles; or cause an epidural hematoma (colloquially known as "swelling in the brain," this refers to bleeding in the space between the dura, which surrounds the brain, and the skull), which can carry a substantial risk of death. Further, should a strike to the face or head knock the subject to the ground, the impact of the subject's head against the ground may foreseeably cause substantial injury even if the strike itself did not. We are not aware of any legitimate police training that instructs officers to strike subjects in the head or face; indeed, police agencies commonly instruct officers to avoid such strikes unless the circumstances justify the application of deadly force.[16]

The risk that a strike to the face or head will result in serious or fatal injury is heightened when the subject's movement is restricted. When the subject is free to move upon being struck, the subject's movement can mitigate some of the force of the impact. The instinctive reaction to being punched in the face is to flinch, which involves recoiling by pulling one's head away from the punch and twisting the hips and shoulders in a way that sheds or escapes the force of the blow. When the subject's movement is restricted, however, they are substantially less able to recoil or compensate for the punch, which means they absorb the power of the punch without being able to shed or avoid it.

Takedowns. Takedowns are techniques that officers use to force a subject to the ground, which officers sometimes euphemistically refer to as "guiding" someone to the ground. Takedowns can be an effective way for an officer to establish a dominant or tactically advantageous position vis-à-vis the subject. Takedowns typically require the officer to disrupt the subject's balance by bringing the subject's shoulders out of alignment with their hips, then to take advantage of the disruption in the subject's balance to bring them to the ground. There are a wide variety of takedowns that draw from a range of martial arts, with some of the most common being an armbar takedown (in which the officer forces the subject to the ground by putting downward and forward pressure on the subject's elbow), a leg-sweep takedown (in which the officer uses one of their own legs to knock one or both legs out from under-neath the subject), and a supinating wristlock takedown (in which the officer twists the subject's wrist outward until the subject is forced to follow the mo-tion to reduce the pain in the wrist).

One relevant consideration is the potential that a takedown technique will, intentionally or accidentally, result in the officer falling on top of the prone subject. A common hip throw, the *uchi mata* from judo, involves the officer disrupting the subject's balance by lifting the subject partially onto the of-ficer's hip and, using one leg to lift the subject's feet into the air, throwing the subject to the ground. If an officer loses their balance or intentionally drops their body weight onto the falling or fallen subject, the subject can be effectively compressed between the officer—including the officers' protrud-ing equipment—and the ground. Physically small or frail subjects may be particularly prone to injury in such circumstances.

Before using a particular takedown, officers must consider the environ-ment in which the encounter is taking place as well as the subject's physi-cal and mental state. Relevant environmental factors include the surface on which the subject will land and any obstacles that the subject may hit during the course of the takedown. A takedown on asphalt or cement may be far more dangerous than the same takedown on grass or carpet, for example, and a takedown that requires a large, circular movement may be inappropri-ate in the limited confines of a narrow hallway or holding cell. The subject's physical and mental state are relevant considerations because takedowns gen-erally depend on the subject compensating, to some extent, for the motion. An intoxicated subject who lacks the presence of mind to put their hand up when he is thrown to the ground, for example, is far more likely to strike their head or face on the ground than is a sober subject. Similarly, a physically frail subject may be unable to break their fall or may be injured in the attempt to do so, and smaller subjects may be vulnerable to injuries that can result from officers intentionally falling on top of subjects during a takedown.

Physically Holding a Subject Down

After bringing a subject to the ground, officers commonly use their own body weight to mechanically disrupt the subject's attempts to rise; they do so by, for example, putting a knee on the subject's back or shoulder. Officers should avoid putting their body weight on the subject's neck or head; the pressure of such a position can fracture the hyoid bone or cervical spine, depending on the position of the subject's head. Even when officers do prop-erly brace themselves against a subject's back or shoulder, such a position should be transitory; as soon as officers can restrain the individual, all weight should be removed and the subject should be placed into an upright or seated position.

Officers must be attuned to the amount and duration of any weight they place on the subject. At least one court has held that an officer's use of body weight can constitute excessive force. In *Drummond v. City of Anaheim*, two officers, one of whom weighed 225 pounds, brought a 160-pound subject to the ground and pressed their weight against his neck and torso for approximately twenty minutes even though the subject did not resist after the takedown. The subject ultimately experienced respiratory distress and died of compressional asphyxia, which the court, quoting an expert, defined as the "inability to breathe caused by mechanical compression of his chest wall such that he could not inhale and exhale in a normal manner." The court found that the officer's use of their body weight to hold the subject down constituted a use of severe force that exceeded the minimal amount of force that was justified by the circumstances.[17]

Officers must also be attuned to environmental factors, including the nature and temperature of the surface against which they are pressing the subject. A mentally ill robbery suspect suffered second- and third-degree burns across his face and torso after California officers held him down against the asphalt of a parking lot for at least five minutes at around 4:00 pm in June 2017, when temperatures were over one hundred degrees.[18] The subject was not wearing a shirt at the time, and, according to the National Weather Service, the temperature of the blacktop was likely close to 170 degrees, almost twenty-five degrees hotter than the temperature at which an egg starts to fry.[19] The subject ultimately spent seven weeks in the hospital and two weeks in a rehabilitation unit and was left with permanent scarring.

"Chokeholds": Respiratory Chokes and Vascular Neck Restraints

In casual usage, a "chokehold" puts pressure on a subject's neck. In policing, however, a more precise definition is required because there is a substantial distinction between a respiratory chokehold and a vascular neck restraint.

A respiratory choke, sometimes referred to as a pulmonary choke, restricts or completely cuts off the flow of air to and from the lungs through the application of pressure to the cartilaginous structures of and near the trachea (the windpipe) or larynx (the voice box). A respiratory choke is an inherently dangerous technique that carries a substantial risk of causing great bodily harm (damaging the structure of the throat itself) or death (through asphyxiation). The inherent dangers of a respiratory choke have led two states—Colorado and Illinois—to prohibit such techniques except in circumstances where deadly force is appropriate.[20]

A vascular neck restraint, in contrast, is performed by wrapping an arm around a subject's neck with the inside of the elbow joint below the subject's chin. This ensures that there is space around the subject's trachea and, proximately, the suspect's esophagus. The vascular neck restraint is applied by clamping the subject's neck between the forearm and bicep, compressing the sides of neck with the encircling arm without putting pressure on the trachea. With this basic positioning, there are multiple variations in the way a vascular neck restraint can be applied, including the three levels of the "lateral vascular neck restraint" taught by the National Law Enforcement Training Center, a private training organization.[21] Regardless of the minutiae, the purpose of a properly applied vascular neck restraint is to compress the veins and arteries that carry blood to and from the brain. By reducing blood flow, a vascular neck restraint can cause discomfort and disorientation, and can be used to render subjects unconscious (i.e., to be "choked out") within a matter of seconds. At the point where the subject submits or is rendered unconscious, of course, the officer should release the hold and apply a control hold for handcuffing.

Properly applied, the technique does not twist or torque the neck, does not put pressure on a subject's trachea, and does not interfere with breathing—although even a properly applied restraint has inherent risks. However, vascular neck restraints do present real dangers to the subject. The primary danger of a vascular neck restraint is that it will be applied improperly. Poor positioning, the application of too much pressure, failure to properly brace the subject's head and body, and other factors can lead an officer to push, pull, or twist a subject's neck beyond the normal range of rotation, potentially causing paralysis or death. Similarly, even a properly applied vascular neck restraint has the potential to shift into a respiratory choke as the officer and subject move in the course of a struggle.

Even when a vascular neck restraint is properly applied, the potential for harm to the subject merits additional consideration. After a vascular neck restraint has been applied, officers should check and monitor the subject's breathing and pulse. Many police agencies require medical clearance after a vascular neck restraint, either by a paramedic or an Emergency Medical Services response, or the transportation of the subject to a hospital. At a minimum, officers should monitor subjects for a period of time, typically twenty minutes, prior to transporting a subject in a nonmedical vehicle (such as a police vehicle or prisoner transport van).

There is little consensus in policing about the propriety of vascular neck restraints. Some agencies, including the New York City Police Department, prohibit the use of such techniques altogether. Other agencies restrict vascular neck restraints to situations in which deadly force would be justified.[22] Yet other agencies classify vascular neck restraints as an application of intermediate force.

Weaponry

Weapons are devices specifically intended to cause physical harm. In this section, we discuss some of the most common police weapons, along with a few that are rarer. Any list of police weaponry is doomed to fall short of being exhaustive; reviewers should keep in mind that officers may use weapons other than the ones we discuss, but in substantially the same fashion as the weapons listed below. So-called "weapons of opportunity" often, although not always, have clear parallels to the weapons we describe. For example, for purposes of evaluation, an officer's use of a large-cell flashlight as an impact weapon may be analogized to the use of a baton.

Drawing and Presenting a Weapon

Officers draw and display weapons for two separate reasons: first, so that the weapon is more easily accessible should the officer need to use it, and second, to intimidate the subject into abandoning any resistance and submitting to an officer's commands. When assessing the proportionality of a use of force, reviewers should keep in mind the general principle that officers should only threaten to use weapons in circumstances in which the use of the weapon is either justified or likely to be immediately justified. For example, an officer should not threaten to use a baton unless the use of a baton would be justified under the circumstances or a reasonable officer would think that the circumstances are about to worsen to the point at which the use of a baton would be justified. When weapons are drawn and presented in circumstances that would not justify the use of the weapon and are unlikely to immediately evolve to the point where the use of the weapon would be justified, some courts have held that drawing and presenting a weapon can itself constitute excessive force even in the absence of any attempt to use the weapon to make physical contact with the subject.[23] This makes good sense in light of the discussion in chapter 5; the drawing of a weapon inherently limits an officer's ability to use other force options, making the use of the drawn weapon more likely. The drawing of a weapon can *increase* the danger to the officer and the subject; in a physical altercation, an officer is far more likely to lose control, or fear losing control, of a weapon in their hand than they are of a weapon that is properly secured in a holster.

Firearms present something of a limited exception to that general rule, as modern police training often directs officers to draw their firearms in situations involving substantial uncertainty. For example, officers who are clearing a building are typically instructed to have their firearms drawn as they do so. Similarly, officers who stop a stolen vehicle are typically instructed to follow a "felony stop" or "high-risk stop" protocol which involves, *inter alia*, drawing firearms and potentially pointing them at vehicle occupants. In both cases, the use of a firearm is not at that point justified, nor is there any specific reason to believe that the use of a firearm is likely to be immediately justified. Instead, police training directs officers to have their weapons drawn and presented to mitigate the risk of being taken by surprise. It is worth noting that while clearing a building or making a high-risk traffic stop can inherently involve substantial uncertainty, most encounters between officers and individual subjects do not. In the vast majority of face-to-face encounters, the general rule that applies to other weapons also applies to firearms: drawing and presenting a weapon is appropriate only when the use of the weapon is justified or likely to be justified in the immediate future. Assertions that officers lacked some information about the subject or that the situation "had the potential" to escalate or the subject "was potentially dangerous" or other such universally applicable descriptions are insufficient.

Firearms are also used to provide "lethal cover" while alternative force options such as a TASER (or other electronic control weapons) are attempted. Lethal cover refers to officers who have taken preparatory steps for discharging a firearm—drawing and often pointing a firearm at the subject—so that, should a less-lethal option prove ineffective, the cover officer can employ lethal force in the event that it becomes necessary to protect the officer using less-lethal force. For example, while one or more officers use a kinetic energy weapon or an electronic control weapon (both discussed below) to respond to a knife-wielding subject, another officer (or officers) may have their firearms drawn and pointed at or toward the subject as a precaution in the event that the less-lethal weapon fails to have the desired result and the situation escalates.

Batons and Other Impact Weapons

Perhaps no weapon is more associated with policing than the baton.[24] Over the years, the basic baton has seen a surprising number of iterations. The first batons were nothing more than short lengths of hardwood, while specialty or "riot" batons were simply longer, heavier versions. Gradually, manufacturers began to make batons out of other materials, including polycarbonate and metal. Monadnock introduced the PR-24 side-handle baton based on the *tonfa*, a traditional Japanese martial arts weapon. The PR-24 modified the standard baton by adding a short, perpendicular handle about a third of the way up the shaft.

Traditionally, batons were carried on a ring that hung from the officer's gunbelt. The desire for an impact weapon that was easier to carry and less likely to get in the way when it was not needed led to the creation of expandable batons. Today, a variety of manufacturers sell expandable batons, where the shaft of the baton and striking surface telescope out of the handle. By necessity, though, expandable batons are hollow, which limits their kinetic force when used. Further, most expandable batons lack a locking mechanism, which can lead a baton to collapse at an inopportune moment.

There are also a range of less common impact weapons. One early impact weapon that has almost disappeared from modern policing is the sap, a short-handled, flat leather pouch shaped like a beaver tail and weighted with lead or some other substance. Like the PR-24, several police impact weapons have drawn inspiration from traditional Japanese martial arts. In the 1960s and 1970s, Takayuki Kubota trained LAPD officers to use a *yawara*, a traditional Japanese martial art weapon that resembles a small dumbbell (usually less than six inches in length), creating a weapon he called the *kubotan*. Starting in the late 1980s, a few police agencies have allowed officers to carry "police nunchucks" based on the *nunchaku*, two short batons connected by a chain or flexible cord. Such weapons require a very high level of technical proficiency to be used safely and effectively. In the late 1990s, Roy Bedard drew inspiration from another traditional martial arts weapon, the *sai*, to create the "rapid rotation baton," a standard (non-expanding) baton with slightly angled cross guard-like protrusions just above the handle.

Batons and other impact weapons may be used as pain compliance tools, as when officers strike a resisting subject until the subject complies with an officer's commands, or, more rarely, as mechanical disruption tools, as when batons are used to apply leverage or for joint locks. As an impact weapon, batons may be used to push, so that the contact surface is a large portion of the baton shaft; they may be swung, so that the striking surface is a small part of the baton shaft (ideally the last few inches of the baton shaft); or they may be used to jab, so that the striking surface is the tip or butt of the shaft. Because a jab concentrates the kinetic force of a baton strike into a much smaller area, it typically creates a higher likelihood of injury than a swinging strike or a push.

When used to push, batons are generally low-level force options. When swung or jabbed, however, the likelihood of injury is substantial enough to generally merit classifying impact weapons as a use of intermediate force. Target areas for the police baton are typically broken into three zones, sometimes designated by color. The "Green Zone" is the safest for officers to strike; it includes the large muscles of the arms, legs, and upper back. The "Yellow Zone" is more vulnerable to injury; it includes the joints, the bony areas of the arms and legs, and the rib cage and pectorals. The "Red Zone" is highly vulnerable to injury and thus not to be targeted except when deadly force is justified; it includes the head, neck, throat, spine, kidneys, groin, and sternum.

Chemical Munitions and Sprays

Chemical munitions and sprays may reduce or eliminate the need for substantial physical force to make an arrest or gain custody.[25] Thus, they may reduce the potential for injuries to officers and suspects relative to physically engaging with the subject. Police have access to a range of chemical sprays, most commonly oleoresin capsicum (OC) or "pepper" spray, but which may also include CS gas (with the active ingredient of 2-chlorobenzalmalononitrile), CN gas (ω-chloroacetophenone), and other lacrimatory agents and tear gases.

Capsaicin, the active chemical ingredient in OC spray, can cause significant pain and temporary blindness through involuntary eye closure; it activates the lachrymator glands causing the eyes to tear, causes a burning sensation that causes mucus to come out of the nose, activates the gagging reflex, and creates the subjective sensation of shortness of breath as well as disorientation, anxiety, or panic. The chemical is emulsified into a water- or alcohol-based solution and pressurized in containers until use. When activated, the spray is propelled by pressure. The effective distance of a chemical spray depends on the nature of the dispersal mechanism; the small canisters that officers often carry on their belt may generally be safely used from about three feet away, while the larger canisters that are more often deployed in crowd-control situations should generally be used from at least nine feet away. Applying a chemical spray at less than its minimum safe distance can propel the solution or chemical components into the subject's skin or eyes, potentially causing eye injuries (including corneal epithelial defects and edema).[26] Because of its effects when properly applied, as well as the risk of misapplication, chemical sprays are typically classified as intermediate force.[27] At least one court has held that OC spray should generally only be used as a defensive weapon.[28]

Officers should generally issue a verbal warning to the subject, other officers, and other individuals present that OC spray will be used, and should generally delay the actual application of OC spray for a reasonable amount of time to allow the subject to comply in light of the warning. Officers must also be attuned to the extent to which a chemical spray will affect parties other than the subject, including themselves. Chemical sprays are liable to cause secondary contamination by being transmitted through physical contact with the contaminated subject. They are also likely to cause some degree of environmental contamination; not all of the microscopic particulates that are propelled through the air will land on or stay on the subject.

After the application of a chemical spray, officers should use a basic decontamination protocol. At a minimum, officers should rinse affected parties' faces and eyes with clean water, then expose them to fresh air. If the chemical spray was applied in a confined space, officers should ensure that everyone exits the contaminated area as promptly as possible. Officers must request medical response or assistance for subjects exposed to chemical spray if they complain of continued effects after having been decontaminated, or if they indicate that they have a pre-existing condition (such as asthma, emphysema, bronchitis, or a heart ailment) that may be aggravated by chemical spray. Officers should then monitor exposed subjects for changes in their condition while in police custody and request medical evaluation as needed. The failure to appropriately decontaminate a subject to whom a chemical munition has been applied can constitute excessive force, even when the initial application of the chemical was justified at the time.[29]

Although chemical munitions and sprays are typically projected from a canister or launched in the form of a grenade, they may also be applied in other ways. In one case, protestors had secured themselves together with self-releasing lock-down devices (known as "black bears"). Officers applied a chemical spray to Q-tips, then applied the Q-tips to the corners of the protestors' closed eyes, refusing to give them water to wash out their eyes unless they released themselves from the "black bears." In that case, the United States Court of Appeals for the Ninth Circuit held that the use of OC spray against passive resistance violated protestors' constitutional rights and that any reasonable officer would have known that the refusal to alleviate the chemicals' harmful effects constituted excessive force.[30]

Kinetic Energy Weapon

Kinetic energy weapons are essentially impact weapons applied from a distance. They include beanbags or projectiles formed from plastic or rubber that are typically fired from a shotgun or large-bore (37mm or 40mm) launcher. Although kinetic energy devices are not designed to cause serious injury or death, kinetic energy devices are properly considered a "less-lethal" weapon—as opposed to a nonlethal weapon—because the projectiles can cause serious injury or death if they hit a sensitive area of the body such as the head, throat, neck, spleen, liver, kidneys, or groin. For the same reasons, officers should avoid using kinetic energy devices on children as well as on adult subjects who are physically disabled or have obvious medical conditions. Unlike a firearm, which is generally aimed at the center or upper chest, kinetic energy weapons should be aimed at the lower abdomen, thighs, or forearms. Impacts to the chest from a distance of less than twenty-five feet may cause serious bodily injury.

Some kinetic energy weapons resemble firearms, which creates the potential for confusion and reflex fire. Reflex fire, also called contagious fire and sympathetic fire, refers to the longstanding observation that officers sometimes fire their weapons in response to what they perceive to be gunfire, including gunfire that they know to originate from another officer, rather than in response to an independently perceived threat. To ensure that other officers, including officers providing lethal cover, are aware that the kinetic energy weapon is *not* a firearm, launchers that resemble firearms should be painted or otherwise marked to make them easily discernible. Further, officers should provide a loud verbal announcement that identifies the less-lethal weapon (e.g., "Beanbag, beanbag, beanbag!") before firing a kinetic energy weapon.

Kinetic Energy/Chemical Munition Weapons

Several manufacturers, including Pepperball Systems and Fabrique Nationale de Herstal (better known by its initials, FN), market kinetic energy weapons that can be or primarily are also used to deliver chemical munitions. Pepperball projectiles are plastic spheres that are typically filled with a chemical powder[31] and projected with compressed gas out of a weapon system that resembles paintball guns. Pepperballs are, in essence, a combination of a kinetic energy weapon (through the impact of the projectiles themselves) and a chemical munition (the chemical irritant powder that is dispersed when the projectile ruptures). Pepperball systems are marketed toward and used primarily in mobile field-force or crowd control operations. The FN 303, made by Fabrique Nationale de Herstal, is a kinetic energy weapon that can be loaded with rounds that contain OC powder.

Because the compressed gas launcher delivers the projectiles with enough force to burst the projectiles on impact and release the chemical powder, there is the potential for a projectile that strikes the head, neck, spine, or groin to inflict serious injury or death. In April 2004, police officers employed by the University of California, Davis deployed a Pepperball system to break up a crowd of more than 1,000 people at an apartment complex. A projectile struck Timothy Davis, a student who was, at the time, standing with friends, causing permanent damage to his eye. The United States Court of Appeals for the Ninth Circuit wrote: "A reasonable officer would have known that firing projectiles, including pepper balls, in the direction of individuals suspected of, at most, minor crimes, who posed no threat to the officers or others, and who engaged in only passive resistance, was unreasonable."[32] Later that year, Boston police officers used the FN 303 weapon system to break up the crowds that assembled in response to the defeat of the New York Yankees by the Boston Red Sox. One of the projectiles struck Virginia Snelgrove in the face, creating a three-quarter-inch hole in the bone behind her right eye, then broke into pieces, inflicting fatal injuries. As with kinetic energy weapons, officers using kinetic energy/chemical munitions projectiles should avoid deliberately targeting vulnerable areas of the body except when the officer reasonably believes the subject poses an imminent threat of serious bodily injury or death to the officer or others. Also as with kinetic energy weapons, officers should clearly announce the nature of the weapon prior to use to avoid reflex fire.

Electronic Control Weapons

Electronic control weapons (ECWs), also known as conductive electrical weapons (CEWs) and other variations, have received considerable attention since the Rodney King incident in 1991. Prior to and through the 1990s, police used relatively crude devices to shock suspects. In the period since, these weapons have been re-engineered multiple times. The most popular ECW is the TASER,[33] manufactured by Axon (formerly TASER International), although police agencies also have access to stun batons, stun shields, and stun belts. TASER adoption by police agencies has increased in recent years; according to the manufacturer, more than 18,000 law enforcement and military agencies around the world now use their weapons. A TASER can be deployed in two ways: in a traditional "probe" mode or in a "drive stun" mode. In a probe deployment, compressed nitrogen launches two barbed darts out of the weapon tip to penetrate the subject's clothing and skin. Each dart has a thin wire, ranging from 15 to 35 feet long (depending on the type of cartridge), which remains connected to the weapon. The barbs are designed to generate an arcing pulse, which creates a conductive path for the electricity that will travel through the human body. When the probes connect properly, the TASER will produce involuntary muscular contractions that are likely to immobilize the subject while the weapon is activated; this is called "neuromuscular incapacitation." The further apart the two probes are, the more of the body the electricity will move through and, thus, the more muscles will be affected by involuntary contraction. While highly painful, neuromuscular incapacitation serves as a form of mechanical disruption; a subject who is actively being "tased" is easier to control and handcuff, although officers must be careful to avoid getting between the two leads or they, too, can be shocked. When the device is powered down, the pain quickly subsides and the subject regains voluntary muscular control. There is some research suggesting that subjects may suffer from at least short-term cognitive impairment in the aftermath of an ECW application.[34]

In a drive stun, the front of the handheld TASER weapon is pushed against the subject directly. The drive stun mode has two purposes. First, when one probe has properly connected, but the other has not, the application of the weapon itself serves to complete the electrical circuit. In this context, a drive stun is functionally identical to a standard probe deployment. Second, a drive stun can be used without any probe deployment as a pain compliance tool; it can cause minor muscular contractions, but the limited contact area means that such effects are highly localized and will not result in incapacitation.

Although ECW models differ, TASER's default application is a five-second stun cycle. Thus, once the trigger is pulled, the device will actively produce electrical impulses for five seconds. Officers may reduce that time by manually deactivating the weapon (by engaging the safety) or expand that time by holding the trigger down for a longer period.

Research on the consequences of ECW use tends to show that, when deployed properly, they reduce the rate and severity of injuries to both officers and subjects relative to other force options.[35] However, the relative ease of use—one simply draws, points, and pulls the trigger—has led some officers to deploy ECWs in situations in which other options may be more appropriate.[36] In part for that reason, ECWs generally and TASERs specifically have been subject to various criticisms, including criticisms that manufacturer funding skewed the results of device safety research[37] and criticisms by the American Civil Liberties Union and Amnesty International.[38] We will not review here the substantial body of literature about the effects of ECW use.[39] It is worth noting, however, that the application of a TASER is intensely painful. The darts themselves cause small punctures, and the electrical discharge that causes neuromuscular incapacitation is excruciating and can cause burns at the application site. In *Armstrong v. Village of Pinehurst*, the Fourth Circuit described the TASER effects as follows:

The [TASER] weapon is designed to "caus[e] . . . excruciating pain," *Cavanaugh v. Woods Cross City*, 625 F.3d 661, 665 (10th Cir. 2010), and application can burn a subject's flesh, see *Orem v. Rephann*, 523 F.3d 442, 447-48 (4th Cir. 2008) *abrogated on other grounds by Wilkins v. Gaddy*, 559 U.S. 34, 37, 130 S. Ct. 1175, 175 L.Ed.2d 995 (2010); cf. *Commonwealth v. Caetano*, 470 Mass. 774, 26 N.E.3d 688, 692 (2015) ("[W]e consider the stun gun a per se dangerous weapon at common law."). We have observed that a taser "inflicts a painful and frightening blow." *Orem*, 523 F.3d at 448 (quoting *Hickey v. Reeder*, 12 F.3d 754, 757 (8th Cir. 1993)). Other circuits have made similar observations. See, e.g., *Estate of Booker v. Gomez*, 745 F.3d 405, 414 n. 9 (10th Cir. 2014) ("A taser delivers electricity into a person's body, causing severe pain."); *Abbott v. Sangamon Cnty.*, 705 F.3d 706, 726 (7th Cir. 2013) ("This court has acknowledged that one need not have personally endured a taser jolt to know the pain that must accompany it, and several of our sister circuits have likewise recognized the intense pain inflicted by a taser." (Internal citations and quotation marks omitted.); *Bryan*, 630 F.3d at 825 ("The physiological effects, the high levels of pain, and foreseeable risk of physical injury lead us to conclude that the X26 and similar devices are a greater intrusion than other non-lethal methods of force we have confronted.").[40]

Although the TASER application at issue in *Armstrong* involved a drive-stun rather than a standard (probe) application, the Fourth Circuit clarified that its description was equally applicable to a TASER application in standard mode (the court uses the term "dart mode"):

Our conclusions about the severity of taser use, however, would be the same had he used dart mode. Dart mode, no less than drive stun mode, inflicts extreme pain. *See* David A. Harris, *Taser Use by Law Enforcement: Report of the Use of Force Working Group of Allegheny County, Pennsylvania*, 71 U. Pitt. L. Rev. 719, 726-27 (2010) ("I remember only one coherent thought in my head while this was occurring: STOP! STOP! GET THIS OFF ME! Despite my strong desire to do something, all through the Taser exposure I was completely paralyzed. I could not move at all." (Emphasis in original.)). And the risk of injury is increased because a paralyzed subject may be injured by the impact from falling to the ground. See *Bryan*, 630 F.3d at 824. Taser use is severe and injurious regardless of the mode to which the taser is set.[41]

Because of its severity, the Fourth Circuit held—and other circuits have suggested—that TASERs satisfy the constitutional "objective reasonableness" test only when used defensively, to protect the officer or another person from a violent attack.[42] The Police Executive Research Forum (PERF) has recommended that "ECWs should be used only against subjects who are exhibiting active aggression or who are actively resisting in a manner that, in the officer's judgment, is likely to result in injuries to themselves or others. ECWs should not be used against a passive subject."[43] Further, "[f]leeing should not be the sole justification for using an ECW against a subject."

Several issues related to ECW use are worth specific mention. First, several ECWs, including most TASER models, look very similar to firearms. On several occasions, officers have drawn and fired their sidearm when, they allege, they intended to draw and fire their TASER. To reduce the likelihood of so-called "TASER confusion," the PERF has recommended that agencies adopt ECWs that are visually distinct from firearms (e.g., brightly colored ECWS) and that officers not wear or draw ECWs in the same way that they wear or draw their firearms. Specifically, they recommend that officers should keep ECWs in a weak-side holster (that is, a holster that sits on the side of an officer's body opposite their firearm and dominant hand), and should be trained to perform either a weak-side draw (drawing the weapon with the nondominant hand and, if necessary, transitioning it to the dominant hand) or a cross-draw (drawing the weapon by reaching the dominant hand across the body).[44]

Second, there is the potential for ECW overuse. Overuse can occur when officers deploy ECWs in situations in which other options, including nonphysical options, may be more appropriate, a phenomenon colloquially referred to as "lazy Tazy" or "lazy cop syndrome."[45] Overuse can also occur when officers continue to activate the weapon even though the subject's resistance has ended. PERF recommends that agencies train officers to re-evaluate the situation after every standard cycle (which, for a TASER, is a five-second activation). Further, training should emphasize that officers should generally avoid multiple cycles or longer cycles, which can increase the risk of serious injury or death. Overuse can also occur when officers use or rely on drive stun mode as a form of pain compliance, especially against subjects against whom pain compliance techniques are less likely to be effective (individuals with a "mind-body disconnect"). For that reason, PERF recommends that agencies discourage officers from using drive stun as pain compliance, reserving that technique only to complete a neuromuscular incapacitation circuit or, when necessary, to create distance between the officer and the subject. Finally, overuse can occur when officers fail to take advantage of neuromuscular incapacitation by restraining the subject, leading to unnecessary additional activations. For this, PERF recommends training officers to attempt appropriate hands-on control tactics during ECW activations, potentially including grabbing a subject's arms and legs or handcuffing the subject. Such training must teach officers that they will not be exposed to an electric discharge *unless* they make contact with the electrical circuit (i.e., by touching the subject between the probes).

Third, the activation of an ECW with a projectile function makes a sound that may be mistaken for gunfire, which can cause other officers to fire their own firearms in reflex. As with kinetic energy weapons, officers should minimize the potential for reflex fire by providing a loud verbal announcement—"TASER, TASER, TASER" is an industry norm—before activating an ECW.

Fourth, as with some other force options, officers should generally avoid using ECWs against particularly vulnerable subjects—such as pregnant women, the elderly, young children, and subjects with identifiable physical frailties—and should avoid applying ECWs to especially sensitive areas, such as the head, neck, or groin. The neuromuscular incapacitation effect of ECW deployment means that affected subjects may lose their ability to maintain their balance or other gross motor functions. As TASER training documents have stated, neuromuscular incapacitation "frequently causes subject to fall," and those "[f]alls are often uncontrolled [such that the] subject is often unable to protect or catch himself." This can increase the risks entailed in ECW deployment, as "[f]alls, even from ground level, can cause serious injuries or death." For that reason, officers should "[c]onsider the environment (including the ground surface) and the likelihood of a fall related injury[,]" and should "optimize choice of landing zone" when it is practical to do so.[46] Officers should also avoid using an ECW on an individual in an elevated position, such as at the top of a set of stairs or on a tree. At least one court has held that the application of a TASER against a subject who was 10 to 15 feet above the ground can be considered a use of deadly force and is subject to being analyzed as such.[47] For substantially the same reasons, officers should not generally use ECWs against a subject who is operating or in physical control of a vehicle in motion.

Firearms

Officers regularly carry handguns, shotguns, and rifles in the course of their duties. We will not here generally describe firearms and their operation in any great depth; it is sufficient to acknowledge that officers in the United States are trained to use firearms to terminate an existing threat, which they do by shooting at the upper portion of a subject's torso, known as the "center mass," or first at the subject's center mass and then at the subject's head. The remainder of our discussion is limited to three particularly relevant issues: reflex fire, shooting at moving vehicles, and warning shots.

Reflex fire, also called contagious fire and sympathetic fire, is when officers fire in response to what they perceive to be gunfire, including gunfire that they know to originate from another officer, rather than in response to an independently perceived threat. Although reflex fire is often offered as a way to explain a high volume of shots, reflex fire is not, in most situations, a sufficient justification for intentionally using deadly force. Each application of force—that is, each shot, or each set of shots in a compressed period—must be justified by the circumstances that observably exist at the time.

Over time, police training and agency policies related to shooting at moving vehicles have evolved. Originally, there were few, if any, restrictions on the practice. As a result, there were multiple occasions in which officers positioned themselves in front of or behind vehicles, then shot to address the threat of being run over. On other occasions, officers would shoot at a vehicle during or after a high-speed pursuit, hoping to terminate the pursuit by disabling the vehicle or the driver. The movement to generally prohibit officers from using firearms against moving vehicles began in August 1972, when New York City Police Officer Timothy Murphy spotted a stolen vehicle occupied by an 11-year-old and two 14-year-old boys, and engaged in a high-speed chase. The pursuit ended when Officer Murphy shot six times at the car, striking it twice. His shots also hit two boys who were sitting on a stoop nearby. Police Commissioner Patrick Murphy responded the next day by prohibiting officers from shooting at moving vehicles. He was the first major city chief to do so.[48] Today, generally accepted practices prohibit shooting at a moving vehicle unless a person in the vehicle presents a threat of death or great bodily harm by means other than the vehicle itself. In most situations, officers should avoid placing themselves in a vehicle's path[49] or should terminate the threat by moving out of the path rather than using deadly force. Among the relatively few exceptions are when an officer is trapped, such as in a narrow alley, or unable to get out of the way, as may be the case when the officer has fallen down in the vehicle's path. These restrictions are appropriate, in our opinion, for at least three distinct reasons. First, shooting at a moving vehicle is a relatively ineffective way of actually stopping the vehicle. Second, if the driver of the vehicle *is* injured, disabled, or killed, the vehicle becomes, in effect, an unguided missile that can still present a high degree of threat to the officer or others. Third, shooting at a vehicle presents a high risk that passengers or other individuals in the line of fire may be injured or killed by the officer's bullets or by an eventual crash. There is a growing trend recognizing a narrow exception to the general rule that precludes officers from shooting at a vehicle when the vehicle itself is being used as a weapon: when the vehicle is being used as a weapon against pedestrians or bystanders, especially crowds. In such circumstances, the predictable results of injuring, disabling, or killing the driver can be effectively less harmful than the predictable results of *not* using deadly force.

Police thinking on warning shots has also evolved over time. Originally permitted and unregulated, conventional police training banned warning shots in the tactical revolution of the late-1960s and early 1970s. The rationale was relatively straightforward; there was little indication that warning shots had the intended effect, and a significant risk that a warning shot, often fired with little attempt to carefully aim, would strike an unintended target. The prohibition on warning shots was, essentially, a settled component of police tactical orthodoxy until January 2017, when the International Association of Chiefs of Police (IACP) released its *National Consensus Policy on Use of Force*. In that document, the IACP wrote:

> Warning shots are inherently dangerous. Therefore, a warning shot must have a defined target and shall not be fired unless
>
> (1) the use of deadly force is justified;
> (2) the warning shot will not pose a substantial risk of injury or death to the officer or others; and
> (3) the officer reasonably believes that the warning shot will reduce the possibility that deadly force will have to be used.[50]

This change was greeted with significant skepticism in law enforcement.[51] The concerns about warning shots essentially mirror the justifications for their prohibition.

Special Weaponry

Police weaponry has been refined over the past several decades, but it has overwhelmingly relied on familiar concepts like impact (e.g., batons and kinetic energy weapons), electricity (e.g., ECWs), chemicals (e.g., chemical munitions), and sheer bodily trauma (firearms). Such weaponry will almost certainly continue to evolve, and we expect that most, if not all, future iterations will be easily analogized to modern versions. However, it is short-sighted to believe that the future of police weaponry will be so limited. In the past decade, several new weapons have gone beyond merely modifying an existing device, instead introducing newer technologies into the policing context, including acoustic weaponry, light-based weaponry, directed-energy weapons, and weaponized drones.

Acoustic weaponry. Manufactured by the LRAD Corporation, the Sound Cannon emits high-volume sounds that can be used for communications (broadcasting messages in a particular direction at high volume) or to induce painful headaches. "Human discomfort starts when a sound hits 120 dB, well below the LRAD's threshold. Permanent hearing loss begins at 130 dB, and if the device is turned up to 140 dB, anyone within its path would not only suffer hearing loss, they could potentially lose their balance and be unable to move out of the path of the audio."[52] Acoustic weaponry first saw action in military operations overseas, but it has already made its way to the home front. According to media reports, a police agency first used acoustic weaponry in 2009, during the G20 summit in Pittsburgh, PA, and then again during the Superbowl two years later.[53]

Light-based weaponry. The tactical use of light is nothing new in policing, as the "wall of light" concept discussed in chapter 5 aptly demonstrates. For over a decade, officers have also used pulsing or flashing tactical lights that are intended to disorient a subject. The most recent iteration of light-based weaponry are devices like the GLARE Enforcer and the Dazer Laser, laser dazzlers that emit intensely bright pulses of visible light that can temporarily blind subjects and induce nausea.[54]

Directed-energy weapons. Directed-energy weapons use tightly focused energy emissions known as millimeter waves to induce extreme pain, which has led to their colloquial nicknames: heat rays or pain rays.

> When the wave enters a water or fat molecule, the encounter produces a significant amount of heat. The device is capable of raising the temperature of water and fat molecules in the skin by as much as 50°C, or 122°F. One individual who was subjected to testing described the feeling as "unbearably uncomfortable, like opening a roasting hot oven door." Any individual caught in the beam instinctively moves away from the beam, and with haste. The United States military reports that most individuals could not stand in the beam for more than three seconds, and no one tested resisted the beam for more than five seconds.[55]

The United States military tested the Active Denial System, a directed-energy weapon used for crowd control situations in Afghanistan, but ultimately rejected it as inappropriate to the mission. In 2010, the Los Angeles County Sheriff's Department instituted a six-month trial program in which a smaller-scale version of the weapon was installed in its Pitchess Detention

Center, where it was intended to be used during inmate-on-inmate assaults. We have been unable to identify the results of that trial, but directed-energy weapons remain potentially available for use in the policing context. They function at ranges far beyond the limited distances of ECWs or kinetic-impact weapons, making them potentially attractive for crowd-control situations.

Weaponized remote-operated delivery systems. In 2016, a gunman ambushed and killed five Dallas Police Department officers, then fled to a parking garage and continued to engage officers in a gunfight. Officers attached an explosive device to a remote-controlled robot, maneuvered the robot close to the subject, and detonated the explosives.[56] Although robots had previously been used to introduce nonlethal force options, including chemical munitions, the Dallas incident was the first known report of a robot being used to deliver lethal force. Later that year, at the annual International Association of Chiefs of Police conference, TASER International (now known as Axon) discussed the possibility of mounting their ECW weapons on remote-operated drones.[57] As robot and drone technology develops, police will almost inevitably have access to more remote force-delivery systems, conceivably including autonomous weaponry. While there may not be unique concerns with regard to the effects of such weapons—an ECW mounted on a drone is likely to function similarly to an ECW carried by an officer—the potential for officers to use force remotely may prompt a rethinking of the applicability of officer safety as a sufficient justification for force. Most obviously, officers cannot use force to address a threat to their safety if there is no imminent threat to officers (because the subject lacks the opportunity to harm officers, who are outside the range of the subject's weapon). The more difficult question is the extent to which officers should be expected to deploy remote-controlled weapon delivery systems, including aerial drones, as a way of intentionally avoiding putting themselves in harm's way, effectively using technology to avoid officer-created jeopardy.[58]

Police Canines

Police canines are used in a variety of ways; they detect various substances (such as narcotics and explosives), clear buildings (essentially by smelling out any people in the location being searched), track subjects, and, most relevantly for our purposes, are a force option used in the course of apprehending a subject. The deployment of a canine is best thought of as occurring in three stages: pre-deployment announcements, deployments, and post-bite interventions.

Dog bites are, at a minimum, intermediate uses of force, and may rise to the level of deadly force when deployed for a prolonged length of time (as the canine bites repeatedly or bites and begins thrashing their head back and forth) or against vulnerable subjects (e.g., children, the elderly, or physically frail subjects). Courts have found the deployment of a police canine to be excessive when the canine is inadequately trained,[59] when the canine was deployed against a nonresisting subject,[60] and in the absence of explicit verbal warnings in advance of the deployment.[61] In the absence of a serious crime, police canines should not be deployed to apprehend subjects suspected to be under the influence of drugs or alcohol or to apprehend mentally disturbed or disabled subjects; such subjects are less likely to respond predictably to a canine bite and thus more likely to be bitten repeatedly or more severely. Police agencies should generally prohibit the use of canines as crowd-control tools in the context of peaceful demonstrations.

Typically, canine handlers are trained to make a verbal announcement prior to deploying a canine against a subject or into any structure or enclosed area. Indeed, at least one court has held that the pre-deployment announcement is a critical component in determining whether a police canine deployment was constitutionally reasonable.[62]

This announcement is intended to notify the subject, or any persons within the containment area, of the intent to deploy a police canine, affording the subject, or any individuals in the area to be searched, the opportunity to surrender. To that end, the announcement should be clearly audible in the affected area; the use of an in-car public address system is often appropriate. To assess whether the warning was clearly audible, officers on perimeter positions can be asked to confirm hearing the announcements. If the area is too large for a single announcement to be clearly audible throughout—such as a warehouse or multi-room office building—announcements should be repeated as the search proceeds. When there is reason to believe that any subject(s) may speak a language other than English, the announcements should be made in the other language, if the situation allows. There is no universally accepted script for this warning, but police training consistently instructs officers to announce their presence and identity (e.g., "This is the city police department.")—unless the circumstances make such an announcement unnecessary—and to announce that a trained police canine will be released into the area and may bite individuals who do not surrender promptly. After each set of announcements, the officers should give any subject(s) a reasonable amount of time to respond before deploying the canine.[63]

When used for apprehension, canines are generally trained to engage in either a "bark and hold" (also called "circle and bark") approach, where the dog circles its target and barks until officers arrive to apprehend the subject, or a "bite and hold" approach, where the dog bites its intended target and maintains the bite until ordered to release by its handler. Canine handlers can deploy a canine either on-leash or off-leash. On-leash deployments allow the handler significantly more control; beyond responding to verbal commands, a canine can be physically held in place or pulled away as the situation requires. Off-leash deployments introduce an element of uncertainty. Although many police canines are highly trained, there is always the possibility for a canine to not hear or not obey a verbal command that would prevent a bite. Because off-leash deployments allow for less handler control, they carry a correspondingly higher degree of risk. For that reason, off-leash canine deployments and searches should generally be limited to searches for armed subjects, subjects wanted for serious or violent crimes, or when alternative options would create a clear danger of death or serious physical injury to the officers or others. Outside of those scenarios, canine deployments should generally be on-leash. Similarly, when there is reason to believe that the subject is particularly vulnerable, alternatives to off-leash deployment should be seriously considered. Canines should not be deployed at all during peaceful protests, and canines deployed to address crowd-control situations during a riot or other dangerous unlawful assembly should remain on-leash at all times.

In the event that a canine deployment results in a bite, the canine handler's response is dependent on whether the subject was armed. If so, the handler should call off the canine at the earliest opportunity to do so safely; this may involve allowing a bite to persist while officers attempt to separate the subject from the weapon. If the subject is unarmed, the handler should order the canine to release the bite immediately, even if the subject is struggling. The contrary approach—typically termed "bite and hold"—relies in large part on the dubious assumption that the canine's bite will, through pain compliance, induce a subject to stop moving or to follow officers' verbal commands. Experience and common sense call this assumption into question; individuals bitten by dogs, including police canines, may reasonably be expected to react to a bite by physically struggling to escape the bite, rather than becoming quietly compliant. This observation has led many police agencies to instruct handlers to keep in mind that struggling is the natural result of a dog bite and should therefore not be used as a reason to maintain the bite.[64]

Police Vehicles

Although not typically thought of as such, vehicles can be used as force options in appropriate situations.[65] Vehicles can effectively be used as force options in two ways: to engage in a PIT maneuver or to ram a subject or target vehicle.

The acronym PIT stands for, variously, precision immobilization technique, pursuit immobilization technique, pursuit intervention technique, or precision intervention tactic. Regardless of the designation, a PIT maneuver can force a fleeing vehicle to abruptly turn 180 degrees, causing the target vehicle to stall and come to a stop. To accomplish this maneuver, the officer pulls their vehicle alongside the fleeing vehicle, so that the officer's front wheels are roughly aligned with the fleeing vehicle's rear wheels. The officer then gently directs the front quarter-panel of his vehicle (the area in front of his front tires) against the rear quarter-panel of the subject vehicle (the area behind the rear tires), then steers into the subject vehicle. At the same time, the officer maintains pressure on the subject vehicle by accelerating; otherwise, the officer's bumper may slide off the subject vehicle. Taken from race car driving, the technique reduces the friction between the lead car's rear wheels and the road surface. As soon as the fleeing vehicle's rear tires lose traction and start to skid, the officer continues to turn in the same direction until clear of the subject vehicle. When performed properly, a PIT causes the subject's vehicle to spin and skid while the officer maintains control of his vehicle.

The relative safety of the PIT maneuver for officers, bystanders, and any individuals in the subject vehicle depends on the nature of the vehicles involved, the location, roadway conditions, vehicle traffic, pedestrians, and weather. When conducted under the proper circumstances and at speeds under 35 miles per hour, the PIT may be considered an intermediate-level force. At higher speeds or when circumstances are unfavorable (e.g., on a narrow road flanked by a ditch or when the target vehicle has a high center of gravity, a narrow wheelbase, or other configurations that increase the likelihood of the subject vehicle flipping or rolling), a PIT maneuver is better categorized as deadly force.

A vehicle ram is when an officer intentionally drives into a subject or target vehicle. Where the PIT maneuver is, when properly performed, fairly elegant, a vehicle ram is anything but. Ramming an individual with a vehicle, even at relatively low speeds, is likely to cause serious bodily injury or death, although an exact determination will depend on the totality of the circumstances. Ramming another vehicle is more dependent on context. At high speeds, for example, ramming a vehicle can disable the target vehicle driver's ability to steer or guide the vehicle, making an uncontrolled crash highly likely. At lower speeds, a rammed vehicle can be forced to travel in any number of directions, depending on the angle, height, and speed of the vehicles.

In *Scott v. Harris*, the Supreme Court had little trouble accepting the proposition that an officer "ramm[ed]" the subject's vehicle by using his front bumper to push the fleeing vehicle's rear bumper, and that such a maneuver "place[d the] fleeing motorist at risk of serious injury or death."[66] The constitutional question, the Court wrote, was whether the officer's use of force was objectively reasonable.[67] The Court ultimately held that it was, finding that the high-speed pursuit (which had reached speeds of 85mph and had lasted for some six minutes) presented a threat of death or great bodily harm to the officers and bystanders. In so holding, the Court downplayed the possibility that the fleeing driver would have driven more safely had the police terminated their pursuit, although the majority specifically stated:

> [W]e do not "assum[e] that dangers caused by flight from a police pursuit will continue after the pursuit ends," nor do we make any "factual assumptions," with respect to what would have happened if the police had gone home. We simply point out the *uncertainties* regarding what would have happened, in response to respondent's factual assumption that the high-speed flight would have ended.[68]

The opinion is regrettably silent with respect to any commentary on the established dynamics of pursuit; the Court's emphasis on "uncertainties" ignores published social science research findings on the likelihood that, when the police terminate a pursuit, the subject will slow down and reduce the risk to the public, the police, and the subject themselves.[69] Further, the Court appears to have adopted one of the classic myths about pursuit driving: if the police refrain from pursuing, more individuals will flee from them.[70] There is no known support for this characterization. To the contrary, there has been no rash of attempts to flee in the jurisdictions that have adopted prohibitive or restrictive pursuit policies (under which officers are not or are only rarely allowed to engage in vehicle pursuits). Further, while the Court bases its opinion on the need to protect innocent third parties, the fact remains that, even under the Court's own factual analysis, the uncontrolled result of the officer's vehicle ram could have as easily injured those parties as protected them. The irony of the Court's factual re-evaluation in the case is that the analysis does precious little to provide protection to a potentially endangered public and a great deal to "green light" unrestrained police vehicular tactics in those agencies not holding a tight rein on their officers.

Conclusion

Officers have access to a wide variety of tools, techniques, and weapons that they can employ in use-of-force situations. Properly evaluating any given use of force under any of the analytical frameworks discussed in the first four chapters of this book requires understanding the force option under review. In this chapter, we provided a brief overview of the common, and many of the less common, force options, discussing the particular risks that can apply depending on how each option is employed.

Conclusion

The use of physical force by officers is perhaps the most defining and controversial aspect of modern policing. At an abstract level, the use of force is controversial because it implicates the tension between the individual interest in liberty and personal autonomy on the one hand, and the societal interest in order on the other. Modern democracies cannot exist unless constituents enjoy a degree of freedom from coercive government intervention, but neither can they exist without demanding and receiving a degree of submission to government authority. To a significant extent, public controversies about police uses of force are the result of disagreements about the appropriate degrees of freedom from and submission to government control. Those disagreements are sharpest in the context of specific cases. At a granular level, a particular use of force can prove controversial when officers are perceived to have used force when they should not have or as having used more force than the situation required.

How, then, are police uses of force properly evaluated to determine whether, in any given incident, an officer's use of force was appropriate? That question appears to solicit a simple answer, but the answer is actually quite complex, as is indicated by the number and scope of analytical frameworks developed to evaluate police uses of force. We have described those frameworks in this text, beginning with the traditional frameworks of constitutional law, state law, and administrative regulation. We then described a less formal analytical framework: community expectations. The analyses and discussion in the first four chapters cover relevant legal and social aspects of police violence.

That said, we do not mean to suggest that it will always be easy to apply any of the analytical frameworks we discussed. Doing so reliably requires a certain level of information about how officers approach and actually use force in real-world incidents. The last two chapters of this book provide that information, offering a detailed overview of tactical concepts and the tools, techniques, and weaponry that officers employ in use-of-force situations. Even with that necessary knowledge, however, applying the various analytical frameworks can be challenging. The stressful nature of a violent encounter and limitations that exist even with regard to otherwise "objective" forms of evidence, such as video cameras,[1] can leave the facts of any given incident subject to dispute, which invariably generates the possibility for both factual and interpretative disagreements to color the evaluation of a violent incident.[2]

Beyond the potential challenges of application, it is appropriate to question the propriety of the analytical frameworks as they currently exist. In light of the wide variation that can exist between states' laws and agencies' policies, we heartily endorse the view that policy makers, police leaders, and academics should take an active approach to assessing the strengths and weaknesses of the evaluative frameworks that they might otherwise accept without critical analysis. While there is almost certainly a substantial range of reasonable approaches, serious inquiry may well determine that common flaws exist and that improvements are possible.

We can think of three such common flaws and corresponding improvements that can and should be implemented immediately. First, there is a tendency to apply the various analytical frameworks myopically, focusing exclusively or primarily on the moment, or perhaps a few short seconds before the moment, when officers actually use force. By narrowing the relevant time period, this approach undoubtedly simplifies the task of evaluation. However, artificially limiting the scope of analysis also omits from consideration the varied and important ways events that precede the use of force can affect the ultimate outcome, potentially skewing the evaluative conclusion. It is imperative to adopt a true "totality of the circumstances" approach by taking into consideration the information available to and the actions taken by both the officer(s) and the subject(s) prior to the moment force is used.

Second, the traditional approaches to evaluating a use-of-force incident focus primarily on the subject's resistance—that is, the nature of the subject's physical actions—to determine whether an officer's use of force was appropriate. Properly understood, however, officers do not use force to address a subject's actions; they use force to prevent or address the predictable *results* of a subject's actions. For that reason, it is the nature of the threat that the subject presents, not the characteristics of their resistance, that should be central to the evaluation of police uses of force.

Finally, while this book has focused on evaluating individual uses of force, we recognize the need for more informed analysis of police violence in the aggregate. Unfortunately, the paucity of available information makes it difficult to have evidence-based policy discussions about police training, statutory or administrative regulation, and a host of related issues. More and better information is sorely needed to inform future public policy making. In the remaining pages, we briefly discuss each of these imperatives.

Taking the "Totality of the Circumstances" Seriously

Uses of force are only very rarely spontaneous occurrences. Generally speaking, an officer is not dropped, suddenly and without warning, into a situation that presents a fully formed threat to the governmental interests in law enforcement, public safety and order, or officer safety. Typically, an officer uses force only after a series of iterative transactions, a sometimes lengthy exchange of information and communicative signals shared between and among officers, subjects, and bystanders. An officer's use-of-force decision, then, will almost always be affected by events that occur prior to use of force itself, and often prior to the subject's noncompliance, resistance, or other physical actions upon which the use of force is immediately predicated.

Unfortunately, some analysts, including federal courts, have limited the scope of their evaluative review to the moment in which force was used, or perhaps a few seconds prior. In the constitutional context, for example, the United States Courts of Appeals for the Fourth and Seventh Circuits have held that an officer's conduct prior to the use of force—what is referred to as "pre-seizure conduct"—is not properly part of the analysis.[3] In our view, and in the view of other federal appellate courts,[4] this limitation is not only self-defeating, it also runs counter to the Supreme Court's acknowledgment that meaningful review "requires careful attention to the facts and circumstances of each particular case."[5] The problem with artificially narrowing the framework through which the use of force is reviewed is that such an approach will inevitably omit facts and circumstances that are highly relevant to determining the propriety of that force.

Consider, for example, an incident in which an officer shoots a subject who, while within arms' reach of the officer, aggressively stabs and slashes at the officer with a knife that, in an effort to avoid being disarmed, the subject had duct-taped to their hand. In that moment, the subject had the ability, opportunity, and apparent intention to attack the officer with a weapon in a manner that creates a substantial likelihood of death or great bodily harm. Under such circumstances, the use of deadly force seems at least plausibly appropriate. But there may well be more to the encounter. If the incident occurred in the middle of an otherwise empty parking lot, and if the subject was confined to a wheelchair that was visibly in disrepair (with, say, a broken wheel), then one might ask how and why the officer came to be so physically close to the effectively immobilized subject. Answering that question is essential to determining whether the officer's approach contributed to creating the dangerous situation—the very situation that deadly force was used to address—and, if so, whether the officer's threat-creating actions were appropriate under the circumstances. As is clear from the discussion of officer-created jeopardy,[6] an officer's reckless actions can precipitate a use of force that sound tactics could have avoided. The ultimate result of an officer's actions—here, the use of deadly force—cannot be properly evaluated without considering its proximate predicates.

Beyond the issue of officer-created jeopardy, another relevant consideration forestalled by an artificially narrow evaluative framework is the availability of alternative methods of addressing an existing threat. The consideration of alternatives is properly limited to those that do not unreasonably increase the risk of harm to the officer or others, of course, but focusing exclusively on the moment in which force is used may overlook even reasonable alternatives. To return to the above example, the spatial limitations—both the subject's immobility and the knife being duct-taped to the subject's hand—mean that the officer could have effectively eliminated the subject's opportunity to cause any harm with the knife by backing away. Any evaluation that fails to consider the availability and likely success of alternative measures should be viewed as incomplete, at best.

The assertions in the prior paragraphs are not without controversy. Police unions, among others, have objected to including in the evaluative framework the events that preceded a use of force and to taking into account the availability of alternatives. Such arguments tend to be rather one-sided; even the most vehement "final frame" advocate would include in the scope of analysis the *subject's* actions that preceded the use of force, including, for example, the severity of the crime the subject is suspected of having committed and their words and actions prior in the encounter. Further, we anticipate that the "final frame" advocate would also point out that the subject can avoid or terminate a use of force either by not resisting or by ending their resistance. In other words, the argument goes, the subject's failure to implement available alternatives should be considered relevant to the analysis. We happily concede both points and, in light of that that concession, we stress the need to take the "totality of the circumstances" seriously by including the officer's prior actions and available alternatives.[7]

This approach has at least two key advantages. First, a true totality of the circumstances review aligns with the philosophical approach to policing that thoughtful police leaders have endorsed[8] and that the public demands. Second, and just as importantly, holistic evaluation can contribute to better outcomes. By recognizing the role that communication and sound tactics can play in use-of-force situations, comprehensive analyses can promote the safety of officers and civilians alike. To the extent that the evaluative frameworks can shape police training, affect agency culture, and influence officer decision making, looking beyond the final frame of an encounter can measurably improve officer performance in real-world situations.

From Resistance to Threat

As suggested in part I, the more formal analytical frameworks—constitutional law, state law, and agency policy—have traditionally reviewed, compared, and proposed types and levels of force as methods for controlling or overcoming types and levels of resistance. In the constitutional law context, the Supreme Court has directed lower courts to assess, *inter alia*, whether the subject is actively resisting or attempting to flee.[9] State laws typically authorize officers to use force to overcome a subject's resistance to arrest[10] or to protect themselves from attack.[11] Police agency policies follow suit. The traditional uses-of-force models—models that have set the standards for policing since police uses of force were first systematically regulated almost fifty years ago and that remain popular with agencies today—instruct officers to make use-of-force decisions by referring to the nature of the subject's actions.

The academic literature has similarly been dominated by comparing police uses of force with subject resistance. Criminologists developed the "force factor" to analyze police–citizen encounters according to the force continuum, assigning numerical values to levels of force and resistance and subtracting one from the other.[12] In essence, the force factor uses these numerical values and tolerances to determine whether a particular incident should be reviewed more thoroughly. When the levels of force and resistance are within pre-established parameters—such as within ±1, for example—the force is likely to have been proportionate to the resistance, but when the levels of force and resistance are outside of those parameters—say ±3—the disparity between the subject's actions and the officer's actions is likely to require a more thorough analysis.[13]

The traditional approach to analyzing police uses of force has the benefit of simplicity: in most cases, it will be fairly easy to describe the subject's physical actions. In our view, however, the traditional approach has crossed the line that separates useful simplification and unreliable oversimplification. An evaluative framework that weighs the propriety of an officer's actions primarily against the subject's resistance is predisposed to omitting other meaningful and relevant considerations that can and should affect an officer's use-of-force decisions, including whether to use force and, if so, what levels or types of force are appropriate.

For example, a linear force continuum, which remains the dominant model informing administrative regulation at individual police agencies,[14] may suggest a more forceful response than a more holistic consideration of the totality of the circumstances would permit. Consider, for example, two suspects who, after committing the same low-level and nonviolent crime, are both attempting to flee on foot. One suspect is college-aged and athletic. The other suspect is a morbidly obese octogenarian toting a portable oxygen machine. Both subjects are unquestionably engaged in "active resistance," a term that the Supreme Court identified in *Graham v. Connor* as a particularly relevant factor and one that most police agencies have adopted into their administrative policies. If the primary consideration in evaluating officers' uses of force is the nature of the subject's actions—their "active resistance," in this example—it would be appropriate for officers attempting to arrest the two subjects to use the same force option.

That approach, however, is deeply flawed. Focusing exclusively or primarily on the nature of the subjects' actions overlooks a relevant difference between the two incidents; namely, the way the two subjects' physical characteristics affect the context of their actions. Indeed, the traditional, resistance-oriented approach implicates, but then fails to address, the ultimate question: was the use of force appropriate to address a threat to a valid governmental interest? While both subjects may be engaged in what are, in effect, identical physical acts, they do not present identical threats to the government's interest in apprehension. All other things being equal, the collegiate athlete threatens that interest in a way that the morbidly obese octogenarian most assuredly does not. Any analytical framework that fails to take into account those relevant distinctions is fundamentally broken *ab initio*.

That logic is equally applicable to governmental interests other than the interest in apprehending criminal offenders. The government has a strong interest in officer safety, for example, but two subjects engaged in similar actions do not necessarily threaten that interest in similar ways. A young adult with a muscular build who attempts to strike an officer with a closed fist presents a very different threat profile than a frail 85-year-old who relies on a walker for support or a physically diminutive seven-year-old, even if all three are engaged in what are, in essence, the same physical actions. Because the elderly and child subjects do not pose much of a threat, if any, to a governmental interest, officers would not be justified in using the same level or type of force that they might employ against the muscular young adult.

The fact that some analytical frameworks would come to opposite conclusions stands as an indictment of how those frameworks are conceptualized or have been applied. Although there is an unfortunate tendency to assess officers' uses of force by referring to the subjects' resistance, the proper referent is the extent to which the subject presents an immediate threat to a valid governmental interest. Regardless of whether a use of force can be explained or justified by charting the subject's physical resistance on a force continuum, each of the analytical frameworks discussed in this book should be applied with an eye toward determining whether and to what extent the subject posed an articulable threat to a legitimate governmental interest. Resistance is, of course, a relevant consideration, but only insofar as it informs the threat assessment.

Properly identifying whether the subject presented a threat to a governmental interest and, if so, the nature and extent of that threat requires a substantial degree of deference to an officer's reasonable factual perceptions. Blind acceptance of the conclusions that an officer draws from those perceptions, however, is unacceptable. Threat, as we have explained, exists only when the subject has—or, at the time, reasonably appears to have—the ability, opportunity, and apparent intention to cause a particular harm (i.e., escaping an arrest or injuring the officer or another person).

The Need for Better Information

With the advent of the internet, there is a plethora of information available at our fingertips. A quick query can yield information that, in prior years, would have been limited to a relatively small audience of interested experts. For example, a simple Google search can provide detailed information about the economic profile of the United States, including the metric tons of beef and pork, the head of cattle and hogs,[15] or the number of passenger vehicles and light trucks[16] that the country imports and exports. Similarly available is data about the number of baccalaureate degrees awarded in the United States, including a breakdown by race and sex;[17] census data about the many different cities in the United States;[18] occupational data;[19] and information about arrests, crime, and crime victims.[20] Anyone who looks for reliable data about police uses of force, however, is quickly frustrated; even dedicated researchers—men and women who have spent their career in policing or who specialize in studying the use of force—have found themselves stymied. This has proven true even at the highest levels of government. In his October 2015 testimony before the House Judiciary Committee, then-Director of the FBI James Comey called the lack of information about police shootings "embarrassing,"[21] saying, "We can't have an informed discussion because we don't have data. . . . I cannot tell you how many people were shot by police in the United States last month, last year, or anything about the demographic. And that's a very bad place to be."[22]

Worse still, what little official information does exist appears highly unreliable. Since 2015, when the *Washington Post* began gathering information from media sources about fatal police shootings—a statistic that both represents a small percentage of police uses of force and is underinclusive, at least to some degree, of officer-involved homicides more generally—it has identified an average of 985.75 such incidents every year. That number is far higher than the official statistics reflected in the Centers for Disease Control and Prevention's National Violent Death Reporting System[23] (which reported an annual average of 283.4 incidents from 2012 to 2016) or the FBI's Crime in the United States, Justifiable Homicide survey (reporting an annual average of 451.2 incidents from 2013 to 2017).[24] National data collection efforts have been lackadaisical, ineffective, or both. The Death in Custody Reporting Act of 2000 was allowed to expire in 2006. Although the Bureau of Justice Statistics continued to collect the relevant data, and although their efforts were reinvigorated by the Death in Custody Reporting Act of 2013, the law requires *states* to report certain kinds of data to the federal government, but it does not require *individual police agencies* to report that data to the states, nor does it obligate states to impose such a requirement. Since the law's re-enactment, it has proven, as Matt Apuzzo and Sarah Cohen have reported, "almost useless":

> Nearly all departments said they kept track of their shootings, but in accounting for all uses of force, the figures varied widely.
>
> Some cities included episodes in which officers punched suspects or threw them to the ground. Others did not. Some counted the use of less lethal weapons, such as beanbag guns. Others did not.
>
> And many departments, including large ones such as those in New York, Houston, Baltimore and Detroit, either said they did not know how many times their officers had used force or simply refused to say. That made any meaningful analysis of the data impossible.[25]

State efforts to collect data on police uses of force have been similarly limited. In Texas, for example, a state law requires police agencies to report "officer-involved injur[ies] or death[s]," but defines that term to mean "an incident during which a peace officer discharges a firearm causing injury or death to another."[26] Further, over a ten-year period, one study found, agencies in Texas failed to report hundreds of fatal encounters.[27]

The need for official sources of reliable information about police uses of force, including but not limited to lethal force, is obvious. And there is some reason for optimism, however guarded. In January 2019, after almost four years of preparation and an 18-month pilot project, the FBI launched a National Use-of-Force Data Collection effort. That initiative will collect reports about "any use of force that results in the death or serious bodily injury of a person, as well as when a law enforcement officer discharges a firearm at or in the direction of a person," including a range of valuable information that has been omitted from prior efforts.[28]

What is less obvious, but no less critical, is the need for other information that can help inform the development of law and policy regulating the use of force. We lack information about the relationship, if any, between a states' statutory regime and instances when officers actually use force. Florida, for example, provides broad statutory authorization for officers to use deadly force when it is reasonably necessary to prevent the escape of a fleeing felon.[29] Tennessee, in contrast, has a restrictive statute that requires officers to have probable cause, does not allow officers to use deadly force unless all other reasonable means of apprehension have been exhausted or are infeasible, and requires officers to inform subjects of their identity when feasible.[30] Yet the available data suggests that officers in Tennessee use deadly force more often per capita than officers in Florida.[31] As that contrast demonstrates, the impact of the statutes on officer behavior, if any, is unclear.

The same thing is true of police agencies' policies. There are both broad commonalities and significant variations among policies, as we discussed in chapter 3. A 2011 study concluded that 80 percent of agencies used some type of force continuum, but that there were a "total of 123 different permutations."[32] These policies were developed with little, if any, empirical foundation; instead, "[d]epartments pick and choose, and tweak and adapt in a multitude of ways—all unfortunately, with no empirical evidence as to which approach is best or even better than another."[33] In short, no one has yet conducted a proper study on the impact of the various types of use-of-force policies to determine their relative effects.

There also exists a need for a more robust understanding of the correlates of force and how they might be addressed through training, policy, and culture. A number of studies, for example, have looked at the objective characteristics of officers or subjects, such as race, age, sex, and education.[34] These studies have not kept up with contemporary conversations about policing and the use of force. Over the past few years, for example, there has been significant attention paid to cognitive biases and implicit associations. Race, perceived class, and a variety of other factors are implicated in the web of unconscious mental frameworks that shape our perceptions and conclusions. The available evidence for the existence of implicit biases is quite strong, but the empirical evidence detailing how such biases affect human decision making generally, and use-of-force decisions specifically, is lacking. Further, a number of police agencies have adopted training intended to inform officers of the concept or, more problematically, to counter the purported effects of implicit biases. Unfortunately, such training programs have generally not been subjected to rigorous scrutiny to determine whether they are having the claimed effect. One meta-analysis reviewed 492 studies (with 87,418 total participants) and found that "changes in measured implicit bias are possible, but those changes do not necessarily translate into changes in explicit bias or behavior."[35]

Obtaining the relevant data and conducting the necessary studies may prove challenging. Historically, neither policing as an industry nor most individual police agencies have been particularly enthusiastic to share information with academics or a broader audience. Often there have been rational justifications, if not good reasons, for this reluctance: no police executive wants their agency come in "last" by reporting more uses of force than peer agencies, and officers can be loath to subject themselves to what they view as unfair criticisms by outsiders.[36] Nevertheless, answering open questions about how police are currently using force, the role of regulation in shaping behavior, and how training and culture can impact officer decision making may prove invaluable not just to policy makers, police executives, and academics, but also to the officers and community members who are personally affected by the use of force.

Summing Up

The use of force by police has proven to be a challenging and divisive issue in the United States, and for good reason. Philosophically, the government's use of violence against civilians runs counter to basic democratic norms of individual freedom, liberty, and autonomy. Police uses of force, in microcosm, represent broader and longstanding concerns about governmental overreach. The reality is that the use of force is a regular occurrence in the United States; the best available data indicate that officers are using force more than once a minute, every minute, all year round. Police violence also plays an important role in shaping public attitudes toward government generally and policing more specifically; community trust and confidence in policing is undermined by the perception that officers are using force unnecessarily, too frequently, or in problematically disparate ways. And yet, the public discussion about the use of force all too often overlooks critical aspects of accountability.

In this book, we have built upon and gone beyond existing academic work in order to address an important, but largely overlooked, facet of the difficult and controversial issue of police violence and accountability. In the first part of this book, we dedicated a chapter to each of four evaluative standards that are used to assess the propriety of an officer's uses of force, engaging in a detailed discussion of the analytical frameworks represented by constitutional law, state law, administrative regulation, and community expectations. In the second part of the book, we provided information about police tactics and tactical concepts as well as the various techniques, tools, and weapons that make up the range of force options that officers have available to them. The first and second parts of the book are interrelated; one cannot begin to apply one of the evaluative frameworks without understanding police practices, nor can one apply that information, in and of itself, to assess a use of force in the absence of an evaluative framework.

Finally, we do not intend for this book to be an instructive guide for rank-and-file officers regarding whether and how to use force in any given situation, although we do believe that officers would certainly benefit from the material we present. Rather, we seek to offer scholars, policy makers, and police executives a detailed and thorough examination of a narrow question: namely, how individual police uses of force are evaluated in the United States.

ACKNOWLEDGMENTS

With great appreciation for the research assistance of Jacob Lampke, the attentive editorial assistance of Inge Lewis, Paul Sager, and Carl Jenkinson, and the guidance of Clara Platter and Martin Coleman.

APPENDIX OF STATE LAWS

This appendix identifies the section and title of state statutes and, when statutes are lacking, the case name and citation of judicial opinions that set out the state standards for the use of force by police, quoting the relevant language of each statute and briefly summarizing the relevant portion of each case. (We summarize only the portions of the rules that relate to police uses of force against non-incarcerated persons. We intentionally omit statutes and portions of statutes that relate to the use of force by the public generally and by correctional officers or guards at detention facilities.)

Alabama

Ala. Code. § 13A-3-27. Use of force in making an arrest or preventing an escape.

(a) A peace officer is justified in using that degree of physical force which he reasonably believes to be necessary, upon a person in order:

    (1) To make an arrest for a misdemeanor, violation or violation of a criminal ordinance, or to prevent the escape from custody of a person arrested for a misdemeanor, violation or violation of a criminal ordinance, unless the peace officer knows that the arrest is unauthorized; or

    (2) To defend himself or a third person from what he reasonably believes to be the use or imminent use of physical force while making or attempting to make an arrest for a misdemeanor, violation or violation of a criminal ordinance, or while preventing or attempting to prevent an escape from custody of a person who has been legally arrested for a misdemeanor, violation or violation of a criminal ordinance.

(b) A peace officer is justified in using deadly physical force upon another person when and to the extent that he reasonably believes it necessary in order:

    (1) To make an arrest for a felony or to prevent the escape from custody of a person arrested for a felony, unless the officer knows that the arrest is unauthorized; or

    (2) To defend himself or a third person from what he reasonably believes to be the use or imminent use of deadly physical force.

(c) Nothing in subdivision (a)(1), or (b)(1) . . . constitutes justification for reckless or criminally negligent conduct by a peace officer amounting to an offense against or with respect to persons being arrested or to innocent persons whom he is not seeking to arrest or retain in custody.

(d) A peace officer who is effecting an arrest pursuant to a warrant is justified in using the physical force prescribed in subsections (a) and (b) unless the warrant is invalid and is known by the officer to be invalid.

ENACTED IN 1979; NO SUBSEQUENT AMENDMENTS.

Alaska

Alaska Stat. § 11.81.370. Justification: Use of force by a peace officer in making an arrest or terminating an escape.

(a) In addition to using force justified under other sections of this chapter, a peace officer may use nondeadly force and may threaten to use deadly force when and to the extent the officer reasonably believes it necessary to make an arrest, to terminate an escape or attempted escape from custody, or to make a lawful stop. The officer may use deadly force only when and to the extent the officer reasonably believes the use of deadly force is necessary to make the arrest or terminate the escape or attempted escape from custody of a person the officer reasonably believes

    (1) has committed or attempted to commit a felony which involved the use of force against a person;

    (2) has escaped or is attempting to escape from custody while in possession of a firearm on or about the person; or

    (3) may otherwise endanger life or inflict serious physical injury unless arrested without delay.

(b) The use of force in making an arrest or stop is not justified under this section unless the peace officer reasonably believes the arrest or stop is lawful.

(c) Nothing in this section prohibits or restricts a peace officer in preparing to use or threatening to use a dangerous instrument.

ENACTED IN 1978; NO SUBSEQUENT AMENDMENTS.

Arizona

Ariz. Rev. Stat. § 13–409. Justification; use of physical force in law enforcement.

A person is justified in threatening or using physical force against another if in making or assisting in making an arrest or detention or in preventing or assisting in preventing the escape after arrest or detention of that other person, such person uses or threatens to use physical force and all of the following exist:

1. A reasonable person would believe that such force is immediately necessary to effect the arrest or detention or prevent the escape.
2. Such person makes known the purpose of the arrest or detention or believes that it is otherwise known or cannot reasonably be made known to the person to be arrested or detained.
3. A reasonable person would believe the arrest or detention to be lawful.

ENACTED IN 1977; NO SUBSEQUENT AMENDMENTS.

Ariz. Rev. Stat. § 13–410. Justification; use of deadly physical force in law enforcement.

A. The threatened use of deadly physical force by a person against another is justified pursuant to § 13–409 only if a reasonable person effecting the arrest or preventing the escape would believe the suspect or escapee is:
   1. Actually resisting the discharge of a legal duty with deadly physical force or with the apparent capacity to use deadly physical force; or
   2. A felon who has escaped from lawful confinement; or
   3. A felon who is fleeing from justice or resisting arrest with physical force.
B. [Concerning private persons.]
C. The use of deadly force by a peace officer against another is justified pursuant to § 13 409 only when the peace officer reasonably believes that it is necessary:
   1. To defend himself or a third person from what the peace officer reasonably believes to be the use or imminent use of deadly physical force.
   2. To effect an arrest or prevent the escape from custody of a person whom the peace officer reasonably believes:
      (a) Has committed, attempted to commit, is committing or is attempting to commit a felony involving the use or a threatened use of a deadly weapon.
      (b) Is attempting to escape by use of a deadly weapon.
      (c) Through past or present conduct of the person which is known by the peace officer that the person is likely to endanger human life or inflict serious bodily injury to another unless apprehended without delay.
      (d) Is necessary to lawfully suppress a riot if the person or another person participating in the riot is armed with a deadly weapon.
D. Notwithstanding any other provisions of this chapter, a peace officer is justified in threatening to use deadly physical force when and to the extent a

reasonable officer believes it necessary to protect himself against another's potential use of physical force or deadly physical force.

ENACTED IN 1989; NO SUBSEQUENT AMENDMENTS.

Arkansas

Ark. Code Ann. § 5-2-610. Use of physical force by law enforcement officers.

(a) A law enforcement officer is justified in using nondeadly physical force or threatening to use deadly physical force upon another person if the law enforcement officer reasonably believes the use of nondeadly physical force or the threat of use of deadly physical force is necessary to:
  (1) Effect an arrest or to prevent the escape from custody of an arrested person unless the law enforcement officer knows that the arrest is unlawful; or
  (2) Defend himself or herself or a third person from what the law enforcement officer reasonably believes to be the use or imminent use of physical force while effecting or attempting to effect an arrest or while preventing or attempting to prevent an escape.

(b) A law enforcement officer is justified in using deadly physical force upon another person if the law enforcement officer reasonably believes that the use of deadly physical force is necessary to:
  (1) Effect an arrest or to prevent the escape from custody of an arrested person whom the law enforcement officer reasonably believes has committed or attempted to commit a felony and is presently armed or dangerous; or
  (2) Defend himself or herself or a third person from what the law enforcement officer reasonably believes to be the use or imminent use of deadly physical force.

PREVIOUSLY CODIFIED IN 1947; CURRENT STATUTE ENACTED IN 1975; LAST AMENDED IN 2005.

California

Cal Penal Code § 196. Justifiable homicide; public officers limited

Homicide is justifiable when committed by peace officers and those acting by their command in their aid and assistance, under either of the following circumstances—

(a) In obedience to any judgment of a competent court.
(b) When the homicide results from a peace officer's use of force that is in compliance with Section 835a.

ENACTED IN 1872; AMENDED IN 2019.

Cal Penal Code § 835a. Use of force to effect arrest, prevent escape, or overcome resistance.

(a) The Legislature finds and declares all of the following:

(1) . . .

(2) As set forth below, it is the intent of the Legislature that peace officers use deadly force only when necessary in defense of human life. In determining whether deadly force is necessary, officers shall evaluate each situation in light of the particular circumstances of each case, and shall use other available resources and techniques if reasonably safe and feasible to an objectively reasonable officer.

(3) That the decision by a peace officer to use force shall be evaluated carefully and thoroughly, in a manner that reflects the gravity of that authority and the serious consequences of the use of force by peace officers, in order to ensure that officers use force consistent with law and agency policies.

(4) That the decision by a peace officer to use force shall be evaluated from the perspective of a reasonable officer in the same situation, based on the totality of the circumstances known to or perceived by the officer at the time, rather than with the benefit of hindsight, and that the totality of the circumstances shall account for occasions when officers may be forced to make quick judgments about using force.

(5) . . .

(b) Any peace officer who has reasonable cause to believe that the person to be arrested has committed a public offense may use objectively reasonable force to effect the arrest, to prevent escape, or to overcome resistance.

(c) (1) Notwithstanding subdivision (b), a peace officer is justified in using deadly force upon another person only when the officer reasonably believes, based on the totality of the circumstances, that such force is necessary for either of the following reasons:

(A) To defend against an imminent threat of death or serious bodily injury to the officer or to another person.

(B) To apprehend a fleeing person for any felony that threatened or resulted in death or serious bodily injury, if the officer reasonably believes that the person will cause death or serious bodily injury to another unless immediately apprehended. Where feasible, a peace officer shall, prior to the use of force, make reasonable efforts to identify themselves as a peace officer and to warn that deadly force may be used, unless the officer has objectively reasonable grounds to believe the person is aware of those facts.

(2) A peace officer shall not use deadly force against a person based on the danger that person poses to themselves, if an objectively reasonable officer would believe the person does not pose an imminent threat of death or serious bodily injury to the peace officer or to another person.

(d) A peace officer who makes or attempts to make an arrest need not retreat or desist from their efforts by reason of the resistance or threatened resistance of the person being arrested. A peace officer shall not be deemed an aggressor or lose the right to self-defense by the use of objectively reasonable force in compliance with subdivisions (b) and (c) to effect the arrest or to prevent escape or to overcome resistance. For the purposes of this subdivision, "retreat" does not mean tactical repositioning or other deescalation tactics.

(e) For purposes of this section, the following definitions shall apply:

(1) "Deadly force" means any use of force that creates a substantial risk of causing death or serious bodily injury, including, but not limited to, the discharge of a firearm.

(2) A threat of death or serious bodily injury is "imminent" when, based on the totality of the circumstances, a reasonable officer in the same situation would believe that a person has the present ability, opportunity, and apparent intent to immediately cause death or serious bodily injury to the peace officer or another person. An imminent harm is not merely a fear of future harm, no matter how great the fear and no matter how great the likelihood of the harm, but is one that, from appearances, must be instantly confronted and addressed.

(3) "Totality of the circumstances" means all facts known to the peace officer at the time, including the conduct of the officer and the subject leading up to the use of deadly force.

ENACTED IN 1957; AMENDED IN 2019.

Colorado

Colo. Rev. Stat. § 18-1-707. Use of physical force in making an arrest or in preventing an escape—definitions.

(1) Except as provided in subsections (2) and (2.5) of this section, a peace officer is justified in using reasonable and appropriate physical force upon another person when and to the extent that he reasonably believes it necessary:

(a) To effect an arrest or to prevent the escape from custody of an arrested person unless he knows that the arrest is unauthorized; or

(b) To defend himself or a third person from what he reasonably believes to be the use or imminent use of physical force while effecting or attempting to effect such an arrest or while preventing or attempting to prevent such an escape.

(2) A peace officer is justified in using deadly physical force upon another person for a purpose specified in subsection (1) of this section only when he reasonably believes that it is necessary:

    (a) To defend himself or a third person from what he reasonably believes to be the use or imminent use of deadly physical force; or

    (b) To effect an arrest, or to prevent the escape from custody, of a person whom he reasonably believes:

        (I) Has committed or attempted to commit a felony involving the use or threatened use of a deadly weapon; or

        (II) Is attempting to escape by the use of a deadly weapon; or

        (III) Otherwise indicates, except through a motor vehicle violation, that he is likely to endanger human life or to inflict serious bodily injury to another unless apprehended without delay.

(2.5)

    (a) A peace officer is justified in using a chokehold upon another person for the purposes specified in subsection (1) of this section only when he or she reasonably believes that it is necessary:

        (I) To defend himself or herself or a third person from what he or she reasonably believes to be the use or imminent use of deadly physical force or infliction of bodily injury; or

        (II) To effect an arrest, or to prevent the escape from custody, of a person whom he or she reasonably believes:

            (A) Has committed or attempted to commit a felony involving or threatening the use of a deadly weapon; or

            (B) Is attempting to escape by the use of physical force; or

            (C) Indicates, except through a motor vehicle, that he or she is likely to endanger human life or to inflict serious bodily injury to another unless he or she is apprehended without delay.

    (b) For the purposes of this subsection (2.5), "chokehold" means a method by which a person holds another person by putting his or her arm around the other person's neck with sufficient pressure to make breathing difficult or impossible and includes, but is not limited to, any pressure to the throat or windpipe, which may prevent or hinder breathing or reduce intake of air.

(3) Nothing in subsection (2) (b) or subsection (2.5) of this section shall be deemed to constitute justification for reckless or criminally negligent con-

duct by a peace officer amounting to an offense against or with respect to innocent persons whom he is not seeking to arrest or retain in custody.

(4) For purposes of this section, a reasonable belief that a person has committed an offense means a reasonable belief in facts or circumstances that if true would in law constitute an offense. If the believed facts or circumstances would not in law constitute an offense, an erroneous though not unreasonable belief that the law is otherwise does not render justifiable the use of force to make an arrest or to prevent an escape from custody. A peace officer who is effecting an arrest pursuant to a warrant is justified in using the physical force prescribed in subsections (1), (2), and (2.5) of this section unless the warrant is invalid and is known by the officer to be invalid.

ENACTED IN 1975; AMENDED IN 2016 (ADDING SECTION 2.5).

Connecticut

Conn. Gen. Stat. § 53a-22. Use of physical force in making arrest or preventing escape.

(a) For purposes of this section, a reasonable belief that a person has committed an offense means a reasonable belief in facts or circumstances which if true would in law constitute an offense. If the believed facts or circumstances would not in law constitute an offense, an erroneous though not unreasonable belief that the law is otherwise does not render justifiable the use of physical force to make an arrest or to prevent an escape from custody. A peace officer, special policeman appointed under section 29-18b, motor vehicle inspector designated under section 14-8 and certified pursuant to section 7-294d or authorized official of the Department of Correction or the Board of Pardons and Paroles who is effecting an arrest pursuant to a warrant or preventing an escape from custody is justified in using the physical force prescribed in subsections (b) and (c) of this section unless such warrant is invalid and is known by such officer to be invalid.

(b) Except as provided in subsection (a) of this section, a peace officer, special policeman appointed under section 29-18b, motor vehicle inspector designated under section 14-8 and certified pursuant to section 7-294d or authorized official of the Department of Correction or the Board of Pardons and Paroles is justified in using physical force upon another person when and to the extent that he or she reasonably believes such to be necessary to: (1) Effect an arrest or prevent the escape from custody of a person whom he or she reasonably believes to have committed an offense, unless he or she knows that the arrest or custody is unauthorized; or (2) defend himself or herself or a third person from the use or imminent use of physical force while effecting or attempting to effect an arrest or while preventing or attempting to prevent an escape.

(c) A peace officer, special policeman appointed under section 29-18b, motor vehicle inspector designated under section 14-8 and certified pursuant to section 7-294d or authorized official of the Department of Correction or the Board of Pardons and Paroles is justified in using deadly physical force upon another person for the purposes specified in subsection (b) of this section only when he or she reasonably believes such to be necessary to: (1) Defend himself or herself or a third person from the use or imminent use of deadly physical force; or (2) effect an arrest or prevent the escape from custody of a person whom he or she reasonably believes has committed or attempted to commit a felony which involved the infliction or threatened infliction of serious physical injury and if, where feasible, he or she has given warning of his or her intent to use deadly physical force.

ENACTED IN 1969; AMENDED IN 1971, 1986, 1992, 1994, 2004, 2005, 2008, AND 2010.

Delaware

Del. Code Ann. tit. 11, § 467. Justification—Use of force in law enforcement.

(a) The use of force upon or toward the person of another is justifiable when:

    (1) The defendant is making an arrest or assisting in making an arrest and believes that such force is immediately necessary to effect the arrest; or

    (2) The defendant is attempting to arrest an individual that has taken a hostage, and refused to comply with an order to release the hostage; and

        a. The defendant believes that the use of force is necessary to prevent physical harm to any person taken hostage; or

        b. The defendant has been ordered by an individual the defendant believes possesses superior authority or knowledge to apply the use of force.

(b) The use of force is not justifiable under this section unless:

    (1) The defendant makes known the purpose of the arrest or believes that it is otherwise known or cannot reasonably be made known to the person to be arrested; and

    (2) When the arrest is made under a warrant, the warrant is valid or believed by the defendant to be valid; or

(3) When the arrest is made without a warrant, the defendant believes the arrest to be lawful.

(c) The use of deadly force is justifiable under this section if all other reasonable means of apprehension have been exhausted, and:

  (1) The defendant believes the arrest is for any crime involving physical injury or threat thereof, and the deadly force is directed at a vehicle to disable it for the purpose of effecting the arrest, or the defendant believes the arrest is for a felony involving physical injury or threat thereof;

  (2) The defendant believes that the force employed creates no substantial risk of injury to innocent persons; and

  (3) The defendant believes that there is a substantial risk that the person to be arrested will cause death or serious physical injury, or will never be captured if apprehension is delayed.

(d) The use of force to prevent the escape of an arrested person from custody is justifiable when the force could justifiably have been employed to effect the arrest under which the person is in custody, except that a guard or other person authorized to act as a peace officer is justified in using any force, including deadly force, which the person believes to be immediately necessary to prevent the escape of a person from a jail, prison or other institution for the detention of persons charged with or convicted of a crime.

(e) The use of force upon or toward the person of another is justifiable when the defendant believes that such force is immediately necessary to prevent such other person from committing suicide, inflicting serious physical injury upon the person's self or committing a crime involving or threatening physical injury, damage to or loss of property or a breach of the peace, except that the use of deadly force is not justifiable under this subsection unless:

  (1) The defendant believes that there is a substantial risk that the person whom the defendant seeks to prevent from committing a crime will cause death or serious physical injury to another unless the commission of the crime is prevented and that the use of deadly force presents no substantial risk of injury to innocent persons; or

  (2) The defendant believes that the use of deadly force is necessary to suppress a riot or mutiny after the rioters or mutineers have been ordered to disperse and warned, in any manner that the law may require, that such force will be used if they do not obey.

(f) The use of deadly force is justifiable under this section if the defendant is attempting to arrest an individual that has taken a hostage, and has refused to comply with an order to release the hostage; and

    (1) The defendant believes that the use of force is necessary to prevent physical harm to any person taken hostage, or the defendant has been ordered by an individual the defendant believes possesses superior authority or knowledge to apply the use of force; and

    (2) The defendant believes that the force employed creates no substantial risk of injury to innocent persons; and

    (3) The defendant or a person of superior authority or knowledge who order the use of deadly force believes that there is a substantial risk that the person to be arrested will cause death or serious physical injury.

ENACTED IN 1972; AMENDED IN 1973, 1995, AND 2005.

Del. Code Ann. tit. 11, § 470. Provisions generally applicable to justification.

(a) When the defendant believes that the use of force upon or toward the person of another is necessary for any of the purposes for which such relief would establish a justification under §§ 462-468 of this title but the defendant is reckless or negligent in having such belief or in acquiring or failing to acquire any knowledge or belief which is material to the justifiability of the use of force, the justification afforded by those sections is unavailable in a prosecution for an offense for which recklessness or negligence, as the case may be, suffices to establish culpability.

(b) When the defendant is justified under §§ 462-468 of this title in using force upon or toward the person of another but the defendant recklessly or negligently injures or creates a risk of injury to innocent persons, the justification afforded by those sections is unavailable in a prosecution for an offense involving recklessness or negligence towards innocent persons.

ENACTED IN 1972; AMENDED IN 1982 AND 1995.

Florida

Fla. Stat. § 776.05. Law enforcement officers; use of force in making an arrest.

A law enforcement officer, or any person whom the officer has summoned or directed to assist him or her, need not retreat or desist from efforts to make a lawful arrest because of resistance or threatened resistance to the arrest. The officer is justified in the use of any force:

(1) Which he or she reasonably believes to be necessary to defend himself or herself or another from bodily harm while making the arrest;

(2) When necessarily committed in retaking felons who have escaped; or

(3) When necessarily committed in arresting felons fleeing from justice. However, this subsection shall not constitute a defense in any civil action for damages brought for the wrongful use of deadly force unless the use of deadly force was necessary to prevent the arrest from being defeated by such flight and, when feasible, some warning had been given, and:

    (a) The officer reasonably believes that the fleeing felon poses a threat of death or serious physical harm to the officer or others; or

    (b) The officer reasonably believes that the fleeing felon has committed a crime involving the infliction or threatened infliction of serious physical harm to another person.

ENACTED IN 1974; AMENDED IN 1975, 1987, 1988, AND 1997.

Georgia

Mullis v. State, 196 Ga. 569, 577–79 (1943) (officers can "use no more force than is reasonably necessary" to make an arrest and "cannot use unnecessary violence disproportionate to the resistance offered")

Ga. Code Ann. § 17-4-20. Arrest without warrant; use of deadly force; training recommendations; authority of nuclear power facility security officers.

(a) [Setting out when officers may make arrests.]

(b) Sheriffs and peace officers who are appointed or employed in conformity with Chapter 8 of Title 35 may use deadly force to apprehend a suspected felon only when the officer reasonably believes that the suspect possesses a deadly weapon or any object, device, or instrument which, when used offensively against a person, is likely to or actually does result in serious bodily injury; when the officer reasonably believes that the suspect poses an immediate threat of physical violence to the officer or others; or when there is probable cause to believe that the suspect has committed a crime involving the infliction or threatened infliction of serious physical harm. Nothing in this Code section shall be construed so as to restrict such sheriffs or peace officers from the use of such reasonable nondeadly force as may be necessary to apprehend and arrest a suspected felon or misdemeanant.

(c) Nothing in this Code section shall be construed so as to restrict the use of deadly force by employees of state and county correctional institutions, jails, and other places of lawful confinement or by peace officers of any agency in the State of Georgia when reasonably necessary to prevent escapes or apprehend escapees from such institutions.

(d) No law enforcement agency of this state or of any political subdivision of this state shall adopt or promulgate any rule, regulation, or policy which prohibits a peace officer from using that degree of force to apprehend a suspected felon which is allowed by the statutory and case law of this state.

PREVIOUSLY CODIFIED IN 1863, 1868, 1873, 1882, 1895, 1910, AND 1933; CURRENT STATUTE ENACTED IN 1975; AMENDED IN 1981, 1986, 1988, 1991, 1997, 2006, AND 2013.

Hawaii

Haw. Rev. Stat. § 703-307. Use of force in law enforcement.

(1) Subject to the provisions of this section and of section 703-310, the use of force upon or toward the person of another is justifiable when the actor is making or assisting in making an arrest and the actor believes that such force is immediately necessary to effect a lawful arrest.

(2) The use of force is not justifiable under this section unless:

(a) The actor makes known the purpose of the arrest or believes that it is otherwise known by or cannot reasonably be made known to the person to be arrested; and

(b) When the arrest is made under a warrant, the warrant is valid or believed by the actor to be valid.

(3) The use of deadly force is not justifiable under this section unless:

(a) The arrest is for a felony;

(b) The person effecting the arrest is authorized to act as a law enforcement officer or is assisting a person whom he believes to be authorized to act as a law enforcement officer;

(c) The actor believes that the force employed creates no substantial risk of injury to innocent persons; and

(d) The actor believes that:

(i) The crimes for which the arrest is made involved conduct including the use or threatened use of deadly force; or

(ii) There is a substantial risk that the person to be arrested will cause death or serious bodily injury if his apprehension is delayed.

(4) The use of force to prevent the escape of an arrested person from custody is justifiable when the force could justifiably have been employed to effect the arrest under which the person is in custody, except that a guard or other person authorized to act as a law enforcement officer is justified in using force which he believes to be immediately necessary to prevent the escape from a detention facility.

ENACTED IN 1972; AMENDED IN 2001.

Haw. Rev. Stat. § 703-310. Provisions generally applicable to justification.

(1) When the actor believes that the use of force upon or toward the person of another is necessary for any of the purposes for which such belief would establish a justification under sections 703-303 to 703-309 but the actor is reckless or negligent in having such belief or in acquiring or failing to acquire any knowledge or belief which is material to the justifiability of the actor's use of force, the justification afforded by those sections is unavailable in a prosecution for an offense for which recklessness or negligence, as the case may be, suffices to establish culpability.

(2) When the actor is justified under sections 703-303 to 703-309 in using force upon or toward the person of another but the actor recklessly or negligently injures or creates a risk of injury to innocent persons, the justification afforded by those sections is unavailable in a prosecution for such recklessness or negligence toward innocent persons.

ENACTED IN 1972; AMENDED IN 1984.

Idaho

Idaho Code Ann. § 19-610. What force may be used.

When the arrest is being made by an officer under the authority of a warrant or when the arrest is being made without a warrant but is supported by probable cause to believe that the person has committed an offense, after information of the intention to make the arrest, if the person to be arrested either flees or forcibly resists, the officer may use all reasonable and necessary means to effect the arrest and will be justified in using deadly force under conditions set out in section 18-4011, Idaho Code.

PREVIOUSLY CODIFIED IN 1887, 1909, AND 1919; CURRENT STATUTE ENACTED IN 1986; AMENDED IN 1987.

Idaho Code Ann. § 18-4011. Justifiable homicide by officer.

Homicide is justifiable when committed by public officers and those acting by their command in their aid and assistance, either:

1. In obedience to any judgment of a competent court; or

2. When reasonably necessary in overcoming actual resistance to the execution of some legal process, or in the discharge of any other legal duty including suppression of riot or keeping and preserving the peace. Use of deadly force shall not be justified in overcoming actual resistance unless the officer has probable cause to believe that the resistance poses a threat of death or serious physical injury to the officer or to other persons; or

3. When reasonably necessary in preventing rescue or escape or in retaking inmates who have been rescued or have escaped from any jail, or when reasonably necessary in order to prevent the escape of any person charged with or suspected of having committed a felony, provided the officer has probable cause to believe that the inmate, or persons assisting his escape, or the person suspected of or charged with the commission of a felony poses a threat of death or serious physical injury to the officer or other persons.

ENACTED IN 1972; AMENDED IN 1986.

Illinois

720 Ill. Comp. Stat. 5/7-5. Peace officer's use of force in making arrest.

(a) A peace officer, or any person whom he has summoned or directed to assist him, need not retreat or desist from efforts to make a lawful arrest because of resistance or threatened resistance to the arrest. He is justified in the use of any force which he reasonably believes to be necessary to effect the arrest and of any force which he reasonably believes to be necessary to defend himself or another from bodily harm while making the arrest. However, he is justified in using force likely to cause death or great bodily harm only when he reasonably believes that such force is necessary to prevent death or great bodily harm to himself or such other person, or when he reasonably believes both that:

    (1) Such force is necessary to prevent the arrest from being defeated by resistance or escape; and

    (2) The person to be arrested has committed or attempted a forcible felony which involves the infliction or threatened infliction of great bodily harm or is attempting to escape by use of a deadly weapon, or otherwise indicates that he will endanger human life or inflict great bodily harm unless arrested without delay.

(b) A peace officer making an arrest pursuant to an invalid warrant is justified in the use of any force which he would be justified in using if the warrant were valid, unless he knows that the warrant is invalid.

ENACTED IN 1961; AMENDED IN 1986.

720 Ill. Comp. Stat. 5/7-5.5. Prohibited use of force by a peace officer.

(a) A peace officer shall not use a chokehold in the performance of his or her duties, unless deadly force is justified under Article 7 of this Code.

(b) A peace officer shall not use a chokehold, or any lesser contact with the throat or neck area of another, in order to prevent the destruction of evidence by ingestion.

(c) As used in this Section, "chokehold" means applying any direct pressure to the throat, windpipe, or airway of another with the intent to reduce or prevent the intake of air. "Chokehold" does not include any holding involving contact with the neck that is not intended to reduce the intake of air.

ENACTED IN 2016; AMENDED IN 2016.

Indiana

Ind. Code § 35-41-3-3. Use of force relating to arrest or escape.

(b) A law enforcement officer is justified in using reasonable force if the officer reasonably believes that the force is necessary to effect a lawful arrest. However, an officer is justified in using deadly force only if the officer:
  (1) has probable cause to believe that that deadly force is necessary:
      (A) to prevent the commission of a forcible felony; or
      (B) to effect an arrest of a person who the officer has probable cause to believe poses a threat of serious bodily injury to the officer or a third person; and
  (2) has given a warning, if feasible, to the person against whom the deadly force is to be used.

(c) A law enforcement officer making an arrest under an invalid warrant is justified in using force as if the warrant was valid, unless the officer knows that the warrant is invalid.

(d) A law enforcement officer who has an arrested person in custody is justified in using the same force to prevent the escape of the arrested person from custody that the officer would be justified in using if the officer was arresting that person. However, an officer is justified in using deadly force only if the officer:
  (1) has probable cause to believe that deadly force is necessary to prevent the escape from custody of a person who the officer has probable cause to believe poses a threat of serious bodily injury to the officer or a third person; and
  (2) has given a warning, if feasible, to the person against whom the deadly force is to be used.

(e) [addressing guards and officers using force to prevent the escape of a detainee].

(f) Notwithstanding subsection (b), (d), or (e), a law enforcement officer who is a defendant in a criminal prosecution has the same right as a person who is not a law enforcement officer to assert self-defense under IC 35-41-3-2.

ENACTED IN 1976; AMENDED IN 1977, 1979, AND 1993.

Iowa

Iowa Code § 804.8. Use of force by peace officer making an arrest.

1. A peace officer, while making a lawful arrest, is justified in the use of any force which the peace officer reasonably believes to be necessary to effect the arrest or to defend any person from bodily harm while making the arrest. However, the use of deadly force is only justified when a person cannot be captured any other way and either of the following apply:
   a. The person has used or threatened to use deadly force in committing a felony.
   b. The peace officer reasonably believes the person would use deadly force against any person unless immediately apprehended.
2. A peace officer making an arrest pursuant to an invalid warrant is justified in the use of any force which the peace officer would be justified in using if the warrant were valid, unless the peace officer knows that the warrant is invalid.

ENACTED IN 1976; AMENDED IN 1977, 1978, AND 2013.

Kansas

Kan. Stat. Ann. § 21-5227. Same; law enforcement officer making arrest.

(a) A law enforcement officer, or any person whom such officer has summoned or directed to assist in making a lawful arrest, need not retreat or desist from efforts to make a lawful arrest because of resistance or threatened resistance to the arrest. Such officer is justified in the use of any force which such officer reasonably believes to be necessary to effect the arrest and the use of any force which such officer reasonably believes to be necessary to defend the officer's self or another from bodily harm while making the arrest. However, such officer is justified in using deadly force only when such officer reasonably believes that such force is necessary to prevent death or great bodily harm to such officer or another person, or when such officer reasonably believes that such force is necessary to prevent the arrest from being defeated by resistance or escape and such officer has probable cause to believe that the person to be arrested has committed or attempted to commit a felony involving death or great bodily harm or is attempting to escape by use of a deadly weapon, or otherwise indicates that such person will endanger human life or inflict great bodily harm unless arrested without delay.

(b) A law enforcement officer making an arrest pursuant to an invalid warrant is justified in the use of any force which such officer would be justified in using if the warrant were valid, unless such officer knows that the warrant is invalid.

ENACTED IN 2010; AMENDED 2011.

Kentucky

Ky. Rev. Stat. Ann. § 503.090. Use of physical force in law enforcement.

(1) The use of physical force by a defendant upon another person is justifiable when the defendant, acting under official authority, is making or assisting in making an arrest, and he:
   (a) Believes that such force is necessary to effect the arrest;
   (b) Makes known the purpose of the arrest or believes that it is otherwise known or cannot reasonably be made known to the person to be arrested; and
   (c) Believes the arrest to be lawful.

(2) The use of deadly physical force by a defendant upon another person is justifiable under subsection (1) only when:
   (a) The defendant, in effecting the arrest, is authorized to act as a peace officer; and
   (b) The arrest is for a felony involving the use or threatened use of physical force likely to cause death or serious physical injury; and
   (c) The defendant believes that the person to be arrested is likely to endanger human life unless apprehended without delay.

(3) The use of physical force, including deadly physical force, by a defendant upon another person is justifiable when the defendant is preventing the escape of an arrested person and when the force could justifiably have been used to effect the arrest under which the person is in custody, except that a guard or other person authorized to act as a peace officer is justified in using any force, including deadly force, which he believes to be necessary to prevent the escape of a person from jail, prison, or other institution for the detention of persons charged with or convicted of a crime.

ENACTED IN 1974; NO SUBSEQUENT AMENDMENTS.

Louisiana

La. Code. Crim. Proc. Ann. art. 220. Submission to arrest; use of force.

A person shall submit peaceably to a lawful arrest. The person making a lawful arrest may use reasonable force to effect the arrest and detention, and also to overcome any resistance or threatened resistance of the person being arrested or detained.

PREVIOUSLY CODIFIED IN 1928; CURRENT STATUTE ENACTED IN 1966; NO SUBSEQUENT AMENDMENTS.

Maine

Me. Rev. Stat. tit. 17-A, § 107. Physical force in law enforcement.

1. A law enforcement officer is justified in using a reasonable degree of non-deadly force upon another person:

    A. When and to the extent that the officer reasonably believes it necessary to effect an arrest or to prevent the escape from custody of an arrested person, unless the officer knows that the arrest or detention is illegal; or

    B. In self-defense or to defend a 3rd person from what the officer reasonably believes to be the imminent use of unlawful nondeadly force encountered while attempting to effect such an arrest or while seeking to prevent such an escape.

2. A law enforcement officer is justified in using deadly force only when the officer reasonably believes such force is necessary:

    A. For self-defense or to defend a 3rd person from what the officer reasonably believes is the imminent use of unlawful deadly force; or

    B. To effect an arrest or prevent the escape from arrest of a person when the law enforcement officer reasonably believes that the person has committed a crime involving the use or threatened use of deadly force, is using a dangerous weapon in attempting to escape or otherwise indicates that the person is likely to endanger seriously human life or to inflict serious bodily injury unless apprehended without delay; and

        (1) The law enforcement officer has made reasonable efforts to advise the person that the officer is a law enforcement officer attempting to effect an arrest or prevent the escape from arrest and the officer has reasonable grounds to believe that the person is aware of this advice; or

        (2) The law enforcement officer reasonably believes that the person to be arrested otherwise knows that the officer is a law enforcement officer attempting to effect an arrest or prevent the escape from arrest.

        For purposes of this paragraph, "a reasonable belief that another has committed a crime involving use or threatened use of deadly force" means such reasonable belief in facts, circumstances and the law that, if true, would constitute such an offense by that person. If the facts and circumstances reasonably believed would not constitute such an offense, an erroneous but reasonable belief that the law is otherwise justifies the use of deadly force to make an arrest or prevent an escape.

3. [Concerning the use of force by private persons acting at the direction of a law enforcement officer.]
4. [Concerning private persons acting on their own behalf.]
5. [Concerning the use of force in confinement facilities.]
5-A [Concerning the use of deadly force in the Maine State Prison].
6. Repealed. 1975, c. 740, § 32, eff. May 1, 1976.
7. Use of force that is not justifiable under this section in effecting an arrest does not render illegal an arrest that is otherwise legal and the use of such unjustifiable force does not render inadmissible anything seized incident to a legal arrest.
8. Nothing in this section constitutes justification for conduct by a law enforcement officer or a private person amounting to an offense against innocent persons whom the officer or private person is not seeking to arrest or retain in custody.

ENACTED IN 1975; AMENDED IN 1976, 1979, 1989, 1995, 2003, AND 2007.

Maryland

Richardson v. McGriff, 361 Md. 437, 452 (2000) (adopting *Graham v. Connor* as the "touchstone of the analysis" for claims brought "under Article 26 of the Maryland Declaration of Rights and for the common law claims of battery and gross negligence").

State v. Pagotto, 762 A.2d 97, 108–09, 112 (2000) (determining gross negligence for purposes of an involuntary manslaughter conviction requires reviewing a defendant officer's conduct "from the perspective of a reasonable police officer similarly situated").

Massachusetts

Julian v. Randazzo, 380 Mass. 391, 396 n.1 (1980) (allowing officers to use "reasonably necessary" force to effect an arrest, permitting deadly force only when "'(a) the arrest is for a felony; and (b) the officer reasonably believes that the force employed creates no substantial risk to innocent persons; and (c) the officer reasonably believes that: (i) the crime for which the arrest is made involved conduct including the use or threatened use of deadly force; or (ii) there is a substantial risk that the person to be arrested will cause death or serious bodily harm if his apprehension is delayed.'" (quoting § 120.7 of the Model Code of Pre-Arraignment Procedure (1975)).

Michigan

Young v. Barker, 158 Mich. App. 709, 723 (1987) ("[A]n arresting officer may use such force as is reasonably necessary to effect a lawful arrest.")

Ealey v. City of Detroit, 144 Mich. App. 324, 332 (1985) ("Reasonable and good faith belief in the necessity of police action is a defense to a civil rights claim.").

Jenkins v. Starkey, 95 Mich. App. 685 (1980) ("A peace officer may use deadly force in defense of his own life, in defense of another, or in pursuit of a fleeing felon.")

People v. Doss, 406 Mich. 90, 102 (1979) ("[P]olice officers making a lawful arrest may use that force which is reasonable under the circumstances in self-defense, and unlike the private citizen a police officer, by the necessity of his duties, is not required to retreat before a display of force by his adversary.").

Op. Atty. Gen. 1976, 5068, September 3, 1976, p. 591 ("A peace officer may not use deadly force when attempting to stop or arrest a person who has committed a misdemeanor. A peace officer may use deadly force to effect the arrest of a felon unless a safe and speedy capture can be made without using deadly force.")

Minnesota

Minn. Stat. § 629.33. When force may be used to make arrest.

If a peace officer has informed a defendant that the officer intends to arrest the defendant, and if the defendant then flees or forcibly resists arrest, the officer may use all necessary and lawful means to make the arrest but may not use deadly force unless authorized to do so under section 609.066. After giving notice of the authority and purpose of entry, a peace officer may break open an inner or outer door or window of a dwelling house to execute a warrant if:

(1) the officer is refused admittance;

(2) entry is necessary for the officer's own liberation; or

(3) entry is necessary for liberating another person who is being detained in the dwelling house after entering to make an arrest.

ENACTED IN 1978, AMENDED IN 1985.

Minn. Stat. § 609.06. Authorized use of force.
Subdivision 1. When authorized.

Except as otherwise provided in subdivision 2, reasonable force may be used upon or toward the person of another without the other's consent when the following circumstances exist or the actor reasonably believes them to exist:

(1) when used by a public officer or one assisting a public officer under the public officer's direction:

    (a) in effecting a lawful arrest; or

    (b) in the execution of legal process; or

    (c) in enforcing an order of the court; or

    (d) in executing any other duty imposed upon the public officer by law; or

(2) [Concerning private persons]; or

(3) [Concerning private persons; defense of others]; or

(4) [Concerning private persons' defense of property]; or

(5) when used by any person to prevent the escape, or to retake following the escape, of a person lawfully held on a charge or conviction of a crime; or

(6) [Concerning the use of force to restrain or correct a child or pupil];

(7) [Concerning school employees and school bus drivers]; or

(8) [Concerning common carriers]; or

(9) when used to restrain a person with a mental illness or a person with a developmental disability from self-injury or injury to another or when used by one with authority to do so to compel compliance with reasonable requirements for the person's control, conduct, or treatment; or

(10) [Concerning persons committed for custody and treatment.]

Subdivision 2. Deadly force used against peace officers.

Deadly force may not be used against peace officers who have announced their presence and are performing official duties at a location where a person is committing a crime or an act that would be a crime if committed by an adult.

ENACTED IN 1963; AMENDED IN 1986, 1993, 1996, 2002, AND 2013.

Minn. Stat. § 609.066. Authorized use of deadly force by peace officers.
Subdivision 1. Deadly force defined.

For the purposes of this section, "deadly force" means force which the actor uses with the purpose of causing, or which the actor should reasonably know creates a substantial risk of causing, death or great bodily harm. The intentional discharge of a firearm, other than a firearm loaded with less-lethal munitions and used by a peace officer within the scope of official duties, in the direction of another person, or at a vehicle in which another person is believed to be, constitutes deadly force. "Less lethal munitions" means projectiles which are designed to stun, temporarily incapacitate, or cause temporary discomfort to a person. "Peace officer" has the meaning given in section 626.84, subdivision 1.

Subdivision 2. Use of deadly force.

Notwithstanding the provisions of section 609.06 or 609.065, the use of deadly force by a peace officer in the line of duty is justified only when necessary:

(1) to protect the peace officer or another from apparent death or great bodily harm;

(2) to effect the arrest or capture, or prevent the escape, of a person whom the peace officer knows or has reasonable grounds to believe has committed or attempted to commit a felony involving the use or threatened use of deadly force; or

(3) to effect the arrest or capture, or prevent the escape, of a person whom the officer knows or has reasonable grounds to believe has committed or attempted to commit a felony if the officer reasonably believes that the person will cause death or great bodily harm if the person's apprehension is delayed.

Subdivision 3. No defense.

This section and sections 609.06, 609.065 and 629.33 may not be used as a defense in a civil action brought by an innocent third party.

ENACTED IN 1978, AMENDED IN 1986 AND 2001.

Mississippi

City of Jackson v. Powell, 917 So. 2d 59, 71-72 (Miss. 2005) (permitting "reasonably necessary" force).

Miss. Code Ann. § 97-3-15. Justifiable homicide.

(1) The killing of a human being by the act, procurement or omission of another shall be justifiable in the following cases:

    (a) When committed by public officers, or those acting by their aid and assistance, in obedience to any judgment of a competent court;

(b) When necessarily committed by public officers, or those acting by their command in their aid and assistance, in overcoming actual resistance to the execution of some legal process, or to the discharge of any other legal duty;

(c) When necessarily committed by public officers, or those acting by their command in their aid and assistance, in retaking any felon who has been rescued or has escaped;

(d) When necessarily committed by public officers, or those acting by their command in their aid and assistance, in arresting any felon fleeing from justice;

(e) [Concerning private persons.]

(f) [Concerning private persons.]

(g) When necessarily committed in attempting by lawful ways and means to apprehend any person for any felony committed;

(h) When necessarily committed in lawfully suppressing any riot or in lawfully keeping and preserving the peace; and

(i) [Concerning "church or place of worship security programs."]

(2)(a) As used in subsection (1)(c) and (d) of this section, the term "when necessarily committed" means that a public officer or a person acting by or at the officer's command, aid or assistance is authorized to use such force as necessary in securing and detaining the felon offender, overcoming the offender's resistance, preventing the offender's escape, recapturing the offender if the offender escapes or in protecting himself or others from bodily harm; but such officer or person shall not be authorized to resort to deadly or dangerous means when to do so would be unreasonable under the circumstances. The public officer or person acting by or at the officer's command may act upon a reasonable apprehension of the surrounding circumstances; however, such officer or person shall not use excessive force or force that is greater than reasonably necessary in securing and detaining the offender, overcoming the offender's resistance, preventing the offender's escape, recapturing the offender if the offender escapes or in protecting himself or others from bodily harm.

(b) As used in subsection (1)(c) and (d) of this section the term "felon" shall include an offender who has been convicted of a felony and shall also include an offender who is in custody, or whose custody is being sought, on a charge or for an offense which is punishable, upon conviction, by death or confinement in the Penitentiary.

     (c) [Defining "dwelling."]

(3) [Concerning the use of defensive force by private persons].

(4) A person who is not the initial aggressor and is not engaged in unlawful activity shall have no duty to retreat before using deadly force under subsection (1)(e) or (f) of this section if the person is in a place where the person has a right to be, and no finder of fact shall be permitted to consider the person's failure to retreat as evidence that the person's use of force was unnecessary, excessive or unreasonable.

(5) [Concerning the use of defensive force by private persons].

ENACTED IN 1983; AMENDED IN 2006 AND 2016.

Missouri

Mo. Rev. Stat. § 563.046. Law enforcement officer's use of force in making an arrest.

1. A law enforcement officer need not retreat or desist from efforts to effect the arrest, or from efforts to prevent the escape from custody, of a person he or she reasonably believes to have committed an offense because of resistance or threatened resistance of the arrestee. In addition to the use of physical force authorized under other sections of this chapter, a law enforcement officer is, subject to the provisions of subsections 2 and 3, justified in the use of such physical force as he or she reasonably believes is immediately necessary to effect the arrest or to prevent the escape from custody.

2. The use of any physical force in making an arrest is not justified under this section unless the arrest is lawful or the law enforcement officer reasonably believes the arrest is lawful, and the amount of physical force used was objectively reasonable in light of the totality of the particular facts and circumstances confronting the officer on the scene, without regard to the officer's underlying intent or motivation.

3. In effecting an arrest or in preventing an escape from custody, a law enforcement officer is justified in using deadly force only:

    (1) When deadly force is authorized under other sections of this chapter; or

    (2) When the officer reasonably believes that such use of deadly force is immediately necessary to effect the arrest or prevent an escape from custody and also reasonably believes that the person to be arrested:

        (a) Has committed or attempted to commit a felony offense involving the infliction or threatened infliction of serious physical injury; or

(b) Is attempting to escape by use of a deadly weapon or dangerous instrument; or

(c) May otherwise endanger life or inflict serious physical injury to the officer or others unless arrested without delay.

4. The defendant shall have the burden of injecting the issue of justification under this section.

ENACTED IN 1977; AMENDED IN 2014 AND 2016.

Montana

Mont. Code Ann. § 45-3-106. Use of force to prevent escape.

1. A peace officer or other person who has an arrested person in custody is justified in the use of force to prevent the escape of the arrested person from custody that the officer or other person would be justified in using if the officer or other person were arresting the person.

2. A guard or other peace officer is justified in the use of force, including force likely to cause death or serious bodily harm, that the guard or officer reasonably believes to be necessary to prevent the escape from a correctional institution of a person whom the guard or officer reasonably believes to be lawfully detained in the institution under sentence for an offense or awaiting trial or commitment for an offense.

PREVIOUSLY CODIFIED IN 1947; CURRENT STATUTE ENACTED IN 1973; AMENDED IN 2009.

Mont. Code Ann. § 46-6-140. Method of arrest.

1. An arrest is made by an actual restraint of the person to be arrested or by the person's submission to the custody of the person making the arrest.

2. All necessary and reasonable force may be used in making an arrest, but the person arrested may not be subject to any greater restraint than is necessary to hold or detain that person.

3. All necessary and reasonable force may be used to effect an entry into any building or property or part thereof to make an authorized arrest.

PREVIOUSLY CODIFIED IN 1947; CURRENT STATUTE ENACTED IN 1967; AMENDED IN 1991.

Nebraska

Neb. Rev. Stat. § 28-1412. Use of force in law enforcement.

(1) Subject to the provisions of this section and of section 28-1414, the use of force upon or toward the person of another is justifiable when the actor is

making or assisting in making an arrest and the actor believes that such force is immediately necessary to effect a lawful arrest.

(2) The use of force is not justifiable under this section unless:

    (a) The actor makes known the purpose of the arrest or believes that it is otherwise known by or cannot reasonably be made known to the person to be arrested; and

    (b) When the arrest is made under a warrant, the warrant is valid or believed by the actor to be valid.

(3) The use of deadly force is not justifiable under this section unless:

    (a) The arrest is for a felony;

    (b) Such person effecting the arrest is authorized to act as a peace officer or is assisting a person whom he believes to be authorized to act as a peace officer;

    (c) The actor believes that the force employed creates no substantial risk of injury to innocent persons; and

    (d) The actor believes that:

        (i) The crime for which the arrest is made involved conduct including the use or threatened use of deadly force; or

        (ii) There is a substantial risk that the person to be arrested will cause death or serious bodily harm if his apprehension is delayed.

(4) The use of force to prevent the escape of an arrested person from custody is justifiable when the force could justifiably have been employed to effect the arrest under which the person is in custody, except that a guard or other person authorized to act as a peace officer is justified in using any force, including deadly force, which he believes to be immediately necessary to prevent the escape of a person from a jail, prison, or other institution for the detention of persons charged with or convicted of a crime.

(5) [Concerning private persons summoned by officers to assist.]

(6) [Concerning private persons not summoned by officers to assist.]

(7) The use of force upon or toward the person of another is justifiable when the actor believes that such force is immediately necessary to prevent such other person from committing suicide, inflicting serious bodily harm upon himself, committing or consummating the commission of a crime involving or threatening bodily harm, damage to or loss of property or a breach of the peace, except that:

    (a) Any limitations imposed by the other provisions of sections 28-1406 to 28-1416 on the justifiable use of force in self-protection, for the protection of others, the protection of property, the effectuation of an arrest or the prevention of an escape from custody shall apply notwithstanding the criminality of the conduct against which such force is used; and

  (b) The use of deadly force is not in any event justifiable under this subsection unless:

    (i) The actor believes that there is a substantial risk that the person whom he seeks to prevent from committing a crime will cause death or serious bodily harm to another unless the commission or the consummation of the crime is prevented and that the use of such force presents no substantial risk of injury to innocent persons; or

    (ii) The actor believes that the use of such force is necessary to suppress a riot or mutiny after the rioters or mutineers have been ordered to disperse and warned, in any particular manner that the law may require, that such force will be used if they do not obey.

(8) The justification afforded by subsection (7) of this section extends to the use of confinement as preventive force only if the actor takes all reasonable measures to terminate the confinement as soon as he knows that he safely can do so, unless the person confined has been arrested on a charge of crime.

ENACTED IN 1972; NO SUBSEQUENT AMENDMENTS.

Neb. Rev. Stat. Ann. § 28-1414. Mistake of law; reckless or negligent use of force.

(1) The justification afforded by sections 28-1409 to 28-1412 is unavailable when:

  (a) The actor's belief in the unlawfulness of the force or conduct against which he employs protective force or his belief in the lawfulness of an arrest which he endeavors to effect by force is erroneous; and

  (b) His error is the result of ignorance or mistake as to the provisions of sections 28-1406 to 28-1416, any other provision of the criminal law, or the law governing the legality of an arrest or search.

(2) When the actor believes that the use of force upon or toward the person of another is necessary for any of the purposes for which such belief would establish a justification under sections 28-1408 to 28-1413 but the actor is reckless or negligent in having such belief or in acquiring or failing to acquire any knowledge or belief which is material to the justifiability of his use of force, the justification afforded by those sections is unavailable in a

prosecution for an offense for which recklessness or negligence, as the case may be, suffices to establish culpability.

(3) When the actor is justified under sections 28-1408 to 28-1413 in using force upon or toward the person of another but he recklessly or negligently injures or creates a risk of injury to innocent persons, the justification afforded by those sections is unavailable in a prosecution for such recklessness or negligence towards innocent persons.

ENACTED IN 1972; NO SUBSEQUENT AMENDMENTS.

Nevada

Nev. Rev. Stat. § 171.1455. Use of deadly force to effect arrest: Limitations.

If necessary to prevent escape, an officer may, after giving a warning, if feasible, use deadly force to effect the arrest of a person only if there is probable cause to believe that the person:

1. Has committed a felony which involves the infliction or threat of serious bodily harm or the use of deadly force; or
2. Poses a threat of serious bodily harm to the officer or to others.

ENACTED IN 1993; NO SUBSEQUENT AMENDMENTS.

Yada v. Simpson, 112 Nev. 254, 913 P.2d 1261, 1262-63 (1996), superseded by statute on other grounds as recognized by RTTC Commc'ns, LLC v. Saratoga Flier, Inc., 121 Nev. 34, 110 P.3d 24, 29 (2005) (holding that it is a battery for officers to use more than "reasonably necessary" force).

New Hampshire

N.H. Rev. Stat. Ann. § 627:5. Physical Force in Law Enforcement.

I. A law enforcement officer is justified in using non-deadly force upon another person when and to the extent that he reasonably believes it necessary to effect an arrest or detention or to prevent the escape from custody of an arrested or detained person, unless he knows that the arrest or detention is illegal, or to defend himself or a third person from what he reasonably believes to be the imminent use of non-deadly force encountered while attempting to effect such an arrest or detention or while seeking to prevent such an escape.

II. A law enforcement officer is justified in using deadly force only when he reasonably believes such force is necessary:

(a) To defend himself or a third person from what he reasonably believes is the imminent use of deadly force; or

(b) To effect an arrest or prevent the escape from custody of a person whom he reasonably believes:

   (1) Has committed or is committing a felony involving the use of force or violence, is using a deadly weapon in attempting to escape, or otherwise indicates that he is likely to seriously endanger human life or inflict serious bodily injury unless apprehended without delay; and

   (2) He had made reasonable efforts to advise the person that he is a law enforcement officer attempting to effect an arrest and has reasonable grounds to believe that the person is aware of these facts.

(c) Nothing in this paragraph constitutes justification for conduct by a law enforcement officer amounting to an offense against innocent persons whom he is not seeking to arrest or retain in custody.

III. [Concerning private persons directed by an officer to assist.]

IV. [Concerning private persons acting on their own.]

V. [Concerning guards and officers in confinement facilities.]

VI. A reasonable belief that another has committed an offense means such belief in facts or circumstances which, if true, would in law constitute an offense by such person. If the facts and circumstances reasonably believed would not constitute an offense, an erroneous though reasonable belief that the law is otherwise does not make justifiable the use of force to make an arrest or prevent an escape.

VII. Use of force that is not justifiable under this section in effecting an arrest does not render illegal an arrest that is otherwise legal and the use of such unjustifiable force does not render inadmissible anything seized incident to a legal arrest.

VIII. Deadly force shall be deemed reasonably necessary under this section whenever the arresting law enforcement officer reasonably believes that the arrest is lawful and there is apparently no other possible means of effecting the arrest.

ENACTED IN 1971; AMENDED IN 1981.

New Jersey

N.J. Rev. Stat. § 2C:3-7. Use of force in law enforcement.

a. Use of force justifiable to effect an arrest.

   Subject to the provisions of this section and of section 2C:3-9, the use of force upon or toward the person of another is justifiable when the actor is making or assisting in making an arrest and the actor reasonably believes that such force is immediately necessary to effect a lawful arrest.

b. Limitations on the use of force.

    (1) The use of force is not justifiable under this section unless:

        (a) The actor makes known the purpose of the arrest or reasonably believes that it is otherwise known by or cannot reasonably be made known to the person to be arrested; and

        (b) When the arrest is made under a warrant, the warrant is valid or reasonably believed by the actor to be valid.

    (2) The use of deadly force is not justifiable under this section unless:

        (a) The actor effecting the arrest is authorized to act as a peace officer or has been summoned by and is assisting a person whom he reasonably believes to be authorized to act as a peace officer; and

        (b) The actor reasonably believes that the force employed creates no substantial risk of injury to innocent persons; and

        (c) The actor reasonably believes that the crime for which the arrest is made was homicide, kidnapping, an offense under 2C:14-2 or 2C:14-3, arson, robbery, burglary of a dwelling, or an attempt to commit one of these crimes; and

        (d) The actor reasonably believes:

            (i) There is an imminent threat of deadly force to himself or a third party; or

            (ii) The use of deadly force is necessary to thwart the commission of a crime as set forth in subparagraph (c) of this paragraph; or

            (iii) The use of deadly force is necessary to prevent an escape.

c. Use of force to prevent escape from custody. The use of force to prevent the escape of an arrested person from custody is justifiable when the force could, under subsections a. and b. of this section, have been employed to effect the arrest under which the person is in custody. A correction officer or other person authorized to act as a peace officer is, however, justified in using any force including deadly force, which he reasonably believes to be immediately necessary to prevent the escape of a person committed to a jail, prison, or other institution for the detention of persons charged with or convicted of an offense so long as the actor believes that the force employed creates no substantial risk of injury to innocent persons.

d. [Concerning the use of force by private persons assisting an unlawful arrest.]

e. Use of force to prevent suicide or the commission of a crime. The use of force upon or toward the person of another is justifiable when the actor reasonably believes that such force is immediately necessary to prevent such other person from committing suicide, inflicting serious bodily harm upon himself, committing or consummating the commission of a crime involving or threatening bodily harm, damage to or loss of property or a breach of the peace, except that:

(1) Any limitations imposed by the other provisions of this chapter on the justifiable use of force in self-protection, for the protection of others, the protection of property, the effectuation of an arrest or the prevention of an escape from custody shall apply notwithstanding the criminality of the conduct against which such force is used; and

(2) The use of deadly force is not in any event justifiable under this subsection unless the actor reasonably believes that it is likely that the person whom he seeks to prevent from committing a crime will endanger human life or inflict serious bodily harm upon another unless the commission or the consummation of the crime is prevented and that the use of such force presents no substantial risk of injury to innocent persons.

ENACTED IN 1978; AMENDED IN 1979 AND 1981.

New Mexico

N.M. Stat. Ann. § 30-2-6. Justifiable homicide by public officer or public employee.

A. Homicide is justifiable when committed by a public officer or public employee or those acting by their command and in their aid and assistance:

(1) in obedience to any judgment of a competent court;

(2) when necessarily committed in overcoming actual resistance to the execution of some legal process or to the discharge of any other legal duty;

(3) when necessarily committed in retaking felons who have been rescued or who have escaped or when necessarily committed in arresting felons fleeing from justice; or

(4) when necessarily committed in order to prevent the escape of a felon from any place of lawful custody or confinement.

B. For the purposes of this section, homicide is necessarily committed when a public officer or public employee has probable cause to believe he or another is threatened with serious harm or deadly force while performing those lawful duties described in this section. Whenever feasible, a public officer or employee should give warning prior to using deadly force.

ENACTED IN 1963; AMENDED IN 1989.

Mead v. O'Connor, 1959-NMSC-077, ¶ 4, 66 N.M. 170, 173, 344 P.2d 478, 479–80 (permitting "reasonably necessary" force and setting out that an officer's good faith will be a defense, but that "it devolves upon the jury . . . to resolve these questions").

New York

N.Y. Penal Law § 35.30. Justification; use of physical force in making an arrest or in preventing an escape.

1. A police officer or a peace officer, in the course of effecting or attempting to effect an arrest, or of preventing or attempting to prevent the escape from custody, of a person whom he or she reasonably believes to have committed an offense, may use physical force when and to the extent he or she reasonably believes such to be necessary to effect the arrest, or to prevent the escape from custody, or in self-defense or to defend a third person from what he or she reasonably believes to be the use or imminent use of physical force; except that deadly physical force may be used for such purposes only when he or she reasonably believes that:
   (a) The offense committed by such person was:
      (i) a felony or an attempt to commit a felony involving the use or attempted use or threatened imminent use of physical force against a person; or
      (ii) kidnapping, arson, escape in the first degree, burglary in the first degree or any attempt to commit such a crime; or
   (b) The offense committed or attempted by such person was a felony and that, in the course of resisting arrest therefor or attempting to escape from custody, such person is armed with a firearm or deadly weapon; or
   (c) Regardless of the particular offense which is the subject of the arrest or attempted escape, the use of deadly physical force is necessary to defend the police officer or peace officer or another person from what the officer reasonably believes to be the use or imminent use of deadly physical force.
2. The fact that a police officer or a peace officer is justified in using deadly physical force under circumstances prescribed in paragraphs (a) and (b) of subdivision one does not constitute justification for reckless conduct by such police officer or peace officer amounting to an offense against or with

respect to innocent persons whom he or she is not seeking to arrest or retain in custody.

3. A person who has been directed by a police officer or a peace officer to
   assist such police officer or peace officer to effect an arrest or to prevent
   an escape from custody may use physical force, other than deadly physical
   force, when and to the extent that he or she reasonably believes such to be
   necessary to carry out such police officer's or peace officer's direction, unless he or she knows that the arrest or prospective arrest is not or was not
   authorized and may use deadly physical force under such circumstances
   when:

   (a) He or she reasonably believes such to be necessary for self-defense or
       to defend a third person from what he or she reasonably believes to
       be the use or imminent use of deadly physical force; or

   (b) He or she is directed or authorized by such police officer or peace
       officer to use deadly physical force unless he or she knows that the
       police officer or peace officer is not authorized to use deadly physical
       force under the circumstances.

4. [Concerning private persons.]

5. [Concerning the guarding of prisoners in a detention facility.]

ENACTED IN 1968; AMENDED IN 1972, 1973, 1975, 1980, 2003, AND
2004.

North Carolina

N.C. Gen. Stat. § 15A-401. Arrest by law-enforcement officer.

(a) [Concerning when officers can make arrests pursuant to an arrest warrant.]

(b) [Concerning when officers can make arrests without an arrest warrant.]

(c) [Concerning how arrests are made.]

(d) Use of Force in Arrest.—

   (1) Subject to the provisions of subdivision (2), a law-enforcement officer
       is justified in using force upon another person when and to the extent
       that he reasonably believes it necessary:

       a. To prevent the escape from custody or to effect an arrest of a
          person who he reasonably believes has committed a criminal
          offense, unless he knows that the arrest is unauthorized; or

       b. To defend himself or a third person from what he reasonably
          believes to be the use or imminent use of physical force while
          effecting or attempting to effect an arrest or while preventing or
          attempting to prevent an escape.

(2) A law-enforcement officer is justified in using deadly physical force upon another person for a purpose specified in subdivision (1) of this subsection only when it is or appears to be reasonably necessary thereby:

    a. To defend himself or a third person from what he reasonably believes to be the use or imminent use of deadly physical force;

    b. To effect an arrest or to prevent the escape from custody of a person who he reasonably believes is attempting to escape by means of a deadly weapon, or who by his conduct or any other means indicates that he presents an imminent threat of death or serious physical injury to others unless apprehended without delay; or

    c. To prevent the escape of a person from custody imposed upon him as a result of conviction for a felony.

      Nothing in this subdivision constitutes justification for willful, malicious or criminally negligent conduct by any person which injures or endangers any person or property, nor shall it be construed to excuse or justify the use of unreasonable or excessive force.

(e) Entry on Private Premises or Vehicle; Use of Force.—

    (1) [Concerning when an officer may enter private premises or a vehicle to effect an arrest.]

    (2) The law-enforcement officer may use force to enter the premises or vehicle if he reasonably believes that admittance is being denied or unreasonably delayed, or if he is authorized under subsection (e)(1)c to enter without giving notice of his authority and purpose.

(vi) [Concerning the use of deadly force to resist arrest.]

(vii) [Concerning the care of arrestees' minor children.]

ENACTED IN 1973; AMENDED IN 1979, 1983, 1985, 1991, 1995, 1997, 1999, 2002, 2004, 2009, AND 2010.

North Dakota

N.D. Cent. Code § 12.1-05-02. Execution of public duty.

1. Conduct engaged in by a public servant in the course of the person's official duties is justified when it is required or authorized by law.

2. [Concerning private persons acting at the direction of a public official.]

3. [Concerning arrests by private persons.]

4. [Concerning private persons acting at the direction of a public official.]

N.D. Cent. Code § 12.1-05-07. Limits on the use of force—Excessive force—
Deadly Force.

1. An individual is not justified in using more force than is necessary and appropriate under the circumstances.
2. Deadly force is justified in the following instances:
   a. When it is expressly authorized by law or occurs in the lawful conduct of war.
   b. When used in lawful self-defense, or in lawful defense of others, if
   such force is necessary to protect the actor or anyone else against
   death, serious bodily injury, or the commission of a felony involving violence. The use of deadly force is not justified if it can be
   avoided, with safety to the actor and others, by retreat or other
   conduct involving minimal interference with the freedom of the
   individual menaced. An individual seeking to protect another
   individual must, before using deadly force, try to cause the other
   individual to retreat, or otherwise comply with the requirements
   of this provision, if safety can be obtained thereby. However, the
   duty to retreat or avoid force does not apply under the following
   circumstances:
      (1) A public servant justified in using force in the performance of
      the public servant's duties or an individual justified in using
      force in assisting the public servant need not desist from the
      public servant's or individual's efforts because of resistance or
      threatened resistance by or on behalf of the other individual
      against whom the public servant's or individual's action is di-
      rected; and
      (2) [concerning private persons].
   c. [Concerning a private person's defense of habitation.]
   d. When used by a public servant authorized to effect arrests or prevent escapes, if the force is necessary to effect an arrest or to prevent
   the escape from custody of an individual who has committed or attempted to commit a felony involving violence, or is attempting to
   escape by the use of a deadly weapon, or has otherwise indicated that
   the individual is likely to endanger human life or to inflict serious
   bodily injury unless apprehended without delay.
   e. [Concerning guards in the context of detention facilities.]
   f. [Concerning the use of force in the medical context.]
   g. [Concerning private persons acting at the direction of a public official.]

ENACTED IN 1973; AMENDED IN 2007.

Ohio

State v. White, 29 N.E.3d 939, 944–45, 947, 950, 952 (Ohio 2015) (permitting the use of "'reasonable force in the course and scope of [an officer's] duties,'" (quoting *State v. Sells*, 30 Ohio Law Abs. 355, 1939 WL 3272 (2d Dist.1939), and adopting *Graham v. Connor* and *Tennessee v. Garner* in the context of "reviewing criminal convictions arising from a police officer's use of deadly force.").

Oklahoma

Okla. Stat. tit. 21 § 732. Justifiable homicide by officer.

A peace officer, correctional officer, or any person acting by his command in his aid and assistance, is justified in using deadly force when:

1. The officer is acting in obedience to and in accordance with any judgment of a competent court in executing a penalty of death; or
2. In effecting an arrest or preventing an escape from custody following arrest and the officer reasonably believes both that:
   a. such force is necessary to prevent the arrest from being defeated by resistance or escape, and
   b. there is probable cause to believe that the person to be arrested has committed a crime involving the infliction or threatened infliction of serious bodily harm, or the person to be arrested is attempting to escape by use of a deadly weapon, or otherwise indicates that he will endanger human life or inflict great bodily harm unless arrested without delay; or
3. The officer is in the performance of his legal duty or the execution of legal process and reasonably believes the use of the force is necessary to protect himself or others from the infliction of serious bodily harm; or
4. The force is necessary to prevent an escape from a penal institution or other place of confinement used primarily for the custody of persons convicted of felonies or from custody while in transit thereto or therefrom unless the officer has reason to know:
   a. the person escaping is not a person who has committed a felony involving violence, and
   b. the person escaping is not likely to endanger human life or to inflict serious bodily harm if not apprehended.

ENACTED IN 1910; AMENDED IN 1990.

Morales v. City of Oklahoma City *ex rel*. Oklahoma City Police Dep't, 2010 OK 9, ¶¶ 26–27, 230 P.3d 869, 880 (stipulating that officers may "use only such force in making an arrest as a reasonably prudent police officer would use in light of the objective circumstances confronting the officer at the time of the arrest," and identifying seven factors that inform that inquiry: "[1] the severity of the crime of which the arrestee is suspected; [2] whether the suspect poses an immediate threat to the safety of the officers or others, [3] whether the suspect is actively resisting arrest or attempting to evade arrest; [4] the known character of the arrestee; [5] the existence of alternative methods of accomplishing the arrest; [6] the physical size, strength and weaponry of the officers compared to those of the suspect; and [7] the exigency of the moment").

Oregon

Or. Rev. Stat. § 161.235. Making arrest or preventing escape.

Except as provided in ORS 161.239, a peace officer is justified in using physical force upon another person only when and to the extent that the peace officer reasonably believes it necessary:
(1) To make an arrest or to prevent the escape from custody of an arrested person unless the peace officer knows that the arrest is unlawful; or
(2) For self-defense or to defend a third person from what the peace officer reasonably believes to be the use or imminent use of physical force while making or attempting to make an arrest or while preventing or attempting to prevent an escape.

ENACTED IN 1971; NO SUBSEQUENT AMENDMENTS.

Or. Rev. Stat. § 161.239. Deadly physical force; making arrest or preventing escape.
(1) Notwithstanding the provisions of ORS 161.235, a peace officer may use deadly physical force only when the peace officer reasonably believes that:
   (a) The crime committed by the person was a felony or an attempt to commit a felony involving the use or threatened imminent use of physical force against a person; or
   (b) The crime committed by the person was kidnapping, arson, escape in the first degree, burglary in the first degree or any attempt to commit such a crime; or
   (c) Regardless of the particular offense which is the subject of the arrest or attempted escape, the use of deadly physical force is necessary to defend the peace officer or another person from the use or threatened imminent use of deadly physical force; or

(d) The crime committed by the person was a felony or an attempt to commit a felony and under the totality of the circumstances existing at the time and place, the use of such force is necessary; or

(e) The officer's life or personal safety is endangered in the particular circumstances involved.

(2) Nothing in subsection (1) of this section constitutes justification for reckless or criminally negligent conduct by a peace officer amounting to an offense against or with respect to innocent persons whom the peace officer is not seeking to arrest or retain in custody.

ENACTED IN 1971; NO SUBSEQUENT AMENDMENTS.

Pennsylvania

Pa. Cons. Stat. § 508. Use of force in law enforcement.

(a) Peace officer's use of force in making arrest.—

(1) A peace officer, or any person whom he has summoned or directed to assist him, need not retreat or desist from efforts to make a lawful arrest because of resistance or threatened resistance to the arrest. He is justified in the use of any force which he believes to be necessary to effect the arrest and of any force which he believes to be necessary to defend himself or another from bodily harm while making the arrest. However, he is justified in using deadly force only when he believes that such force is necessary to prevent death or serious bodily injury to himself or such other person, or when he believes both that:

(i) such force is necessary to prevent the arrest from being defeated by resistance or escape; and

(ii) the person to be arrested has committed or attempted a forcible felony or is attempting to escape and possesses a deadly weapon, or otherwise indicates that he will endanger human life or inflict serious bodily injury unless arrested without delay.

(2) A peace officer making an arrest pursuant to an invalid warrant is justified in the use of any force which he would be justified in using if the warrant were valid, unless he knows that the warrant is invalid.

(b) [Concerning private persons' use of force to make arrest.]

(c) Use of force regarding escape.—

(1) A peace officer, corrections officer or other person who has an arrested or convicted person in his custody is justified in the use of such force to prevent the escape of the person from custody as the

  officer or other person would be justified in using under subsection
(a) if the officer or other person were arresting the person.

  (2) [Concerning escape from correctional institutions.]

  (3) [Concerning correctional officers.]

(d) Use of force to prevent suicide or the commission of crime.—

  (1) The use of force upon or toward the person of another is justifiable
when the actor believes that such force is immediately necessary
to prevent such other person from committing suicide, inflicting
serious bodily injury upon himself, committing or consummating
the commission of a crime involving or threatening bodily injury,
damage to or loss of property or a breach of the peace, except
that:

   (i) Any limitations imposed by the other provisions of this chapter
on the justifiable use of force in self-protection, for the protection of others, the protection of property, the effectuation of an
arrest or the prevention of an escape from custody shall apply
notwithstanding the criminality of the conduct against which
such force is used.

   (ii) The use of deadly force is not in any event justifiable under this
subsection unless:

    (A) the actor believes that there is a substantial risk that the
person whom he seeks to prevent from committing a crime
will cause death or serious bodily injury to another unless
the commission or the consummation of the crime is prevented and that the use of such force presents no substantial risk of injury to innocent persons; or

    (B) the actor believes that the use of such force is necessary
to suppress a riot or mutiny after the rioters or mutineers
have been ordered to disperse and warned, in any particular manner that the law may require, that such force will be
used if they do not obey.

  (2) The justification afforded by this subsection extends to the use of
confinement as preventive force only if the actor takes all reasonable
measures to terminate the confinement as soon as he knows that he
safely can, unless the person confined has been arrested on a charge
of crime.

ENACTED IN 1972; AMENDED IN 2007.

Rhode Island

R.I. Gen. Laws § 12-7-8. Restraint and force used.

No greater restraint than is necessary shall be used for the detention of any person, and no unnecessary or unreasonable force shall be used in making an arrest.

ENACTED IN 1938; AMENDED IN 1941.

R.I. Gen. Laws § 12-7-9. Conditions justifying force dangerous to life.

A police officer may use force dangerous to human life to make a lawful arrest for committing or attempting to commit a felony, whenever he or she reasonably believes that force dangerous to human life is necessary to effect the arrest and that the person to be arrested is aware that a peace officer is attempting to arrest him or her.

ENACTED IN 1938; AMENDED IN 1941.

South Carolina

State v. Weaver, 265 S.C. 130, 136 (1975) ("When an officer has a right to make an arrest, he may use whatever force is reasonably necessary to apprehend the offender or effect the arrest.")

Sheppard v. State, 594 S.E.2d 462, 473 (2004) (citing *Tennessee v. Garner* for the statement that "an officer may use whatever force is necessary to effect the arrest of a felon including deadly force to effect that arrest.")

South Dakota

S.D. Codified Laws § 22-16-33. Justifiable homicide—Apprehending felon—Suppressing riot—Preserving peace.

Homicide is justifiable if necessarily committed in attempting by lawful ways and means to apprehend any person for any felony committed, or in lawfully suppressing any riot, or in lawfully keeping and preserving the peace.

ENACTED IN 1939; AMENDED IN 2003 AND 2005.

S.D. Codified Laws § 22-18-2. Justifiable force used by public officer in performance of duty—Assistance or direction of officer.

To use or attempt to use or offer to use force or violence upon or toward the person of another is not unlawful if necessarily committed by a public of-

ficer in the performance of any legal duty or by any other person assisting the public officer or acting by the public officer's direction.
ENACTED IN 1939; AMENDED IN 2005.

S.D. Codified Laws § 22-18-3. Lawful force in arrest and delivery of felon.

To use or attempt to use or offer to use force or violence upon or toward the person of another is not unlawful if necessarily committed by any person in arresting someone who has committed any felony or in delivering that person to a public officer competent to receive him or her in custody.
ENACTED IN 1939; AMENDED IN 2005.

Tennessee

Tenn. Code Ann. § 39-11-613. Suicide or self-inflicted injury; prevention.

A person is justified in threatening or using force, but not deadly force, against another, when and to the degree the person reasonably believes the force is immediately necessary to prevent the other from committing suicide or from the self-infliction of serious bodily injury.
ENACTED IN 1989; NO SUBSEQUENT AMENDMENTS.

Tenn. Code Ann. § 39-11-620. Deadly force; law enforcement officers.
(a) A law enforcement officer, after giving notice of the officer's identity as such, may use or threaten to use force that is reasonably necessary to accomplish the arrest of an individual suspected of a criminal act who resists or flees from the arrest.
(b) Notwithstanding subsection (a), the officer may use deadly force to effect an arrest only if all other reasonable means of apprehension have been exhausted or are unavailable, and where feasible, the officer has given notice of the officer's identity as such and given a warning that deadly force may be used unless resistance or flight ceases, and:
  (1) The officer has probable cause to believe the individual to be arrested has committed a felony involving the infliction or threatened infliction of serious bodily injury; or
  (2) The officer has probable cause to believe that the individual to be arrested poses a threat of serious bodily injury, either to the officer or to others unless immediately apprehended.
ENACTED IN 1989; AMENDED IN 1990.

Tenn. Code Ann. § 40-7-108. Resisting arrest; law enforcement officer; powers and duties.

(a) A law enforcement officer, after giving notice of the officer's identity as an officer, may use or threaten to use force that is reasonably necessary to accomplish the arrest of an individual suspected of a criminal act who resists or flees from the arrest.

(b) Notwithstanding subsection (a), the officer may use deadly force to effect an arrest only if all other reasonable means of apprehension have been exhausted or are unavailable, and where feasible, the officer has given notice of the officer's identity as an officer and given a warning that deadly force may be used unless resistance or flight ceases, and:

    (1) The officer has probable cause to believe the individual to be arrested has committed a felony involving the infliction or threatened infliction of serious bodily injury; or

    (2) The officer has probable cause to believe that the individual to be arrested poses a threat of serious bodily injury, either to the officer or to others unless immediately apprehended.

(c) All law enforcement officers, both state and local, shall be bound by this section and shall receive instruction regarding implementation of this section in law enforcement training programs.

PREVIOUSLY CODIFIED IN 1858; CURRENT STATUTE ENACTED IN 1985; AMENDED IN 1990.

Texas

Tex. Penal Code Ann. § 9.51. Arrest and search.

(a) A peace officer, or a person acting in a peace officer's presence and at his direction, is justified in using force against another when and to the degree the actor reasonably believes the force is immediately necessary to make or assist in making an arrest or search, or to prevent or assist in preventing escape after arrest, if:

    (1) the actor reasonably believes the arrest or search is lawful or, if the arrest or search is made under a warrant, he reasonably believes the warrant is valid; and

    (2) before using force, the actor manifests his purpose to arrest or search and identifies himself as a peace officer or as one acting at a peace officer's direction, unless he reasonably believes his purpose and identity are already known by or cannot reasonably be made known to the person to be arrested.

(b) [Concerning the use of force by private persons.]

(c) A peace officer is justified in using deadly force against another when and to the degree the peace officer reasonably believes the deadly force is immediately necessary to make an arrest, or to prevent escape after arrest, if the use of force would have been justified under Subsection (a) and:

    (1) the actor reasonably believes the conduct for which arrest is authorized included the use or attempted use of deadly force; or

    (2) the actor reasonably believes there is a substantial risk that the person to be arrested will cause death or serious bodily injury to the actor or another if the arrest is delayed.

(d) [Concerning the use of deadly force by private persons.]

(e) There is no duty to retreat before using deadly force justified by Subsection (c) or (d).

(f) Nothing in this section relating to the actor's manifestation of purpose or identity shall be construed as conflicting with any other law relating to the issuance, service, and execution of an arrest or search warrant either under the laws of this state or the United States.

(g) Deadly force may only be used under the circumstances enumerated in Subsections (c) and (d).

ENACTED IN 1973; AMENDED IN 1993.

Utah

Utah Code Ann. § 76-2-403. Force in arrest.

Any person is justified in using any force, except deadly force, which he reasonably believes to be necessary to effect an arrest or to defend himself or another from bodily harm while making an arrest.

ENACTED IN 1973; NO SUBSEQUENT AMENDMENTS.

Utah Code Ann. § 76-2-404. Peace officer's use of deadly force.

(1) A peace officer, or any person acting by the officer's command in providing aid and assistance, is justified in using deadly force when:

    (a) the officer is acting in obedience to and in accordance with the judgment of a competent court in executing a penalty of death under Subsection 77-18-5.5(2), (3), or (4);

    (b) effecting an arrest or preventing an escape from custody following an arrest, where the officer reasonably believes that deadly force is necessary to prevent the arrest from being defeated by escape; and

        (i) the officer has probable cause to believe that the suspect has committed a felony offense involving the infliction or threatened infliction of death or serious bodily injury; or

(ii) the officer has probable cause to believe the suspect poses a threat of death or serious bodily injury to the officer or to others if apprehension is delayed; or

(c) the officer reasonably believes that the use of deadly force is necessary to prevent death or serious bodily injury to the officer or another person.

(2) If feasible, a verbal warning should be given by the officer prior to any use of deadly force under Subsection (1)(b) or (1)(c).

ENACTED IN 1986; AMENDED IN 1987, 2004, AND 2015.

Vermont

Coll v. Johnson, 161 Vt. 163, 164–66 (1993) (adopting *Graham v. Connor* to govern state law claims).

Vt. Stat. Ann. § 2305. Justifiable homicide.

If a person kills or wounds another under any of the circumstances enumerated below, he or she shall be guiltless:

(1) In the just and necessary defense of his or her own life or the life of his or her husband, wife, parent, child, brother, sister, master, mistress, servant, guardian or ward; or

(2) In the suppression of a person attempting to commit murder, sexual assault, aggravated sexual assault, burglary, or robbery, with force or violence; or

(3) In the case of a civil officer; or a military officer or private soldier when lawfully called out to suppress riot or rebellion, or to prevent or suppress invasion, or to assist in serving legal process, in suppressing opposition against him or her in the just and necessary discharge of his or her duty.

ORIGINALLY CODIFIED IN 1787, 1797, 1818, 1840, 1862, 1880, 1894, 1906, 1917, 1933, AND 1947; CURRENT STATUTE ENACTED IN 1983.

Virginia

Crosswhite v. Barnes, 139 Va. 471 (1924) (officers may not inflict serious bodily injury against fleeing misdemeanants).

Buck v. Commonwealth, 20 Va. App. 298, 304 (1995) (officers may use "reasonable" force).

Couture v. Commonwealth, 656 S.E.2d 425, 427–31 (Va. Ct. App. 2008) (officers can use force that is reasonable in relation to a perceived threat, including deadly force when reasonably necessary, but "[t]o the extent [the officer's] responsibility for creating the perception of danger[] . . . rendered his perception unreasonable or his use of force excessive, then the privilege to defend himself with deadly force would not be available. On the other hand, if [the officer's] responsibility for creating the perception of danger did not undermine the reasonableness of his use of force or of his apprehension of danger, then" the officer could validly use deadly force in self-defense [internal quotation marks omitted]).

Washington

Wash Rev. Code § 9A.16.040. Justifiable homicide or use of deadly force by public officer, peace officer, person aiding.

(1) Homicide or the use of deadly force is justifiable in the following cases:

    (a) When a public officer applies deadly force in obedience to the judgment of a competent court; or

    (b) When necessarily used by a peace officer meeting the good faith standard of this section to overcome actual resistance to the execution of the legal process, mandate, or order of a court or officer, or in the discharge of a legal duty; or

    (c) When necessarily used by a peace officer meeting the good faith standard of this section or person acting under the officer's command and in the officer's aid:

       (i) To arrest or apprehend a person who the officer reasonably believes has committed, has attempted to commit, is committing, or is attempting to commit a felony;

       (ii) To prevent the escape of a person from a federal or state correctional facility or in retaking a person who escapes from such a facility;

       (iii) To prevent the escape of a person from a county or city jail or holding facility if the person has been arrested for, charged with, or convicted of a felony; or

       (iv) To lawfully suppress a riot if the actor or another participant is armed with a deadly weapon.

(2) In considering whether to use deadly force under subsection (1)(c) of this section, to arrest or apprehend any person for the commission of any crime, the peace officer must have probable cause to believe that the suspect, if not apprehended, poses a threat of serious physical harm to the officer or a threat of serious physical harm to others. Among the circumstances which

may be considered by peace officers as a "threat of serious physical harm" are the following:

    (a) The suspect threatens a peace officer with a weapon or displays a weapon in a manner that could reasonably be construed as threatening; or

    (b) There is probable cause to believe that the suspect has committed any crime involving the infliction or threatened infliction of serious physical harm.

    Under these circumstances deadly force may also be used if necessary to prevent escape from the officer, where, if feasible, some warning is given, provided the officer meets the good faith standard of this section.

(3) A public officer covered by subsection (1)(a) of this section shall not be held criminally liable for using deadly force without malice and with a good faith belief that such act is justifiable pursuant to this section.

(4) A peace officer shall not be held criminally liable for using deadly force in good faith, where "good faith" is an objective standard which shall consider all the facts, circumstances, and information known to the officer at the time to determine whether a similarly situated reasonable officer would have believed that the use of deadly force was necessary to prevent death or serious physical harm to the officer or another individual.

(5) The following good faith standard is adopted for law enforcement officer use of deadly force:

    (a) The good faith standard is met only if both the objective good faith test in (b) of this subsection and the subjective good faith test in (c) of this subsection are met.

    (b) The objective good faith test is met if a reasonable officer, in light of all the facts and circumstances known to the officer at the time, would have believed that the use of deadly force was necessary to prevent death or serious physical harm to the officer or another individual.

    (c) The subjective good faith test is met if the officer intended to use deadly force for a lawful purpose and sincerely and in good faith believed that the use of deadly force was warrant in the circumstance.

    (d) Where the use of deadly force results in death, substantial bodily harm, or great bodily harm, an independent investigation must be completed to inform the determination of whether the use of deadly force met the objective good faith test established by this section and satisfied other applicable laws and policies.

(6) For the purpose of this section, "law enforcement officer" means any law enforcement officer in the state of Washington, including by not limited to law enforcement personnel and peace officers as defined by RCW 43.101.010.

(7) This section shall not be construed as:

    (a) Affecting the permissible use of force by a person acting under the authority of RCW 9A.16.020 or 9A.16.050; or

    (b) Preventing a law enforcement agency from adopting standards pertaining to its use of deadly force that are more restrictive than this section.

ENACTED IN 1986, AMENDED IN 2018.

Wash Rev. Code § 10.31.050. Officer may use force.

If after notice of the intention to arrest the defendant, he or she either flee or forcibly resist, the officer may use all necessary means to effect the arrest.

ENACTED IN 2010; NO SUBSEQUENT AMENDMENT.

West Virginia

Maston v. Wagner, 236 W. Va. 488, 504 (2015) (officers may use force when it is "objectively reasonable in light of the facts and circumstances confronting them, without regard to their underlying intent or motivation" [internal quotation marks omitted]).

Wisconsin

Wis Stat. § 939.45. Privilege.

The fact that the actor's conduct is privileged, although otherwise criminal, is a defense to prosecution for any crime based on that conduct. The defense of privilege can be claimed under any of the following circumstances:

(1) [Concerning coercion and necessity];

(2) [Concerning defense of persons or property]; or

(3) When the actor's conduct is in good faith and is an apparently authorized and reasonable fulfillment of any duties of a public office; or

(4) When the actor's conduct is a reasonable accomplishment of a lawful arrest; or

(5) [Concerning child welfare.]

(6) When for any other reason the actor's conduct is privileged by the statutory or common law of this state.

ENACTED IN 1955; AMENDED IN 1987.

Wirsing v. Krzeminski, 61 Wis. 2d 513, 519–20, 213 N.W.2d 37, 40 (1973) (permitting reasonably necessary force).

McCluskey v. Steinhorst, 45 Wis. 2d 350, 354, 173 N.W.2d 148, 150 (1970) (permitting reasonably necessary force, and defining that issue as a jury question).

Wyoming

Roose v. State, 759 P.2d 478, 479 (Wyo. 1988) (citing and relying on *Tennessee v. Garner*).

NOTES

INTRODUCTION

1 James J. Fyfe, "'Good' Policing," in *The Socio-Economics of Crime and Justice*, ed. Brian Forst (London: Routledge, 2015), 269–90.

2 Egon Bittner, "Florence Nightingale in Pursuit of Willie Sutton: A Theory of Policing," in *The Potential for Reform of Criminal Justice*, ed. Herbert Jacob (Beverly Hills, CA: Sage 1974).

3 Geoffrey Alpert and Roger Dunham, *Understanding Police Use of Force: Officers, Suspects and Reciprocity* (Cambridge: Cambridge University Press, 2004); Elizabeth Davis, Anthony Whyde, and Lynn Langton, *Contacts Between Police and the Public, 2015* (Washington DC: U.S. Department of Justice, 2018).

4 U.S. Department of Justice, Community Relations Service, *Principles of Good Policing: Avoiding Violence Between Police and Citizens* (Washington, DC, September 2003), www.justice.gov.

5 Daniel Bukszpan, *America's Most Destructive Riots of All Time*, CNBC (Feb. 1, 2011), www.cnbc.com.

6 Oral Argument, Plumhoff v. Rickard, 572 U.S. 765 (2014) (No. 12-1117).

7 Dennis P. Rosenbaum, Amie M. Schuck, Sandra K. Costello, Darnell F. Hawkins, and Marianne K. Ring, "Attitudes Toward the Police: The Effects of Direct and Vicarious Experience," *Police Quarterly* 8 (2005): 343–65.

8 Justin Nix, "A Bird's Eye View of Civilians Killed by Police in 2015: Further Evidence of Implicit Bias," *Criminology and Public Policy* 16, no. 1 (2017): 309–40.

9 Robert J. Friedrich, "Police Use of Force: Individuals, Situations, and Organizations," *Annals of the American Academy of Political and Social Science* 452 (1980): 82–97.

10 Alpert and Dunham, *Understanding Police Use of Force.*

11 Rémi Boivin and Maude Lagacé, "Police Use-of-Force Situations in Canada: Analyzing the Force or Resistance Ratio Using a Trichotomous Dependent Variable," *Police Quarterly* 19 (2016): 180–98.

CHAPTER 1. THE CONSTITUTIONAL LAW STANDARD

1 Jackson v. City of Joilet, 715 F.2d 1200, 1203 (7th Cir. 1983).

2 Legal scholars have criticized the conclusion that the Constitution should be read as a document of negative rights on both descriptive and normative grounds. See, e.g., Michael J. Gerhardt, "The Ripple Effects of *Slaughter-House*: A Critique of a Negative Rights View of the Constitution," *Vanderbilt Law Review* 43, no. 2 (1990):

409–50; Susan Bandes, "The Negative Constitution: A Critique," *Michigan Law Review* 88 (1990): 2271–2347; David P. Currie, "Positive and Negative Constitutional Rights," *University of Chicago Law Review* 53 (1986): 864–90; Seth F. Kreimer, "Allocational Sanctions: The Problem of Negative Rights in a Positive State," *University of Pennsylvania Law Review* 132 (1984): 1293–1397.

3 Tennessee v. Garner, 471 U.S. 1 (1985).

4 Graham v. Connor, 490 U.S. 386 (1989). Uses of force against pretrial detainees are analyzed under the Fourteenth Amendment's protection of the substantive due process right to be secure in one's person. In that context, as in the policing context, the jail official's subjective intention is irrelevant; "a pretrial detainee must show only that the force purposely or knowingly used against him was objectively unreasonable," taking into account "the 'legitimate interests that stem from [the government's] need to manage the facility in which the individual is detained,' appropriately deferring to 'policies and practices that in th[e] judgment' of jail officials 'are needed to preserve internal order and discipline and to maintain institutional security.'" Kingsley v. Hendrickson, 135 S.Ct. 2466, 2473 (2015) (quoting Bell v. Wolfish, 441 U.S. 520, 540, 547 (1979)).

   Uses of force against incarcerated convicts is evaluated under the Eighth Amendment's prohibition against cruel and unusual punishment, which incorporates a subjective analysis. Under this standard, the inmate must suffer a non-trivial injury as the result of force applied maliciously and sadistically rather than as part of a good-faith effort to maintain or restore discipline. Wilkins v. Gaddy, 599 U.S. 34 (2010). The question is "whether force was applied in a good-faith effort to maintain or restore discipline, or maliciously and sadistically to cause harm." Hudson v. McMillian, 503 U.S. 1, 4 (1992). Inadvertence and good faith errors do not offend this standard. Jeffers v. Gomez, 267 F.3d 895 (9th Cir. 2001).

5 Bivens v. Six Unknown Named Agents of the Federal Bureau of Narcotics, 403 U.S. 388 (1971).

6 Haywood v. Drown, 556 U.S. 729 (2009).

7 State Farm Mutual Automobile Insurance Company v. Campbell, 538 U.S. 408, 416 (2003) (citing *Restatement (Second) of Torts* §903 (1979)).

8 Smith v. Wade, 461 U.S. 30, 36 (1983).

9 Stephen Rushin, *Federal Intervention in American Police Departments* (Cambridge: Cambridge University Press, 2017), 141–42.

10 Monroe v. Pape, 365 U.S. 167 (1961).

11 David Alan Sklansky, "What the Feds Can and Cannot Do in the *Brown* and *Garner* Cases," *Stanford Law School Blogs*, December 5, 2014, https://law.stanford.edu.

12 United States v. Acosta, 470 F.3d 132 (2d Cir. 2006).

13 The Fourth Amendment also regulates searches, but the manifold search doctrines that the Supreme Court has articulated are not relevant to the use of force.

14 California v. Hodari D., 499 U.S. 621, 628 (1991).

15 Brower v. County of Inyo, 489 U.S. 593 (1989).

16 *Hodari D.,* 499 U.S. at 621.

17 Scott v. Harris, 550 U.S. 372, 383 (2007).

18 Geoffrey P. Alpert and William C. Smith, "How Reasonable Is the Reasonable Man? Police and Excessive Force," *Journal of Criminal Law & Criminology* 85, no. 2 (1994): 486.

19 Graham v. Connor, 490 U.S. 386 (1989).

20 Bittner, "Florence Nightingale."

21 James Q. Wilson, *Varieties of Police Behavior* (Cambridge, MA: Harvard University Press, 1978).

22 Samuel Walker and Charles M. Katz, *The Police in America: An Introduction,* 9th ed. (New York: McGraw-Hill, 2018); Roger B. Parks, Stephen D. Mastrofski, Christina DeJong, and M. Kevin Gray, "How Officers Spend Their Time With the Community," *Justice Quarterly* 16 (1999): 483.

23 Madison Troyer, "15 Hilarious Police Blotter Entries That Will Make You ROFL," The Things.com (Oct. 28, 2017), www.thethings.com.

24 Troyer, "15 Hilarious Police Blotter Entries."

25 Associated Press, "Bum Wrap," NBC News (Apr. 29, 2005), www.nbcnews.com; La Nota Loca, "Bomb Threat Called in for Tin Foil-Wrapped Burrito in Oklahoma," Fox News (Nov. 27, 2013), www.foxnews.com.

26 Troyer, "15 Hilarious Police Blotter Entries."

27 Egon Bittner, *Aspects of Police Work* (Boston: Northeastern University Press, 1990).

28 Terry v. Ohio, 392 U.S. 1, 15 (1968); see also William Terrill and Michael Reisig, "Neighborhood Context and Police Use of Force," *Journal of Research in Crime and Delinquency* 40, no. 3 (2003): 291–321; Robert E. Worden and Sarah J. McClean, "Police Legitimacy, Procedural Justice, and the Exercise of Police Authority," *Police Chief* 82 (November 2015): 14–16.

29 Rachel A. Harmon, "When Is Police Violence Justified?," *Northwestern University Law Review,* 102, no. 3 (2008): 1119–87.

30 David W. Neubauer and Henry F. Fradella, *America's Courts and the Criminal Justice System* (Belmont, CA: Wadsworth, 2011).

31 Harmon, "When Is Police Violence Justified?"

32 Harmon, "When Is Police Violence Justified?," 34.

33 Harmon, "When Is Police Violence Justified?," 38.

34 See, e.g., Wackwitz v. Roy, 418 S.E.2d 861, 864 (Va. 1992).

35 Harmon, "When Is Police Violence Justified?," 36.

36 We discuss an officer's ability to invoke the generally available legal principles of self-defense at greater length in chapter 2.

37 Harmon, "When Is Police Violence Justified?," 38.

38 Draper v. United States, 358 U.S. 307 (1959).

39 Brinegar v. United States, 338 U.S. 160 (1949).

40 Illinois v. Gates, 462 U.S. 213 (1983).

41 Beck v. Ohio, 379 U.S. 89 (1964).

42 *Brinegar*, 338 U.S. at 160.

43 Wayne R. LaFave, *Search and Seizure: A Treatise on the Fourth Amendment,* 5th ed. (Eagan, MN: Thomson West, 2012), 2:83.

44 Terry v. Ohio, 392 U.S. 1 (1968).

45 United States v. Sokolow, 490 U.S. 1, 7–8 (1989).

46 *Sokolow*, 490 U.S. at 7.

47 Wayne LaFave, *Search and Seizure: A Treatise on the Fourth Amendment,* 5th ed. (Eagan, MN: Thomson West, 2012), 4: 671.

48 While the nature of the threat is certainly critical to the overall use-of-force determination, it is not relevant to the question of governmental interest. Instead, it is relevant to the issue of proportionality, which we discuss later in this chapter.

49 Although some commentators distinguish between "imminent" threat and "immediate" threat, we use those terms synonymously.

50 See, e.g., International Association of Chiefs of Police, *National Consensus Policy and Discussion Paper on Use of Force* (2017), 11, http://noblenational.org ("An immediate, or imminent, threat can be described as danger from an individual whose *apparent intent* is to inflict serious bodily injury or death and the individual has the *ability and opportunity* to realize this intention." Emphasis added.)

51 Young v. County of Los Angeles, 655 F.3d 1156 (9th Cir. 2011).

52 Henderson v. Roberson, 2017CP0400636 (S.C. C.P. March 28, 2017).

53 See Mattos v. Agarano, 661 F.3d 433, 444 n.5 (9th Cir. 2011) (en banc); Winterrowd v. Nelson, 480 F.3d 1181, 1185 (9th Cir. 2007).

54 See Elliott v Leavitt, 99 F.3d. 640, 643 (4th Cir. 1996).

55 Mantoute v Carr, 114 F.3d 181 (11th Cir. 1997).

56 Estate of Hill v. Miracle, 853 F.3d 306, 314 (6th Cir. 2017).

57 *Miracle*, 853 F.3d at 314 (6th Cir. 2017).

58 Cady v. Dombrowski, 413 U.S. 433 (1973).

59 Debra Livingston, "Police, Community Caretaking, and the Fourth Amendment," *University of Chicago Legal Forum* 1 (1998): 261–313.

60 Brigham City v. Stuart, 547 U.S. 398 (2006).

61 Ames v. King County, 846 F.3d 340, 349 (9th Cir. 2017).

62 Bryan v. MacPherson, 620 F.3d 805 (9th Cir. 2010); see also Estate of Armstrong v. Village of Pinehurst, 810 F.3d 892 (4th Cir. 2016).

63 Graham v. Connor, 490 U.S. 386 (1989). Internal quotation marks omitted.

64 Glenn v. Washington County, 661 F.3d 460, 471–74 (9th Cir. 2011).

65 Tennessee v. Garner, 471 U.S. 1 (1985).

66 *Garner*, 471 U.S. at 3.

67 *Garner*, 471 U.S. at 9–12. Citations and footnotes omitted.

68 Scott v. Harris, 550 U.S. 372 (2007).

69 *Harris*, 550 U.S. at 372.

70 *Harris*, 550 U.S. at 372.

71 Welsh v. Wisconsin, 466 U.S. 740 (1984).

72 Warden v. Harden, 387 U.S. 294 (1967).

73   See, e.g., Hesterberg v. United States, 71 F. Supp. 3d 1018, 1029 (N.D. Cal. 2014).

74   We discuss the various "levels" of resistance, as they are commonly used in policing, at length in chapter 3.

75   California Commission on Peace Officer Standards and Training: Basic Course Workbook Series (2007), 2-6, 7, https://post.ca.gov.

76   Peter Scharf and Arnold Binder, *The Badge and the Bullet: Police Use of Deadly Force* (New York: Praeger, 1983).

77   See Young v. City of Providence, 404 F.3d 4 (1st Cir. 2005); Abraham v. Raso, 183 F.3d 279 (3rd Cir. 1999); Dickerson v. McClellan, 101 F.3d 1151, 1161 (6th Cir. 1996); Allen v. Muskogee, 119 F.3d 837 (10th Cir. 1997).

78   Billington v. Smith, 292 F.3d 1177 (9th Cir. 2001).

79   County of Los Angeles v. Mendez, 137 S. Ct. 1539 (2017).

80   See Greenidge v. Ruffin, 927 F.2d 789, 792 (4th Cir. 1991); Carter v. Buscher, 973 F.2d 1328, 1332 (7th Cir. 1992).

81   Gardner v. Buerger, 82 F.3d 248, 253 (8th Cir. 1996).

82   See chapter 5.

CHAPTER 2. THE STATE LAW STANDARD

1   *See* Brian A. Reaves, U.S. Department of Justice, *Local Police Departments, 2013: Personnel, Policies, and Practices* (2015), www.bjs.gov; Brian A. Reaves, U.S. Department of Justice, *Census of State and Local Law Enforcement Agencies, 2008* (2011), www.bjs.gov; Brian A. Reaves, U.S. Department of Justice, *Federal Law Enforcement Officers, 2008* (2012), www.bjs.gov.

2   Eric T. Schneiderman, *Biennial Report of the Office of the Attorney General's Special Investigations and Prosecutions Unit* (New York: New York Office of the Attorney General, 2017), https://ag.ny.gov.

3   Lindsey Devers, *Plea and Charge Bargaining: Research Summary* (Arlington, VA: Bureau of Justice Assistance, January 2011), www.bja.gov.

4   Literally, "no contest." Under a *nolo contendere* plea—which is also known as an "Alford plea" or, in West Virginia, a "Kennedy plea"—the defendant does not admit guilt, but acknowledges that the state has sufficient evidence to obtain a conviction.

5   The Henry A. Wallace Police Crime Database, Police Integrity Research, accessed December 7, 2018, https://policecrime.bgsu.edu/.

6   We define "official capacity" as follows: "Most all police crime committed by an officer while on-duty is considered as having occurred in the officer's official capacity. Numerous factors are considered in determining whether an officer's alleged crime was committed while he or she was off-duty, including whether: (1) there was an ordinance that deemed officers on-duty 24-hours per day; (2) officer identified him or herself as a police officer: (3) officer was wearing a police uniform; (4) officer showed service weapon (e.g., pistol or revolver) or other agency lethal or less-lethal weapon; (5) officer flashed a badge; (6) officer conducted a search while off-duty; (7) officer made an arrest while off-duty; and/

or (8) officer intervened in an existing dispute pursuant to agency policy." The Henry A. Wallace Police Crime Database, Glossary, accessed December 7, 2018, https://policecrime.bgsu.edu.

7 Alpert and Dunham, *Understanding Police Use of Force*; Tom McEwen, U.S. Department of Justice, *National Data Collection on Police Use of Force* (Alexandria, CA: Bureau of Justice Statistics, 1996), www.bjs.gov.

8 See, e.g., *California Rules of Professional Conduct* 5-110(A).

9 See, e.g., American Bar Association, *Criminal Justice Standards for the Prosecution Function*, Standard 3-4.3(a).

10 28 U.S.C. § 1441.

11 28 U.S.C. § 1442.

12 Revised Code of Washington 43.101.450 (2018).

13 Revised Code of Washington 43.101.452 (2018).

14 Revised Code of Washington 43.101.452(2) (2018).

15 Roger L. Goldman, "Importance of State Law in Police Reform," *Saint Louis University Law Journal* 60, no. 3 (2016): 363–90.

16 N.J. Rev. Stat. § 2C:51-2.

17 Conn. Gen. Stat. § 7-291c(a).

18 Conn. Gen. Stat. § 7-291c(d).

19 California's Assembly Bill 392 provides one example. If passed and signed into law, that bill would radically amend the two oldest, unamended use-of-force statutes in the country.

20 Chad Flanders and Joseph Welling, "Police Use of Deadly Force: State Statutes 30 Years after *Garner*," *Saint Louis University Public Law Review* 35, no. 1 (2016): 109–56.

21 Hayes v. City of San Diego, 57 Cal. 4th 622, 639 (2013).

22 Russell *ex rel.* J.N. v. Virg-In, 258 P.3d 795, 802 (Alaska 2011).

23 Caudillo v. City of Phoenix, No. 1 CA-CV 09-0467, 2010 WL 2146408, at *2 n.6 (Ariz. Ct. App. May 27, 2010).

24 Ewells v. Constant 2012 Ark. 148 at 4.

25 Hernandez v. City of Pomona, 46 Cal. 4th 501, 513-15 (2009).

26 Martinez v. Harper, 802 P.2d 1185, 1187 (Colo. App. 1990).

27 State v. Saturno, 322 Conn. 80, 114 (2016) ; State v. Smith, 73 Conn. App. 173, 205 (2002).

28 Elliott v. Dunn, No. Civ. A. 94C-04-026, 1995 WL 411406, at *3 (Del. Super. Ct. July 6, 1995); Cornish v. Delaware State Police, No. CIV. A. 94C-12-019, 1996 WL 453304, at *5 (Del. Super. Ct. June 19, 1996) (unpublished opinion).

29 Brown *ex rel.* Brown v. Jenne, 122 So. 3d 881, 885 (Fla. Dist. Ct. App. 2012).

30 Kline v. KDB, Inc., 295 Ga. App. 789, 794 (2009).

31 People v. Mandarino, 2013 IL App (1st) 111772, ¶ 49.

32 Love v. State, 73 N.E.3d 693, 698 (Ind. 2017).

33 State v. Dewitt, 811 N.W.2d 460, 470 (Iowa 2012).

34 State v. Palmer, 2009-0044 (La. 7/1/09); 14 So. 3d 304.

35 Richards v. Town of Eliot, 780 A.2d 281, 287 (2001).

36 Richardson v. McGriff, 361 Md. 437, 452 (2000).

37 Webb v. City of Taylor, No. 236153, 2002 WL 31947931, at *4 (Mich. Ct. App. Dec. 3, 2002).

38 Phillips v. Liberty Mutual Insurance Co., 293 Neb. 123, 132 (2016).

39 Lane v. State, No. 66733, 2015 WL 7283335, at *1 (Nev. Nov. 13, 2015).

40 State v. Mantelli, 2002-NMCA-033, ¶ 23, 131 N.M. 692, 698, 42 P.3d 272, 278 (2002).

41 State v. White, 29 N.E.3d 939, 944–45, 947, 950, 952 (Ohio 2015).

42 Morales v. City of Oklahoma City ex rel. Oklahoma City Police Department, 2010 OK 9, 230 P.3d 869, 880 (2010).

43 Albanese v. Town of Narragansett, 135 A.3d 1179, 1188 (R.I. 2016).

44 Heyward v. Christmas, 357 S.C. 202, 207 (2004).

45 Coll v. Johnson, 161 Vt. 163, 164–65 (1993).

46 Bufford v. Commonwealth, No. 0630-08-4, 2009 WL 2222970, at *8 (Va. Ct. App. July 28, 2009).

47 Maston v. Wagner, 236 W. Va. 488, 504 (2015).

48 Wilson v. State, 2009 WY 1, 199 P.3d 517, 520 n.3 (Wyo. 2009).

49 Richardson v. McGriff, 361 Md. 437, 452 (2000).

50 James v. City of Boise, 160 Idaho 466, 478 (2016).

51 Brown v. Fournier, No. 2015-CA-001429-MR, 2017 WL 2391709, at *4 (Ky. June 2, 2017).

52 Williams v. Lee County Sheriff's Department, 744 So.2d 286, 297 (Miss.1999).

53 McCummings v. New York City Transit Authority, 81 N.Y.2d 923, 927 (1993).

54 Williams v. Lee County Sheriff's Department, 744 So.2d 286, 297 (Miss.1999).

55 McCummings v. New York City Transit Authority, 81 N.Y.2d 923, 927 (1993).

56 Martinez v. Harper, 802 P.2d 1185, 1187 (Colo. App. 1990).

57 Mullis v. State, 196 Ga. 569, 577 (1943); State v. Bunn, 288 Ga. 20, 24 (2010).

58 State v. Dewitt, 811 N.W.2d 460, 469 (Iowa 2012).

59 Washington v. Starke, 173 Mich. App. 230, 236, 433 N.W.2d 834, 836 (1988).

60 Newell v. State, 364 P.3d 602, 604 (2015).

61 State v. Mantelli, 2002-NMCA-033, ¶ 23, 131 N.M. 692, 698, 42 P.3d 272, 278 (2002).

62 McCummings v. New York City Transit Authority, 81 N.Y.2d 923, 924 (1993).

63 State v. White, 29 N.E.3d 939, 944–45, 947, 950, 952 (Ohio 2015).

64 Albanese v. Town of Narragansett, 135 A.3d 1179, 1189 (R.I. 2016).

65 Roose v. State, 759 P.2d 478, 479 (Wyo. 1988).

66 Washington v. Starke, 173 Mich. App. 230, 236, 433 N.W.2d 834, 836 (1988).

67 Newell v. State, 364 P.3d 602, 604 (2015).

68 Caudillo v. City of Phoenix, No. 1 CA-CV 09-0467, 2010 WL 2146408, at *2 n.6 (Ariz. Ct. App. May 27, 2010).

69 Hernandez v. City of Pomona, 46 Cal. 4th 501, 513 (2009).

70 Williams v. State, 539 A.2d 164, 174 (Del. 1988).

71 Holland v. State, 696 So.2d 757, 760 (Fla. 1997).

72 Bell v. Commonwealth, 122 S.W.3d 490, 499 (Ky. 2003).

73 Richardson v. McGriff, 361 Md. 437, 452 (2000).

74 Baker v. Chaplin, 517 N.W.2d 911, 915 (Minn. 1994).

75 Sheppard v. State, 594 S.E.2d 462, 473 (2004).

76 Maston v. Wagner, 236 W. Va. 488, 504 (2015).

77 Williams v. State, 539 A.2d 164, 174 (Del. 1988).

78 Caudillo v. City of Phoenix, No. 1 CA-CV 09-0467, 2010 WL 2146408, at *2 (Ariz. Ct. App. May 27, 2010) ("It appears . . . that [the officer] was 'effectuating an arrest' because his use of deadly force against Celaya constituted a seizure for Fourth Amendment purposes").

79 Ala. Code § 13A-3-27(c).

80 See, e.g., Fla. Stat. § 901.15.

81 Crosswhite v. Barnes, 139 Va. 471 (1924).

82 Compare Me. Rev. Stat. tit. 17-A, § 107 with N.H. Rev. Stat. Ann. § 627:5.

83 Wirsing v. Krzeminski, 61 Wis. 2d 513, 519–20, 213 N.W.2d 37, 40 (1973) ("although force is privileged to effect an arrest, it is not privileged if the means employed are in excess of those which the actor reasonably believes to be necessary." Internal quotation marks omitted).

84 Alaska Stat. § 11.81.370(b).

85 Conn. Gen. Stat. § 53a-22(a).

86 Conn. Gen. Stat. § 53a-22(a).

87 Del. Code Ann. tit. 11, § 467(b)(2), (3).

88 Ky. Rev. Stat. Ann. § 503.090(1)(c).

89 Fla. Stat. § 776.05.

90 La. Code. Crim. Proc. Ann. art 220.

91 S.D. Codified Laws § 22-18-2.

92 Julian v. Randazzo, 380 Mass. 391, 396 & n.1, 403 N.E.2d 931, 934 & n.1 (1980).

93 People v. Doss, 406 Mich. 90, 102, 276 N.W.2d 9, 14 (1979); Young v. Barker, 158 Mich. App. 709, 723, 405 N.W.2d 395, 402 (1987). But see Ealey v. City of Detroit, 144 Mich. App. 324, 332, 375 N.W.2d 435, 438 (1985) ("Reasonable and good faith belief in the necessity of police action is a defense to a civil rights claim.").

94 Yada v. Simpson, 112 Nev. 254, 913 P.2d 1261, 1262–63 (1996), *superseded by statute on other grounds* as recognized by RTTC Commc'ns, LLC v. Saratoga Flier, Inc., 121 Nev. 34, 110 P.3d 24, 29 (2005) ("[A] police officer who uses more force than is reasonably necessary to effect a lawful arrest commits a battery upon the person arrested").

95 Idaho Code Ann. § 19-610.

96 Mullis v. State, 196 Ga. 569, 579, 27 S.E.2d 91, 98 (1943).

97 Minn. Stat. § 629.33.

98 Fla. Stat. § 776.05(2).

99 N.D. Cent. Code § 12.1-05-02.

100 S.D. Codified Laws § 22-18-2.

101 Ala. Code § 13A-3-27.

102 Del. Code Ann. tit. 11, § 467(a)(2).

103 Ind. Code § 35-41-3-3(f).

104 See chapter 1, The Constitutional Law Standard.

105 Mullis v. State, 196 Ga. 569, 579, 27 S.E.2d 91, 98 (1943).

106 Julian v. Randazzo, 380 Mass. 391, 396 & n.1, 403 N.E.2d 931, 934 & n.1 (1980).

107 Young v. Barker, 158 Mich. App. 709, 723, 405 N.W.2d 395, 402 (1987).

108 City of Jackson v. Powell, 917 So. 2d 59, 71–72 (Miss. 2005).

109 Yada v. Simpson, 112 Nev. 254, 913 P.2d 1261, 1262–63 (1996), superseded by statute
on other grounds as recognized by RTTC Commc'ns, LLC v. Saratoga Flier, Inc.,
121 Nev. 34, 110 P.3d 24, 29 (2005).

110 Mead v. O'Connor, 1959-NMSC-077, ¶ 4, 66 N.M. 170, 173, 344 P.2d 478, 479–80.

111 State v. White, 29 N.E.3d 939, 944-45, 947, 950, 952 (Ohio 2015).

112 State v. Weaver, 265 S.C. 130, 136, 217 S.E.2d 31, 34 (1975).

113 R.I. Gen. Laws § 12-7-8.

114 Or. Rev. Stat. § 161.235.

115 Pa. Cons. Stat. § 508.

116 Pa. Cons. Stat. § 501.

117 Haw. Rev. Stat. §§ 703-300, 703-307.

118 Del. Code Ann. tit. 11, § 467(a)(1).

119 Del. Code Ann. tit. 11, § 470(a).

120 State v. Thompson, 244 Neb. 189, 505 N.W.2d 673 (1993); Wagner v. City of
Omaha, 236 Neb. 843, 464 N.W.2d 175 (1991).

121 Prince v. Com., 987 S.W.2d 324 (Ky. Ct. App. 1997).

122 Fla. Stat. § 776.05(1).

123 Richardson v. McGriff, 361 Md. 437, 452, 762 A.2d 48, 56 (2000).

124 Morales v. City of Oklahoma City ex rel. Oklahoma City Police Dep't, 2010 OK 9,
¶¶ 26-27, 230 P.3d 869, 880.

125 Coll v. Johnson, 161 Vt. 163, 164–66, 636 A.2d 336, 338-39 (1993).

126 Buck v. Commonwealth, 20 Va. App. 298, 304, 456 S.E.2d 534, 537 (1995).

127 Maston v. Wagner, 236 W. Va. 488, 504, 781 S.E.2d 936, 952 (2015).

128 Fla. Stat. § 776.05(2), (3).

129 N.D. Cent. Code § 12.1-05-02.

130 Ga. Code Ann. § 17-4-20.

131 Me. Rev. Stat. tit. 17-A, § 107(7); N.H. Rev. Stat. Ann. § 627:5(VII).

132 Ariz. Rev. Stat. § 13-1203(A)(2).

133 Ariz. Rev. Stat. § 13-409(a).

134 Idaho Code Ann. § 19-610; Minn. Stat. Ann. § 629.33; Wash. Rev. Code §10.31.050;
Wis. Stat. Ann. § 939.45(4).

135 Idaho Code Ann. § 19-610.

136 Ark. Code Ann. § 5-2-610(a).

137 There is some variation as to the definition of "great bodily harm" or, as it is
sometimes alternatively phrased, "serious bodily injury" or "serious bodily harm."
Serious bodily harm may be thought of as "so grave or serious that it is regarded
as differing in kind, and not merely in degree, from other bodily harm."
Restatement (Second) of Torts § 63 (Comment on Subsection (1)). The Model

Penal Code defines "serious bodily injury" as "bodily injury which creates a substantial risk of death or which causes serious, permanent disfigurement, or protracted loss or impairment of the function of any bodily member or organ." Model Penal Code § 210.0(3). Federal law, in contrast, defines "serious bodily injury" to mean an injury that involves "a substantial risk of death, extreme physical pain, protracted and obvious disfigurement, or protracted loss or impairment of the function of a bodily member, organ, or mental faculty." 18 U.S.C.A. § 1365(h)(3). State law may adopt a different definition of serious bodily injury. For example, the California Penal Code defines serious bodily injury as a "serious impairment of physical condition, including, but not limited to, the following: loss of consciousness, concussion, bone fracture, protracted loss or impairment of function of any bodily member or organ, a wound requiring extensive suturing, and serious disfigurement." Ca. Penal Code § 243(f)(4).

138 Flanders and Welling, "Police Use of Deadly Force."

139 Tennessee v. Garner, 471 U.S. 1 (1985).

140 Flanders and Welling, "Police Use of Deadly Force."

141 A number of states also authorize or provide a justification defense to public officers who use lethal force pursuant to the judgment of a competent court by, for example, carrying out a lawfully imposed death penalty. Such situations are outside of the context in which we are examining the use of force, so we will not further discuss the use of force as a punishment.

142 Or. Rev. Stat. § 161.239(1)(a).

143 City of Princeton vex rel. Barber v. Fidelity & Cas. Co. of New York, 118 W.Va. 89, 188 S.E. 757, 758 (1936).

144 Mullis v. State, 196 Ga. 569, 579, 27 S.E.2d 91, 98 (1943).

145 Mich. Op. Atty. Gen. 1976, No. 5068, p. 591.

146 Ind. Code § 35-31.5-2-138.

147 N.Y. Penal Law § 35.30(1)(a)(ii); Or. Rev. Stat. § 161.239(1)(b).

148 N.J. Rev. Stat. § 2C:3-7(b)(2)(c).

149 R.I. Gen. Laws § 12-7-9.

150 Ky. Rev. Stat. Ann. § 503.090(2).

151 CA Penal Code § 835a(e)(2).

152 Julian v. Randazzo, 380 Mass. 391, 396 n.1 (1980).

153 Iowa Code § 804.8(1).

154 N.H. Rev. Stat. Ann. § 627:5(VIII).

155 CA Penal Code 835a(a)(2).

156 Colo. Rev. Stat. § 18-1-707(2)(b)(III).

157 Mont. Code Ann. § 45-3-106.

158 Sheppard v. State, 594 S.E.2d 462, 473 (2004).

159 Ariz. Rev. Stat. § 13-410(c)(2)(d); Wash Rev. Code § 9A.16.040(1)(c)(4).

160 Del. Code Ann. tit. 11, § 467(e)(2); Neb. Rev. Stat. § 28-1412(7)(b)(ii). Pennsylvania follows a very similar approach, but the wording differs slightly. See Pa. Cons. Stat. § 508(d)(1)(ii)(B).

161 720 Ill. Comp. Stat. 5/7-5.5.

162 See chapter 1, The Constitutional Law Standard.

163 Prince v. Commonwealth, 987 S.W.2d 324 (Ky. Ct. App. 1997).

164 State v. Thompson, 244 Neb. 189, 505 N.W.2d 673 (1993); Wagner v. City of Omaha, 236 Neb. 843, 464 N.W.2d 175 (1991).

165 Prince v. Commonwealth, 987 S.W.2d 324 (Ky. Ct. App. 1997).

166 State v. Thompson, 244 Neb. 189, 505 N.W.2d 673 (1993); Wagner v. City of Omaha, 236 Neb. 843, 464 N.W.2d 175 (1991).

167 Idaho Code Ann. § 18-4011(2).

168 Wash Rev. Code § 9A.16.040(1)(b).

169 Nev. Rev. Stat. § 171.1455.

170 Julie Tate, Jennifer Jenkins, Steven Rich, John Muyskens, Kennedy Elliott, Ted Mellnik, and Aaron Williams, "How the *Washington Post* Is Examining Police Shooting in the United States," *Washington Post*, July 7, 2016, www.washingtonpost.com.

171 Ala. Code. § 13A-3-27(c).

172 N.C. Gen. Stat. § 15A-401(iv).

173 Minn. Stat. § 609.066, subd. 3.

174 Me. Rev. Stat. tit. 17-A, § 107(8); N.H. Rev. Stat. Ann. § 627:5(II)(C).

175 Ore. Rev. Stat. § 161.239(2).

176 Colo. Rev. Stat. § 18-1-707(3).

177 Fla. Stat. § 776.05(3) (emphasis added).

178 Paul H. Robinson and Tyler Scot Williams, *Mapping American Criminal Law: Variations Across the 50 States* (California: Praeger Press, 2018), 151.

179 Robinson and Williams, *Mapping American Criminal Law*, 151.

180 Robinson and Williams, *Mapping American Criminal Law*, 153.

181 Robinson and Williams, *Mapping American Criminal Law*, 154.

182 Robinson and Williams, *Mapping American Criminal Law*, 153-54.

183 Ind. Code § 35-41-3-3.

184 Andy Reid, "Nouman Raja Second-Guessed His Approach to Corey Jones' Car After Shooting, Records Show," *South Florida Sun Sentinel*, January 17, 2017, www.sun-sentinel.com; Francis Robles and Christine Hauser, "Lawyers Provide Details in Police Shooting of Corey Jones in Florida," *New York Times*, October 22, 2015, www.nytimes.com; Palm Beach Gardens Police, "Officer-Involved Shooting," Official Website for the City of Palm Beach Gardens, accessed February 7, 2019, www.pbgfl.com.

185 Tracy Connor, "Photo Raises Doubts About Police Shooting of Jermaine McBean," NBC News, May 30, 2015, www.nbcnews.com; Tracy Connor, "Florida Deputy Indicted for Killing Jermaine McBean," NBC News, December 11, 2015, www.nbcnews.com.

186 Florida v. Peraza, No. SC17-1978 (Fla. Dec. 13, 2018).

CHAPTER 3. THE ADMINISTRATIVE STANDARD

1 Matthew J. Hickman and Brian A. Reaves, U.S. Department of Justice, *Local Police Departments 2000* (2003), iv, Bureau of Justice Statistics, www.bjs.gov.

2 Brian A. Reaves, U.S. Department of Justice, *State and Local Law Enforcement Training Academies, 2006* (2009), 6, Bureau of Justice Statistics, www.bjs.gov.

3 See, e.g., International Association of Chiefs of Police/COPS Office Use of Force Symposium, *Emerging Use of Force Issues: Balancing Public & Officer Safety* (2012), International Association of Chiefs of Police, www.theiacp.org; Police Executive Research Forum, *Guiding Principles on Use of Force* (2016), Police Executive Research Forum, www.policeforum.org.

4 William Terrill, Eugene A. Paoline III, and Jason Ingram, *Final Technical Report Draft: Assessing Police Use of Force Policy and Outcomes* (2011), iii, National Criminal Justice Reference Service, www.ncjrs.gov.

5 Arlington Police Department, *General Order* 401.00(401.05).

6 *Atlanta Police Department Policy Manual* APD.COP.3010(4.5).

7 Monell v. Department of Social Services, 436 U.S. 658 (1978).

8 Stephen Rushin, "Structural Reform Litigation in American Police Departments," *Minnesota Law Review* 99, no. 4 (2015): 1343–1422; Stephen Rushin, "Federal Enforcement of Police Reform," *Fordham Law Review* 82, no. 6 (2014): 3189–3247; Rachel A. Harmon, "Promoting Civil Rights Through Proactive Policing Reform," 62 *Stanford Law Review* 62 (2009): 1–68.

9 Ga. Code Ann. § 17-4-20(d) (2010).

10 Ludwig v. Anderson, 54 F.3d 465, 472 (8th Cir. 1995) (internal quotation marks omitted).

11 Lorie A. Fridell, Steve Ijames, and Michael Berkow, "Taking the Strawman to the Ground: Arguments in Support of the Linear Use-of-Force Continuum," *Police Chief* 78 (December 2011): 20–25.

12 Brandon Garrett and Seth Stoughton, "A Tactical Fourth Amendment," *Virginia Law Review* 103, no. 2 (2017): 284.

13 Thomas Frank, "High-Speed Police Chases Have Killed Thousands of Innocent Bystanders: Victims Include Small Children, Teenage Drivers and the Elderly," *USA Today*, July 30, 2015, www.usatoday.com.

14 Gregory J. Connor, "Use of Force Continuum: Phase 11," *Law and Order* 39 (1991): 30–3; Franklyn Graves and Gregory J. Connor "The FLETC Use-of-Force Model," *Police Chief* 59 (1992): 56–58.

15 Terrill, Paoline, and Ingram, *Final Technical Report Draft*.

16 Garrett and Stoughton, "A Tactical Fourth Amendment," 270.

17 Email correspondence; on file with authors.

18 See Fridell, Ijames, and Berkow, "Taking the Strawman to the Ground."

19 Fridell, Ijames, and Berkow, "Taking the Strawman to the Ground."

20 "Planning," in this context, does not necessarily mean drafting out a formal tactical plan. Instead, it refers to an officer's responsibility to go beyond reactively responding to a suspect's resistance by proactively approaching the situation in a way that maximizes a successful resolution.

21 Michael Williams and Jenny Lloyd, *A Review of the Literature on Police Use of Force Models* (Victoria, Australia, 2012), 11.

22 Seth W. Stoughton, "Law Enforcement's 'Warrior' Problem," *Harvard Law Review Forum* 128 (2015): 225–34.

23 We are aware of no academic work that has attempted to identify the effect of policy components on the use of less-lethal force. The only analysis of lethal force that we are aware of comes from Campaign Zero, an advocacy organization that has published an analysis of eight different policy components related to the use of deadly force: comprehensive reporting, an exhaustion requirement, a prohibition on chokeholds, the adoption of a force continuum, a de-escalation requirement, a duty to intervene, restricting shooting into moving vehicles, and requiring a verbal warning before deadly force is used. Campaign Zero, *Police Use of Force Project*, Analysis, http://useofforceproject.org/#analysis. By comparing rates of lethal shootings at agencies with different policies, Campaign Zero has offered a calculation of the effect of each component, writing, "After taking into account other factors, each additional use of force policy [component] was associated with a 15% reduction in killings by police. According to our analysis, the average police department would have 54% fewer killings and a police department with none of these policies currently in place would have 72% fewer killings by implementing all eight of these policies." (emphasis omitted).

24 Fridell, Ijames, and Berkow. "Taking the Strawman to the Ground"; Alpert and Smith, "How Reasonable Is the Reasonable Man?"

25 Terrill, Paoline, and Ingram, *Final Technical Report Draft*.

26 Garrett and Stoughton, "A Tactical Fourth Amendment," 278–86.

27 Graham v. Connor, 490 U.S. 386 (1989).

CHAPTER 4. THE COMMUNITY EXPECTATIONS STANDARD

1 U.S. Department of Justice, *Final Report of the President's Task Force on 21st Century Policing* (Washington, DC: U.S. Department of Justice, 2015), 1, www.cops.usdoj.gov.

2 Robert J. Kane, "Compromised Police Legitimacy as a Predictor of Violent Crime in Structurally Disadvantaged Communities," *Criminology* 43 (2005): 469, 492.

3 U.S. Department of Justice, *Community Relations Service FY 2003 Annual Report*, 2003, www.justice.gov.

4 Daniel Bukszpan, "America's Most Destructive Riots of All Time," CNBC, February 1, 2011, www.cnbc.com.

5 John Graveline, "Steve Young Quote," YouTube, November 22, 2012, https://youtu.be/tqhdDhoZPEo?t=32.

6 Nick Selby, Ben Singleton, and Ed Flosi, *In Context: Understanding Police Killings of Unarmed Civilians* (St. Augustine, FL: Contextual Press, 2016). Emphasis added.

7 Tom R. Tyler, Kenneth A. Rasinski, and Nancy Spodick, "Influence of Voice on Satisfaction With Leaders: Exploring the Meaning of Process Control," *Journal of Personality and Social Psychology* 48, no. 1 (1985): 72–81; Tom R. Tyler, Jonathon Jackson, and Ben Bradford, "Procedural Justice and Cooperation," in *Encyclopedia*

of Criminology and Criminal Justice, ed. Gerben Bruinsma and David Weisburd (New York: Springer, 2014), 4011–24.

8   See Tom R. Tyler and Jeffrey Fagan, "Legitimacy and Cooperation: Why Do People Help the Police Fight Crime in Their Communities?," *Ohio State Journal of Criminal Law* 6 (2008): 231, 262; Tom R. Tyler and Cheryl Wakslak, "Profiling and Police Legitimacy: Procedural Justice, Attributions of Motive, and Acceptance of Police Authority," *Criminology* 42 (2004): 253, 255; Tom R. Tyler and Yuen J. Huo, *Trust in the Law: Encouraging Public Cooperation With the Police and Courts* (New York: Russell Sage Foundation, 2002); Raymond Paternoster, Robert Brame, Ronet Bachman, and Lawrence W. Sherman, "Do Fair Procedures Matter? The Effect of Procedural Justice on Spouse Assault," *Law and Society Review* 31 (1997): 163–204.

9   Tracy L. Meares et al., "Lawful or Fair? How Cops and Laypeople View Good Policing," Yale Law School, Public Law Working Paper No. 255, August 11, 2014, https://papers.ssrn.com.

10 Tracy L. Meares and Peter Neyroud, "Rightful Policing," *New Perspectives in Policing* (February 2015): 1-16, National Criminal Justice Reference Service, www.ncjrs.gov.

11 Meares and Neyroud, "Rightful Policing."; Tom R. Tyler, "Enhancing Police Legitimacy," *Annals of the American Academy of Political and Social Science* 593 (2004): 84–99, 94.

12 John R. Baseheart and Terry C. Cox, "Effects of Police Use of Profanity on a Receiver's Perceptions of Credibility," *Journal of Police and Criminal Psychology* 9, no. 2 (1993): 9–19.

13 Christina L. Patton Michael Asken, William J. Fremouw, and Robert Bemis, "The Influence of Police Profanity on Public Perception of Excessive Force," *Journal of Police and Criminal Psychology* 32, no. 4 (2017): 340–57.

14 "The Origin of the LAPD Motto," Los Angeles Police Department, accessed February 7, 2019, www.lapdonline.org.

15 Kären M. Hess and Christine Hess Orthmann, *Introduction to Law Enforcement and Criminal Justice*, 10th ed. (Boston: Cengage Learning, 2012), 129.

16 "To Protect and Serve All," Officer.com, October 1, 2008, www.officer.com.

17 See, e.g., Deshaney v. Winnebago County Department of Social Services, 489 U.S. 189 (1989).

18 Madeline Buckley, Gregory Pratt, Matthew Walberg and Paige Fry, "'You Should Not Be Wearing That,' Man Screams at Woman in Puerto Rican Flag Shirt; Cop's Response Under Investigation," *Chicago Tribune*, July 10, 2018, www.chicagotribune.com.

19 Manny Fernandez, "After Walter Scott Shooting, Scrutiny Turns to 2nd Officer," *New York Times*, April 17, 2015, www.nytimes.com.

20 Lucy Steigerwald, "NYPD and EMS Workers Failed to Help Eric Garner After Cop Choked Him," *Bad Cop Blotter*, July 21, 2014, www.vice.com.

21 Shaila Dewan and Richard A. Oppel Jr., "In Tamir Rice Case, Many Errors by Cleveland Police, Then a Fatal One," *New York Times*, January 22, 2015, www.nytimes.com.

22 Emily Saul, "Cop: I Couldn't Save Shooting Victim Because NYPD Helped Me Cheat on CPR Test," *New York Post*, February 4, 2016, https://nypost.com.

23 Richard Pérez-Peña, "Why First Aid Is Often Lacking in the Moments After a Police Shooting," *New York Times*, September 21, 2016, www.nytimes.com.

24 Erin M. Harley, "Hindsight Bias in Legal Decision Making," *Social Cognition* 25, no. 1 (2007): 48–63.

25 Brian A. Reaves, U.S. Department of Justice, *Census of State and Local Law Enforcement Agencies, 2008* (2011), 2.

26 Rich Morin and Renee Stepler, Pew Research Center, *The Racial Confidence Gap in Police Performance*, September 29, 2016, https://www.pewsocialtrends.org.

27 Giri Nathan, "Eric Garner Died From Chokehold While in Police Custody," *Time*, August 1, 2014, http://time.com.

28 Nick Gillespie, "Eric Garner Was Choked to Death for Selling Loosies," *Daily Beast*, December 3, 2014, www.thedailybeast.com.

29 Rachel Harmon, "Why Arrest?," *Michigan Law Review*, 115 (2016).

30 One of the authors of this text, Jeff Noble, served as a consultant in the Tamir Rice case.

31 Los Angeles Times Staff, "Hear the 911 Call About Tamir Rice: Gun Is 'Probably Fake,' Caller Says," *Los Angeles Times*, November 26, 2014, www.latimes.com.

32 Rebecca Stone and Kelly M. Socia, "Boy With Toy or Black Male With Gun: An Analysis of Online News Articles Covering the Shooting of Tamir Rice," *Race and Justice*, (2017): 1–29.

33 Rheana Murray, "Video of Police Shooting Boy Holding Toy Gun Is Released," ABC News, November 26, 2014, https://abcnews.go.com.

34 Evan MacDonald, "Four Things You Forgot About Timothy Loehmann, the Cleveland Police Officer Who Shot Tamir Rice," Cleveland.com, May 30, 2017, www.cleveland.com.

35 Djvlad, "Full Surveillance Video Released of Tamir Rice Shot by Police," YouTube, December 1, 2014, www.youtube.com/watch?v=sdAYPQd1H1A.

36 Teddy Kulmala, "Judge Sentences Ex-S.C. Trooper to Prison for 2014 Shooting of Black Motorist," *The State*, August 15, 2017, www.thestate.com.

37 Amanda Sakuma, "Taser vs. Gun: Why Police Choose Deadly Force Despite Non-Lethal Options," NBC News, September 29, 2016, www.nbcnews.com. "Experts acknowledge the temptation to train police to shoot to wound, rather than to kill. Why not subdue a suspect by shooting them in the arm or the leg, but not the chest?"

38 Lindsey Bever, "School Officer Fired After Video Showed Him Body-Slamming a 12-Year-Old Girl," *Washington Post*, April 12, 2016, www.washingtonpost.com.

39 Jack Levin and Alexander R. Thomas, "Experimentally Manipulating Race: Perceptions of Police Brutality in an Arrest: A Research Note," *Justice Quarterly* 14, no. 3 (1997): 581.

40 Levin and Alexander R. Thomas, "Experimentally Manipulating Race," 581.

41 Levin and Alexander R. Thomas, "Experimentally Manipulating Race," 581.

42 In each video, the "officers" were the same two campus security guards wearing light- or dark-colored panty hose over their heads. Distance and poor-quality recording turned the mask into the officer's "race." Levin and Alexander R. Thomas, "Experimentally Manipulating Race," 579.

43 Levin and Thomas, "Experimentally Manipulating Race," 582.

44 German Lopez, "There are Huge Racial Disparities in How US Police Use Force," *Vox*, November 14, 2018, www.vox.com.

45 "Officer Caught Fighting Homeless Man Given Verbal Reprimand," *Wesh* 2, March 12, 2016, www.wesh.com.

46 Seth Stoughton, "Cop Expert: Why Sandra Bland's Arrest Was Legal but Not Good Policing," *Talking Points Memo*, July 24, 2015, http://talkingpointsmemo. com.

47 Joe Coscarelli, "How Anonymous Cops Online Are Reacting to the Death of Eric Garner," *New York Intelligencer*, July 21, 2014, http://nymag.com.

48 Sunil Dutta, "I'm a Cop. If You Don't Want to Get Hurt, Don't Challenge Me.," *Washington Post*, August 19, 2014, www.washingtonpost.com.

49 Seth Stoughton, "A Former Cop on What Went Wrong in McKinney," *Talking Points Memo*, June 9, 2015, https://talkingpointsmemo.com.

50 Doug Wyllie, "Why the 'Pool Party' Arrest Hysteria Is (Again) Dead Wrong," *PoliceOne.com*, June 10, 2015, www.policeone.com.

51 Matt Walsh, "Blame the Teenagers for What Happened in McKinney, Not the Police," *The Blaze*, June 09, 2015, www.theblaze.com.

52 Brandon Brooks, "Cops Crash Pool Party (Original)," YouTube, June 6, 2015, https://youtu.be/R46-XTqXkzE.

CHAPTER 5. TACTICAL CONSIDERATIONS

1 This chapter contains material adapted from Brandon Garrett and Seth Stoughton, "A Tactical Fourth Amendment," *Virginia Law Review* 103, no. 2 (2017): 211; Seth W. Stoughton, "Principled Policing: Warrior Cops and Guardian Officers," *Wake Forest Law Review* 51, no. 3 (2016): 611; and Seth Stoughton, "Modern Police Practices: *Arizona v. Gant's* Illusory Restriction of Vehicle Searches Incident to Arrest," *Virginia Law Review* 97, no. 7 (2011): 1727.

2 Arnold Binder and Peter Scharf, "The Violent Police–Citizen Encounter," 452 *Annals of American Academy of Political and Social Sciences* 452, no. 1 (1980): 116; Scharf and Binder, *The Badge and the Bullet*.

3 Merriam-Webster Dictionary, s.v. "tactics" 1(a).

4 We discussed the distinction between risk and threat in chapter 1, but a brief reminder may be valuable. A threat exists when an individual has the apparent ability, opportunity, and intention to cause a specific and identifiable type of harm. "Ability" refers to the subject's physical capability to cause a particular harm; "opportunity" refers to the availability of the object of that harm, and "intention" refers to the subject's apparent objective to cause that harm. Consider, for example, a subject who is physically able to flee from officers, who has the

opportunity to flee because the situation is such that officers cannot grab him to prevent his flight, and whose actions—running away—demonstrate an intention to flee. In that case, it may easily be concluded that the subject presents a threat to the government's interest in apprehension.

Risk is a distinct concept that may be understood as a potential threat; a risk exists when a subject has one or two, but not all three, components of a threat. An individual who has the physical ability to run from officers and the opportunity to do so, but who has taken no actions indicating any intention to flee, may present a risk to the government's interest in apprehension, but such an individual does not present an active threat to that interest.

5 Jeffrey J. Noble, and Geoffrey P. Alpert, "State-Created Danger: Should Police Officers Be Accountable for Reckless Tactical Decision Making?," in *Critical Issues in Policing: Contemporary Readings*, ed. Roger G. Dunham and Geoffrey P. Alpert, 7th ed. (Long Grove, IL: Waveland Press, 2015), 568.

6 Binder and Scharf, "The Violent Police-Citizen Encounter," 116; Scharf and Binder, *The Badge and the Bullet*.

7 Lorie A. Fridell and Arnold Binder, "Police Officer Decisionmaking in Potentially Violent Confrontations," *Journal of Criminal Justice* 20, no. 5 (1992): 393.

8 Scharf and Binder later revised their taxonomy to add a fifth phase, the "Aftermath" phase, which includes everything that happens after a use of force, from the officer providing first aid to a possible judicial inquiry and prosecution.

9 Albert Reiss, for example, divided use of force encounters into two phases: "the last moment when the citizen [has] failed to heed all warnings" and everything that came prior to that point. Albert J. Reiss, Jr., "Controlling Police Use of Deadly Force," *Annals of American Academy of Political and Social Sciences* 452, no. 1 (1980): 127.

10 James Fyfe has suggested that an officer's decision to use force was influenced not just by case-specific information, but also by environment, organization, and situational variables that shape the officer's working environment. James J. Fyfe, "Police Shooting: Environment and License," in *Controversial Issues in Crime and Justice*, ed. Joseph E. Scott and Travis Hirschi (Newbury Park, CA: Sage Publications, 1988), 79–94; James J. Fyfe, "Police Use of Deadly Force: Research and Reform," *Justice Quarterly* 5, no. 2 (1988): 165–205.

11 John Spencer and Matt Larsen, "A Gun Won't Give You the Guts to Run Toward Danger," *Washington Post*, March 5, 2018, www.washingtonpost.com; Jonathan J. Cooper, "Cops: Slain Sheriff's Sergeant Was Talking to His Wife When Shooting Call Came In," *Chicago Tribune*, November 8, 2018, www.chicagotribune.com (describing a "sheriff's sergeant who was killed trying to stop a shooting rampage at a California bar as a 'cop's cop' who didn't hesitate to run toward danger.").

12 Abraham v. Raso, 183 F.3d 279, 285 (3d Cir. 1999).

13 See Young v. City of Providence, 404 F.3d 4 (1st Cir. 2005); *Raso*, 183 F.3d at 279; Dickerson v. McClellan, 101 F.3d 1151, 1161 (6th Cir. 1996); Allen v. Muskogee, 119 F.3d 837 (10th Cir. 1997); Hayes v. County of San Diego, 57 Cal. 4th 622, 639 (2013).

14 Denver Police Department, Operations Manual § 105.01(1)(a) (2010), www. denvergov.org.

15 Graham v. Connor, 490 U.S. 386, 397 (1989).

16 Louise E. Porter, Justin Ready, and Geoffrey P. Alpert, "Officer-Involved Shootings: Testing the Effect of Question Timing on Memory Accuracy for Stressful Events," *Journal of Experimental Criminology* No. 1 (2019): 1–28; David A. Klinger and Rod K. Brunson, "Police Officers' Perceptual Distortions During Lethal Force Situations: Informing the Reasonableness Standard," *Criminology and Public Policy* 8, no. 1 (2009): 123; see also Dean T. Olson, "Improving Deadly Force Decision Making," *FBI Law Enforcement Bulletin* 67, no. 2 (1998): 1–9, 7 (discussing "the deterioration of fine and complex motor skills under survival stress"); Bobby Westmoreland and Billy D. Haddock, "Code '3' Driving: Psychological and Physiological Stress Effects," *Law and Order* 37, no. 11 (1989): 29–31, 30 (describing how the stress of an emergency can lead to tunnel vision); Seth D. DuCharme, Note, "The Search for Reasonableness in Use-of-Force Cases: Understanding the Effects of Stress on Perception and Performance," *Fordham Law Review* 70 (2002): 2541–42 (explaining three categories of distorted sensory perception).

17 Judith P. Andersen and Harri Gustafsberg, "A Training Method to Improve Police Use of Force Decision Making: A Randomized Controlled Trial," *SAGE Open* 6 (2016): 1–13, 2–3 http://sgo.sagepub.com/content/6/2/2158244016638708; DuCharme, "Search for Reasonableness," 2546–48.

18 Noble and Alpert, "State-Created Danger," 574; Seth W. Stoughton, "Policing Facts," *Tulane Law Review* 88, no. 5 (2014): 864–69.

19 See Tracy A. Hightower, "Boyd's O.O.D.A. Loop and How We Use It," *Tactical Response Blog*, October 20, 2016, https://tacticalresponse.com; J. Pete Blair and M. Hunter Martaindale, *Evaluating Police Tactics: An Empirical Assessment of Room Entry Techniques*, ed. Joycelyn M. Pollock and Michael C. Braswell (Oxford and Waltham, MA: Elsevier, 2014), 41.

20 Amaury Murgado, "Why the OODA Loop Is Still Relevant," *Police*, January 10, 2013, www.policemag.com.

21 Donald A. MacCuish, "Orientation: Key to the OODA Loop—The Culture Factor," *Journal of Defense Resources Management* 3, no. 2 (2012): 67–74, 70.

22 MacCuish, "Orientation," 70.

23 Ray Hyman, "Stimulus Information as a Determinant of Reaction Time," *Journal of Experimental Psychology* 45, no. 3 (1953): 188–96; William Edmund Hick, "On the Rate Gain of Information," *Quarterly Journal of Experimental Psychology* 4 (1952): 11–26, 12.

24 Hightower, "Boyd's O.O.D.A. Loop."

25 Charles "Sid" Heal, *Sound Doctrine: A Tactical Primer* (New York: Lantern Books, 2000), 79.

26 Jack R. Greene ed., *The Encyclopedia of Police Science*, 3rd ed. (New York and London: Routledge, 2007), 792.

27 Charles Remsberg, *The Tactical Edge: Surviving High-Risk Patrol* (Glen Ellyn, IL: Calibre Press, 1986), 229.

28 See Radley Balko, *Overkill: The Rise of Paramilitary Police Raids in America* 1–4 (Washington DC: Cato Institute, 2006), 1–4 (documenting examples).

29 Remsberg, *The Tactical Edge*, 237.

30 Daniel Kahneman, *Thinking, Fast and Slow* (New York: Farrar, Straus and Giroux, 2011), 20.

31 Kahneman, *Thinking, Fast and Slow*, 21; see also Gideon Keren and Yaacov Schul, "Two Is Not Always Better Than One: A Critical Evaluation of Two-System Theories," *Perspectives on Psychological Science* 4 (2009): 546 (discussing the role of both systems in problem solving).

32 Kahneman, *Thinking, Fast and Slow*, 19–20.

33 Kahneman, *Thinking, Fast and Slow*, 19–20.

34 See, e.g., William R. Lovallo, *Stress and Health: Biological and Psychological Interactions*, 2nd ed (Thousand Oaks, CA: Sage Publications, 2005), 89–98; Raffael Kalisch, Marianne B. Müeller, and Oliver Tüscher, "A Conceptual Framework for the Neurobiological Study of Resilience," *Behavioral and Brain Sciences* 38 (2015): 1–79, 3.

35 Kalisch et al., "A Conceptual Framework," 3.

36 See generally Gerd Gigerenzer, *Simply Rational: Decision Making in the Real World* (Oxford and New York: Oxford University Press, 2015), 107–39 (exploring methods for enabling rational decision making through heuristics).

37 Ronald J. Adams, Thomas A. McTernan, and Charles Remsberg, *Street Survival: Tactics for Armed Encounters* (Glen Ellyn, IL: Calibre Press, 1997), 79.

38 Portland Police Bureau, *Manual of Policy and Procedure* (Portland: Portland Police Bureau, 2010), 162 (instructing officers to provide, when plausible, certain information, "Before making a traffic stop, [including]: 1. Unit number and [the radio signal indicating a traffic stop]. 2. Vehicle license plate or description. 3. Location.").

39 Adams et al., *Street Survival*, 69–76.

40 Adams et al., *Street Survival*, 75.

41 Adams et al., *Street Survival*, 155.

42 Adams et al., *Street Survival*, 395.

43 Remsberg, *The Tactical Edge*, 437, 440.

44 Amaury Murgado, "Closing the Gap," *Police*, July 10, 2013, www.policemag.com.

45 Dennis Tueller, "How Close Is Too Close?" *The Police Policy Studies Council* (2004), www.theppsc.org.

46 Lawrence Mower, "Police Shootings: Deputies Shielded by the Badge," *Palm Beach Post*, April 29, 2015.

47 Ron Martinelli, "Revisiting the '21-Foot Rule,'" *Police*, September 18, 2014.

48 Steven Albrecht and John Morrison, *Contact & Cover: Two-Officer Suspect Control* (Springfield, IL: Charles C. Thomas, 1992).

49 Mike "Ziggy" Siegfried, "Video: Cars, Cover, and Concealment," *Police*, October 1, 2011, www.policemag.com ("Every well-trained cop can explain the difference

between cover and concealment. One common summary I have heard is[:] 'Cover stops the bullets that are being fired at you[,] and concealment hides you from the suspect but does not stop bullets.'").

50 Anthony J. Pinizzotto et al., *Violent Encounters: A Study of Felonious Assaults on Our Nation's Law Enforcement Officers* (Washington, DC: U.S. Department of Justice, 2006), 19; John Bennett, "How Command Presence Affects Your Survival," *PoliceOne.com*, October 7, 2010, www.policeone.com.

51 Erwin Chemerinsky, "An Independent Analysis of the Los Angeles Police Department's Board of Inquiry Report on the Rampart Scandal," *Loyola of Los Angeles Law Review* 34, no. 2 (2001): 563.

52 Indeed, the criticisms emphasize the potential for command presence to lend itself to gender discrimination when included as part of an evaluative process. Women's Advisory Council to the L.A. Police Commission, *A Blueprint for Implementing Gender Equity in the Los Angeles Police Department* (Los Angeles: Women's Advisory Council, 1993), 39–41; Frank Rudy Cooper, "'Who's the Man?': Masculinities Studies, *Terry* Stops, and Police Training," *Columbia Journal of Gender and Law* 18, no. 3 (2009): 671–742.

53 Stoughton, "Principled Policing," 652–58.

54 Independent Commission on the L.A. Police Department, *Report of the Independent Commission on the Los Angeles Police Department* (Los Angeles: Independent Commission on the L.A. Police Department, 1991), 99; Chemerinsky, "An Independent Analysis," 596; Thomas M. Riordan, "Copping an Attitude: Rule of Law Lessons From the Rodney King Incident," *Loyola of Los Angeles Law Review*, 27 (1994): 675, 727–28.

55 Marcel F. Beausoleil, "Police Abuse," in *The Social History of Crime and Punishment in America: An Encyclopedia,* ed. Wilbur R. Miller (Los Angles: Sage Publishing, 2012), 3: 1372, 1375.

56 Beausoleil, "Police Abuse," 1375.

57 John Van Maanen, "The Asshole," in *Policing: A View from the Street,* ed. Peter K. Manning and John Van Maanen (New York: Random House, 1978), reprinted in *Police and Society: Touchstone Readings*, ed. Victor E. Kappeler, 2nd ed. (Prospect Heights, IL: Waveland Press, 1999).

58 Jack L. Colwell and Charles Huth, *Unleashing the Power of Unconditional Respect: Transforming Law Enforcement and Police Training* (Boca Raton, FL: CRC Press, 2010), 45, 89 ("It has become fashionable for officers to adopt an adversarial perspective toward the public, especially when they perceive the public as being unsupportive or overly critical of their actions. This distorted perception reinforces the idea that the police are a separate entity from the public and can result in a pattern of self-justification that can be used to legitimize rudeness, a lack of empathy, and, in some cases, illegal behavior. This kind of unconscious programming—reaffirmed over hundreds of interactions and years of typecasting—is the inevitable result of a police culture that has slowly drifted away from a service mentality.").

59 Beausoleil, "Police Abuse," 1375.

60 Alpert and Dunham, *Understanding Police Use of Force*, 41.

61 Stoughton, "Principled Policing," 655–56.

62 Kristin Precoda, "Key Findings for Interpersonal Skills," *SSIM TA1A Final Report* (November 2013), 13–14.

63 Seth Stoughton, "Guardians of Our Galaxy—What Is Good Policing?" TEDxUofSC, YouTube, January 10, 2019, https://youtube.com/uJrBuo3lo5s?t=618.

64 Unfortunately, officers are still widely taught to take command of any given situation. See Stoughton, "Principled Policing," 652–58.

65 George J. Thompson and Jerry B. Jenkins, *Verbal Judo: The Gentle Art of Persuasion* (New York: William Morrow, 2013), 62–63.

66 Thompson and Jenkins, *Verbal Judo*, 63.

67 Thompson and Jenkins, *Verbal Judo*, 63.

68 Sue Rahr et al., "The Four Pillars of Justice Based Policing: Listen and Explain with Equity and Dignity," *The Loyalty Solutions Group*, March 9, 2014, http://loyaltysolutionsgroup.com.

69 Sue Rahr et al., "The Four Pillars of Justice Based Policing."

70 Conn. Gen. Stat. § 53a-167a (2005).

71 State v. Williams, 110 Conn. App. 778, 793 (2008) ("[T]he state must prove that the defendant had the specific intent to interfere with an officer." (citing State v. Nita, 27 Conn App. 103, 111–12 (1992)).

72 Darwin BondGraham, "Oakland Police Release Video of Officers Fatally Shooting a Homeless Man," *East Bay Express*, November 1, 2018, www.eastbayexpress.com.

73 Scott Morris, "After Three Years, Oakland Police Release Body-Camera Video of Demouria Hogg Shooting," *East Bay Express*, September 17, 2018, www.eastbayexpress.com.

74 Jim Glennon, "$#it that Cops Say: Profanity and Public Perception," PoliceOne.com, December 8, 2010, www.policeone.com.

75 Gary T. Klugiewicz, "Should You Swear at Suspects?" PoliceOne.com, July 27, 2005, www.policeone.com; Dan Marcou, "Why Profanity Directed Toward Suspects Isn't Worth It," PoliceOne.com, December 3, 2014, www.policeone.com.

76 Baseheart and Cox, "Effects of Police Use of Profanity," 9–19.

77 Patton et al., "The Influence of Police Profanity."

78 Courtney Han, "Police Officer Shouts 'Pretend Like We're Going to Shoot You' During Traffic Stop," ABC News, May 21, 2018, https://abcnews.go.com.

79 Bernard D. Rostker, Lawrence M. Hanser, William M. Hix, Carl Jensen, Andrew R. Morral, Greg Ridgeway, and Terry L. Schel, *Evaluation of the New York City Police Department Firearm Training and Firearm-Discharge Review Process* (Santa Monica, CA: Rand Corporation, 2008), www.nyc.gov (quoting NYPD Police Academy, *Physical Training and Tactics Department Recruit Tracking Booklet* (New York: NYPD, 2007a), 17).

80 Rostker et al., *Evaluation of the New York City Police Department* (quoting NYPD Police Academy, *Physical Training*, 18).

81 William Terrill and Stephen D. Mastrofski, "Situational and Officer-Based Determinants of Police Coercion," *Justice Quarterly* 19, no. 2 (2002): 234–35 (suggesting that having multiple officers on scene may decrease the need to use force).

82 Terrill and Mastrofski, "Situational and Officer-Based Determinants," 234–35.

83 See Jonathan Rubenstein, "Controlling People," in *Policing: A View from the Street*, ed. Peter K. Manning and John Van Maanen (New York: Random House, 1978), 255–65.

84 See, e.g., McCullough v. Quarterman, No. H-06-3974, 2008 WL 5061512, at *7 (S.D. Tex. Nov. 24, 2008) (inmate who was being handcuffed began physically resisting after one handcuff had been applied).

85 See Parker v. Gerrish, 547 F.3d 1, 5–6 (1st Cir. 2008); United States v. Steptoe, 126 F. App'x 47, 49 (3d Cir. 2005); Cooper v. Rakers, No. 09-556-GPM, 2010 WL 1241530, at *1 (S.D. Ill. Mar. 23, 2010); *McCullough*, 2008 WL 5061512 at *7; Crystal Poole v. Gee, No. 8:07-CV-912-EAJ, 2008 WL 3367548, at *8–*10 (M.D. Fla. Aug. 8, 2008); Owens v. Chrisman, No. 3:07-0021, 2008 WL 217118, at *8 (M.D. Tenn. Jan. 23, 2008); Parker v. City of South Portland, No. 06-129-P-S, 2007 WL 1468658, at *11 n.50 (D. Me. May 18, 2007); Riddle v. Baber, No. 2:05CV00031, 2005 WL 2605545, at *2 (W.D. Va. Oct. 14, 2005); Birdine v. Gray, 375 F. Supp. 2d 874, 876 n.2 (D. Neb. 2005).

86 Remsberg, *The Tactical Edge*, 487.

87 Remsberg, *The Tactical Edge*, 498–506 ("Remember: EVERY arrestee should be handcuffed with hands behind him—and stay handcuffed—regardless of how cooperative he appears to be."); Portland Police Bureau, *Manual of Policy and Procedure* § 870.20, Custody and Transportation of Subjects (2009); John Wills, "Officer . . . It Hurts," *LawOfficer.com*, April 30, 3008, www.lawofficer.com ("It is not tactically sound to cuff someone in the front.").

88 Officers may apply additional restraints to arrestees who remain combative after being handcuffed, such as four-point restraints or hobbles that prevent the arrestee from freely moving his arms or legs. See, e.g., Portland Police Bureau, *Manual of Policy and Procedure* § 870.20 ("Members are authorized to use hobble restraint cords when necessary to subdue or secure a violent or unruly person. Restraint cords should not be used in lieu of handcuffs.").

89 Melissa Morabito et al., "Crisis Intervention Teams and People With Mental Illness Exploring the Factors that Influence the Use of Force," *Crime & Delinquency* 58 (2012): 57–77; James Arey et al., "Crisis Intervention Teams: An Evolution of Leadership in Community and Policing," *Policing* 10 (2016): 143–40.

90 Robert T. Flint, "Crisis Intervention Training," *FBI Law Enforcement Bulletin* 43 (1974): 6.

91 Lou Hayes, Jr., "Police Crisis Intervention & Illinois Model," *The Illinois Model: Thinking Like a Tactical Philosopher*, August 14, 2015, www.theillinoismodel.com.

92 "CIT Is More than Just Training . . . It's a Community Program," CIT International, Inc., accessed February 8, 2019, www.citinternational.org.

93 See Randolph Dupont, Sam Cochran, and Sarah Pillsbury, *Crisis Intervention Team Core Elements* (2007), http://cit.memphis.edu; U.S. Department of Justice, *Final Report of the President's Task Force on 21st Century Policing* (Washington, DC: U.S. Department of Justice, 2015), 2, www.cops.usdoj.gov; Amy C. Watson and Anjali J. Fulambarker, "The Crisis Intervention Team Model of Police Response to Mental Health Crises: A Primer for Mental Health Practitioners," *Best Practices in Mental Health* 8, no. 2 (2012): 71–81, www.ncbi.nlm.nih.gov.

94 Michael T. Compton, Berivan N. Demir Neubert, Beth Broussard, Joanne A. McGriff, Rhiannon Morgan, and Janet R. Oliva, "Use of Force Preferences and Perceived Effectiveness of Actions Among Crisis Intervention Team (CIT) Police Officers and Non-CIT Officers in an Escalating Psychiatric Crisis Involving a Subject With Schizophrenia," *Schizophrenia Bulletin* 37, no. 4 (2011): 742; Jennifer Skeem and Lynne Bibeau, "How Does Violence Potential Relate to Crisis Intervention Team Responses to Emergencies?," *Psychiatric Services* 59, no. 2 (2008): 201–04; Paul W. Spait and Mark S. Davis, *The Mentally Ill and the Criminal Justice System: A Review of Programs* (Columbus, OH: NAMI Ohio, June 2005), 17–23, www.namiohio.org.

95 Henry J. Steadman, Martha Williams, Randy Borum, and Joseph Morrissey, "Comparing Outcomes of Major Models of Police Responses to Mental Health Emergencies," *Psychiatric Services* 51, no. 5 (2000): 645–49 (finding that officers in Memphis who had received training in the Memphis CIT model were less likely to arrest persons with mental illnesses than officers who used a different specialized response in two other jurisdictions); Jennifer L. S. Teller et al., "Crisis Intervention Team Training for Police Officers Responding to Mental Disturbance Calls," *Psychiatric Services* 57, no. 2 (2006): 232–37.

96 Police Executive Research Forum, *Critical Issues in Policing Series: The Police Responses to Active Shooter Incidents* (Washington, DC: Police Executive Research Forum, 2014), Police Executive Research Forum, www.policeforum.org.

97 Some agencies train officers to enter an active shooting scene individually and without backup, while other agencies train officers to work in pairs or small groups. *See* Police Executive Research Forum, *The Police Responses*, 8–10.

98 Police Executive Research Forum, *The Police Responses*, 6.

99 Police Executive Research Forum, *The Police Responses*, 13.

CHAPTER 6. FORCE OPTIONS

1 18 U.S. Code § 1365 (h)(3).

2 Ca. Penal Code § 243(f)(4); California Commission on Peace Officer Standards and Training, *Basic Course Workbook Series, Student Materials, Learning Domain 20, Use of Force, Version 4.0* (2005), San Francisco Police Officers Association, https://sfpoa.org.

3 The application of handcuffs will not automatically convert a *Terry* stop into an arrest for Fourth Amendment purposes, but reviewers are cautioned to keep in

mind that, like other aspects of an investigative detention, the use of restraints must be justified when they are initially applied and throughout the duration of their application. Even if initially justified, it can become constitutionally unreasonable to keep a subject in handcuffs for a prolonged length of time. Fisher v. City of Las Cruces, 584 F.3d 888 (10th Cir. 2009).

4 Mlodzinski v. Lewis, 648 F.3d 24 (1st Cir. 2011).

5 Morrison v. Board of Trustees, 583 F.3d 394 (6th Cir. 2009); *Mlodzinski*, 648 F.3d at 24.

6 Cruz v. City of Laramie, 239 F.3d 1183 (10th Cir. 2001).

7 Centers for Disease Control and Prevention, *Loud Noise Can Cause Hearing Loss*, accessed February 11, 2019, www.cdc.gov.

8 The tactical aspects of such disorientation and confusion are discussed more fully in chapter 5.

9 The Safariland Group, Defense Technology, *Low Roll™ Distraction Device® 12-Gram, Non-Reloadable*, Defense Technology, accessed February 15, 2019, www.defense-technology.com.

10 Boyd v. Benton County, 374 F.3d 773 (9th Cir. 2004).

11 Steve Ijames, "6 Safety Considerations for Flashbangs," *PoliceOne.com*, March 18, 2011, www.policeone.com/.

12 Office of Professional Accountability, *Closed Case Summary*, December 8, 2015, website of the City of Seattle, www.seattle.gov.

13 Christine Eith and Matthew R. Durose, "Contacts Between Police and the Public, 2008," *Bureau of Justice Statistics* (October 2011): 11, *Bureau of Justice Statistics*, http://bjs.ojp.usdoj.gov.

14 Patrick McGreevy, "Bratton Bans Use-of-Force Term 'Distraction Strike' But Not Force," *Los Angeles Times*, November 18, 2006, www.latimes.com.

15 Ed Flosi, "When a Cop Throws a Punch to the Face," *PoliceOne.com*, November 11, 2010, www.policeone.com.

16 See, e.g., Omaha Police Department General Order 10-13, defining the head generally as an "area[] of the body that when struck with an empty hand tactic . . . ha[s] a high risk of causing serious bodily injury."

17 Drummond *ex rel* Drummond v. City of Anaheim, 343 F.3d 1052 (9th Cir. 2003).

18 Cynthia Hubert, "Police Held a Man Down on the Hot Pavement. He Ended up Burned, Fighting for His Life," *Miami Herald*, July 20, 2017, www.miamiherald.com; Cynthia Hubert, "He Suffered 3rd-Degree Burns While Police Held Him on Pavement. Now, He's Due to Report to Jail," *Sacramento Bee*, September 6, 2017, www.sacbee.com.

19 Hubert, "Police Held a Man Down."

20 720 Ill. Comp. Stat. 5/7-5.5; Colo. Rev. Stat. § 181-1-707(2.5).

21 The National Law Enforcement Training Center has trademarked the phrase "lateral vascular neck restraint," but it remains in common use as a generic term for vascular neck restraints. Other common phrasing for vascular neck restraints

include "sleeper hold," "carotid hold," "carotid sleeper hold," "blood choke," "rear naked choke," "naked choke," "naked strangle," and *hadaka jime*.

22 *Seattle Police Department Policy* § 8.300-POL-10.

23 Robinson v. Solano County, 278 F.3d 1007 (9th Cir. 2002).

24 Joshua A. Ederheimer and Lroe A. Fridell, eds., *Chief Concerns: Exploring the Challenges of Police Use of Force* (Washington DC: Police Executive Research Forum, April 2005), Police Executive Research Forum, www.policeforum.org.

25 Michael R. Smith and Geoffrey P. Alpert. "Pepper Spray: A Safe and Reasonable Response to Suspect Verbal Resistance," *Policing: An International Journal of Police Strategies and Management* 23 (2000): 233–45.

26 Bob Greenlee, "Eyes Get Peppered With Problems," *Review of Optometry* 141, no. 2 (March 9, 2004), www.reviewofoptometry.com.

27 Smith and Alpert, "Pepper Spray."

28 Young v. County of Los Angeles, 655 F.3d 1156 (9th Cir. 2011).

29 LaLonde v. County of Riverside, 204 F.3d 947, 961 (9th Cir.2000).

30 Headwaters Forest Defense v. County of Humboldt, 276 F.3d 1125 (9th Cir. 2002).

31 Pepperball markets projectiles filled with OC powder, CS powder, and a blend of CS and Pava powder. Other projectile types include malodorant rounds, rounds filled with colorful or ultraviolet marking dye, solid plastic rounds (for breaking windows), and training rounds filled with talc or water.

32 Nelson v. City of Davis, 685 F.3d 867 (9th Cir. 2012).

33 The name of the weapon is an acronym of the "Thomas A. Swift Electric Rifle," which references a weapon invented by Tom Swift, a fictional teenager made famous by Victor Appleton in a series of juvenile adventure novels published between 1910 and 1941.

34 Michael D. White, Justin T. Ready, Robert J. Kane, and Lisa M. Dario, "Examining the Effects of the TASER on Cognitive Functioning: Findings From a Pilot Study with Police Recruits," *Journal of Experimental Criminology* 10, no. 3 (2014): 267–90.

35 Geoffrey P. Alpert and Roger G. Dunham, "Policy and Training Recommendations Related to Police Use of CEDs: Overview of Findings From a Comprehensive National Study," *Police Quarterly* 13, no. 3 (2010): 235–59; Geoffrey P. Alpert, Michael R. Smith, Robert J. Kaminski, Lorie A. Fridell, John MacDonald, and Bruce Kubu, "Police Use of Force, Tasers and Other Less-Lethal Weapons," *National Institute of Justice, Research in Brief* (May 2011), National Criminal Justice Reference Service, www.ncjrs.gov; Christina A. Hall, "Public Risk from Tasers: Unacceptably High or Low Enough to Accept?," *Canadian Journal of Emergency Medicine* 11, no. 1 (2009): 84–86; Mark W. Kroll and Jeffrey D. Ho, eds., *TASER® Conducted Electrical Weapons: Physiology, Pathology, and Law* (New York: Springer Science + Business Media, 2009); In the Circuit Court of the Eleventh Judicial Circuit of Florida in and for the County of Miami-Dade, Final Report of the Miami-Dade County Grand Jury, *Tasers: Deadly Force?* February 2, 2006, Miami-Dade State Attorney, www.miamisao.com.

36 Alpert and Dunham, "Policy and Training Recommendations."

37 Gary. M. Wilke, Christian M. Sloane, and Theodore C. Chan, "Funding Source and Author Affiliation in TASER Research Are Strongly Associated With a Conclusion of Device Safety," *American Heart Journal* 162, no. 3 (2011): 533–37.

38 See Phillip Matthew Stinson, Bradford W. Reyns, and John Liederbach, "Police Crime and Less-Than-Lethal Coercive Force: A Description of the Criminal Misuse of TASERs," *International Journal of Police Science and Management* 14, no. 1 (2012): 1–19; New York Civil Liberties Union, *Report: Taking Tasers Seriously: The Need for Better Regulation of Stun Guns in New York*, October 17, 2011, New York Civil Liberties Union, www.nyclu.org.

39 Alpert and Dunham, "Policy and Training Recommendations"; Kroll and Ho, *TASER® Conducted Electrical Weapons*; *Tasers: Deadly Force?*

40 Armstrong v. Village of Pinehurst, 810 F.3d 892, 902 (2016) (footnote omitted).

41 *Armstrong*, 810 F.3d at 902 n.8.

42 *Armstrong*, 810 F.3d at 892; Cyrus v. Town of Mukwonago, 624 F.3d 856, 863 (7th Cir. 2010); Mattos v. Agarano, 661 F.3d 433, 446 (9th Cir. 2011) (en banc); Brown v. City of Golden Valley, 574 F.3d 491, 497 (8th Cir. 2009); Bryan v. MacPherson, 630 F.3d 805 (9th Cir. 2010); Smith v. LePage, 834 F.3d 1285 (11th Cir. 2016).

43 *2011 Electronic Control Weapon* (Washington DC: Police Executive Research Forum and COPS: Community Oriented Policing Services, U.S. Department of Justice, 2011), Guidelines, Police Executive Research Forum, www.policeforum.org.

44 *2011 Electronic Control Weapon.*

45 Alpert and Dunham, "Policy and Training Recommendations."

46 *TASER Training Version 19.* In a more recent version of TASER user training, the manufacturer states, "Falls are often uncontrolled and subjects are often unable to protect or catch themselves," and, "Falls, even from ground level, can cause serious injuries or death (especially on a hard surface)." *TASER X2 Training Version 21.*

47 Jackson v. County of San Bernardino, 191 F.Supp.3d 1100 (C.D. Cal. 2016).

48 Jon Swaine, Jamiles Lartey, and Oliver Laughland, "Moving Targets," *Guardian (US)*, accessed February 11, 2019, www.theguardian.com.

49 See the discussion of "officer-created jeopardy" in chapter 5.

50 *National Consensus Policy and Discussion Paper on Use of Force*, October 2019, National Organization of Black Law Enforcement Executives, http://noblenational.org.

51 Doug Wyllie, "Why Warning Shots Are a Terrible Idea," *PoliceOne.com*, April 4, 2017, www.policeone.com; Martin Kaste, "Police Warning Shots May Be in for a Comeback," NPR, March 28, 2017, www.npr.org.

52 Roberto Baldwin, "What Is the LRAD Sound Cannon?," *Gizmodo*, August 14, 2014, https://gizmodo.com.

53 Baldwin, "What Is the LRAD Sound Cannon?"

54 Liz Klimas, "Laser Dazzler Unveiled for Use by Law Enforcement—So How Does It Work?," *Blaze*, February 14, 2012, www.theblaze.com; Chris Matyszczyk, "Police to Experiment With Blinding 'Dazer Laser'?," *cnet.com*, July 23, 2010, www.cnet.com.

55 Brad Turner, "Cooking Protestors Alive: The Excessive-Force Implications of the Active Denial System," *Duke Law and Technology Review* 11, no. 2 (2012): 332–56.

56 David A. Graham, "The Dallas Shooting and the Advent of Killer Police Robots," *Atlantic*, July 8, 2016, www.theatlantic.com.

57 Zusha Elinson, "Taser Explores Concept of Drone Armed With Stun Gun for Police Use," *Wall Street Journal*, October 20, 2016, www.wsj.com.

58 See chapter 5.

59 Campbell v. City of Springboro, Ohio, 700 F.3d 779 (6th Cir. 2012).

60 Edwards v. Shanley, 666 F.3d 1289 (11th Cir. 2012).

61 Vathekan v. Prince George's County, 154 F.3d 173 (4th Cir. 1998). However, other courts have clarified that officers need not issue a verbal warning when it would be unsafe to do so. Crenshaw v. Lister, 556 F.3d 1283 (11th Cir. 2009).

62 Kuha v. City of Minnetonka, 365 F.3d 590 (8th Cir. 2003).

63 See, e.g., *Seattle Police Department Policy* § 8.300-POL-2.

64 Seattle Police Department Policy § 8.300-POL-2.

65 Geoffrey P. Alpert and Lorie A. Fridell, *Police Vehicles and Firearms: Instruments of Deadly Force*, (Prospect Heights, IL, Waveland Press, 1992).

66 Scott v. Harris, 550 U.S. 372 (2007).

67 See chapter 1.

68 Scott v. Harris, 550 U.S. 372 (2007) at 385, fn. 11.

69 California Highway Patrol, *Pursuit Study* (Sacramento: California Highway Patrol, 1983); Roger G. Dunham, Geoffrey Alpert, Dennis Jay Kenny, and Paul Cromwell, "High Speed Pursuit: The Offender's Perspective," *Criminal Justice and Behavior* 20 (1998): 30-45; Geoffrey P. Alpert and Cynthia Lum, *Police Pursuit Driving: Policy and Research* (New York: Springer, 2014).

70 *Harris*, 550 U.S. at 385 ("It is obvious the perverse incentives such a rule would create: Every fleeing motorist would know that escape is within his grasp, if only he accelerates to 90 miles per hour, crosses the double-yellow line a few times, and runs a few red lights.").

CONCLUSION

1 Seth W. Stoughton, "Police Body-Worn Cameras," *North Carolina Law Review* 96 (2018): 1363.

2 As described in chapter 1, factual disagreements arise when individuals disagree about the underlying facts, while interpretive disagreements arise when individuals agree on the underlying facts but disagree as to the conclusions that can be drawn from those facts.

3 See Greenridge v. Ruffin, 927 F.2d 789, 792 (4th Cir. 1991); Carter v. Buscher, 973 F.2d 1328, 1332 (7th Cir. 1992).

4 See Young v. City of Providence, 404 F.3d 4 (1st Cir. 2005); Abraham v. Raso, 183 F.3d 279 (3rd Cir. 1999); Dickerson v. McClellan, 101 F.3d 1151, 1161 (6th Cir. 1996); Allen v. Muskogee, 119 F.3d 837 (10th Cir. 1997).

5 Graham v. Connor, 490 U.S. 386, 396 (1989).

6 See chapter 5.

7 We are cognizant of the argument that the analytical frameworks we discuss in this text suffer from the same criticisms that we level at the "final frame" approach; namely, that they do not go far enough by considering all of the relevant contributing factors. A police agency's failure to properly train officers to use a particular weapon, for example, can certainly contribute to an officer's misuse of that weapon. Similarly, an agency's failure to adequately supervise officers and review uses of force in prior cases can contribute to the inappropriate use of force in the future. We fully acknowledge the value of assessing how systemic and institutional factors can affect officers' use-of-force decisions. That inquiry, however, goes beyond the question that we seek to answer in this text: How can society reliably evaluate the propriety of an officer's use of force in an individual encounter?

8 See *Final Report of the President's Task Force on 21st Century Policing* (Washington, DC: Office of Community Oriented Policing Services, 2015), https://cops.usdoj.gov/.

9 *Graham*, 490 U.S. at 386.

10 Idaho Code Ann. § 9-610 (authorizing officers to use force when making an arrest "if the person to be arrested either flees or forcibly resists").

11 See Ala. Code. § 13A-3-27 (authorizing an officer to use force "[t]o defend himself or a third person from what he reasonably believes to be the use or imminent use of physical force while making or attempting to make an arrest for a misdemeanor, violation or violation of a criminal ordinance").

12 Alpert and Dunham, "Understanding Police Uses of Force."

13 Matthew J. Hickman, Loren T. Atherley, Patrick G. Lowery, and Geoffrey P. Alpert, "Reliability of the Force Factor Method in Police Use-of-Force Research," *Police Quarterly* 18, no. 4 (2015): 368–96.

14 Research in 2006 estimated that about 70 percent of police agencies used an incremental model force matrix. William Terrill and Eugene A. Paoline, "Force Continuums: Moving Beyond Speculation and Toward Empiricism," *Law Enforcement Executive Forum* 7, no. 4 (2007): 27, 28. Additional research in 2011 estimated that number at more than eighty percent. William Terrill, Eugene A. Paoline III, and Jason Ingram, "Final Technical Report Draft: Assessing Police Use of Force Policy and Outcomes" (Rockville, MD: NCJRS (National Criminal Justice Reference Service), May 2011), ii, www.ncjrs.gov.

15 U.S. Department of Agriculture, Economic Research Service, *Livestock and Meat International Trade Data*, United States Department of Agriculture Economic Research Service, accessed February 22, 2019, www.ers.usda.gov.

16 U.S. Department of Commerce, International Trade Administration, *Office of Transportation and Machinery, Automotive Team: Industry Trade Data*, International Trade Administration, accessed February 22, 2019, www.trade.gov.

17 National Center for Education Statistics, *Fast Facts*, accessed February 22, 2019, https://nces.ed.gov.

18 U.S. Census Bureau, *American Fact Finder,* accessed February 22, 2019, https://factfinder.census.gov.

19 U.S. Department of Labor, Bureau of Labor Statistics, accessed February 22, 2019, https://stats.bls.gov.

20 U.S. Department of Justice, Bureau of Justice Statistics, accessed February 22, 2019, https://bjs.gov.

21 Aaron C. Davis and Wesley Lowery, "FBI Director Calls Lack of Data on Police Shootings 'Ridiculous,' 'Embarrassing,'" *Washington Post,* October 7, 2015, www.washingtonpost.com.

22 Eric Lichtblau, "Justice Department to Track Use of Force by Police Across U.S.," *New York Times,* October 13, 2016, www.nytimes.com.

23 Centers for Disease Control and Prevention, *National Violent Death Reporting System (NVDRS),* accessed February 22, 2019, www.cdc.gov.

24 U.S. Department of Justice, Federal Bureau of Investigation, *2017 Crime in the United States, Expanded Homicide Data Table 14: Justifiable Homicide by Weapon, Law Enforcement,* Uniform Crime Reporting (UCR) Program, accessed February 22, 2019, https://ucr.fbi.gov.

25 Matt Apuzzo and Sarah Cohen, "Data on Use of Force by Police Across U.S. Proves Almost Useless," *New York Times,* August 11, 2015, www.nytimes.com.

26 Texas Code of Crim. Pro. § 2.139.

27 Howard E. Williams, Scott W. Bowman, and Jordan Taylor Jung, "The Limitations of Government Databases for Analyzing Fatal Officer-Involved Shootings in the United States," *Criminal Justice Policy Review* 30, no. 2 (2016): 201–22.

28 Federal Bureau of Investigation, Criminal Justice Information Services, Uniform Crime Reporting (UCR) Program, *National Use-of-Force Data Collection,* accessed February 22, 2019, www.fbi.gov.

29 Fla. Stat. § 776.05(2), (3).

30 Tenn. Code Ann. § 39-11-620.

31 See chapter 2.

32 Terrill et al., *Final Technical Report Draft,* iii.

33 Terrill et al., *Final Technical Report Draft,* 28.

34 Charles F. Klahm, IV and Rob Tillyer, "Understanding Police Use of Force: A Review of the Evidence," *Southwest Journal of Criminal Justice* 7 (2010): 214–39.

35 Patrick S. Forscher, Calvin K. Lai, Jordan R. Axt, Charles R. Ebersole, Michelle Herman, Patricia G. Devine, and Brian A. Nosek, "A Meta-Analysis of Procedures to Change Implicit Biases," *Preprint,* August 15, 2016, https://psyarxiv.com.

36 Jeff Rojek, Peter Martin, and Geoffrey P. Alpert, *Developing and Maintaining Police-Researcher Partnerships to Facilitate Research Use* (New York: Springer, 2015), 37.

INDEX

ABOUT THE AUTHORS

Seth W. Stoughton is an Associate Professor at the University of South Carolina School of Law and an affiliate of the Rule of Law Collaborative. He researches the regulation of policing, including the use of force. He previously served as an officer with the Tallahassee Police Department and an investigator with the Florida Department of Education, Office of Inspector General.

Jeffrey J. Noble is a police consultant and expert in the use of force, including police tactics, procedures, and investigations. He has worked on several high-profile use-of-force incidents, including the shootings of Tamir Rice, Philando Castille, and Keith Scott. He is an attorney licensed in California. In 2012, he retired as the Deputy Chief of the Irvine Police Department.

Geoffrey P. Alpert is a Professor of Criminology at the University of South Carolina and Griffith University. His research interests include high-risk policing activities. He is the recipient of multiple research grants and has taught at the FBI National Academy and the Federal Law Enforcement Training Center. He was a Federal Monitor for the New Orleans Police Department, and he has testified before Congress and the President's Task Force on 21st Century Policing.